This companion will prove an invaluable resource for all those engaged in research or teaching on Jacob Boehme and his readers, as historians, philosophers, literary scholars or theologians. Boehme is "on the radar" of many researchers, but often avoided as there are relatively few aids to understanding his thought, its context and subsequent appeal. This book includes a fine spread of topics and specialists.

Cyril O'Regan, University of Notre Dame, USA

An Introduction to Jacob Boehme

This volume brings together for the first time some of the world's leading authorities on the German mystic Jacob Boehme to illuminate his thought and its reception over four centuries for the benefit of students and advanced scholars alike. Boehme's theosophical works have influenced Western culture in profound ways since their dissemination in the early seventeenth century, and these interdisciplinary essays trace the social and cultural networks as well as the intellectual pathways involved in Boehme's enduring impact. The chapters range from situating Boehme in the sixteenth-century Radical Reformation to discussions of his significance in modern theology. They explore the major contexts for Boehme's reception, including the Pietist movement, Russian religious thought, and Western esotericism. In addition, they focus more closely on important readers, including the religious radicals of the English Civil Wars and the later English Behmenists, literary figures such as Goethe and Blake, and great philosophers of the modern age such as Schelling and Hegel. Together, the chapters illustrate the depth and variety of Boehme's influence, and a concluding chapter addresses directly an underlying theme of the volume, asking why Boehme matters today and how readers in the present might be enriched by a fresh engagement with his apparently opaque and complex writings.

Ariel Hessayon is Senior Lecturer in the Department of History at Goldsmiths, University of London. He has published extensively on a variety of early modern topics, including antiscripturism, book burning, communism, environmentalism, esotericism, extra-canonical texts, heresy, crypto-Jews, Judaizing, millenarianism, mysticism, prophecy, and religious radicalism.

Sarah Apetrei is Departmental Lecturer in Ecclesiastical History at the University of Oxford. She is the author of *Women, Feminism and Religion in Early Enlightenment England* and is currently working on a book dealing with the place of mystical theology in seventeenth-century British religion.

Routledge Studies in Religion

1 **Judaism and Collective Life**
Self and Community in the Religious Kibbutz
Aryei Fishman

2 **Foucault, Christianity and Interfaith Dialogue**
Henrique Pinto

3 **Religious Conversion and Identity**
The Semiotic Analysis of Texts
Massimo Leone

4 **Language, Desire, and Theology**
A Genealogy of the Will to Speak
Noëlle Vahanian

5 **Metaphysics and Transcendence**
Arthur Gibson

6 **Sufism and Deconstruction**
A Comparative Study of Derrida and Ibn 'Arabi
Ian Almond

7 **Christianity, Tolerance and Pluralism**
A Theological Engagement with Isaiah Berlin's Social Theory
Michael Jinkins

8 **Negative Theology and Modern French Philosophy**
Arthur Bradley

9 **Law and Religion**
Edited by Peter Radan, Denise Meyerson and Rosalind F. Atherton

10 **Religion, Language, and Power**
Edited by Nile Green and Mary Searle-Chatterjee

11 **Shared Idioms, Sacred Symbols, and the Articulation of Identities in South Asia**
Edited by Kelly Pemberton and Michael Nijhawan

12 **Theology, Creation, and Environmental Ethics**
From *Creatio Ex Nihilo* to *Terra Nullius*
Whitney Bauman

13 **Material Religion and Popular Culture**
E. Frances King

14 **Adam Smith as Theologian**
Edited by Paul Oslington

15 **The Entangled God**
Divine Relationality and Quantum Physics
Kirk Wegter-McNelly

16 **Aquinas and Radical Orthodoxy**
A Critical Inquiry
Paul J. DeHart

17 **Animal Ethics and Theology**
The Lens of the Good Samaritan
Daniel K. Miller

18 **The Origin of Heresy**
A History of Discourse in Second Temple Judaism and Early Christianity
Robert M. Royalty, Jr.

19 **Buddhism and Violence**
Militarism and Buddhism in Modern Asia
Edited by Vladimir Tikhonov and Torkel Brekke

20 Popular Music in Evangelical Youth Culture
Stella Sai-Chun Lau

21 Theology and the Science of Moral Action
Virtue Ethics, Exemplarity, and Cognitive Neuroscience
Edited by James A. Van Slyke, Gregory R. Peterson, Kevin S. Reimer, Michael L. Spezio and Warren S. Brown

22 Abrogation in the Qur'an and Islamic Law
Louay Fatoohi

23 A New Science of Religion
Edited by Gregory W. Dawes and James Maclaurin

24 Making Sense of the Secular
Critical Perspectives from Europe to Asia
Edited by Ranjan Ghosh

25 The Rise of Modern Jewish Politics
Extraordinary Movement
C. S. Monaco

26 Gender and Power in Contemporary Spirituality
Ethnographic Approaches
Anna Fedele and Kim E. Knibbe

27 Religions in Movement
The Local and the Global in Contemporary Faith Traditions
Robert W. Hefner, John Hutchinson, Sara Mels and Christiane Timmerman

28 William James's Hidden Religious Imagination
A Universe of Relations
Jeremy Carrette

29 Theology and the Arts
Engaging Faith
Ruth Illman and W. Alan Smith

30 Religion, Gender, and the Public Sphere
Edited by Niamh Reilly and Stacey Scriver

31 An Introduction to Jacob Boehme
Four Centuries of Thought and Reception
Edited by Ariel Hessayon and Sarah Apetrei

An Introduction to Jacob Boehme

Four Centuries of Thought and Reception

Edited by Ariel Hessayon and Sarah Apetrei

Routledge
Taylor & Francis Group
LONDON AND NEW YORK

First published 2014 by Routledge

2 Park Square, Milton Park, Abingdon, Oxfordshire OX14 4RN
711 Third Avenue, New York, NY 10017

Routledge is an imprint of the Taylor & Francis Group, an Informa Business

First issued in paperback 2018

Library of Congress Cataloging-in-Publication Data

An introduction to Jacob Boehme : four centuries of thought and reception /
edited by Ariel Hessayon and Sarah Apetrei. — 1st [edition].
pages cm. — (Routledge studies in religion ; 31)
Includes bibliographical references and index.
1. Böhme, Jakob, 1575-1624. 2. Mysticism—History.
I. Hessayon, Ariel, editor of compilation.
BV5095.B7I64 2013
230'.044092—dc23
2013008795

ISBN: 978-0-415-84357-7 (hbk)
ISBN: 978-1-138-54915-9 (pbk)

Typeset in Sabon
by Apex CoVantage, LLC

Dedication
To our students
(past, present, and future)

Contents

Figures

Acknowledgments

This volume emerged from the conference "'Teutonic Philosophy': Jacob Boehme (1575–1624) in context, his life and the reception of his writings" held at St Edmund Hall, University of Oxford from September 16–18, 2010. The editors wish to thank all of the speakers at this conference and all of those who attended for their enthusiasm and interest. We are also grateful to the trustees of the Panacea Society and the Fell Fund (University of Oxford) for their generous financial support in hosting this event. Additional gratitude is due to the Panacea Society, which has very generously supported the larger research project on the prophetic thought and legacies of Jacob Boehme and Jane Lead, of which this volume is the first outcome. Thanks, too, to Laura Stearns, Lauren Verity, and the rest of the staff at Taylor & Francis for their courtesy, kindness, and efficiency. Finally, we extend special thanks first to Jennifer Smyth for her invaluable help in the very last stages and second to our contributors for their unstinting cooperation and unfailing patience.

1 Introduction

Boehme's Legacy in Perspective

Ariel Hessayon and Sarah Apetrei[1]

I

Jacob Boehme has variously been called "the illuminated Instrument of God," "the prince of divine philosophers," "the most comprehensive, abundant and multifaceted of all mystics," "the greatest and most famous of all Theosophists in the world," "the greatest of the mystics, and the father of German philosophy," "a giant in intelligence," "a religious and philosophical genius" rarely with "equal in the world's history," "the most imaginative genius" of the early seventeenth century—indeed "one of the greatest geniuses of mankind," and, by no less a figure than the cultural critic Walter Benjamin, "one of the greatest allegorists."[2]

Writing in German from about 1600 until shortly before his death in 1624 he was—by his first biographer's reckoning—the author of thirty works, several of which are extremely long. In addition, Boehme's extensive correspondence survives for the period from January 1618 to June 1624. A Lutheran by birth, by formative religious instruction, and steadfastly at his death, Boehme's major theological concerns were with the nature of creation and how it came into being, the origin and presence of evil, and the attainment of salvation through a process of inward spiritual regeneration and rebirth. Nonetheless, influenced initially by the teachings of Paracelsus and the spiritual reformers Caspar Schwenckfeld and Valentin Weigel as well as by popular alchemical and astrological texts, and then, following the clandestine circulation of his first incomplete book in manuscript, by a widening social network of friends, learned correspondents, and noble patrons, Boehme began developing certain heterodox views that were furiously denounced by a local clergyman. These included his understanding of the Trinity, which he was accused of denying through his introduction of a fourth "person," Sophia (symbolizing the Noble Virgin of Divine Wisdom); his explanations for the fall of Lucifer and the rebel angels (constituting a first fall preceding the second fall of humanity from paradise); Adam's prelapsarian androgynous nature; the existence of seven qualities (dry, sweet, bitter, fire, love, sound, and *corpus*); and the three principles that corresponded to the dark world (God the Father), the light world (God the Son), and our temporal visible world (the Holy Spirit). Moreover, having settled and established himself as a cobbler at Görlitz in Upper Lusatia and writing against a backdrop of vibrant scientific, astronomical, and medical enquiry, damaging regional political struggles, religious polemic, apocalyptic speculation, and, from 1618, the earliest phase of the Thirty Years' War, Boehme interposed himself—ignorantly and presumptuously according to his better educated critics—in important doctrinal debates over the nature of free will and the sacraments of Baptism and the Lord's Supper by expounding an irenic, anticlerical message. This culminated in his announcement of an impending Great Reformation—a new age of love, patience, peace, and joy.

Boehme's writings divided nineteenth- and twentieth-century commentators. On the one hand, he was praised as an "independent, bold and profoundly penetrating thinker," with an "amazing range of thought and depth of experience," whose "majestic symbols drawn from the Bible" and contemporary chemistry expressed particular doctrines of "wondrous beauty" to produce, in the words of the existentialist philosopher Paul Tillich, "one of the most profound and strangest systems of Western thought."[3] Furthermore, this "illiterate and untrained," "simple" "peasant shoemaker" was regarded as "one of the giants," "one of the most amazing phenomena in the history of mysticism." The "great sweep" of his vision, with its "immense heights and deeps," led to comparisons with other Christian poets, notably Dante, while "a natural genius for the transcendent" also enabled this "theosophist" and "myth-creator" to leave his "mark upon German philosophy."[4] On the other, even Boehme's admirers acknowledged that, however memorable his concepts, they were nonetheless expressed obscurely. This "notorious opacity," this "coagulated cyclone of language," which understandably deterred generations of potential readers, has made Boehme, to quote Cyril O'Regan, "one of the most difficult reads in the history of Christian thought."[5] Less generously, it was suggested that few, if any, were "able to pierce the clouds in which his meaning has been charitably presumed to lie hid."[6] The "fantastic disorder" of his "chaotic and shapeless" notions supposedly came from an inability to "winnow and arrange" the outpourings of a heated imagination, while Boehme was also "constantly doing violence to language" by impetuously attempting to "express the inexpressible" through the introduction of barbarous neologisms. Consequently, the French idealist philosopher Émile Boutroux regarded Boehme's work as "a mixture of abstruse theology, alchemy, speculations on the indiscernible, and the incomprehensible, fantastic poetry and mystic effusions"; in short, "a dazzling chaos."[7]

This tendency to polarize opinion was nothing new. As the nineteenth-century Danish theologian Hans Martensen observed, Boehme:

> had to pass, not only during his lifetime, but also after his death, through honour and dishonour, good report and evil report. Many have regarded him as a visionary, and have placed his teaching in the history

> of human follies. In many libraries his writings are to be found under the rubric *Fanatici*. Others have extolled him to the skies, and have believed that they have found in him all the treasures of knowledge and all enigmas solved.[8]

To illustrate Martensen's point, the day after Boehme's burial, one of the physicians who had attended him on his deathbed lamented the loss of "a precious, enlightened, and highly God-taught" man who should have been revered by his fellow citizens rather than openly reviled as "a *Fanatic*, *Enthusiast*, and *Visionary*."[9] Indeed, a spectrum ranging from adulation to exasperation to repulsion characterized the main reactions to Boehme's thought—either in the original German or in Latin, Dutch, English, Welsh, French, and Russian translations—from the second quarter of the seventeenth- to the mid-nineteenth century.[10]

Thus, Pierre Poiret, a French devotee of the mystics, believed it was Boehme alone to whom God had "uncovered the foundation of nature, of spiritual as well as corporeal things, and who, with an utterly penetrating insight into matters theological or supernatural, also knew the origin of the true principles of metaphysical and pneumatic, as well as purely physical, philosophy." In the same vein, Boehme's early nineteenth-century French translator Louis Claude de Saint-Martin ("le philosophe inconnu") urged readers to "dip courageously" into his "numerous writings, which contain . . . extraordinary and astonishing expositions of our primitive nature; of the source of evil; of the essence and laws of the universe; of the origin of gravity; of what he calls . . . the seven powers of nature; of the origin of water; . . . of the nature of the disobedience of the angels of darkness; . . . of the way of reconciliation which eternal love employed to reinstate man in his inheritance."[11] Then, there was the German Catholic philosopher Franz von Baader, who had arrived at Boehme through reading Saint-Martin and who defended Boehme from the "absurd" charge of reviving the "blasphemous ancient Gnostic error, which would have the Devil as the cook and seasoning, and the stimulant in God as well as in Creation." On the contrary, insisted von Baader, Boehme should be recognized for having established more profoundly than anyone else before him or since, the fundamental teaching of a supernatural, supra-worldly, and uncreated God.[12]

More ambivalent was the attitude of Georg Christoph Lichtenberg, an eighteenth-century German scientist who, in a remark subsequently popularized by Sigmund Freud in a book on the joke's relation to the unconscious, likened the prose of Boehme's "immortal works" to particular odes in that they are "a kind of picnic, where the author provides the words (the sound) and the reader the meaning."[13] For the poet Samuel Coleridge, Boehme was "the great German Theosopher." Although his "delusions" may have been "gross" and easily controverted, and although as a visionary he frequently mistook "the dreams of his own overexcited Nerves, the phantoms and witcheries from the cauldron of his own seething Fancy, for parts or symbols of a universal Process," as a philosopher, he surprises rather than perplexes. For according to Coleridge, the "unlearned" shoemaker "contemplated Truth and the forms of Nature thro' a luminous Mist, the vaporous darkness rising from his Ignorance and accidental peculiarities of fancy and sensation, but the Light streaming into it from his inmost Soul."[14] Similarly, the nineteenth-century American essayist and Transcendentalist Ralph Waldo Emerson regarded Boehme as a poet, sage, and mystic who, "tremulous with emotion," listened "awestruck with the gentlest humanity to the Teacher" whose lessons he conveyed. Notwithstanding his "mystical narrowness," "incommunicableness," and "vague, inadequate" propositions, Boehme's "excellence" was merited by his "comprehensiveness": "It is his aim that is great. He will know, not one thing, but all things."[15]

At the other extreme, Boehme was denounced as an "ingenious madman" by the eighteenth-century theologian John Wesley. In his journal and correspondence, Wesley fulminated against what he deemed to be Boehme's unscriptural, irrational, contradictory, crude, and indigestible blending of religion with philosophy. On reading part of Boehme's allegorical exposition of Genesis, he spluttered, "it is most sublime nonsense; inimitable bombast; fustian not to be paralleled!"[16] A German church historian agreed: those who honored Boehme as an "*inspired messenger of heaven*" or admired him as a "judicious and wise philosopher" were "deceived and blinded in a very high degree; for never did there reign such obscurity and confusion in the writings of any mortal, as in the miserable productions of Jacob Behmen, which exhibit a motley mixture of chemical terms, crude visions, and mystic jargon."[17] Such censure chimed with the objections of two eighteenth-century English bishops. William Warburton, bishop of Gloucester, believed that heavenly and earthly wisdom should be communicable and easily understood. Accordingly, he dismissed Boehme as an imposter, a "pretender" to divine inspiration, whose effusions were nothing but a "heap of unmeaning," "unintelligible words," "the jargon of the *spirit of infatuation*."[18] Likewise, George Horne, bishop of Norwich, objected to these "stupendous reveries": either Boehme's scheme was a "*new revelation*, or an explanation of the *old*." If the latter, why was it wrapped up in "*mystic jargon*" unheard of before in the Christian church and not given in plain "*Scripture language*"? If the former, it was "an *imposture* and *delusion*" since "*extraordinary inspirations*" were only to be credited if supported by miracles.[19]

Modern scholarship has generally focused on three complementary approaches in an effort to comprehend Boehme: the taxonomic, the genealogical, and the contextual. The first asks how we should define Boehme; the second, which intellectual and religious traditions he inherited and contributed towards; and the third, what milieu he should be situated within. As we have seen, various Protestant clergymen and church historians tended to label Boehme a heretic, fanatic, enthusiast, visionary, or impostor, discrediting his unwelcome plebeian challenge to ecclesiastical power structures and doctrinal orthodoxy by ridiculing him as an ignorant, delusional artisan venting derivative, impenetrable gibberish. By contrast, Boehme's followers generally revered him as a divine instrument, sanctified figure, prophet, illuminate, sincere teacher, and genius. Others, including those intrigued but frustrated by his writings, have usually classed him either a mystic, Theosopher, philosopher, or prodigy. Boehme, however, does not readily conform to a specific type. Nor are these neutral terms, because each discloses—albeit to different degrees—the reader's perspective. So it may be unhelpful to categorize Boehme as one thing or another and more useful to envisage him as an exceptional hybrid.

Similar issues arise from the second approach. Here, investigators run the risk of repeating the methodology of both heresiographers and hagiographers, who sought to damage or enhance Boehme's reputation by seeking precedents—though rarely with sufficient attention to subtle doctrinal distinctions or indeed an adequate explanation for how ideas were transmitted to and received by him. All the same, Boehme's concepts clearly did not originate from nothing, so it is worthwhile to briefly review these traditions and his potential sources. Writing approximately a century after the German Reformation and calling for a Great Reformation, Boehme was occasionally likened to a second Luther, and Lutheran thought—especially as mediated in Görlitz—clearly had a big impact on his development. Boehme has also been positioned within a tradition of German mysticism, with roots going back to pseudo-Dionysius the Areopagite, which attempted to understand and describe the divine nature by emphasizing what God was not. Moreover, he has been regarded as an independently-minded successor of the spiritual reformers, notably Caspar Schwenckfeld and Valentin Weigel. Then there is Paracelsus, whose influence is undeniable. Through him and his interpreters, Boehme became acquainted with the wider alchemical tradition, while his knowledge of heliocentrism shows familiarity with astrological texts. These resonances, in conjunction with perceived pantheistic elements, have prompted suggestions that Boehme drew ultimate inspiration from an ancient theology that embraced currents of Gnosticism, Neoplatonism, Hermeticism, and Christian adaptations of the Jewish Kabbalah. In addition, although not a staunch millenarian, Boehme expected an imminent period of great tribulation, and hence his apocalyptic thought has been compared with Joachim of Fiore's eschatological scheme.

Despite the paucity of evidence, the third approach, namely the painstaking recovery of Boehme's milieu, has been instrumental in overturning enduring misconceptions. Here, biographical discoveries have supplemented and corrected the familiar, idealized portrait, while important research on the backdrop—Görlitz's lively intellectual scene; contemporary religious controversies between Catholics, Lutherans, Calvinists and assorted sectarians; the local impact of the Thirty Years' War; not to mention Boehme's circle of physicians, alchemists, prophets, Rosicrucian sympathizers, customs officials, tradesmen, and noblemen—has considerably enhanced our understanding of how his work was informed by and responded to wider contexts.

Unquestionably, as the essays in this volume indicate, Boehme's rich and diverse legacy spans the four centuries since a legible manuscript copy of his first if incomplete book (later entitled "Aurora") was made.[20] Encouragingly, Andrew Weeks's modern English translation with accompanying original German text and critical apparatus is nearing completion. Together with relatively recent published work and other ongoing projects, this should go some way towards "rescuing Boehme's thought and discourse from the oblivion" into which it has regrettably fallen in Anglophone historical, theological, and philosophical scholarship.[21] Beyond the academy, there is a popular audience for Boehme as a simple internet search attests. Some, like certain theosophists at the turn of the twentieth century, are undoubtedly drawn by a quest for "Higher Wisdom" or an interest in esoteric philosophy and mysticism more generally; others, perhaps with a view to his teachings about the existence of evil, God's presence within the creation, and the noble virgin Sophia, might see potential for stimulating debates on aspects of moral philosophy, environmentalism, poetic expression, and female-centered spirituality.[22] Whatever the reason, Evelyn Underhill's hyperbolical observation is worth repeating: Boehme "remains one of those cloud-wrapped immortals who must be rediscovered and reinterpreted by the adventurers of every age."[23]

II

As Nigel Smith suggests in Chapter Six of this volume, the interpretation of Boehme has been developmental: a kind of "progressive revelation." For this reason, our book is designed to illustrate that diachronic exegetical process, stopping at significant landmarks along the pathway towards understanding. Several of the essays are concerned with the essential paradox at the heart of Boehme's thought and its reception: the interplay between what Andrew Weeks describes as "his anomalous status as a simple shoemaker and the incommensurate complexities of his writing." Ariel Hessayon's introductory chapter attempts to provide a balanced account of Boehme's life by stripping away both hagiographic myths perpetuated by his earliest biographer and negative stereotypes conversely maintained in the heresiography. He then contextualizes Boehme's thought, highlighting the process whereby he acquired specialist knowledge through a combination of reading and conversation. The result was the sophisticated works of Boehme's intellectual maturity (1619–1624). In Chapter Three, Andrew Weeks burrows deeply into the theological and cultural soil in which Boehme himself was embedded. His synoptic interpretation of Boehme's intellectual formation illuminates how traditions of anticlerical dissent, medieval and Renaissance cosmogony, and Lutheran metaphysics interact in the Teutonic Philosopher's vastly ambitious project. With sensitivity to the immediate political situation of the Empire at the turn of the seventeenth century as well as intellectual inheritance, Weeks also looks forward to explain how Boehme's "liminality" between epochs, and between lay and elite culture, resonated so powerfully in later modernism. The contemporary environment, in which any three-dimensional portrait of Boehme must be grounded, is further excavated in Leigh Penman's chapter on his intellectual networks in the early seventeenth century. Definitively, Penman explodes the myth of Boehme as a prodigious "voice crying in the wilderness," reconstructing through careful prosopographical study the heterodox networks of contemporary Görlitz. Just as Weeks maps out the broader intellectual influence of the Radical Reformation, so Penman illustrates with microscopic precision the patronal and personal relationships that linked Boehme with antinomian, Paracelsian, Kabbalistic, chiliast, and spiritualist thinkers.

The extent and limit of Boehme's English reception, particularly during the politically explosive period of the Civil Wars and Revolution, are explored in the fifth chapter. Here, Hessayon points to the pitfalls of tracing too linear a Behmenist genealogy, showing that the English translations must be understood as part of a more diffuse dissemination of mystical and occult literature. He challenges the assumption that it was primarily a radical sectarian audience to which Boehme appealed, showing that the impulse for translation came rather from irenic and politically moderate milieus. Boehme's significance in seventeenth-century England, Hessayon argues, does not lie in the formative contribution he made to the incendiary religious politics of the Revolution, but rather in the way that he was enlisted in the service of existing agendas and intellectual trends. In the following chapter, Nigel Smith analyses the appeal of Boehme's writings, especially to English readers, in the decades after their earliest publication. He suggests that part of the initial attraction of Boehme's prose lay in its inherent difficulty and obscurity: its refusal to yield up readily its meaning to rational scrutiny. As the earlier chapters demonstrate and as Smith indicates, the long process of digesting and contextualizing Boehme over centuries has exposed a coherency in his thought, which even the most well-read of early modern interpreters were unable to unravel at first glance. However, it was precisely this opacity in Boehme's writing that helped to confirm its status as authentic prophecy and which encouraged experimental types of inspired speech and poetry pointing precociously towards Blake's distinctive mystical register.

The role of English readers in keeping Boehme's thought alive into the eighteenth century was crucial, as Sarah Apetrei's epilogue on the London Philadelphian Society (founded in the 1690s) indicates. Jane Lead, the visionary matriarch of the Philadelphians, helped to consolidate Boehme's reputation as inspired magus while establishing herself as his successor. Lead's distinctive interpretations of Boehme—for example, reconfiguring his doctrine of "Sophia" or Divine Wisdom or carrying through his eschatological discourse to a vision of universal salvation—shaped the preoccupations of the next generation of his readers, including radical Pietists and mystical readers in France, England, and Scotland. This reinforces Smith's conclusion that Lead provided a crucial point of reference for all prophetic and anti-scholastic (perhaps also anticlerical) appropriations of Boehme in the post-Enlightenment age. This legacy provides part of the context for Lucinda Martin's discussion of German Pietism in Chapter Seven. Martin examines the channels through which Pietists became reacquainted with Boehme and maps out the diverse and vibrant landscape of Pietist interpretations. These range from the deeply idiosyncratic, chiliastic, and sectarian, such as Johann Georg Gichtel's celibate "Angel Brothers" or the sexually invasive and controlling "Mother Eva Society," to Gottfried Arnold's more intellectually mainstream and widely-disseminated exposition of Sophia doctrine. The anthropological implications of Sophianic thought suggested by the English Behmenists, chiefly John Pordage and Jane Lead, stimulated in Pietism not only the disturbing attitudes to sexuality manifested in certain sects, but also, Martin concludes, renewed prospects for female authority.

The versatility of Boehme's thought, potentially amenable to both rigorist and antinomian readings, emerges once again in Alan Gregory's treatment of one of his most critical and complex yet also most celebrated interpreters, the eighteenth-century English mystic William Law. Gregory shows how Law used Boehme to construct a spiritual system centered on the doctrine of regeneration and identifies two significant hermeneutical moves. First, within a distinctively Anglican apologetic tradition, Law re-deploys Boehme for the orthodox cause, showing how his integrated narrative of creation resists both the radically dualist and radically monist implications of contemporary philosophies. However, as Gregory argues, Law's use of Boehme is not merely opportunistic. As any truly faithful interpreter must, he recognizes that Boehme's prose is essentially performative, written with intent upon the reader, not so much to unveil mysteries as to engender change. Such an appreciation of the generative quality of Boehme's writing is characteristic of the Romantic reception of Boehme, discussed in the following chapters by Kristine Hannak and Elisabeth Jessen. Hannak and Jessen trace the historical channels of Boehme's reception among seminal figures in German and English Romanticism and also analyze the aesthetic, intellectual, and emotional appeal of Boehme's prophetic discourse for a formative generation in the history of Western literature. Hannak asks how and why Boehme was read as a *poet* in the German Romantic movement, explaining that for critics of rationalism, such as Novalis and Friedrich Schlegel, their project was to "poeticize" society, or make visible the spiritual. Turning to the English Romantics, Jessen contrasts the Behmenism of William Blake and Samuel Taylor Coleridge, arguing that the former's deeply felt, sensually animated, and anti-institutional engagement with Boehme made him the more authentic reader, while the latter's assessment was altogether more critically circumspect.

Blake found inspiration in Boehme for a radical ecclesiology. In distant Russia, however, it was the established Orthodox Church that provided the most receptive audience for his ideas. Since the arrival in Moscow of the Behmenist prophet Quirinus Kuhlmann in the late seventeenth century, Russian thought was continually nourished by Boehme's influence. In Chapter Eleven, Oliver Smith examines not only the intellectual impact of Boehme, initially through Masonic circles and later in Russian religious philosophy, but also his role in shaping the ideal landscapes of aristocratic estates in the later eighteenth century. Smith's analysis also illuminates the central importance of Boehme's Sophiology for the great Russian theologians of the late nineteenth and early twentieth centuries, concluding with the surprising interest in Boehme shown by Marxists and Soviet dissidents. Above all, this survey of the Russian reception illustrates the extraordinary variety of contexts in which Boehme has resonated as well as the astonishing range of modern thinkers to whom his writing has sounded prophetic.

A more familiar legacy, though equally significant, is the debt owed to Boehme by the German idealist philosophers. In Chapter Twelve, Glenn Magee reassesses his influence on perhaps the greatest of these, Georg Wilhelm Friedrich Hegel. As Magee illustrates, mystical influences on Hegel, and especially that of Boehme, have been somewhat marginalized in accounts of his philosophical development. In many respects, Magee's narrative picks up where Hannak's ends—with Schelling, Novalis, and Schlegel in Jena, representing the increasingly recognizable pattern of an intellectual network collectively seduced by Boehme's writings. The significance of this circle for Hegel, and especially his mentor and friend Schelling, forms the starting point for Magee's contention that Boehme supplied the watershed moment in Hegel's thought. Taking into account Hegel's own stated ambivalence, he nonetheless suggests that Hegel's writings continued to be fertilized by Boehme throughout his career. George Pattison pursues the evolutions of Boehme beyond German idealism, further into the nineteenth century and the work of the Danish Hegelian theologian, Hans Martensen. During a period in which theosophy and Darwinism became dominant conversation partners for theologians, Martensen's long engagement with Boehme came to fruition in his monograph on Boehme, published at the end of his life in 1881. Pattison suggests that, unlike some other readers of Boehme, Martensen's theosophical trajectory strayed from the apophatic center of Christian mysticism—the "wisdom of unknowing"—and towards a kind of gnosis.

It is the positive and uncompromising truth claims made by Boehme, especially the "initiatory" quality of his prose, which, as Arthur Versluis explains in Chapter Fourteen, present such a challenge to contemporary scholarship. A leading historian and theorist of Western esotericism, Versluis maps out the different prospects for Boehme's role in the modern field of esoteric studies. Of particular difficulty for scholars working in this area is the ambiguity of Boehme's intellectual identity: he draws together threads from alchemical, astrological, Kabbalistic, and mystical traditions, some of which are more congenial to the epistemological assumptions of modern esotericism than others. However, Versluis shows that this dynamic status helpfully draws attention to the taxonomical problems inherent in the category of the "esoteric" itself. Bringing the question of influence and appropriation forward to the present moment, the concluding chapter by Bruce Janz asks why Boehme matters today. Writing from the perspective of a philosopher, Janz suggests that it is the uncontained creativity of Boehme's thinking that provides a source of inspiration for contemporary readers. Refusing to be inhibited by conventions of language or conceptual organization, Boehme is relentless in his appetite for fresh solutions to renewed questions. The legacy of this startling originality is not only to be found in direct intellectual genealogies or explicit adherence. Janz suggests, "The most interesting Boehme today is the one we don't know is there, the one who has become part of the backdrop against which other concepts strive for manifestation."

Pathways in the reception history of Boehme—not all of which are covered in this volume—are bewildering in their variety and divergent courses. There is far more to say, of course, about Boehme's impact on philosophy (Nietzsche and Schopenhauer), literature (Emerson, Lawrence, and Yeats), psychoanalysis (Jung) and religion (theosophy and Pentecostalism). These essays are intended to provide a stimulus for further research and the beginning of a coherent narrative explaining the place that Boehme occupies in the "backdrop" of modernity. Our volume underscores the irreducible specificity of historical context in Boehme's reception, while also highlighting some themes that transcend the particular. The mysteriousness of the visionary genre, its transformative potency combined with its obstinate opacity, has resonated counter-culturally in intellectual environments increasingly dominated by positivism and distaste for mystery. But rather than placing a traditionalist harness on rampant modernity, Boehme offers a dynamic alternative, as much in tune with postmodern critical theory as with seventeenth-century prophecy: the creative striving for new ways of speaking that will open up new ways of thinking.

NOTES

1. We are grateful to Jennifer Smyth for her translations from the French and German.
2. William Law, *The Spirit of Love* (London: W. Innys, 1752), 37; Louis Claude de Saint-Martin, *Le ministère de l'homme-esprit* (Paris, 1802), 43; Friedrich von Schlegel, *Philosophische vorlesungen aus den jahren 1804 bis 1806* (Bonn: Eduard Weber, 1836), 424; Hans Martensen, *Jacob Boehme: Studies in his Life and Teaching*, trans. T. Rhys Evans, revised Stephen Hobhouse (New York: Harper, 1949), 1; Alexander Whyte, *Jacob Behmen: an Appreciation* (Edinburgh & London: Oliphant, Anderson & Ferrier, 1894), 7; Franz Hartmann, *The Life and Doctrines of Jacob Boehme the God-Taught Philosopher* (Boston: The Occult Publishing Company, 1891), 17; Jacob Boehme, *Concerning the Three Principles of the Divine Essence*, ed. C.J. Barker

(London: John Watkins, 1910), xxxvi; K. Francke, "The place of Sebastian Franck and Jakob Boehme in the history of German Literature," *Germanic Review*, 1 (1926), 4; Nikolai Berdyaev, "Review of Heinrich Bornkamm, *Luther und Boehme* (1925)," *Put'*, 5 (1926), 119, trans. S. Janos, http://www.berdyaev.com/berdiaev/berd_lib/1926_316.html; Walter Benjamin, *The Origin of German Tragic Drama*, trans. John Osborne (1928; London: Verso, 2003), 201.

3. Boehme, *Three Principles*, ed. Barker, li; Rufus Jones, *Spiritual Reformers in the 16th and 17th Centuries* (1914; reprinted Gloucester, MA: Peter Smith, 1971), 171; Harold Höffding, *A Brief History of Modern Philosophy*, trans. Charles Finley Sanders (New York: Macmillan, 1922), 14; Isaak Dorner, *History of Protestant Theology Particularly in Germany*, trans. George Robson and Sophia Taylor (2 vols., Edinburgh: T. & T. Clark, 1871), vol. 2, 184; John Stoudt, *Sunrise to Eternity. A Study in Jacob Boehme's Life and Thought* (Philadelphia: University of Pennsylvania Press, 1957), 8.
4. Caroline Spurgeon, *Mysticism in English Literature* (Cambridge: Cambridge University Press, 1913), 91; Jones, *Spiritual Reformers*, 171; Evelyn Underhill, *Mysticism* (12th edn., 1930, reprinted, Oxford: Oneworld, 1993), 469; Nikolai Berdyaev, "Studies concerning Jacob Boehme. The Teaching about the Ungrund and Freedom," *Put'* 20 (1930), 47–79, trans. S. Janos http://www.berdyaev.com/berdiaev/berd_lib/1930_349.htm.
5. Cyril O'Regan, *Gnostic Apocalypse. Jacob Boehme's Haunted Narrative* (Albany, NY: State University of New York, 2002), 3.
6. Henry Hallam, *Introduction to the Literature of Europe in the Fifteenth, Sixteenth, and Seventeenth Centuries* (4 vols., London: John Murray, 1837–39), vol. 3, 154.
7. Robert Vaughan, *Hours with the Mystics* (6th edn., London: Gibbings & Co., 1893), vol. 2, 120; Dorner, *Protestant Theology*, vol. 2, 184; Martensen, *Boehme*, 1; Emile Boutroux, *Historical Studies in Philosophy*, trans. Fred Rothwell (London: Macmillan, 1912), 169, 171.
8. Martensen, *Boehme*, 1.
9. *Memoirs of the Life, Death, Burial and Wonderful Writings of Jacob Behmen*, trans. Francis Okely (Northampton: James Lackington, 1780), 61.
10. An Italian translation begun in 1684 was abandoned and remained unpublished. There are also eighteenth-century Swedish translations from the German as well as Danish and perhaps also Finnish versions extant in manuscript. Unlike Johann Arndt, however, Boehme does not appear to have been translated into Icelandic.
11. Pierre Poiret, "Lettre," in *La Theologie Réelle Vulgairement ditte La Theologie Germanique* (Amsterdam: Hendrick Wettstein, 1700), 51; Saint-Martin, *Le ministère*, 43.
12. Franz von Baader, *Sämmtliche Werke* (Leipzig: Herrmann Bethmann, 1852), vol. 3, 330n, 382.
13. Paola Mayer, *Jena Romanticism and Its Appropriation of Jacob Böhme: Theosophy, Hagiography, Literature* (McGill-Queen's University Press, 1999), 49n, 72; Sigmund Freud, *The Joke and its Relation to the Unconscious*, trans. Joyce Crick (London: Penguin, 2002), 75.
14. Samuel Coleridge, *A Book I Value. Selected Marginalia*, ed. H.J. Jackson (Princeton, NJ: Princeton University Press, 2003), 28–29; Samuel Coleridge, *Biographia literaria* (2 vols., London: Rest Fenner, 1817), vol. 1, 138–39.
15. Ralph Waldo Emerson, *Journals*, eds. E.W. Emerson and W.E. Forbes (10 vols., London, Boston & New York: Houghton Mifflin Company, 1910–14), vol. 6, 517–18; Ralph Waldo Emerson, *Representative Men*, ed. Andrew Delbanco (Cambridge, MA: Harvard University Press, 1996), 66, 76, 80.

16. John Wesley, *Works of John Wesley* (3rd edn., 14 vols., London: John Mason, 1831), vol. 1, 375–76, vol. 3, 502–03, vol. 9, 509–14.
17. Johann Lorenz Mosheim, *An Ecclesiastical History*, trans. Archibald Maclaine (4 vols., Dublin: Ann Leathley, 1767), vol. 4, 217.
18. William Warburton, *The Doctrine of Grace* (2 vols., London: A. Millar, 1763), vol. 2, 150–52.
19. William Jones, *Memoirs of the Life, Studies, and Writings of . . . George Horne* (London: G. G. and J. Robinson, 1795), 73, 198.
20. The title-page is dated June 12, 1612.
21. O'Regan, *Gnostic Apocalypse*, 1.
22. Rudolf Steiner, *Mystics of the Renaissance*, trans. Bertram Keightley (New York & London: The Knickerbocker Press, 1911), 232.
23. Underhill, *Mysticism*, 469.

2 Boehme's Life and Times

Ariel Hessayon[1]

I BOEHME'S LIFE: DISTINGUISHING TRUTH FROM MYTH

There have been few more polarizing figures in early modern religious history than the German Lutheran mystic Jacob Boehme (ca.1575–1624), who has been regarded as a divinely illuminated genius by his most devoted disciples yet also reviled in equal measure as an incomprehensible, ignorant heretic by his fiercest critics. Partly derived from his reminiscences in conversation, Boehme's earliest biography was posthumously crafted, embroidered, and continually reworked by his principal admirer, the Silesian nobleman Abraham von Franckenberg (1593–1652). It is predominantly hagiographic, the eight extant versions produced between 1631 and 1651, supplementing aspects of Boehme's own carefully self-fashioned identity, which emphasized that though a humble, innocent artisan, he was the recipient of profound God-given knowledge.

Contrary to what has usually been assumed, the date of Boehme's nativity is uncertain. Most likely, he was born sometime between mid-November 1574 and mid-June 1575. Boehme was the fourth of five children of Jacob (d.1618) and his first wife Ursula (d.1607?), Lutheran peasants undoubtedly not of the "poorest sort" as von Franckenberg claimed—they were modest farmers—yet possibly of "sober and honest demeanour." He came from the village of Alt-Seidenberg (modern Zawidów, Poland). This was roughly eight miles from Görlitz, a town in Upper Lusatia of around 10,000 inhabitants by 1600. During his childhood, Boehme was said to have tended cattle and subsequently to have attended school, where he probably received an elementary education. Young Jacob, whose father was a lay jurist, deacon, and vestryman, was, according to von Franckenberg, "addicted to the feare of God" and a "willing hearer" of church sermons.[2] Progressing from shoemaker's apprentice to journeyman, he registered himself as a burgher of Görlitz and purchased a cobbler's shop there for 240 marks on April 24, 1599. Just over two weeks later on May 10th, he married Katharina Kuntzschmann, a wealthy local butcher's daughter. They had four sons: Jacob (bap. January 29, 1600–fl. 1628), Michael (bap. January 8, 1602–fl. March 1608), Tobias (bap. September 11, 1603–fl. 1630), and

Elias (bap. September 4, 1611–d. November 10, 1625).[3] On August 21st, 1599, Boehme bought a large property for three hundred marks on the east bank of the river Neisse, which still stands.[4]

Boehme's earliest premonitions and visionary experiences are undated. While still a boy tending cattle, he climbed the Landeskrone (a hill southwest of Görlitz), where among the big red stones he found a wooden container full of money. Being honest, he left this untouched, and von Franckenberg later interpreted the incident –which may have been invented given its similarity to local legends—as an omen of Boehme's "future spiritual Admission to the Sight of the hidden Treasury of the Wisdom and Mysteries of God and Nature."[5] On another occasion, when an apprentice minding his master's shop, Boehme was said to have been visited by a stranger who predicted greatness for him as well as misery, poverty, and persecution. A different time, Boehme had his first supposed visionary experience when, having "awakened within himself" and at the same time become alarmed by "manifold scholarly quarrelling over religion (to which he could not conform and subject himself)," he was enraptured by a divine light for seven days.[6] Then about 1600, Boehme was again possessed with a divine light and, suddenly seeing a pewter vessel, was "brought to the inward ground or *Centrum* of the hidden *Nature*." Presently going out into an open field he beheld "the *Wonder-workes* of the Creator" in the "Signatures, Shapes, Figures, and Qualities or Properties of all created things," very clearly and manifestly laid open.[7]

In 1610, having vended his property but continuing to live there paying rent, Boehme bought two houses for 375 marks. He sold the smaller and made the other his home. This new dwelling was very close to his old residence, situated within the Neisse Gate at the eastern edge of Görlitz and conveniently on the road to Liegnitz (modern Legnica, Poland). That same year, he also received a third divine illumination. Unwilling to forget what had been imparted to him by the Holy Spirit, he secretly set pen to paper for his own edification. Between January and June of 1612, he made a fair copy of his celebrated "Morgenröthe im Aufgang" or "Aurora" (literally "Morning Glow, Ascending"), a long, unfinished work that seems to have been at least twelve years in the making. But following the clandestine circulation of the manuscript and the transcription of additional copies—probably on the initiative of a good friend, Karl Ender von Sercha (1568–1624), though supposedly without the author's consent—there was trouble. According to von Franckenberg, Boehme was subjected to virulent invective poured out from the pulpit by Pastor Gregor Richter (1560–1624), who stirred up the magistracy against him. Consequently, this humble and "blessed" man was committed to custody, had his book seized, was declared an idiot, and admonished to refrain from writing such books that "*did not belong to his profession and condition*."[8]

These events can be corroborated by the diary of Bartholomäus Scultetus (1540–1614), who, besides being a notable mathematician, astronomer, and advocate of Paracelsian teaching, was then Görlitz's mayor. Although Scultetus's diary is no longer extant, there exist slightly different versions of three extracts referring to Boehme. Thus Scultetus recorded that on Friday, July 26th, 1613:

> Jacob Boehme, a shoemaker living between the gates behind the hospital forge, was summoned to the Senate-House for punishment and asked about his enthusiastic opinions. Thereupon he was put in prison and as soon as his book, written in quarto, was brought from his house by Oswald [Krause], he was released from confinement and warned to cease from such matters.[9]

Then on Sunday, July 28th, Scultetus noted that Richter used a text against false prophets to preach a sharp and "tart" sermon against Boehme the shoemaker. Finally, on Tuesday, July 30th, Boehme was brought before Görlitz's Lutheran ministry and rigorously examined "concerning his Confession of Faith."[10]

By this time, Boehme had already sold his cobbler's bench and begun to engage in small-scale commerce, trading in yarns and gloves. After an interval of several years, he had a fourth spiritual experience that resulted in his most creative period. Supposedly stirred up again by the motion of the Holy Spirit and encouraged by the entreaties of certain God-fearing people, he took up his pen, producing "The Three Principles of the Divine Essence" (1619), "The Threefold Life of Man" (completed and copied by September 1620), "Forty Questions concerning the Soul" (completed by August 1620), "The Incarnation of Jesus Christ" (completed between May and August 1620), "Six Points," both "Great" and "Small" (1620), and a number of other treatises, including "Signatura Rerum" (completed by August 1621) and "Mysterium Magnum" (completed by September 1623). Von Franckenberg claimed that, although Boehme wrote slowly in a plain, legible hand, he never altered nor crossed out a single word in his writing, "but just as it was suggested to his Mind by the Spirit of God, so it stood clear and untranscribed upon the Paper."[11] Unless one believes in divine dictation, such astonishing fluency can be discounted. There are, for example, two different versions of the "Aurora" extant in the hands of various copyists. One is significantly shorter, suggesting that Boehme's method of composition was to elaborate on inchoate drafts. If he then finished these works as the opportunity arose, this explains how he seemingly wrote so much so quickly.

Boehme boasted that his manuscript writings were known throughout Silesia as well as in many places in the Margraviate of Brandenburg, Meissen, and Saxony. Even so, they remained in that form until the beginning of January 1624 when Johann Sigismund von Schweinichen (1590–1664) paid for the unauthorized printing of *Der Weg zu Christo* (Görlitz, 1624), which contained three short pieces: "True Repentance," "True Resignation," and "A Dialogue between a scholar and his master, concerning the Super-sensual life." This transition from scribal publication to print was important. Nevertheless, having a work in the public domain without the approval of Görlitz's town council or clergy antagonized Richter, who denounced Boehme as a "common Disturber of the Peace, a turbulent, restless, sorry Fellow, and a Heretic." So bitter was Richter's tirade that the matter came to the attention of Görlitz's town council.[12] Presented with "manifold" complaints against Boehme's "alleged pernicious doctrine," they decreed that he be summoned before them. Their minute-book of March 26th, 1624 records that:

> the shoemaker and confused enthusiast or visionary, says that he composed the book . . . though he did not have it printed . . . Was warned by the Council to seek fortune elsewhere, or in default of fair means this must be reported to the Illustrious Prince Elector. Thereupon he declared that he would take his departure as soon as possible.[13]

The next day, Richter finished the third and final part of his humanist satire, censuring the "enthusiastic shoemaker's fanatic books." Here, Richter inveighed against Boehme's new manner of speaking and the many blasphemies in his text, which stank "*abominably of* Shoemakers Pitch *and* Blacking." Among these alleged noxious notions were Boehme's denial of God the Father's eternity and his teaching of a Quaternity, or four-fold nature of God. There was also personal vilification: the shoemaker was an unlearned, drunken, rascally knave aspiring to be a new prophet when he was really the Antichrist. Boehme in turn quickly wrote a letter to the council (April 3rd) pleading that he was a simple layman whose divinely inspired work should not be condemned to be burned and including an impassioned defense refuting this horrid libel (10 April).[14]

Although Richter had demanded Boehme's banishment, and although a fanciful story circulating more than twenty-five years later claimed that this falsely accused "patient and blessed" man was banished by majority verdict of the town council only to be recalled the following day, Boehme was admonished rather than commanded by the council to go away for a while.[15] Clearly, it was advisable to leave until the controversy abated; as he put it, "the fire of *Satans* Anger and Rage burneth *at Home*."[16] Initially he headed south to Zittau. There he met with some adherents before traveling west to Dresden at the invitation of certain eminent people attending the court of Johann Georg I, Prince-Elector of Saxony. Setting out on May 9th, 1624, and arriving by May 15th, Boehme stayed at the home of the court's alchemist, Benedikt Hinckelmann (d.1642). Word of his coming soon spread among the Prince-Elector's entourage, and influential figures such as councilor Joachim von Loß (1576–1633); the Marshal of the House, Alexander von Ragewitz (d.1629); and Dietrich von Taube (1594–1639), who was Master of Horse and chief chamberlain, signaled their desire to meet with him. Boehme explained this surprisingly warm reception, which differed sharply from his treatment at Görlitz, by ingenuously remarking that his little printed book was "loved and liked" by these great personages—so much so that many consulted it daily, acknowledging it to be a "*divine Gift.*" Presently, on the feast of Pentecost (Whitsunday), May 26th, Johann Melchior von Schwalbach (1581–1635), von Ragewitz, von Taube, and an unnamed councilor visited Boehme at his lodging. They apparently listened to him very willingly in an atmosphere of love and kindness, promising their "favour and assistance." The following Thursday, May 30th, Boehme was fetched by coach together with Hinckelmann and a physician to von Loß's castle about a mile from Dresden. Von Loß was considered a very learned man and he, too, loved Boehme's "Cause and *Gifts.*" Indeed, Boehme expected von Loß to act as his patron, thereby enabling him to publish his work more freely without fear of retribution. Another noteworthy reader and apparent admirer of Boehme's treatise on "True Repentance" was the Lutheran superintendent Ägidus Strauch (1583–1657), who, together with the court chaplain, Dr Matthias Hoë von Hoënegg (1580–1645), had begun teaching the doctrine of "the New Birth and the *Inward* Man." Even so, Strauch still required clarification on certain abstruse points beyond his comprehension and arranged for a conference with Boehme at his lodging on Sunday, June 16th.[17]

While the details of Boehme's theological discussions at Dresden are unknown, there is no contemporary evidence indicating that he was formally examined about his views. This official silence contrasts with the well-known account of the Breslau physician, Cornelius Weißner, who, after initially rejecting Boehme's ideas, became a follower. Writing in February of 1651, Weißner maintained that Boehme was interviewed in the presence of the Prince-Elector by six Lutheran theologians, including the famous Johann Gerhard (1582–1637), and two professors of mathematics about the "high Mysteries" contained in his writings. He responded to their difficult theological, philosophical, and astrological questions with such "meekness of spirit" and "depth of knowledge" that these eminent men reportedly found nothing objectionable in his "mild" answers.[18] Despite being widely accepted during the seventeenth century and indeed reinforced with a document written by a Görlitz councilor in 1669, modern scholarship has generally questioned the reliability of Weißner's narrative even though there is universal agreement that no judgment was passed against Boehme. All the same, the motivations of the various councilors and court officials mentioned in Boehme's correspondence are not entirely clear, nor do we know what may have happened behind the scenes. It does appear, however, that Boehme's announcement of the dawn of a Great Reformation, of a new age of love, patience, peace and joy, went largely unheeded.

By July, Boehme had returned to Görlitz. Despite probable exhaustion, he then undertook a journey to the family seat of his supporter von Schweinichen at Schweinhaus, Silesia (modern Świny, Poland). There he spent several weeks in the company of von Schweinichen and von Franckenberg. Boehme was in ill health, however, and, despite subsisting on a practically vegetarian diet, fell sick about mid-August of a burning fever which he exacerbated by drinking too much water.[19] At his request, he was taken back to Görlitz, arriving at his house on November 7th, where the Paracelsian physician, Tobias Kober (1587–1625), and his colleague, Melchior Berndt of Zittau, attended him. But they despaired of his symptoms: rumbling bowels, pain in his left side, swollen belly and feet, gaping mouth, great decay of the chest and face, and discolored urine. With the end approaching, Boehme received Pastor Elias Dietrich, who required his assent to questions of faith before administering the sacrament of the Lord's Supper to him. Boehme died about six o'clock in the morning on Sunday, November 17th, 1624. Shortly beforehand, he supposedly called his son Tobias, asking him whether he heard the "sweet" harmonious music without his chamber. Boehme's last recorded words were "*Now go I hence into Paradise*."[20]

At Boehme's request, the funeral arrangements were undertaken by Kober, but the dead man's family and friends were unable to prevent both the shunning of his corpse by the majority of Görlitz's clergy and the subsequent desecration of his grave. Although the text first chosen for Boehme's funeral sermon was Revelation 3:5, the new principal minister Nikolaus Thomas—Richter had predeceased Boehme by three months—washed his hands of it, insisting he would have nothing to do with a man notorious for infecting the region with "*Fanaticism* and *Enthusiasm*." Boehme's widow, Katharina, and his heirs were thus forced to petition the mayor, who convened a meeting of the town council. After much debate and with legal approval, they concluded that it was a humane and pious duty to grant heretics a decent burial and for the deceased to have a funeral sermon. The next day, Katharina and her children petitioned the town council, requesting immediate interment since Boehme's corpse was rapidly decomposing and ready to burst. They consented. Pastor Dietrich who, like his senior colleague, had refused to preach the funeral sermon, was ordered to do so and instructed to pass over Boehme's doctrinal errors in silence. On Wednesday, November 20th, the church bells of St. Nicholas were rung, hymns sung, and Boehme, neatly dressed within his coffin, was solemnly laid to rest. Although the principal minister had excused himself from the occasion by pretending to be sick, three other clergymen were obliged to join the procession to the grave, which was very near the churchyard's center. They slunk off, however, at the nearest opportunity and did not enter church with other mourners as was customary. Despite some mockery amongst the "great concourse" of people present, the cortege of friends, sympathizers, shoemakers, and tanners outnumbered them. Inside, Dietrich began his sermon by saying he would rather be elsewhere, asserting that he did not share Boehme's heterodox beliefs. Having publicly exculpated himself with this unusual preamble, he pointedly chose to preach on Hebrews 9:27, "it is appointed unto men once to die, but after this the judgment." In the evening, Dietrich returned his fee and, fearing censure from his fellow priests for having complied with the council's directive, requested an indemnification from them.[21]

Boehme's grave was originally marked by a black wooden cross sent as a gift by unnamed Silesian friends (probably von Schweinichen and, among others, perhaps also von Franckenberg). Erected at least one day after his burial, it fittingly consisted of an elaborate "Hieroglyphical Monument." At its top was the Hebrew name of Jesus "יהשוה" encompassed by twelve golden beams, under which a reclining child rested its head on a skull. Below were eight initials, V.H.I.L.I.C.I.V., representing Boehme's motto, "Unser Heil Im Leben Jesu Christi In Uns" (*Our Salvation is In the Life of Jesus Christ In Us*). And below that, a broad oval circle on which was inscribed Boehme's epitaph. His last words were written on the vertical shaft reading upwards. Yet the most enigmatic feature was a threefold painted "mystical" device. On the right from the south side was a black eagle on a rock, its left foot treading on a serpent's head, its right clutching a palm, with a lily-twig in its beak (the lily-twig was a symbol of new regeneration affected by Christ's presence within man). On the left from the north side stood a lion with a crown and cross on its head, its right hind-foot on a cube, its left on a globe, its right fore-paw brandishing a flaming sword, and its left grasping a burning heart. In the middle, below the epitaph on the stock of the cross (and resembling the twenty-ninth of Paracelsus's magical figures) was a lamb with a bishop's miter, beneath a palm tree, by a spring in a meadow, feeding among flowers. Each device also bore a single Latin word, "veni," "vidi," "vici;" an apparent allusion to coming into the world, seeing Satan's fall, and conquering Hell. Within a year, however, this elaborate memorial had been "bespattered with Filth," mangled and defaced by the "*blind furious zeale*" of Boehme's hateful persecutors, who, unable to crucify the "blessed" man in life, destroyed his cross after death.[22]

There are no authentic portraits of Boehme. Those likenesses that exist—oddly, his hair tends to get thicker rather than thinner over time while his weight fluctuates alarmingly—appear to be based mainly on contemporary descriptions of his physical appearance. Best known is von Franckenberg's portrayal:

> The external physical form of J. B. was time-worn, of ordinary appearance, small stature, low forehead, raised temples, slightly hooked nose, grey or intensely sky-blue glittering eyes, which, moreover, were like windows to Solomon's Temple, a short and spare beard, and small thin voice; yet gracious of speech, well-bred in manner, humble of conduct, patient of suffering, gentle of heart. His spirit, highly illuminated by God beyond all natural measure, and his utterly pure, comprehensible High German manner of speaking can be judged and recognized from these, his unfalsified writings in the divine light.[23]

Christian Bernhard (d.1649), a toll-collector of Sagan (modern Zagan, Poland), depicted him similarly:

> A middling person, but for the most part smaller rather than larger, lean body, black beard, with a staff and little white sack of books, in which he

had a little bread, a slight black coat, miserable worn clothes, very dirty from pitch, in the manner of a cobbler. The pants wide open at the front.[24]

If the latter sketch is trustworthy, it represents an impecunious individual. While Boehme had evidently enjoyed a period of prosperity and indeed inherited half his father's estate in 1618, he apparently soon forsook his trade, devoting himself with little distraction to his calling. During intermittent periods of deprivation and devastation following the outbreak of

Figure 2.1 Jacob Boehme's house on the east bank of the river Neisse where he lived between 1599 and 1610. The property has undergone restoration since then and today houses a small museum in Zgorzelec, Poland. © Copyright Ariel Hessayon, June 2012

what became known as the Thirty Years' War (1618–1648), he received gifts of corn from his patron Karl Ender, which provided essential sustenance as well as a convenient method of smuggling books hidden within sacks. Other supporters sent him food and money, perhaps in exchange for permission to copy his anonymous manuscripts, whose contents and authorship were sometimes clarified by letters accompanying them. For his part, Boehme served as a go-between, negotiating the purchase of books at the Leipzig fair and the sale of other people's works as well as safe passage to the intended recipients. Although his wife continued the family yarn trading business, this still suggests an almost hand-to-mouth existence. Defending himself against Richter, Boehme claimed to be a poor beer-drinking man,

Figure 2.2 Plaque placed by the Oberlausitzische Gesellschaft der Wissenschaften outside Boehme's house on the tercentenary of his death in 1924. © Copyright Ariel Hessayon, June 2012

unable to afford foreign wine or brandy. Though little is known of his later financial affairs, Boehme may have died in relative poverty since a collection was taken to defray his funeral expenses. Besides property, the only thing of value he bequeathed was his writings, which had been dispersed. He left specific instructions to his son Tobias to collect them from the people they had been lent to, probably intending to deposit his literary remains with von Schweinichen.

Von Franckenberg added that Boehme had a seal consisting of a hand reaching out from heaven holding a stalk of three full-blown lilies. This represented the "Kingdom of the Lily in the Paradise of God," which was to

Figure 2.3 One of Boehme's later gravestones. This was erected in about 1800 on the initiative of Karl Gottlob von Anton, a member of Görlitz city senate, and funded by subscription. © Copyright Ariel Hessayon, June 2012

be manifested in the "last Time, when the End shall have been brought back to it's Beginning, and the Circle closed."[25] Boehme was also fond of signing friends' albums with a stanza:

> To whom Time is as Eternity,
> And Eternity as Time,
> He is freed from all strife.[26]

Figure 2.4 Top: Boehme's black marble gravestone placed by the Oberlausitzische Gesellschaft der Wissenschaften in 1869. The inscription includes a reference to Revelation 3:5, the text initially chosen for Boehme's funeral sermon. Bottom: Philosophische Kügel placed on top of Boehme's grave in 1922. It was donated by American admirers, Mr. Richard A. Beale and an unnamed countrywoman. © Copyright Ariel Hessayon, June 2012

II REAPPRAISING THE DEVELOPMENT OF BOEHME'S THOUGHT IN CONTEXT

Boehme's death served only to increase the aura surrounding this "great Wonder of the *German* Nation." His apparent meekness and piety were presented as a model of sanctity, his humble occupation compared favorably with the lowly trades of Christ's apostles, and his persecution by scholastically-trained clergymen likened to Jesus' fate at the hands of scheming Pharisees. Boehme thus became a "Witness of God," a "rejected Corner-Stone" (Psalm 118:22, Matthew 21:42) who had incurred the displeasure of "the logically-learned School-Gentry, and the Metaphysical Church-Luminaries."[27] Primarily disseminated through von Franckenberg's continually reworked hagiography and a trans-European epistolary network, a legend began to take shape portraying Boehme as a simple, barely literate artisan who had been given the gift of "Universall knowledge of God and Nature," and shown:

> the Centre of all Beings; *how all things arise from God Originally: consist in God, and againe returne, and flow in to him.*[28]

Praising Boehme's "*profound*" and "*deep-grounded*" writings, von Franckenberg also believed they hinted at the great wonders God would perform in future generations.[29]

Towards the end of his life, and certainly by 1620, some of Boehme's readers had begun calling him by the code-name "Teutonicus." Most likely this was a necessary expedient to protect his anonymity rather than, as von Franckenberg claimed, an honorific bestowed by the learned and much travelled Liegnitz physician Balthasar Walther (1558–ca.1630). A student of Paracelsus, alchemy, magic, and Kabbalah, Walther became acquainted with Boehme in 1617 and was subsequently briefly appointed director of the secret laboratory at Dresden. Walther was said to have dubbed Boehme the "*Teutonic* Philosopher," and von Franckenberg speculated that this either referred to the German Dominican friar Johannes Teutonicus (ca.1180–1252), or else indicated Boehme's nationality coupled with the "exceptional gift" of such works being "written in High German."[30] The moniker "Teutonicum Philosophum," however, did not appear in print until a decade after Boehme's death with the publication of an abridged and unreliable German edition of *Aurora* (Amsterdam, 1634). By 1647, the English translator John Sparrow had adopted the nominative form "Teutonicus Philosophus," which became anglicized as the "Teutonick Philosopher."

Significantly, despite declaring that he was a simple man and "no Prophet," "Teutonicus" (alias Boehme) was still regarded by certain followers as a prophet of the Thirty Years' War.[31] Although Boehme was not moved to address the conflict in a specific text, his writings, particularly his epistles, contain many references to contemporary events. Here the work of, among others, John Stoudt and, more recently, Andrew Weeks has done much to resituate Boehme within an historical context that too many—though by no means all—earlier scholars had been inclined to pass over. Thus, in "The Three Principles of the Divine Essence" (1619) Boehme despaired of the multitude of sects and religious controversies, warning that "great hatred," envy, and persecution fomented war and insurrection, which would lead to slaughter, destruction, and ruination.[32] Again, having recently witnessed the coronation at Prague of the Calvinist champion Frederick V of the Palatinate (the ill-fated "Winter King" of Bohemia), Boehme predicted in a letter dated November 14th, 1619, that there would be "great War and Contention" resulting in the desolation of many cities and strongholds. Drawing on the prophecies of Ezekiel, he foresaw "the great Slaughter of the children of *Babel*" at the hands of the Calvinist prince of Transylvania, Gabriel Bethlen (1580–1629), who had captured the Hungarian city Pressburg (modern Bratislava, Slovakia) and was marching on Vienna.[33] Following the passage through Görlitz of the newly elected Holy Roman Emperor Ferdinand II in March of 1620 and then in August of disease-carrying foreign mercenaries, the Catholic Emperor's Lutheran ally Johann Georg I of Saxony invaded western Lusatia on September 3rd. The Elector-Prince initially besieged and bombarded Bautzen, which capitulated on October 5th. Recounting what he had learned from soldiers and civilians fleeing the ruined town, Boehme described how Bautzen was ferociously and relentlessly pounded for three weeks with "terrible" canon fire and a variety of incendiary devices. Reportedly, 1,700 people were killed and more than 1,100 houses destroyed. Many survivors were trapped hidden in cellars among the smoking debris, and those managing to escape were robbed by an enemy intent on plunder. Fearing the loss of Lusatia, Boehme cautioned:

> Babel, the beast and the whore are in flames. He who now hopes to become blessed must gird himself with patience and assume nothing worldly for himself, for he will receive nothing and shall indeed lose his soul.[34]

The apocalyptic mood was pervasive. That summer, a Liegnitz toll-collector named Paul Kaym (d.1634) had written to Boehme enclosing two small treatises. These contained chiliastic interpretations of scriptural passages concerning the "*Last Times*," "the first Resurrection of the dead," the thousand-year Sabbath, the ruin and imminent fall of Babel (which would be utterly destroyed about 1630), and the rebuilding of Zion, which would usher in a golden age. Responding on August 14th, 1620, Boehme cautiously agreed that the growth and imminent destruction of Babel was manifest. All the same, because there were only hints of these events in Revelation and the apocryphal 2 Esdras, he did not know when this would happen; nor did Boehme know whether the world would continue for seven thousand years or if there was to be a millennial Sabbath, since these were mysteries hidden from mankind. Accordingly, he warned against attempting to penetrate God's secrets without divine illumination.[35] This reluctance to become embroiled in the specifics of apocalyptic chronology was consistent with Boehme's understanding of the Last Judgment: he believed that, at the end of time, God would punish the wicked and reward his martyred saints together with the rest of the righteous godly, but he did not risk calculating a date. He eventually enlarged on this subject in what appears to have been a lost book on the "Last Judgment" (1624?)—a work reportedly destroyed during the burning of Gross Glogau, Silesia (modern Głogów, Poland).

Though not a committed millenarian, Boehme nonetheless became convinced as the war progressed that a period of great tribulation had begun; war, uproar, insurrection, calamity, and death were imminent. In an unusual postscript to a letter dated February 20th, 1623, addressed to von Franckenberg, he drew on an established tradition of political prophecy that fused biblical symbols with heraldic devices to make a series of bold predictions: Babel would be destroyed, the Turks would turn Christian, and the Holy Roman Emperor's underlings would turn upon him savagely, clipping his military power.[36]

While the earliest phase of the Thirty Years' War provides a crucial if sometimes neglected backdrop for reading Boehme's letters and later treatises, his engagement with contemporary affairs was of longstanding duration. Thus, he continually despaired of hypocrisy and contention, bemoaning the debilitating effect of intra-denominational religious disputes as well as untrammeled magisterial authority operating in conjunction with clerical self-interest to enforce outward conformity. Moreover, as Weeks has shown, sections of many works can also be read as irenic, anticlerical interventions in heated doctrinal debates over the sacrament of the Lord's Supper and the related issue of scriptural authority. As he notes in our volume, the original fair copy of this text was transcribed during a six-month period between January and June of 1612, coinciding with important political developments and debates about guaranteeing religious toleration in Upper Lusatia.[37] Context, however, is not all. For there is an additional psychological dimension: the transformative illuminative experience that impelled Boehme to compose "Aurora" had been preceded by a prolonged bout of melancholy. This passage from depression to exaltation, suggestive of a troubled soul, was typical of many seventeenth-century Protestant religious autobiographies, which frequently culminated with the spiritual suffering, even death, of the sinful protagonist and their joyful rebirth in the light and love of God.[38]

Boehme maintained in his correspondence that he had written "Aurora" in sudden bursts of inspiration, like a shower of rain which hit "whatsoever it lighteth upon." He could have written in "a more accurate, fair, and plain" manner, yet "the burning fire did often force forward with *speed*; and the hand and pen must hasten directly after it." When deprived of divine knowledge, however, he could scarcely recognize or understand his own writings. Boehme also ingenuously claimed that he was an "illiterate," simple man of little "understanding, and shallow capacity." He had not received instruction from men or learning from reading books, but had written "out of my own Book which was opened in me, being the Noble similitude of God."[39] This self-serving myth was perpetuated by von Franckenberg, who insisted that Boehme wrote secretly for his own benefit and that, when setting pen to paper, he was "furnished with no Books at all but the Holy Bible."[40] Elsewhere, however, Boehme was slightly more candid about his sources. In "Aurora" and then the "Three Principles," he acknowledged having read the writings of "very high Masters, hoping to find therein the ground and true depth." Among these were works by students of physics, mathematics, and astrology. To his dismay, he found nothing his soul lusted after within these "Master-pieces," only "very many contrary opinions," and a "*half dead* Spirit."[41]

Besides texts, Boehme acquired knowledge through an increasingly widening social network of friends, correspondents, and patrons—a milieu fleshed out fully in Leigh's Penman's chapter. Thus, it appears Boehme drew on the same rhetorical techniques as Martin Moller (1547–1606), appointed chief pastor at St. Nicholas, Görlitz in July of 1600.[42] The author of several works, including *Mysterium Magnum* (1595) and *Praxis Evangeliorum* (1601), Moller's teachings emphasized regeneration, Christ within, and the primacy of inward spiritual experience. Although Moller died when Boehme was aged about thirty-one, linguistic parallels suggest that his sermons may have left an impression on Boehme's "Aurora."[43] Whether or not this book was secretly circulated among the remnants of Moller's "Conventicle of God's Real Servants" (of which Boehme was allegedly a member), it is clear that, through scribal publication, it brought him to far wider attention. Repeatedly copied, versions of the text passed through villages, towns, and cities where they were seen by clergymen, physicians, and members of the nobility. Consequently, Boehme was implored by the more receptive of his predominantly well-educated readership to reveal more of his "gifts, knowledge, and confession." Never a lay preacher and uncomfortable in this newly assigned role of teacher, he nonetheless relented, acquiring disciples through a mixture of receiving guests, personal visits, and epistolary exchange.[44]

Among Boehme's circle were physicians, alchemists, mystics, prophets, possessors of magical and Rosicrucian works, various toll collectors, officials, and noblemen. As Weeks, Penman, and others have recognized, this apparently exclusively male network, which was spread across parts of the Margraviate of Brandenburg, Saxony, Lusatia, Silesia, and Bohemia, played an important part in shaping the direction of Boehme's intellectual development. Equally significant were the mercantile journeys that took Boehme to Breslau, Prague, Sagan, and Zittau, bringing him into touch with sympathetic tradesmen. Moreover, from 1621 he began visiting supporters among the Protestant dissenters in Silesia and elsewhere. These additional contacts provided him with news and probably made it easier to acquire writings in his native tongue.[45]

As we have seen, Boehme seldom named his sources. Even so, he appears to have been familiar with a range of doctrines enunciated by Magisterial, Radical, and Spiritual Reformers. Among the most important of these were Martin Luther and mediators of his thought. Boehme had certainly heard Lutheran sermons and hymns; was familiar with Lutheran prayer formula; and upheld Lutheran teaching on the importance of personal faith for salvation, on grace being freely given as a gift by God, on Christ's corporeal presence within the Communion bread and wine, and on the ubiquity of Christ's body. But though Boehme affirmed essential articles of Lutheran faith prior to receiving absolution and the sacrament of the Lord's Supper on his deathbed, he diverged from Luther on several significant points—notably on the crucial question of free will, where he also differed sharply from mainstream Calvinist thinking on predestination. Furthermore, Boehme's allegorical method of scriptural exegesis went against the grain of Luther's predominantly literal biblical commentaries (if not his sermons). Consequently, and without biblical justification, Boehme developed beliefs on the process of creation, the fall of the rebel angels, and Adam's prelapsarian androgynous nature that were fundamentally opposed to Lutheran orthodoxy. In addition, and with a measure of justification, Boehme has been regarded as an independently minded interpreter and continuator of the Spiritual Reformers and an inheritor of a religious tendency—tradition might be too strong—incorporating writings by or attributed to Sebastian Franck (1499–1542), Caspar Schwenckfeld (1490–1561), and Valentin Weigel (1533–1588).

Boehme does not mention or allude to Franck, and if he did happen upon his teachings, then these may have been mediated to him indirectly. But he does engage critically with Schwenckfeld, conspicuously on the connected issues of Christ's nature and how Christ was present in humanity. There had been a substantial and visible Schwenckfelder presence in Görlitz from the 1560s, and since a number of Boehme's most prominent supporters had Schwenckfelder backgrounds, it is unsurprising that Boehme was familiar with some of Schwenkfeld's works.[46] Likewise Boehme knew Weigel, sometimes borrowing—most likely from influential manuscript works on cosmogony—and occasionally controverting. Thus, Boehme asserted that Weigel erred in denying that the Virgin Mary had been entirely human, yet at the same time concurred with Weigel's treatment of the "new birth" and the "union of humanity in Christ." Accordingly, he neither condemned nor despised Weigel's writings, nor those who read them.[47] Boehme may also have read devotional works by the Lutheran theologian Johann Arndt (1555–1621). Drawing on a range of mystical writings, Arndt's teaching emphasized faith, humility, prayer, and true repentance. Examples of similarities of thought, however, may be explained by common dependence on the same sources, notably Weigel and Paracelsus.

Boehme's indebtedness to Paracelsus is indisputable. He drew on him when writing "Aurora" and defended Paracelsus's opinions in correspondence with Paul Kaym. From Paracelsus, either directly or else mediated by his medical acquaintances, Boehme derived the alchemically inflected terms *arcana*, *tincture*, and *turba* together with the three categories of Salt, Mercury, and Sulphur. So extensive was this borrowing that it did not escape the notice of contemporary critics: Christian Beckmann found more than twenty-five instances of words and phrases used by Boehme in a manner similar to Paracelsus and Weigel, while Erasmus Francisci stated that Boehme quoted from Paracelsus on more than thirty occasions.[48] Modern scholars concur. Yet Boehme's treatment of Paracelsus was not slavish. As Howard Brinton observed, he initially contradicted the Paracelsian or pseudo-Paracelsian *Philosophia ad Athenienses* (*Philosophy to the Athenians*) on the question of whether God created heaven and earth out of nothing.[49] Interestingly, the English translation of the Paracelsian *Aurora* was published with a discourse attributed to Johann Siebmacher entitled *Wasserstein der Weysen* (*Water-Stone of the Wise Men*; Frankfurt, 1619). In a letter of July 1622, Boehme commended the printed version of this work as a clear and worthy exposition of the alchemical art.[50]

There were also several comparatively obscure figures with whose writings Boehme engaged: Hans Weyrauch, Balthaser Tilke (fl.1621), Ezechiel Meth (d.1640), Esajas Stiefel (1561–1627), Paul Kaym, and perhaps Paul Nagel. Weyrauch claimed prophetic gifts and was said to have been a weaver from Olmütz, Moravia (modern Olomouc, Czech Republic). Having examined his writings, Boehme conceded that he may be an "honest Brother," but nonetheless rejected Weyrauch's boast of secret knowledge.[51] Tilke was a Silesian nobleman and suspected crypto-Calvinist who wrote a pasquinade against certain notions expounded in Boehme's "Aurora" and then a refutation of Boehme's fifth book. With these libels in hand, Boehme responded with two polemical apologies. Meth was an alchemist with messianic pretensions, some of whose letters survive and against whom Boehme wrote in 1622. These messianic delusions were shared by Meth's uncle Stiefel. An avid follower of Weigel and an antinomian sect-master who believed himself incapable of sinning, Stiefel was among the first to mention Boehme's doctrines in print. The connection was probably established by Stiefel's former supporter, Balthasar Walther. Doubtless through a trusted intermediary, Stiefel sent a treatise on "The Threefold State of Man" with accompanying letter to Boehme. The "Teutonick" completed his response on April 18th, 1621, acknowledging that Stiefel "may indeed, be an honest or vertuous new born or *Regenerate Man*, and in Christ with his *New-birth*." But he fervently denied that Stiefel had attained total perfection, believing it impossible for the outward body to achieve this on earth. Boehme followed this with a response to Stiefel's exposition of four scriptural texts.[52] As for Nagel, he was an alchemist, astrologer, and chiliastic prophet from Torgau, Saxony. A reader of Weigel as well as Boehme's "Aurora" in manuscript, he reproduced extracts from the latter concerning the creation of three angelic kingdoms in his pamphlet *Prodromus astronomiae apocalypticae* (*Herald of apocalyptic astronomy*; Danzig, 1620).[53]

Taken together, these mediated and directly encountered textual and oral sources explain the otherwise problematic presence in the corpus of a non-university educated shoemaker of sophisticated mystical, apocalyptic, alchemical, astrological, and seemingly Gnostic, Neoplatonic, and Kabbalistic ideas—especially since Boehme did not read Hebrew, Greek, or Latin. Thus, through Luther's writings or perhaps Moller's instruction, Boehme may have become acquainted with devotional and mystical works by the German Dominicans Meister Eckhart (ca.1260–1328), Johannes Tauler (ca.1300–1361), and Heinrich Suso (ca.1295–1366); Thomas à Kempis (ca.1380–1471); as well as the anonymous fourteenth-century *Theologia Germanica*. This could account for the current of negative theology and fascination with the abyss in his writings. Certainly von Franckenberg, who became a devotee of these "old *German* enlightened Men," purposefully positioned Boehme within a tradition of German mysticism.[54] Again, Stoudt and, more recently, Cyril O'Regan have suggested that Boehme's apocalyptic thought drew inspiration—however indirectly—from a deeper well, namely the tripartite eschatological scheme announced by the Calabrian-born abbot Joachim of Fiore (ca.1135–1202). Presumably mediated through Paracelsus or Lutheran interpreters more generally, Joachim's conception of three ages corresponding to God the Father (Jewish Law), God the Son (Christian Gospel), and the Holy Ghost (Spirit) must, as O'Regan accepts, have been drastically modified by Boehme; if, that is, he was ever aware of it. For although Boehme declared that the "great Day of Revelation and the Final Judgment" was approaching, he developed a sevenfold divinely-structured periodization of history perhaps taken from the seven seals of Revelation and culminating in the time of Enoch ("the seventh from Adam," Jude 1:14).[55]

With his espousal of Sophia as a symbol of the Noble Virgin of Divine Wisdom, Boehme invited the charge that he was reiterating ancient Gnostic heresies. This was the opinion of some hostile seventeenth-century commentators and, having been taken up by the nineteenth-century German theologian Ferdinand Christian Bauer, subsequently found support among a handful of modern scholars. In this vein, Weeks has written of Boehme's "increasing use of Gnostic symbols and images," while O'Regan has argued that Boehme's body of work is "a privileged site of the return of a Gnostic modality of thought in modernity."[56] As O'Regan admits, however, Boehme "neither cites Gnostic nor Valentinian sources in his texts, nor mentions them in his letters."[57] Indeed, there is scant evidence for continuous and direct transmission of unadulterated Gnostic doctrines through the ages. That said, traces of Gnosticism could have reached Boehme by way of incorporation within Neoplatonism and perhaps also Hermetic literature; though, in the latter instance, the question of Gnostic influence remains open. If this were so, mediation would most likely have been through Paracelsus.

Just as writings under the name Paracelsus may have been a conduit for Gnostic vestiges, so too did they channel streams of Neoplatonism. Running from Plotinus through the Florentine Platonist Marsilio Ficino

(1433–1499), this Neoplatonic current may, in its appropriation and adaptation, partially account for Boehme's elaboration of a process of emanation during the creation as well as what certain commentators regard as a pantheistic imbued conception of nature. More striking still are resemblances in Boehme's thought to some concepts in a key Jewish Kabbalistic work, *Sefer Ha-Zohar* (*The Book of Splendour*), as well as to aspects of later Christian Kabbalistic thought as elaborated in Johannes Reuchlin's *De arte Cabalistica* (Hagenau, 1517). Boehme writes in his unfinished answers to "The 177 Theosophic Questions" (1624) of "Cabala and Magia" and then the "*Holy* Cabala," although by itself this signifies little; the Paracelsian *Aurora* likewise used the term to describe a mystical and prophetic art full of "Divine Mysteries," just as magic contained "natural secrets."[58] Even so, there is convincing evidence that Boehme knew specific Kabbalistic teachings, albeit at several removes. Hence, the Kabbalists' *En-Sof* (the Infinite) has been compared with Boehme's *Ungrund* (mystical being of the Deity); their *Adam Kadmon* (primordial man) with Boehme's androgynous Adam; the highest three attributes of the Zohar's ten *Sefirot* (potencies of the manifest God), that is, *Keter* (crown), *Hokhmah* (wisdom), and *Binah* (intelligence), with Boehme's conception of an imminent Trinity. Penman even demonstrates in this volume a specific instance of Boehme adopting a Kabbalistic scriptural interpretation found in Reuchlin, which was mediated to him through Walther. Cumulatively, these Neoplatonic and Kabbalistic resonances indicate Boehme was no mere plagiarist but a profound and original—if occasionally erratic—thinker who veered towards synthesis on a grand scale.

Allied to Neoplatonism and Kabbalism was belief in magic. Unlike Heinrich Cornelius Agrippa, who in his infamous compendium *De occulta philosophia sive magia libri tres* (Cologne, 1533) delineated three types of magic—divine (the secrets of God), celestial (the influence of stellar bodies), and natural (the properties of things in nature)—Boehme distinguished between divine and natural magic in "Mysterium Magnum." Magic, however, plays a minor role in Boehme's worldview, and what knowledge he had of it probably derived from Walther, who copied and collected Paracelsian, Kabbalistic, and magical texts.[59] Much the same can be said of Boehme's lack of engagement with the *Corpus Hermeticum*, a haphazard body of ancient Greek literature ascribed to the god Hermes and consisting of approximately seventeen dialogues. Widely circulated in Latin and then vernacular translations—including Sebastian Franck's German paraphrase of the first colloquy *Poimandres* (Augsburg, 1538)—these treatises, despite being exposed as forgeries, were nonetheless valued by the English Boehme translators John Sparrow and Charles Hotham. Indeed, they constitute a distinctive feature of the wider milieu in which the Teutonic's writings were sympathetically received: Sparrow glossed Boehme's reference to the "Eternal Mind" with a marginal note to *Poimandres*,[60] while the ardent Behmenist Abraham Willemsz van Beyerland financed his own Dutch translation of Hermetic books published at Amsterdam in 1643. Moreover, the fabled

"Tabula Smaragdina" ("Emerald Tablet") attributed to Hermes was printed in Latin translation with commentary by the Paracelsian Gerhard Dorn in volume one of *Theatrum Chemicum* (Oberursel, 1602; reprinted, Strasbourg, 1613), an enormous alchemical compendium that may have been owned by some of Boehme's wealthier acquaintances.

Another integral element within this milieu was the Rosicrucian manifestos, the earliest of which was an allegory written in 1605 by the Lutheran Johann Valentin Andreae (1586–1654) entitled *Chymische Hochzeit: Christiani Rosencreuz Anno 1459* (*The Chemical wedding*; published anonymously in Strasbourg, 1616). Having been circulated in manuscript, these works began emerging in printed German and Latin editions from 1614 and were, as Penman notes, available in Görlitz through the town's principal bookseller. The most notable advocated a utopian universal reformation akin to Boehme's slightly later vision of a Great Reformation. Their cause was furthered by another Lutheran figure, Michael Maier (1566–1622), who supposed that the Fraternity of the Rosy Cross possessed the secrets of nature and whose own writings blended alchemical motifs with Hermetic wisdom. Further afield was the English physician Robert Fludd (1574–1637), an apologist for the Rosicrucians whose major cosmological works were issued in Latin at Oppenheim from 1617. Significantly, some of Boehme's patrons and followers read and collected these Rosicrucian writings. A few even participated in the ensuing European-wide printed debate.

Then there is the unmistakable adoption of heliocentrism in Boehme's earliest attempt to formulate an explanation for the planets' motion. Despite professing ignorance of the finer points of mathematics and astrology, he rejected the Ptolemaic system, insisting that the Sun did not orbit the Earth in a day and a night. Rather, the Earth imitated the motion of a wheel, revolving around the Sun in the space of a year. So too did the planets closest to the Sun, Mercury and Venus. But the outer planets—Mars, Jupiter, and Saturn—did not complete their revolution in a year because they were too far from the Sun and hence their orbit was of greater circumference. This vision of the heavens corresponded most closely to that advanced by the Polish astronomer Nicolaus Copernicus, though it is unlikely that Boehme had read his *De Revolutionibus Orbium Coelestium* (*On the Revolution of the Heavenly Spheres*; Nuremberg, 1543). More probable is that Boehme was familiar with astrological works then circulating in Görlitz, a town where the sometime mayor Bartholomäus Scultetus had corresponded with the astronomers Tycho Brahe and Johannes Kepler.[61] Some years later, Boehme elaborated on his conception of the cosmos in "The Threefold Life of Man" (1620). Here, the universe was imagined as concentric circles: the outer wheel consisted of the twelve signs of the zodiac together with the other constellations; within were the seven planets; then the Sun; and finally the inner wheels of Fire, the heavenly Tincture, Majesty, and the number three with the cross.[62] This idiosyncratic heliocentric scheme was remarked upon by Christian Beckmann, who dismissed it as an old song.[63]

For Beckmann it was incredible that an "illiterate" common man could have such a profound and extraordinary knowledge of God and Nature. These misgivings made him suspect that Boehme had been incapable of expounding on such abstruse subjects. Nor was he alone in expressing doubts that the books written and circulated under the name "Teutonicus" were the work of a lowly shoemaker.[64] Anticipating the authorship controversy surrounding the plays of his more famous contemporary Shakespeare, the contention that Jacob Boehme did not write Boehme gradually became more pronounced. In the 1690s, for example, the Lutheran pastor and Orientalist Abraham Hinckelmann insisted that Balthasar Walther had been the real author of these works and that Boehme had not written "a single line" of what was attributed to him.[65] Alternatively, some believed it was not a learned associate but the father of lies himself who had dredged up some "old reprobated *Heresy*" from the "bottomless Pit" of Hell and passed off a "visionary Piece of Devilism" under Boehme's name.[66]

Such skepticism surrounding Boehme's authorship was the obverse of the hagiographic tendency we have witnessed. The truth of course was that neither God nor the Devil was responsible. His disciples may have claimed that Boehme had been favored with God's great and secret spirit, which caused him to produce amazing writings that in their clarity and purity were unparalleled since the apostolic age. Yet some were also responsible for educating him in the rudiments of Latin through conversation and correspondence. Hence, whereas "Aurora" was, to quote Stoudt, "a primitive, profound, chaotic, exasperating, prophetic work of cant and rant as well as of insight," the writings of Boehme's intellectual maturity show he had found ways of expressing himself beyond the "barrenness of his mother tongue."[67] These included the invention of German neologisms which, on a cursory reading, made his writings appear "harsh and uncouth," even "obscure and unintelligible." Added to this was Boehme's claim that he knew the "*Language of Nature,*" through which he could ascertain not only the inward virtues and qualities of plants, herbs, and stones, but also understand the gist of conversations in Latin and French—a talent akin to the Pentecostal gift of tongues (Acts 2:1–15). All of which meant his writings were unlike "other men's books."[68]

Indisputably, at stake here was an unwelcome plebeian challenge to scholastic learning, doctrinal orthodoxy, and the jealously guarded clerical monopoly of biblical interpretation. On this point, the various hagiographic and mythopoeic representations of Boehme's persona and concomitant veneration of his almost impenetrable writings converge in agreement with the hostile portrait promoted in the heresiography. Throughout this struggle for interpretative hegemony, Boehme's authority was strengthened in the hagiography by claims of divine illumination while being weakened in the heresiography by charges of arrogance, ignorance, heterodoxy, and presumption. He himself despaired of a wicked world, yet contented himself with knowledge of the approaching apocalypse. Moreover, Boehme justified his lack of learning by drawing parallels with God's "Great" and "Small" prophets, mere "vulgar plain and mean" shepherds and herdsmen, as well with Christ's apostles, who were but "poor, despised illiterate Fishermen." Invoking Luther's first reformation of the church, he declaimed:

> *What were they* that in all Ages in the Church of Christ stood to it most stoutly and constantly? The poor contemptible despised people, who shed their Bloud for the sake of Christ.

Therefore, who but a "poor *Mechanic*" drawn from the "lowest Class" could herald a second reformation?

> *The Spirit sheweth and declareth, that yet before the End, many a Layman, will know and understand more, then now the Wittiest or Cunningest Doctors know.*[69]

A few months before his premature death, Boehme prophesied that although his writings would be discarded by his fellow countrymen, foreign nations would joyfully take them up. This prediction was largely borne out during the seventeenth century as Boehme's works were "vilified and cast away" in his homeland but painstakingly published in Dutch and English translations.[70] Having endured both vehement clerical opposition and suppression, it was, so his followers believed, a posthumous vindication. Indeed, they considered the survival of Boehme's writings providential.[71] And it is remarkable how little has been lost. Besides the book on the "Last Judgment" (1624?) mentioned earlier, there may no longer exist a treatise entitled "The herbs of nature," a work on the noble virgin Sophia, a few minor pieces, and some correspondence. Some writings also remained unfinished: "Aurora" (1612), "The 177 Theosophic Questions" (1624), "The Holy Week or a Prayer Book" (1624), and "The Highly precious Gate of the Divine Vision" (also known as "A little book of Divine Contemplation," 1622–24). Regrettable as these losses and incompletions are, they are nonetheless outweighed by the huge corpus of Boehme's extant writings. Naturally, it was through their effective dissemination by a combination of scribal and print publication, both in the original German and several major European languages, that Boehme's legacy was ensured—a legacy which will be explored in subsequent chapters of this collection.

NOTES

1. I am grateful to Leigh Penman and Andrew Weeks both for clarifying a number of points and their helpful suggestions. All dates are according to the Gregorian calendar. Unless otherwise indicated, quotations in the first section are taken from various versions of Abraham von Franckenberg's life of Boehme. The last and longest of these, completed on September 23, 1651,

was published together with other relevant documents in "De vita et scriptis Jacobi Böhmii," in Johann Wilhelm Ueberfeld (ed.), *Theosophia Revelata* (Leiden, 1730). An English translation of this miscellany by Francis Okely was issued as *Memoirs of the Life, Death, Burial and Wonderful Writings of Jacob Behmen* (Northampton: James Lackington, 1780).
2. *Memoirs*, trans. Okely, 1–2, 4.
3. One son apparently became a goldsmith, a second a shoemaker, and two apprenticed into other trades. Three of them (Jacob, Tobias, and Elias) survived their father although all had died by 1669. A namesake, who was a tanner, with whom Boehme has sometimes been confused, had two daughters.
4. Boehme lived here until 1610. On the three-hundredth anniversary of his death in 1924 a plaque was erected commemorating the fact. Today, the building houses a small museum in Zgorzelec, Poland.
5. *Memoirs*, trans. Okely, 2–3.
6. Ueberfeld (ed.), *Theosophia Revelata*, vol. 1, 8–9. I am grateful to Andrew Weeks for the translation.
7. *Memoirs*, trans. Okely, 7–8.
8. Ibid., 8–9.
9. Howard Brinton, *Mystic Will. Based Upon a Study of the Philosophy of Jacob Boehme* (New York: Macmillan, 1930), 50. An eighteenth-century chronicle added the embellishment that Boehme was placed in the town stocks.
10. *Memoirs*, trans. Okely, 120.
11. Ibid., 16.
12. "Theosophick Letters," in *The Remainder of Books written by Jacob Behme*, trans. John Sparrow (London: Giles Calvert, 1662), 44–48; *Memoirs*, trans. Okely, 40–45.
13. Boehme, *De Electione Gratiæ, and Quæstiones Theosophicæ*, trans. John Rolleston Earle (London: Constable & Co., 1930), liv, lv.
14. "Apologie," in *Remainder*, 5, 12, 14, 21, 25–27, 34, 35; Boehme, *The Epistles of Jacob Behmen*, trans. J[ohn] E[llistone] (London: Giles Calvert, 1649), 33 (203–06); "Theosophick Letters," in *Remainder*, 22, 24–25.
15. *Memoirs*, trans. Okely, 45–47.
16. "Theosophick Letters," in *Remainder*, 28, 33.
17. "Theosophick Letters," in *Remainder*, 27–35; Boehme, *Epistles*, 35.13–17 (214).
18. *Memoirs*, trans. Okely, 39–40, 47–49.
19. Ibid., 23, 51, 52, 64.
20. Ibid., 23–24, 53–54, 64–65.
21. Ibid., 25, 54–58, 60, 65, 66, 67–68, 68–79, 91–98.
22. Ibid., 21, 25–27, 61, 103.
23. Ueberfeld (ed.), *Theosophia Revelata*, vol. 1, 20–21. I am grateful to Andrew Weeks for the translation.
24. Theodor Harmsen (ed.), *Jacob Böhmes Weg in die Welt* (Amsterdam: In de Pelikaan, 2007), 77. I am grateful to Leigh Penman for the translation.
25. *Memoirs*, trans. Okely, 20.
26. Ibid., 21.
27. Ibid., 1, 9, 14, 27, 29, 86, 134.
28. Ibid., 110.
29. Ibid., 112–13.
30. *Memoirs*, trans. Okely, 14; L.T.I. Penman, "Böhme's Student and Mentor: the Liegnitz Physician Balthasar Walther (c.1558–c.1630)," in Wilhelm Kühlmann and Friedrich Vollhardt (eds.), *Offenbarung und Episteme* (Berlin and Boston: Walter de Gruyter, 2012), 47–65.

31. *Memoirs*, trans. Okely, 19, 33.
32. John Stoudt, *Sunrise to Eternity. A Study in Jacob Boehme's Life and Thought* (Philadelphia: University of Pennsylvania Press, 1957); Andrew Weeks, *Boehme: An Intellectual Biography of the Seventeenth-Century Philosopher and Mystic* (Albany, NY: SUNY Press, 1991).
33. Boehme, *Epistles*, 15.39–40 (134–35).
34. Boehme, *Die Urschriften*, ed. Werner Buddecke (2 vols., Stuttgart: Friedrich Frommann Verlag, 1963–66), vol. 2, 399–402. I am grateful to Leigh Penman for the translation.
35. Boehme, *Epistles*, 4.2, 20–21, 26–27, 34–35, 39, 50–51, 73, 87 (47–61).
36. Ibid., 20.23–36 (160–61).
37. Weeks, *Boehme*, 80–81.
38. Boehme, *Aurora*, trans. John Sparrow (London: Giles Calvert, 1656), 19.5 (425).
39. Boehme, *Epistles*, 2.10–14, 3.5–6, 3.35, 4.76–78, 9.27 (20–21, 36, 44, 60, 108).
40. *Memoirs*, trans. Okely, 8.
41. Boehme, *Aurora*, 10.45, 19.4, 19.67, 21.61, 22.9–14, 25.46–48 (184, 425, 438, 492, 512–13, 594); Boehme, *Concerning The Three Principles of The Divine Essence*, trans. J[ohn] S[parrow] (London: Humphrey Blunden, 1648), 10.1 (77).
42. Bo Andersson, "*Du Solst wissen es ist aus keinem stein gesogen.*" *Studien zu Jacob Böhmes Aurora oder Morgen Röte im Auffgang* (Stockholm: Almqvist & Wiksell International, 1986).
43. Stoudt, *Sunrise*, 49–52, 64.
44. Epistle 54 (April 3, 1624), in Stoudt, *Sunrise*, 180–83.
45. Weeks, *Boehme*, 159.
46. Boehme, *Epistles*, 2.54 (30).
47. Boehme, *Epistles*, 2.52–53, 2.59–60 (29–30, 31); Boehme, "Theosophick Letters," in *Remainder*, 5.
48. Christian Beckmann, *Exercitationes theologicæ* (Amsterdam: Johann Janssonius, 1643), 434–59; Daniel Colberg, *Das Platonisch-Hermetische Christenthum* (Leipzig: Weidmanns, 1710), vol. 1, 312–14.
49. Brinton, *Mystic Will*, 89–91;Stoudt, *Sunrise*, 95, 99, 100–01, 142; Weeks, *Boehme*, 29–30, 49–50, 197–98; Cyril O'Regan, *Gnostic Apocalypse. Jacob Boehme's Haunted Narrative* (Albany, NY: State University of New York, 2002), 58–68.
50. Boehme, *Epistles*, 3.33, 23.18 (44, 171).
51. Ibid., 2.51 (29).
52. "Considerations upon Esaiah Stiefel," in *Remainder*, 19, 56–62 (4, 13–14).
53. L.T.I. Penman, "'Repulsive Blasphemies.' Paul Nagel's Appropriation of Unprinted Works of Jacob Böhme and Valentin Weigel in his *Prodromus astronomiae apocalypticae* (1620)," *Daphnis*, 38 (2009), 599–622.
54. *Memoirs*, trans. Okely, 21–22, 37–38.
55. Boehme, *Aurora*, 4.3 (74); Boehme, *Mysterium Magnum*, trans. John Ellistone and John Sparrow (London: Humphrey Blunden, 1654), 30.34–46 (181–84); Stoudt, *Sunrise*, 124, 127–28, 164, 297–98; O'Regan, *Gnostic Apocalypse*, 145, 146, 161–75.
56. Weeks, *Boehme*, 121–22, 144, 148, 175, 182, 204; O'Regan, *Gnostic Apocalypse*, 2, 15.
57. O'Regan, *Gnostic Apocalypse*, 15, 148.
58. "177 Theosophick Questions," in *Several Treatises*, trans. John Sparrow (London: Lodowick Lloyd, 1661), 3.50, 6.11 (41, 49); *Paracelsus His Aurora*, trans. J[ohn] H[arding] (London: Giles Calvert, 1659), 2, 3, 8, 9–10.

59. Boehme, *Mysterium Magnum*, 68.1–8 (505–06).
60. "177 Seven Theosophick Questions," in *Several Treatises*, 6.1 (48).
61. Boehme, *Aurora*, 22.10–15, 25.1, 25.65–66, 25.79, 25.83 (512–13, 583, 598–99, 602, 603).
62. Boehme, *High and Deepe Searching out of The Threefold Life of Man*, trans. John Sparrow (London: Humphrey Blunden, 1650), 9.63–89 (139–44).
63. Beckmann, *Exercitationes theologicæ*, 448.
64. *Memoirs*, trans. Okely, 28, 115, 116–17, 119–20, 121–22.
65. Penman, "Böhme's Student and Mentor," 64.
66. *Memoirs*, trans. Okely, 28.
67. *Memoirs*, trans. Okely, 15–16; Stoudt, *Sunrise*, 79.
68. Boehme, *Epistles*, 2.13, 15.20–27 (21, 132–33); *Memoirs*, trans. Okely, 87–88, 89, 104–05, 111–12, 117–19, 123.
69. Boehme, *Aurora*, 8.127, 8.161–62, 8.173–79, 9.1–13 (147, 154, 157–58, 159–61); *Memoirs*, trans. Okely, 29, 126.
70. Boehme, *Epistles*, 33.25 (206); Ueberfeld (ed.), *Theosophia Revelata*, vol. 1, 109; *Memoirs*, trans. Okely, 140.
71. Ueberfeld (ed.), *Theosophia Revelata*, vol. 1, 106; *Memoirs*, trans. Okely, 135.

3 Radical Reformation and the Anticipation of Modernism in Jacob Boehme

Andrew Weeks

The Nobel Prize-winning postwar German author Günter Grass once wrote a novel that re-imagined the seminal postwar German writers' conference Group 47. Instead of 1947, his *Meeting at Telgte* takes place at the end of the Thirty Years' War. The parallel suggests that thinking people in either era were shipwrecked by history: they were forced to recover a lost culture and restore a language debased by ideological or confessional propaganda. As a *roman à clef*, Grass's *Meeting* requires Baroque counterparts for the Modernists and Realists of his own period. Who could stand in for Franz Kafka as the guiding light of a resurgent German Modernism? In Grass's novel, it is Jacob Boehme who inspires the Baroque Modernists.

The analogy is appealing. Modernism departs from Realism in rendering invisible things visible, as in Paul Klee's dictum, "Art does not reproduce the visible but rather makes visible".[1] Boehme articulated invisible metaphysical realities that made his readers see with the eye of the mind. The mystic as Modernist is a literary joke with a profound meaning. The intricate images that adorn early editions of Boehme's books evoke the world as a symbolic mystery. The puzzle of his life and work encourages us to seek coherence among the seemingly incoherent elements in his writings and between the work, its author, his time, and our own.

The incoherence begins with our image of the shoemaker-mystic. He wants us to believe that his writing is as simple as his self-representation. Yet nothing in German Baroque literature is as complicated. His life, as we know it, was ordinary. Of prosperous peasant origin, he learned the craft of a shoemaker and established a family. Around 1600, his experience of illumination and sense of religious calling propelled him to write for himself and others like him.

We need to uncouple the dual aspects of his paradox: his anomalous status as a simple shoemaker and the incommensurate complexities of his writing with its threefold worlds, seven divine spirits, and vast array of arcane concepts. From the start, Boehme attracted a lay readership consisting of the middle class of his time. How could such daunting expositions serve ordinary readers? To reconcile the discrepancy between his simple person and his intricate mode of expression, we need to understand how simplicity and complexity—tantamount to the anticlericalism and Paracelsism in his work—were, in reality, two sides of the same coin.

A shoemaker practicing theology violated the prerogatives of the clergy. Boehme did so within a long tradition of medieval and Reformation anticlericalism. There has been much recent interest in the rebellion of the lay folk against the power, authority, and privilege of the clerical estate or office. Though there were certainly various motives for early modern anticlericalism, Hans-Jürgen Goertz states convincingly in the *Oxford Encyclopedia of the Reformation* that "Anticlericalism then was much more a matter of criticizing those holding office in the church out of a deep, fundamental religious need."[2] Nineteenth- and twentieth-century anticlericalism is associated with atheism and materialism. Medieval and early modern anticlericalism typically reacted to the failure of religious institutions to measure up to their religious principles. Though more religious than its post-Enlightenment manifestations, Reformation anticlericalism was not less strident. Empowered by Luther's doctrine of the universal lay priesthood and his verbal attacks on the pope and the monastic estate, it culminated in revolutionary violence, in excesses we might associate with atheistic Bolshevism or radical Islam. Images were destroyed, graves desecrated, sacred objects defiled, churches degraded to stables, and the religious harassed and persecuted.[3] Luther retreated from the lay priesthood of the believer,[4] condemning peasant revolt and doctrinal dissent, but radical reformers maintained the anticlerical thrust of his doctrine, even against Luther himself.

Anticlericalism also lay at the heart of a Reformation tendency opposed to externals in religion. The tendency is referred to in German as *Spiritualismus*. The Spiritualists raised the spirit above the letter and disdained what they called the "church of walls."[5] They condemned Pharisees and false teachers. In Luther's German, Pharisees are "Schriftgelehrten," scholars of scripture. The Spiritualists considered them unregenerate authoritarians who imposed the dead letter of doctrine from above. Throughout his writings, Boehme asserted himself in opposition to authoritarian pastors and scholars. *Aurora* denounced the arrogance of "Doctores" who forbid him his theological speculation while instigating conflict with their incessant quarreling.[6] He pillories them as "Maul-Pfaffen" (mouth-priests) who know only the letter of scripture.[7]

The Spiritualists were dissenting individualists with diverse ideas and beliefs. Despite their shared influences and similarities, they constituted something more like a tendency than a tradition. Caspar Schwenckfeld, Sebastian Franck, and their kindred spirit Paracelsus were all born prior to 1500. The notorious revolutionary and mystic Thomas Müntzer is sometimes included, though he was exceptional in advocating force. Toward the end of the sixteenth century, Spiritualist thought matured in Valentin Weigel (1533–1588). The more reflective Spiritualists did not plunder monasteries, harass priests, or circulate woodcuts of monks emerging from the devil's anus. With some justification, they indicted the clergy as the source of strife and dissension. Boehme even blamed the clergy for the exploitation of the poor and the aggression of the secular princes. In his usage, "der Laye," or lay person, is both the clerically unanointed and the materially oppressed.[8] The Spiritualists reinforced their opposition with elaborations of theory that included the paradoxes of Franck, the epistemology and cosmology of Weigel, and the metaphysical speculations of Boehme.

Spiritualist theory responded to the contradictions of a Reformation which had set out to simplify and purify faith but instead created an irresolvable perplexity of contending doctrines. The second half of the sixteenth century was dominated by Protestant internecine quarrels. The Gnesio Lutheran controversies and the disputes between Lutherans and Calvinists raged on in the shadow of a Catholic resurgence. These quarrels were Weigel's point of departure.[9] He was a dissenting Lutheran pastor who read Paracelsus, Franck, and the medieval mystics. Weigel not only raises spirit above letter, he attempts to transcend the superficial understanding of nature, which appears to be a correlative of the superficiality of biblical literalism. His objective is not to propound some new doctrine. He criticizes the terms of theology and the relationship of the knower to the known. Reality itself cries out for spiritualization. Authorized by certain biblical passages (among them 2 Corinthians 3:6, the killing letter and life-giving spirit; Luke 17:21, the kingdom of God within us; and John 1:1–3, the divine creator Word), the theorizing dissent of the Spiritualists seeks the living spirit not only beneath the letter of the Bible and within the believer, but even inside the inert elements of physical nature. The Spiritualist receptiveness to alchemy, nature philosophy, and introspection takes shape in Boehme's complicated positive objectives.

But first we need to consider yet another aspect of his anticlericalism. This was the age of *cuius regio, eius religio*. Dynastic successions resulted in the imposition of new doctrines on territorial populations. Boehme's Lutheran Lusatia was not only threatened by the Catholicism of its Habsburg overlord, it was also destabilized by Lutheran, Crypto-Calvinist, or Philippist rulers who traded places and insults in neighboring Saxony. In the confessional free-for-all of the late sixteenth century, a stable orthodoxy was more elusive than later. In many regions, Lutheranism was considered an achievement of the popular will. The people clung to it. Calvinism was more thorough in eliminating vestiges of Roman Catholicism and imposing discipline on communities, but those tendencies also made its followers more confrontational. When the Calvinist territorial rulers imposed their rational doctrine of the bread and wine, substituting baker's bread for the sacred host, their Lutheran subjects resisted. There were spectacular riots and insurrections.[10]

These events help to explain Boehme's outspoken defense of the controversial Lutheran doctrines of Christ's corporeal presence in Communion and the ubiquity of Christ's body. The Calvinists ridiculed the doctrine of the real bodily presence in the bread and wine and its corollary doctrine of ubiquity. Modern thinking brushes aside such doctrines as residual premodern dogma. We should instead ask what they meant to their defenders.

Boehme defends the real presence, but protests against all quarreling theologians. Divine corporeal presence in the bread and wine confirmed the immediate relationship of the layperson's being to God.[11] In Boehme's Lutheran community surrounded by confessional rivals, these beliefs were more than just doctrine. They embodied personal and popular freedoms, the salvation of the individual soul, and the autonomy and experience of the community.

Boehme's vision of a God omnipresent resonated with Lutheran Lusatians surrounded on three sides by Catholic and Calvinist powers on the eve of the Thirty Years' War:

> Therefore you human child, is it not so that the false shepherds without calling perpetually quarrel, and each of them says: "Come hither to me: Christ is here, Christ is there"; and each of them condemns the other and consigns him to the devil, destroys harmony, and extinguishes the love, in which the spirit of God is born; and engenders nothing but bitterness, and seduces the laity into believing that Christ is a shepherd of quarrelling, attacks his opponents, instigates war and murder: this is supposed to be the spirit of God. This is supposed to be the path to Paradise.[12]

Those exclaiming, "Christ is here, Christ is there!"[13] are the Catholic and Calvinist dogmatists who would impose their exclusive path to salvation. Against their injunctions, Boehme reaffirms the omnipresence of the invisible God. Christ's body with all persons of the Trinity is everywhere because the seven divine source-spirits that constitute nature as the body of God inform all things.

Boehme's simple negatives are balanced by his complex positives. His anticlericalism is complemented by his view of nature as revelation. His *Rising Dawn* or *Aurora* (written in 1612) begins with a tree metaphor. Like the branches of a tree, knowledge of God (the theology of the subtitle) and the knowledge of nature (exemplified by astrology and philosophy, which study the celestial and terrestrial worlds, respectively) possess a common mother or root. Theology and natural science sprout from this same root, and the growth of the tree is the unfolding totality of knowledge. First comes revealed truth. It is falsified by a venal merchant (the pope), who profits from the tree's fruit. When truth is restored (by the Reformation), bitter disputes commence over the root. These are the doctrinal quarrels of the present time. As the tree grows toward the final stage in the life of the world, one last green branch sprouts, not from the proud heights of learning, but from the very root itself. In this last green branch, the final revelation proceeds from all nature. What is revealed in this last greening is nothing other than the content of Boehme's work itself.

To know what is revealed, we therefore have to read his work. After reconstructing the coherence of its elements, I will offer practical suggestions for reading Boehme: where to begin and what to expect. One key component is the new heliocentric cosmology.[14] *Aurora* heralds it ecstatically. Much like anticlericalism, heliocentrism turns the world upside down. It also calls for recognition of force fields that assure order in the free-floating cosmos. However, in the final revelation of nature, one can scarcely overestimate the role of the speculative Paracelsism, which Boehme presumably knew from physicians or scholars in his region, which was a center for collecting and editing his writings. Though Boehme's Paracelsism has long been recognized, it is now becoming more accessible through the edition of the theological writings of Paracelsus by Urs Leo Gantenbein and the translation of the main theoretical writings into English.[15] Just as Luther had placed the Bible in lay hands, Paracelsus appeared to promise a fresh and more direct access to nature.[16] Lutheran anticlericalism and Paracelsian nature theory are therefore two sides of the same paradigm shift toward a new and unmediated knowledge.

Paracelsism made grandiose claims; it is hardly a direct empirical approach to nature. The Paracelsian concepts of microcosm and macrocosm, of the doctrine of signatures, and of the three principles that embody an essential fire in nature have medieval origins.[17] The notion of divine powers in nature is Neo-Platonic and patristic. The Augustinian *rationes seminales* might differ in characterization from the "seeds" and divine influences of Paracelsus, which differ in turn from Boehme's seven source spirits in God, but all these concepts of divine power in nature are vindicated by biblical tropes of God as all things in all and the Word through which all things are created according to the Prologue of the Gospel of John. By whatever name, they confirm that divine powers inform created nature. Nor are Boehme's multiple worlds new. Nicholas of Cusa, Johannes Reuchlin, and Agrippa von Nettesheim could have served as precedents.

This brings us to a pivotal distinction that emerges with Paracelsus and breaks ground for Boehme: the displacement or inversion of medieval hierarchy. Typical for the Middle Ages or the Renaissance, Agrippa's *De occulta philosophia* reproduces a multistoried hierarchy of worlds: the terrestrial, celestial, and divine. Knowledge of their ascending powers is reserved for a hierarchy of elite scholars who hold philosophical, mathematical, and theological qualifications, respectively. The symbolic medieval or Neo-Platonic hierarchy is an architecture of ascending dignity. The spatial and metaphysical hierarchy suggests a pyramid of authorities, crowned by clerical and theological supremacy. This is as true of the canonical hierarchies of Pseudo-Dionysius as it is of the thirteenth-century Dominican preacher Bertold of Regensburg. Bertold's popular sermons projected ten celestial choirs that betokened the ordered ranking of the estates and professions. First and highest was the clergy.[18]

Luther cast scorn upon these celestial and ecclesiastic hierarchies.[19] In the same vein, Paracelsus disputed the special authority of both the learned humanists and the clergy. Teaching and writing in the vernacular, he confidently took up matters of theology, medicine, magic, and astronomy (though the latter is transformed in his hands into something without resemblance to the mathematical science of Copernicus or Kepler). Paracelsus explicitly reclaimed all provinces of knowledge, first for the physician in *Opus Paragranum* (H 2:53; W 191)[20] and subsequently for every human being in his influential *On the Foundation of the Sciences and Wisdom* (*Liber de fundamento scientiarivm, sapientiaeque*, H 9:414). In his worldview, the elements, the *astra* or stellar powers, and the spirit-like influences of God all inhabit an accessible realm of nature.[21] Paracelsus insists that knowledge of nature is immediate. Nowhere in his writings do we find the hierarchy of higher worlds, intelligible only to learned elites. For Weigel as well, knowledge that had been higher now lies deeper within us. The ascending order of elements, astral powers, and God has shifted to an inner hierarchy accessible to the inspired seeker.

For many readers, then and now, the result has seemed dauntingly opaque. Yet in casting off the "fool Aristotle," Paracelsus promised to do for nature what Luther had done for the Bible. The problem was to discover from his widely circulating writings what this meant. Weigel and Boehme were among those attempting to sort out Paracelsus's ill-defined alchemical and astral forces. *Aurora* follows the lead of Martin Ruland by consolidating the Paracelsian forces into a sequence of seven prime qualities.[22] In implicit fulfillment of its subtitle, *Aurora* associates the seven planetary influences with Ruland's seven alchemical spirit qualities. Earthly elements and celestial stars are integrated into the flexible formula of the seven eternal source-spirits and their dynamically intermingling qualities. The atom-like paradigm of the seven evokes both the astral powers and the alchemically disclosed inner forces in the elements and, by extension, heaven and earth, the angels in the former and the elemental entities in the latter. Common to all spheres are the divine source-spirits and their dynamically ordered qualities.[23]

The source-spirits are a utopian model of unity in diversity. Their pattern is a microcosm of all divine and created being. The regenerative harmony of the source spirits is sublimated in the political concord of the angelic kingdoms. The love play of the source spirits is paralleled by the benevolent diplomatic exchanges of the angelic hosts. Without subjugation or banishment, the angels enjoy both freedom of movement and a natural right, "ein Naturrecht," each to its own place of birth. No angelic kingdom begrudges any other its particular qualities. Lest we miss the point, the author cautions us that the angelic world is the mirror of an ideal earthly justice.[24]

The surviving autograph of *Aurora* is dated in the author's own hand. It was written out in the first six months of 1612. This coincided with the interval between the transfer of power in Bohemia and Lusatia from Rudolph II and the crowning of Matthias as the new emperor. During this interval, the Lusatians could hope for an extension to their homeland of the Bohemian letter of religious tolerance, for which they had been lobbying since 1609. When Matthias is crowned without fulfilling their hopes, the *Aurora* fragment breaks off after a note of somber prophecy.[25]

Nevertheless, the universalism of *Aurora* has a cosmic authority, with the source spirits as a microcosm of all divine and created being. The creating, ordering, and transforming power of the source-spirits and their associated qualities gives meaning to Boehme's assertion that the terrestrial and celestial worlds are all of a piece. He claims to have experienced the universality of heavens and earth with his senses aided by the Holy Spirit. The ubiquity of the divine spirits or "essences" negates the cosmic, metaphysical, clerical, and academic hierarchies with a single stroke. Recognition of the sun as the centre of the cosmos reconfirms the homogeneity of the all-encompassing heavens and thereby highlights the divine forces. Without them, the order of the free-floating cosmos would be inconceivable. In scholastic-Aristotelian cosmology, the heavens were substantially distinct from the sublunary realm. Boehme's seminal illumination of 1600 recognizes that "the true heavens are everywhere." He claims that everything else follows from this. Indeed, we can connect the dots in a logical order from his interpretation of his recounted illumination to the stated program of *Aurora* with its heliocentrism and alchemy, its penetration of celestial and elemental realms, and finally to the ubiquitous order of divine spirit and the ecstatic sense of revelation pervading his work. The problem for the reader is that there seems to be no end to the dots: Boehme's concepts and terms multiply as if there were strength in numbers.

His vast arsenal of concepts and symbols supports the simple idea that nature, witnessed by the untutored human being inspired by the Holy Spirit, is a second Bible: a divinely-authored Book of Nature. The light of nature augments scripture. It offers a new revelation that should resolve all disputes. The reader is induced to seek out the harmony between the terms of nature and the truth of scripture. This is somewhat like searching for hidden treasures that have been cleverly concealed for children in places they are sure to look. The contrived mystery is more urgent than the correlation of terms. In Paracelsus, key concepts had been associated with the Bible.[26] Boehme refines their biblical associations. Sulphur, Mercury, and Salt, found already in the fifteenth-century *Book of the Holy Trinity*, had been likened by Paracelsus to the three divine persons.[27] Boehme redeems their latent potential, just as his "signatures of things" expands upon a medieval thinking that had recognized divine signs and vestiges in nature.[28] Medieval alchemy had hardly been foreign to Christian symbolism, nor to the exercise of parsing nature in terms of microcosm and macrocosm. Even Luther had no problem with these terms.[29]

Boehme extends their pattern so that even the smallest circle of nature is said to contain the entire being of the divinity. If this seems unbiblical, it conforms to the Pauline trope of God as all in all.[30] This commonplace of so-called mystical writing captures the facets of his vision and echoes his tradition. The erudite Nicholas of Cusa handled this trope as a syllogism. If all things are in God and God in all, then all things are in all other things.[31] This makes for a vastly enriched conception of divine ubiquity. In search of the complex in the simple and vice versa, the artisan polishes a lens for contemplating nature through faith by construing all things in all.

Boehme applies the lens of *omnes in omnibus* to the elements, vegetation, bodies—human or angelic—and to the heavens. He applies it to our conscious or subliminal inner life of desire, anxiety, unrest, and equilibrium. This results in what can be aptly called a metaphysics of will. Schopenhauer cited pertinent passages in Boehme's *Vom irdischen und himmlischen Mysterio* before he discovered the ancient Hindu thought, which he preferred to claim as his philosophical precursor.[32] Boehme's work imagines a primal cosmic will materializing out of vain longing to grasp the light. His speculative *tour de force* is intentionally mysterious. It has its antecedents.

The first will is called the *matrix* of all being. The Paracelsian medical treatise *On the Matrix* had recycled a medieval gynecology that equated gestation and birth with the creation of the world: macrocosm and microcosm *in statu nascendi*.[33] And what about the light shining in the darkness? We know this trope from John 1:5. Boehme's metaphysics of will adapts and develops the Paracelsian *matrix* to elaborate a riff on the Prologue of John. The light shines in the darkness, but the darkness cannot grasp the light.[34] The self-absorbing concentration of the blind darkness, the reification of its frustrated longing and incomprehension, materializes in the birth of the elemental world out of which stuff we are made. Boehme's cosmic puzzles reward the simple lay reader who knows Luther's Bible chapter and verse.

The identity or congruity of theogony, cosmogony, birth, and spiritual rebirth is not set out discursively. It is intimated, as in poetry or music, by the repetition of motifs: the first will, darkness and light, the spiritual photogeneration of whatever is good in nature. We can only guess in a leap of faith. The correct association might be found in a nearby passage. The inner and outer, spirit and nature, are everywhere allegorical of one another. This leads to an ultimate revelation. The creation of the world and the human being, the fall, the torment of birth, death, and rebirth, and the final resolution of things: these are the alpha and omega of Holy Scripture. Applying his mystical lens of *omnes in omnibus* to the Bible brings Boehme's Spiritualism full circle. His late, massive treatise *Mysterium Magnum* interprets Genesis chapter by chapter in the light of Paracelsian nature philosophy. His exegesis surmounts the despised historical faith by transfiguring each event in ever richer combinatory codes and coordinates. *Mysterium Magnum* surveys all nature, temporal and divine. In a manner of speaking, the quickening spirit resurrects itself from the tomb of the dead letter. Riddles latent from the very beginning of the world are to be clarified in the end of time.

How can we classify Boehme's writings, and how should we read them? He has certainly been a source of religious inspiration and philosophical insight. One could also place him in the sphere of popular religion studied by Robert Scribner.[35] In Boehme, there is a fine line between the naïve and the sublime. Circulating by hand, his writings would have appealed to a popular culture of symbol that flourished without higher learning or codification. Numerology and sacred symbols were important both in popular religion and Boehme's work. But the same habits of mind, the same symmetries and sacred numbers that make him appear naive and popular, infuse Dante as well. Boehme was influenced both by lay piety and learned theological disputation.

Our term "mysticism" is an anachronism that offers little insight into the intentions or thinking behind such writing. No matter how complex and difficult, Boehme's texts can hardly be read as transcripts of spontaneous, passive, or ecstatic experiences (except, of course, insofar as any intense inspiration can be ecstatic and illuminating, even to the most secular writer or reader). Though much can be learned from social history and much gained for the study of the history of philosophy and religion, his writings are a kind of creative literature and must be appreciated as such. Grass's conceit of the Baroque mystic as Modernist was more than whimsy. Boehme had an impact on German Baroque poetry. The attraction of the Baroque for Modernists is borne out by the appeal that John Donne and the metaphysical poets held for T.S. Eliot and of Góngora for the avant-garde Spanish Generation of '27. My remaining remarks are advice for the prospective reader and suggestions about what the student of literature might hope to find in Boehme's work.

Readers should take the author at his word. Of course, we must understand his words in his sense (bearing in mind, for example, that not only Boehme but others of a more practical bent of mind would have claimed the Holy Spirit as the source of whatever was true and good in their efforts). We should respect the sequence of his treatises, beginning with his first, progressing to his second, and so on. Titles, subtitles, and tables of contents reveal much about structures and objectives—without which his work might seem like a trackless labyrinth. Passages taken out of context and offered as oracular pronouncements are not the best guide to his meaning. Like other writers, he has stronger and weaker moments. He has formulae that become depleted. There are lapses and inconsistencies. His sources of inspiration are transformed into extended compositions through what appears to be an experimental trial-and-error process.

I would suggest that the patient reader of *Aurora* begin with the first twenty-six sections of chapter nineteen, roughly its first four pages. They can be read as an account of the seminal experience which Boehme implies took place in 1600 (twelve years prior to his actual writing in the first half of 1612). In his region, those years were a time of dangerous tensions between Saxon Lutherans and Philippists or Crypto-Calvinists. The first six months of 1612, in which Boehme wrote out the long fragment of *Aurora*, coincided with the interregnum between the death of Emperor Rudolph II and the accession of his rival and brother Matthias as the crowned head of the Holy Roman Empire. Several chapters are devoted to the vision of the peaceful and tolerant angelic kingdoms, which the author calls exemplary for the human world.

The broader historical-eschatological perspective is outlined in the beautiful parable in the Preface to *Aurora*: "I will compare all of *philosophia*, *astrologia*, and *theologia*, together with its mother, to a fine tree which grows in a pleasure garden." The symbolic tree, which grows and bears the fruit of revealed truth, despite repeated assaults by the forces of the devil, incorporates three biblical sources (the tree of knowledge of good and evil in Gen. 2–3, the root of Jesse in Isaiah 11:1, and the parable of the wheat and weeds in Matthew 13). The tree alludes to three main intellectual sources of *Aurora*: (1) nature theory derived from alchemical philosophy, (2) cosmic speculation that encompasses astronomy and astrology, and (3) Lutheran theological speculation centered in the doctrines of real presence and divine ubiquity.

Aurora is nothing less than the ultimate fruition of revealed truth. In comprehending the theological convergence of the heavenly and earthly nature, the reader brings about God's final revelation of the eternal secrets of the creation. The self-referential preface, which embodies the knowledge it announces, calls to mind the self-referential meta-narratives of Modernist authors. In *Aurora*, however, the telling of the tale is not about the telling of the tale. Rather, the comprehending of what is being told creates the revelation that it treats of, which is nothing less than the ultimate age of knowledge itself. The prophecy does not predict; it institutes.

After the memoir of chapter nineteen and the parable of the preface, the first few chapters of *Aurora* offer an entirely new mode of writing: Boehme appears intent upon composing a philosophical treatise based on definitions and stated premises. In order to understand what God is, one must regard the forces in nature. Doing so, one recognizes that everywhere on, in, and above the earth there are two qualities: good and evil. Next comes his definition of "Qualität" as "the agitation, emanation, or driving force of a thing" ("die Beweglichkeit, Quallen oder Treiben eines Dinges"). Immediately, he enumerates qualities. He begins like an objective physical observer with the qualities of warmth and cold, but soon it becomes evident that the qualities are personalized and theologized, divided up into mirroring good and evil versions and compounded, insofar as warmth can issue in light and the life-force or exhibit grim, dark destructiveness. The enumeration soon resolves itself into the dual substance referred to as the *Salitter*, the Trinitarian pattern of three, and the no less significant pattern of seven source-spirits or qualities. Not unlike a modern experimental narrative, the play of the seven source-spirit qualities takes on a life of its own in an inner drama, which is as erotic as it is eschatological.

In chapter nine, *Aurora*'s focus and tone shift to deliver an anticlerical manifesto. The lay and the learned are integrated into a sweeping eschatological perspective and insinuated into the sequence of the seven qualities in nature. No mere digression, the thematic turn of chapter nine embodies the revelatory triumph of the humble and thus fulfils the promise couched in the title. What was hidden is dawning. As in Modernism, this experimentalism is revolutionary and utopian. The author proceeds to the angelic utopia and its admonitory contrast with the infernal realm. Later chapters of the fragment discuss the planets. Their coherence in the scheme of the seven qualities confirms the harmonies of the philosophy, astrology, and theology in the subtitle.

Since the *Aurora* manuscript is a fair copy, representing the premature discontinuation of a decade-long compositional process, we are justified in respecting its order of chapters. We are not justified in supposing that their order divulges the chronology of Boehme's interests. Even chapter nineteen, which stands out in its presentation of an experience twelve years prior, cannot be read as a psychological report. It is far too saturated with terms derived from Boehme's reflections and sources to be read as psychological description.

The reader would do well to consider that the various modes of writing found in *Aurora* can be seen as several treatments of the same problem. The memoir recounts how the author had been deeply depressed by his sense of the remoteness of the heavens from the earth and by that of himself from God and the heavenly world. Heavens and heaven in his remembered depression appear as one, as indeed they are designated by the same word in German. The seminal illumination of the author—that the true heavens are everywhere—was therefore an intuition of the object pursued speculatively in the theory of the qualities and forces, a pursuit placed in eschatological context by the Preface parable. In yet another sense, the gulf between the heavens and earth is closed in *Aurora*. The qualities of the alchemically disclosed earthly elements discussed in the first eight chapters coincide with the planetary qualities explicated in the penultimate ones. They implicitly surmount the Aristotelian and scholastic distinction between the qualities of the celestial and terrestrial worlds: everywhere the dynamic pattern of the seven and the Trinitarian three prevail in the substance of nature, in human life, and in the key to all, the divine being.

The Three Principles of Divine Being begins by boldly inquiring after the nature of God: "If we want to speak of God, what He is and where He is, then we indeed must say that God is himself the being of all beings: for from Him have all things been born, created, and proceeded; and everything has its first beginning in God."[36] This expanded corollary of monotheism enables the author to do several things. It allows him to construe Paracelsian alchemy as an allegory of the divine nature while spiritualizing and psychologizing the dynamics of the three principles. It permits him to construe as variants of a single archetypal pattern or event the eternal birth of the divinity, the cosmic birth of the natural world, and the birth and spiritual rebirth of the human being. It licenses him to interject the narrative of "angelic Adam," whose wholeness as a true image of the divine being is to be restored by divine knowledge and rebirth at the end of time.

Aurora and *The Three Principles of Divine Being* are the workshops in which the reader can attend to the concepts and materials that are shaped and adapted for all writings to come. However, the extended substance of his writings also articulates biblical sequences and doctrinal and philosophical concepts. In *Mysterium Magnum,* the entire Book of Genesis is explicated; in *Aurora* and *Three Principles* its initial chapters. The latter work explicates the Paracelsian three "principles." *Aurora* also devotes considerable attention to microcosm and macrocosm, and *De Signatura Rerum* to a meditation on the concept of its title. Writings are directed to devotional matters and to controversial doctrines such as the Lord's Supper, Incarnation, baptism, spiritual rebirth, and the election of grace. Astronomy and the theories of alchemy and nature philosophy enter into a spiritualized synthesis, uniting celestial and elemental realms and yielding what the author himself regards as a new style of discourse. Revealing God everywhere and in all things validates the Lutheran doctrine of real presence and reinforces the notion of lay priesthood.

We only hear the peculiar music of his writing when we become aware of the overtones and harmonies that tie any one theme to its equivalents in other frames of reference, so that the alchemical theme evokes the spiritual, the biblical the astrological, and so on. This lends Boehme a unique style and voice, or actually several of them, each with its own peculiar authority. The voice of *Aurora* combines that of a lay preacher, teller of folk tales, and master of riddles with that of a shrewd Socratic ironist, philosophical inquirer, and ardent people's advocate, lodging protests against the powers that be. The voice of the subsequent writings is more somber, oracular, and at times pretentious. The color and resonance usually echo the historical circumstances and atmosphere of the catastrophic junctures in which he wrote. Boehme's invention of his "language of nature," for interpreting sounds and syllables allegorically, might strike us as a whimsical concoction, but it reinforces his poetic attention to the harmonies of sound and sense.

Written in 1620 when the Bohemian phase of the Thirty Years' War was in full swing in Lusatia, *The Threefold Life of Man* begins with a note of universal introspection that calls to mind the coincidence of the Gnostic with the Existentialist in Hans Jonas. The objectification of despair or hope in extreme images can resemble German Expressionism.

> If we consider the beginning of our life and want to hold it up against the eternal life which is promised to us, we cannot say or conclude that we are at home in this external life. . . . And if we consider life, and [inquire] what it is, we observe that it is a burning fire which consumes; and when it has nothing left to consume, it goes out, as can be seen from all fires. . . . We see clearly that the elemental life is in a state of seething, that it is that very seething; and when it ceases to seethe, it goes out. We also know that the stars ignite the elements and are the fire of the elements; and the sun ignites the stars, thereby causing them to flow forth and seethe into one another. Yet the elemental life is finite and perishable, and the life of the soul eternal.[37]

The exposition of *The Threefold Life of Man* resolves and clarifies the seething cauldron of elements and stars into which the human being is thrust. The complexities of alchemical and astronomical theory again reveal that beneath the puzzle of being, the triune body and spirit of God are omnipresent: "But it is the corporeality of nature in which all seven forms of all nature stand, and in them are the seven spirits of God, manifest as seven burning torches . . . " (3:83). This alchemical-astronomical vision evokes the Book of Revelation (4:5), where seven torches burn before the throne of God. The apocalyptic omnipresence of God offers the antidote to the literalistic "Pfaffen" (clerics) who cry out, "God is here, God is there!" (3:224–25). Of course, divine omnipresence reconfirms that the believer receives the flesh and blood of Christ in the sacrament (3:261).

After rejecting factional adherence to Luther, Calvin, Schwenckfeld, or the pope (3:130), the later chapters of *The Threefold Life* rise to an anticlerical crescendo in exalting the lay-priest (3:254) and condemning "falsche Bischöfe" and "Pfaffen-Teufel," the clergymen-devils whose quarreling has now become religious war (3:277, 278). *The Threefold Life* thus begins with the mystery of human existence, magnifies it into the conundrum of the cosmos, and finally resolves it by reaffirming Boehme's universalistic articles of faith in opposition to all partisan authorities of the time. It can be objected that the author remains partisan while claiming universality. *The Threefold Life* is indeed at once partisan in its Lutheranism and universalistic in declaring even the Indians of remote America better Christians than those ruling Christendom (3:228).

Like Modernism, the literary vision of Boehme is conditioned by the confusions and catastrophes of his age. He is akin not only to the Romantics, whom he influenced, but also to such Modernists as Franz Kafka, Rainer Maria Rilke, or Paul Celan. Like them, though without the modern skepticism in religious matters, Boehme shifts the locus of transcendence inward, into the human psyche and the hidden inner life of the world. He creates hermetic symbols and systems of symbols that draw upon, yet transcend, the conflicts and conundrums of his world.

Boehme is a master of ambiguity, allusion, symbol, and neologism. Consider a passage such as this one from *Aurora*:

> And the seven spirits of God are all together God the Father: for no spirit exists without the other; rather, they give birth to all seven one after the other. If not for the one, the other would not be. Yet the light is a different person [of the deity]: for it is perpetually born from the seven; and the seven perpetually ascend [or rise in force] in the light; and the forces of the seven spirits perpetually proceed out in the radiance of the light into the seventh nature-spirit, and form and shape everything in the seventh spirit; and this going out is the Holy Spirit (1:146).

We notice first of all how he accommodates the Trinity: the totality of the nature spirits is the Father, the light perpetually born from the Father the Son. The Holy Spirit proceeds from the Father *and* Son. So far, so good. This is simply Western Trinitarian orthodoxy. Yet the plurality of the seven is also pluralistic and integrative. It takes all kinds to make a divine whole. It takes the darkness of the Father and the light of the Son to generate the third person of the Trinity. Darkness and light hold keys to the synchronous understanding of the world. The order of spirits is the order of revelation in time. The seventh is the author's ultimate knowledge. As in Johannes Scotus Erigena, history unfolds out of God.

The divine ubiquity is extended in depth. The layers of meaning descend to the opposite end of the Great Chain of Being, from the sublime to the physical and the sensual. We took note that the paradigm of seven spirits resembles the heliocentric world. Boehme is also thinking of the alchemy of niter or potassium nitrate, which he calls *salitter*. Niter was a banal gunpowder ingredient and an object of intense speculation around 1600. In the Latin of Pliny, *nitor* meant splendor or brilliance. The spirit forces in the *salitter* release light and warmth, embodying the solar heart of the cosmos and the Son of God. But it is not all sweetness and light in the inner world of the elements. Benign or malignant forces arise from the mixture of the spirit qualities. Nature is nowhere neutral. Good and evil powers, literally Paradise and Hell, are present in the inert element. There are the powers of light and healing balm, but there are also powers which are dark, explosive, pestilential, and destructive. Most of this was anticipated by Paracelsus.

One of the niter-related qualities hints at how experiential his alchemy might indeed have been. He refers to a triumphant, rising source of laughter, associated with a sweet smell (1:88). These aspects would fit the properties of nitrous oxide or laughing gas which is thought to have been synthesized only much later. The "all in all" of the source spirits is raised back up, from the lowly element to the exalted heights of angelic bliss:

> Observe the depth: Just as when the flash of life rises up in the midst of the divine force, when all the spirits of God receive their life and highly rejoice, there proceeds a loving and holy embracing, kissing, tasting, feeling, hearing, seeing, and smelling; [and] thus it is too with the angels: when the one sees, hears, and feels the other, in its heart the flash of life rises up, and one spirit embraces the other within the divinity (1:152).

After this orgy of love, the life of the spirits is replicated in the harmonies of the angelic world: "Every angel is created like the entire divinity, and is like a small god. For when God created the angels, he created them out of himself. Now God is in one place as he is in the other: everywhere he is the Father, Son, and Holy Spirit" (1:152). This passage introduces a pivotal theme. The angels, their kingdoms, and pristine Adam all replicate the divine ubiquity in depth. Boehme rejects the *creatio ex nihilo* in favor of a *creatio ex se*: God creates everything out of his own being. This explains why we are free and not doomed, as in his caricature of Calvinist theology. It is also why the angels, elements, and human beings reproduce within their respective beings the tensions and dynamics of the divine nature. Everything is created in God's image and out of his being. Everything has God's DNA, so to speak, though the paths of "evolution" were bifurcated in Satan's fall. Yet only an inner, spiritual turn separates the base from the exalted.

In *The Three Principles of Divine Being*, Boehme explains how God created everything out of his own being. We can revisit the theme and see where it takes us: "The true heavens in which God dwells are everywhere, in all places: He encompasses Hell, in which the devil dwells; and there is nothing outside of God . . . all things have been born from him; and God is called God because he alone is the good, the heart, or the best, the light or power, from which nature arises."[38] God is only God because the eternal light of the pure divinity overcomes the darkness in the divine being. Evil is unregenerate or relapsed darkness. So is God everything? Or is God only the good? The author wants to have it both ways. This leads to his theodicy of the *Ungrund*, which influenced Friedrich Schelling and Nikolai Berdyaev, both of whom incorporated the term in their thought. A common response is to declare him a certified mystic and forget about him. We should instead see where his contradictions lead us.

The art of his riddles and paradoxes shifts the focus. Like Weigel, or for that matter like Montaigne, Boehme directs us to regard our inner life. To recognize how nature arises, we have to imagine the eternal darkness outside of God: "[the darkness] has a great yearning for the light, since the light is mirrored in the darkness and shines within itself" (68/721:22). The darkness is nowhere and nothing. Yet, oddly, this nothingness yearns for the light: its yearning becomes the foundation of the world. The author tells us that we can experience this yearning in the depth of our soul. "Depth" is often his key word and signal direction. We know deep down that we are nothing and therefore crave enlightenment. This, of course, makes a different and more modern sense.

Next comes the creation of the human being: Adam was initially created by God as an androgynous creature in the likeness of the angels. Like God, he is whole. This Adam never sleeps. Though androgynous, his impulsive aspect is the male youth who lusts after the female principle within his pristine being: the Noble Virgin of Divine Wisdom. She is the light within his angelic being. He has an improper longing to possess and become pregnant with her. Based on the biblical book of Job, the apocryphal books of the Wisdom of Solomon and Sirach (Ecclesiasticus), as well as on the Paracelsian reification of wisdom in nature, the Noble Virgin embodies truth and goodness in nature. Wisdom is a female aspect of divinity. Again we find the same motifs: the darkness longs for the light but cannot possess or comprehend it. The Noble Virgin of Divine Wisdom flees lustful Adam whereupon he sinks into a male darkness and sleeps the sleep of all mankind. By endeavoring to give voice to the inconceivable, Boehme expands the capacity for reflection and self-recognition. Angelic Adam can be interpreted on many different levels.

The struggle of darkness and light recurs in theogony, cosmogony, astronomy, alchemy, and anthropology, always in allusion to Genesis and John. The cosmos is born when the light shines into the darkness, which cannot comprehend it. The human mission is to overcome the uncomprehending darkness within ourselves by knowing that we cannot possess the beauty and goodness which are the divine light toward which all things grow and mature. All of nature is in agony to give birth to the light. The devil's usurping shortcut to radiant bliss leads to hell.

There are more concrete examples of the tendency of Boehme's thought to coordinate life and nature with the Bible. He supplies his readers with practical advice for daily devotions. Hour by hour, the devout soul reenacts the odyssey of the human race. Getting up out of bed on Monday morning, one's prayers recall the nakedness of Adam and Eve after their fall from grace. Setting off to work recalls the human expulsion from Paradise. Preparing for bed at night means putting on angelic garments in preparation for the return to Paradise. Boehme provides practical advice for the spiritually challenged. The melancholy should avoid Calvinist books about the elect and gird themselves to conquer the devil's outlaw castle, from whence the attacks of melancholy are launched. Boehme's exemplary soul is to Adam and Eve as Joyce's Bloom is to Ulysses (4:237–52).

But the same patterns of thought are extended to the tragic current events. Here is how he responds to the religious war in progress: "You persecute one another, revile and despise one another, [you] instigate war and insurrection, devastating the country and the people . . . [all] for the sake of the true knowledge of God" (which means knowledge disclosed by him): "[Yet] you do not know your own selves. This is why you are furious and fight over God, who is a sustainer and creator of all things, who is the centre in all things. . ." (3:13). As always, God is ubiquitous. As always, the darkness cannot comprehend the light. And as always, the failed *coup d'état* of darkness to seize possession of the light—"Christ is here! Christ is there!"—leads to the hellish fire-world of confessional war. Boehme's quixoticism is overshadowed by historical tragedy.

Modernism signals a crisis of nineteenth-century Realism and progressivism. Boehme's thought signals a crisis of medievalism and Renaissance humanism. Agrippa's humanistic *De occulta philosophia* ascends from the lower to the higher, from the elemental to the celestial to the divine. Instead of a rising hierarchy, Boehme projects an inner one that goes ever deeper into worlds within worlds. Though essential to his meaning, this creates a compositional chaos, as if Dante's architecture of worlds had been shattered by the Reformation and commingled. The dark fire-world and the angelic light world, good and evil, heaven and earth, inner and outer, eternity and time, are said to be "in one another like a single thing." Good and evil are distinct yet inseparable. Our world is heaven and hell in one. Our daily newspaper confirms it.

As for the initial paradox of simplicity and complexity, one might resolve it by assuming that Boehme was only pretending to be simple but was, in reality, utterly steeped in learning and tradition. One can also take him at his word but understand him properly. When he introduces Paracelsian theory, it is to him neither pharisaic dogma nor mystical lore. It is the experienced wisdom of the lay people harmonized with the Bible. One of the aspirations of the Spiritualists, shared by Weigel and Boehme, is to teach the lay believer how to outsmart the better-educated elite. The purpose is served by the paradoxes of Franck and by Boehme's complex puzzles with their simple biblical keys. His worldview is overly complex because it oversimplifies nature.

For future study, we need better access to the literary sources so that readers can decide for themselves and so that we can discern whether "Behmenists" in other countries continued in his path or went off in new directions. We need modern translations with adequate commentary. We need to examine the culture of late-Reformation Germany. Its ambience of polarization and demonization is documented in pamphlets denouncing rival theologians as minions of Satan, in so-called folk songs celebrating the burning of witches, in the *Historia of Dr. Faustus*, and in the compendious *Theatrum Diabolorum*, where everything from natural calamities and peccadilloes to magicians and heretics represents the devil's carnival masquerade. The predominance of the devil in the age of faith was a precondition for Boehme's dialectic of good and evil in God. His writing is a counterpoint voice in and against the dialectic of destructive polarization in the late Reformation.

Without the horrors of his age, Boehme appears pointlessly overwrought.[39] *Aurora* is one of the most unique and beautiful works in the German language. Like any other great and complex literary work, it must be read also as an expression of its moment. German historian Johannes Burkhardt recently described the propagandistic print battle over the centenary of the *Ninety-Five Theses* in 1617 as a significant factor in polarizing the Germans for war.[40] Arguably, one of the earliest public anti-war campaigns began with the circulation of Boehme's manuscripts together with the posthumous publication of Weigel and appeals by Bernegger, Staricius, Opitz, and Kepler. Unfortunately, it was not destined to have any real impact.

On the last pages of Boehme's *Three Principles of Divine Being* (1618), the Noble Virgin of Divine Wisdom draws the hounded soul out of the thorns of its exile and pledges it to spread truth against hatred and war. Stirring as this is, the influence of Boehme in Germany was more cultural than political. He inspired poets and philosophers from Angelus Silesius and Novalis to Schelling, Schopenhauer, and Hegel. Boehme's work remains liminal between the medieval and the modern, between the lay and the learned. Not by chance, he was a product of the same years and epochal shift that gave us another inspired layman: Don Quixote

NOTES

1. Paul Klee, *Schöpferische Konfession* (1920), cited in Max Huggler, *Paul Klee: Die Malerei als Blick in den Kosmos* (Stuttgart: Huber, 1969), 19 ("Kunst gibt nicht das Sichtbare wieder, sondern macht sichtbar").
2. H. J. Goertz, "Anticlericalism," *Oxford Encyclopaedia of the Reformation* (Oxford: Oxford UP, 1996), 46–51.
3. Johannes Janssen, *History of the German People*, trans. A.M. Christie (New York: AMS Press, 1966), vol. 6, 204–5.
4. Bernard Lohse, *Martin Luther: An Introduction to His Life and Work*, trans. Robert T. Schultz (Philadelphia: Fortress Press, 1986), 182.
5. The term had been anticipated by Luther's pejorative "Geisterei," but its use is integrated into the social history of the church by Ernst Troeltsch in *Die Soziallehren der christlichen Kirchen, Gesammelte Schriften*, vol. 1 (Tübingen: Mohr, 1923), 863–64, 898.
6. Jacob Böhme, *Aurora, oder Morgenröthe im Aufgang, Sämtliche Schriften*, ed. Will-Erich Peuckert, vol. 1 (Stuttgart: Frommann-Holzboog, 1955), 325, 326. Subsequent citations of Boehme in this chapter refer to this edition by volume and page.
7. Böhme, *Beschreibung der Drey Principien, Schriften*, 2, 468.
8. Böhme, *Aurora*, 154. The victim, of exploitation by the rich or oppression by the aggressive prince, suffers it as a "layman."
9. On his sources and range of thought, see A. Weeks, *Valentin Weigel (1533–1588): German Religious Dissenter, Speculative Theorist, and Advocate of Tolerance* (Albany: State University of New York Press, 2000). Weigel's main theoretical works are available as Valentin Weigel, *Selected Spiritual Writings*, in *Classics of Western Spirituality*, trans. A. Weeks (New York: Paulist Press, 2003). Weigel recounts his seminal consternation in Chapter 24 of *The Golden Grasp*, 205–06.
10. J. Janssen, in *History of the German People*, vol. 10, 283, 290, 291, gives examples of Lutheran popular resistance to Calvinism during the years in which Boehme was at work on *Aurora*.
11. *Aurora* pillories "Calvinus" for restricting Christ's body in place (294). The next work is even more explicit in its reasoning: Christ has promised to be with the faithful until the end of the world (Matthew 28:20); his body and blood, as the true food and drink, are his promise of eternal life (John 6:54–55). Only those who still suffer the illness of Adam could imagine an absent Christ. See *Beschreibung der Drey Principien*, 402.
12. Böhme, *Beschreibung der Drey Principien, Schriften*, 90–91.
13. This trope echoes the Spiritualist *locus classicus* drawn from Luke 17:21. It is significant for the Spiritualists that the last two words were once translated "within you" (King James Version) or "inwendig in euch" (Luther).
14. Andrew Weeks, *Boehme: An Intellectual Biography of the Seventeenth-Century Philosopher and Mystic* (Albany: SUNY Press, 1991), 5, 54–57.
15. Urs Leo Gantenbein (ed.) in collaboration with Michael Baumann and Detlef Roth, *Paracelsus (Theophrastus Bombast von Hohenheim): Theologische Werke*, vol. 1 (*Vita Beata—Vom seligen Leben*), in *Neue Paracelsus-Edition*, I (Berlin, New York: de Gruyter, 2008); Paracelsus, *Essential Theoretical Writings*, trans. A. Weeks (Leiden: Brill, 2008). Subsequent references to this volume are cited as W by page.
16. Nature can be immediately intuited as a mirror image of the invisible world known in and through the human being: "What is philosophy other than the

invisible nature" (W 113). Knowledge proceeding from the light of nature by virtue of divine illumination supersedes human books. See Paracelsus, *Labyrinthus medicorum errantium*, in *Sämtliche Schriften*, ed. Karl Sudhoff (Munich and Berlin: Oldenbourg, 1928), vol. 11, 201.

17. On the medieval sources of Paracelsus see W 62–63, 89, 112–13, 316–17, 356, 359; cf. A. Weeks, *German Mysticism from Hildegard of Bingen to Ludwig Wittgenstein: A Literary and Intellectual History* (Albany: SUNY Press, 1993), 30–32.
18. Von zehen körn der engele und der cristenheit: simile est regnum celorum," in Berthold von Regensburg, *Vier Predigten* (Stuttgart: Reclam, 1983). Hierarchy is manifest in the pseudo-Dionysian visions of power and authority with the worldly and ecclesiastic realms in parallel ascent.
19. Martin Luther, *Werke* 42 (Weimar: Böhlau, 1908), 174–75.
20. Theophrastus Paracelsus, *Bücher und Schrifften*, ed. Johannes Huser (Basel: Waldkirch, 1589; reprint Hildesheim: Olms, 1971), cited as H by volume and page.
21. W 26, 172–75, 330.
22. Weeks, *Boehme*, 73; cf. Martin Ruland, *Lexicon Alchemiae* (1612) (Hildesheim: Olms, 1964), 442.
23. Weeks, *Boehme*, 70–74, 106–09.
24. Weeks, *Boehme*, 79–80; "Die Welt der Engel als Utopie des Friedens in Böhmes *Aurora*," *Festschrift für Ernst-Heinz Lemper* (1999):63–69.
25. Böhme, *Aurora*, 401.
26. A. Weeks, *Paracelsus: Speculative Theory and the Crisis of the German Reformation* (Albany: SUNY Press, 1997), 118–23.
27. Theophrast von Hohenheim, genannt Paracelsus, *De genealogia Christi*, in *Sämtliche Werke, 2. Abteilung (Theologische und religionsphilosophische Schriften)*, vol. 3, 63.
28. F. Ohly, *Zur Signaturenlehre der frühen Neuzeit: Bemerkungen zur mittelalterlichen Vorgeschichte und zur Eigenart einer epochalen Denkform in Wissenschaft, Literatur und Kunst* (Stuttgart: Hirzel, 1999).
29. Martin Luther, *Werke* (Weimar: Böhlau, 1908), vol. 42, 51. Luther did not object to the concept of microcosm.
30. 1 Corinthians 12:6; 1 Corinthians 15:28; Ephesians 1:23; Colossians 3:10–11.
31. A. Weeks, *German Mysticism* (1993), 107–14, 178–84.
32. A. Weeks, "Schopenhauer und Böhme," *Schopenhauer Jahrbuch* 73 (1992): 7–17.
33. W 616–18; cf. Walter Pagel, *Paracelsus: An Introduction to Philosophical Medicine in the Era of the Renaissance* (Basel: Karger, 1958), 238.
34. Weeks, *Boehme*, 105; *German Mysticism*, 22.
35. R. Scribner, *Popular Culture and Popular Movements in Reformation Germany* (London: Hambledon Press, 1987).
36. Böhme, *Beschreibung der Drey Principien*, 9.
37. *Vom dreyfachen Leben des Menschen*, in *Schriften*, vol. 3, 3, 4.
38. Böhme, *Beschreibung der Drey Principien*, 68.
39. J.M. van der Laan and A. Weeks, eds., *The Faustian Century: German Literature and Culture in the Age of Luther and Faustus* (Rochester, NY: Camden House, 2013).
40. Johannes Burkhardt, *Das Reformationsjahrhundert. Deutsche Geschichte zwischen Medienrevolution und Institutionsbildung (1517–1617)* (Stuttgart: Kohlhammer, 2002), p. 200.

4 Boehme's Intellectual Networks and the Heterodox Milieu of His Theosophy, 1600–1624

Leigh T. I. Penman

Numerous myths have concretized around the Görlitz theosopher Jacob Boehme, which have obscured the true nature and sources of his voluminous works. The most influential of these myths stems from Boehme's own sophisticated rhetorical self-presentation within his books and letters as a simple hand-worker who wrote only for himself, inspired by the grace of God, following a series of divine visions he experienced from 1600.[1] This notion was perpetuated by contemporary supporters eager to shield themselves from charges of heresy and has since also been commonly found in more modern accounts of Boehme and his works. But Boehme's self-presentation, particularly with regard to the sources of his doctrines, was not uniform. In a letter to Martin Moser in March of 1624, for example, Boehme wrote: "I did not receive my scholarship by manner of learning in schools and in books, but rather from the great book of all beings."[2] However, in his earlier *Aurora* (1612), Boehme wrote that "I have read the writings of many high masters."[3] Which statement is true?

Strictly speaking, both might be. There are aspects of Boehme's thought and work that are highly idiosyncratic and original, and aspects that are not. But the two statements are enough in and of themselves to demonstrate that Boehme's corpus, as a philosophical product, did not spring from an intellectual vacuum. The reason why Boehme's work communicated a cosmogony resembling that of the Zschopau pastor Valentin Weigel (1533–1588) and ideas of matter that echoed those of Paracelsus (1493–1541), as well as featured a heterodox eschatology that reflected that of contemporary chiliastic prophets like Paul Nagel (d. 1624) was because Boehme was, most assuredly, influenced by their works. Boehme was a heliocentrist as early as 1612, complained about specific aspects of Calvinist doctrine, and was a critic of Caspar Schwenckfeld (1489–1561), precisely because he knew and engaged with persons and works, both printed and manuscript, which communicated such material to him. In no way is Abraham von Franckenberg's (1593–1652) statement that Boehme only "learnt to read and write a little" to be accepted uncritically.[4] Boehme consistently portrayed himself as a "babe" (Psalms 8:2, Matthew 21:16); a simple, enlightened laborer, specifically in order to increase the appeal of his writings among his fellow men, as well as to insulate himself—unsuccessfully, as several persecutions in Görlitz demonstrate—from charges of heresy.

The present chapter has two major aims. First, it is devoted to presenting some insight into Boehme's intellectual world. It illustrates that, in contrast to his self-representations—and the misleading representations of occultists, novelists, and several historians who have furthered his myth—Boehme emerged from a distinctly heterodox intellectual milieu. Second, it is hoped that this chapter, by finally locating Boehme within a concrete intellectual tradition, will provide a spur to further research concerning his sources and influences. While much ink has been spilled over the possible meanings of Boehme's philosophy, there has been comparatively little effort devoted to situating Boehme within solid historical contexts and identifying the sources of his intellectual debts.[5] Here, I suggest some possible avenues to identifying these further influences.

The chapter is structured in three parts. The first examines the intellectual and religious climate that predominated in Boehme's home town of Görlitz during the theosopher's spiritual awakening in 1600. The second points to a selection of personalities from within Boehme's networks, in particular the several physicians, chymists, and religious enthusiasts with whom Boehme trafficked during his most intensive creative period, between 1619 and 1624. The third presents some examples that demonstrate the impact of these historical traditions and people on Boehme's thought, with particular regard to his reception of Kabbalistic and chiliastic ideas. Thereby, I hope to demonstrate that, despite stories of divine illumination, Boehme was not a man apart from his contemporaries, but very much one of their fellow travelers.

I BOEHME'S GÖRLITZ AROUND 1600

Görlitz today, as Germany's easternmost town, is an isolated place nestled in a crook of the river Neiße on the Polish border. In Boehme's time, however, it was at Europe's heart. Situated in the semi-autonomous territory of Upper Lusatia, administered from distant Prague, Görlitz was located on the *via regia*, Europe's major trading road, which spanned from Krakow to Paris. As such, it was a bustling commercial center and a major marketplace in Europe's woad trade. It was also a major intellectual center. The Reformation reached Görlitz from below in 1524, namely through the wish and striving of the populace. The Görlitz Gymnasium Augustum was established in 1565, and its Philippist curriculum—a humanistic Lutheranism developed by Philipp Melanchthon (1497–1560)—attracted locals and students from Saxony, Thuringia, Bohemia, and the Silesian duchies, creating a late-blooming of humanist culture in the town.[6] With a spiritual ministry subject to the authority of the city council, Görlitz was relatively liberal in confessional terms, and as the second Reformation took hold in surrounding territories, the city received numerous disgruntled and dissatisfied Protestants of Calvinist, Schwenckfeldian, and other backgrounds. By 1600, the population of Görlitz had swelled to some 10,000 inhabitants, making it one of the largest towns in Germany between Erfurt and Breslau (Wrocław). This was the Görlitz in which Boehme lived, worked, and experienced what he believed to be his first encounter with the divine.

As something of a harbor of religious tolerance and a destination of choice for those fleeing their home territories, Görlitz gradually attracted an eclectic assortment of freethinkers, spiritualists, and dissenters during the latter half of the sixteenth century who fled persecution in other territories. The most prominent movement was that of the Paracelsians,[7] and their figurehead was Bartholomäus Scultetus (1540–1614).[8] Eight times mayor of Gorlitz, Scultetus was Görlitz's arch-humanist: a mathematician, astronomer, author, and cartographer, and a correspondent of Tycho Brahe and Johannes Kepler. In addition to issuing an annual astrological almanac, he also authored a tract about the portentous comet of 1577. Furthermore, Scultetus presided over an important collection of Paracelsus's radical theological and medical manuscripts.[9] These he collected from around 1567, and his now lost diaries record his meetings with a host of visitors interested in Paracelsianism as they wandered through the territory, where matters including Paracelsus's teachings on medicine and religion were discussed.[10] In 1570, these gatherings of Paracelsians led city officials to investigate "meetings of physicians of the Paracelsian sect" (*collegium medicorum sectae Paracelsi*) and to attempt to determine whether the group posed a threat in religious matters. The investigation appears to have come to naught and did little to dissuade Scultetus from his interests. Nor did it make the town less attractive to Paracelsian visitors. While Scultetus served as mayor during the first controversy over Boehme's *Aurora* in 1613, the available evidence cannot demonstrate a personal connection between the two men.

As Carlos Gilly has observed, linked by the necessity of secrecy, heterodox and oppositional personalities, together with the writings that they trafficked, tended to move along and through the same channels.[11] And in Görlitz, Paracelsianism went hand in hand with Weigelianism. One visitor to the Paracelsian gatherings in and about Görlitz was the physician Abraham Behem (ca. 1545–1599), Scultetus's brother-in-law. A prominent physician and friend of Conrad Gesner, Behem knew Weigel personally, and in 1579 corresponded with him concerning cosmogony.[12] As Andrew Weeks has shown, several of the ideas presented in this letter were later paralleled in Boehme's works; it is also noteworthy that the extant manuscript derives from the collection of one of Boehme's adherents, Benedikt Hinckelmann.[13] It was not only that Weigel's cosmogony decisively influenced his *Aurora*. In September 1620, Boehme attempted to procure for his disciple Christian Bernhard (d. 1649), toll-collector in Sagan (Zagan), a copy of the Pseudo-Weigelian third part of the *Gnothi seauton* (1619) as well as what may have been a further Pseudo-Weigelian text, *Vom alten und newen Jerusalem*

(1619).[14] Additionally, in a 1621 letter to his Beuthen (Bytom) follower Kaspar Lindner, Boehme wrote:

> Otherwise Weigel accords with our writings concerning the new birth and the union of humanity with Christ quite well, which, while I write about the matter somewhat more clearly in my works, I leave aside here, and do not reject them, nor those who read them.[15]

While Weigel's followers thus exercised some influence in Görlitz, a larger part in the city's spiritual life was played by followers of another radical reformer: Caspar Schwenckfeld von Ossig. Many of these Schwenckfelders had fled to Upper Lusatia during the late sixteenth century on account of persecution in nearby Silesian duchies and ultimately accounted for a substantial minority of the population.[16] The movement's chiefs were sometime mayor Sebastian Hoffmann (d. 1605) and his brother-in-law, Michael Ender (d. 1595).[17]

A direct link between the Paracelsian and Schwenckfeldian communities was the alchemist and physician Balthasar Walther (1558–ca. 1630) of Fraustadt (Wschowa) in the duchy of Liegnitz.[18] Probably of Schwenckfelder stock, in 1587 Walther met Scultetus in Görlitz and received from him a host of Paracelsian, magical, Kabbalistic, and prophetic writings, which he copied the next year while living in the Schwenckfeldian village of Harpersdorf (Twardocice). He was also befriended by the Liegnitz physician Abraham Meffert (d. 1617), who was a copyist of Paracelsus's works and an editor of Paul Lautensack's prophetic texts, which circulated among Boehme's followers. In 1599, after undertaking a trip to the Orient in search of magical knowledge, Walther authored a biography of the Wallachian warlord Michael the Brave (1558–1601) dedicated to both Scultetus and Hoffmann. Although he flirted initially with the antinomian doctrines of the Langensalza prophet Esajas Stiefel (1561–1627), after about 1617, Walther would become perhaps Boehme's foremost follower as well as influence—both as a disciple and teacher.[19] He was a tireless promoter of Boehme's theosophy and furnished the forty questions that inspired one of the theosopher's most influential works. The common intellectual thread that would link the Paracelsian, Weigelian, and Schwenckfeldian traditions to Boehme's outlook was their radical spiritualistic anticlericalism. Like the founders of each of these movements, Boehme rejected the authority of the *Mauerkirche*—the worldly churches of mere walls—and instead claimed direct inspiration from the eternal school of the Holy Spirit.

Finally, an additional name must be mentioned as crucial to the spiritual and intellectual life of Boehme's Görlitz. This was Martin Moller (1547–1606), after 1600, chief evangelical pastor at the *Nikolaikirche*.[20] Along with Philip Nicolai and Johann Arndt, Moller is one of the most prominent figures in the so-called *Frömmigkeitswende* (devotional change) in Lutheran society during the early seventeenth century. A reaction against a dogmatic orthodoxy, Moller's works, in particular his *Mysterium Magnum* (1595) and *Praxis evangelicorum* (1601), offered a meditative approach to practical spiritual Lutheranism. According to a disputed report by the eighteenth-century historian Christian Knauthe—who presided over a library of unpublished material—Boehme was apparently a member of a small conventicle (*Hauß-Convent*) that met regularly at Moller's home to discuss issues of personal devotion, the soul's welfare, and practical Christianity.[21]

This brief sketch therefore illustrates something of the spiritual and intellectual characteristics of Görlitz society when Boehme first emerged there. This was a town where Philippists, Schwenckfelders, Weigelians, and Paracelsians were well-known members of society, and where opportunities to express and discuss these ideas existed in the form of conventicles or meetings in private homes—some of which Boehme is thought to have attended. Boehme's first work "Aurora" (1612) was an attempt to engage with the divine mysteries he believed he had encountered. This unfinished treatise, suffused with Paracelsian and Weigelian notions, speaks directly to the milieu in which it was produced.

II PATRONS, PHYSICIANS, AND PROPHETS: BOEHME'S INTELLECTUAL NETWORK, 1618–1624

The success of Boehme's writings in central Europe after 1618 owed much, naturally, to the inherent appeal of his work, but this appeal was also fostered by broader conditions. The injustices and instabilities of the nascent Thirty Years' War, all too visible in and around Lusatia, had awoken numerous locals to the utility of practical and spiritual theosophical Christianity. Additionally, the climatic disaster of the little ice age, together with rampant inflation, had inspired angst, uncertainty, and unrest among the populace, as well as a longing for insight into God's plans. Furthermore, it also relied upon the tireless efforts of readers, copyists, publicists, and followers, which he attracted from several levels of society. The spread of Boehme's *Aurora* is a prime example. This text was copied before its completion in 1613 by Karl Ender von Sercha (1568–1624). The already familiar figure of Balthasar Walther championed the work on his travels as a physician and, in or around 1618, Walther showed some of Boehme's work to the Sagan (Zagan) revenue collector, Christian Bernhard, who was captivated by what he read. Thereafter, Bernhard became the chief copyist of Boehme's material. The mechanisms behind the spread of *Aurora* epitomizes the interlocking associations of the local gentry, and both the highly educated and mercantile classes, which not only assisted the distribution of Boehme's works, but, I argue, also informed his writings. In the following sections, based primarily on a consideration of Boehme's extant epistles, I aim to outline some of the major figures in Boehme's energetic and sometimes volatile networks and point out the roles that they played in informing and disseminating his writings and ideas. The point here is to demonstrate, in a further context, that Boehme was not a man apart from his contemporaries during his most creative period between 1619 and his death in 1624, but rather was very much connected to the personalities and ideas circulating around him.

III PATRONS AND PROFESSIONALS

The important facilitating role of patronage within Boehme's networks has long been realized. Less frequently acknowledged, however, are the general heterodox inclinations of several of these patrons. Indeed, three of Boehme's foremost supporters among the local gentry were locally educated sons of major figures in Görlitz's Schwenckfelder community. The brothers Karl and Michael Ender von Sercha the younger (1590–1637) of Leopoldshain (Łagów), for example, were sons of the aforementioned Schwenckfelder patriarch Michael.[22] Additionally, Johann Sigismund von Schweinichen the younger (1590–1664), son of another major Schwenckfelder, financed the publication of Boehme's *Weg zu Christo* (Görlitz, 1624) and secured a publication privilege from Georg Rudolf II of Liegnitz (1595–1653).[23]

Further noble supporters of Boehme included Abraham von Sommerfeld (d. 1651), who visited the theosopher on numerous occasions and prepared copies of several of his works, giving them outlandish Latin titles.[24] Another patron, Kaspar von Fürstenau (1572–1649) of Lissa (Lasów), practiced alchemy and read and collected the works of Weigel and the Rosicrucian manifestos.[25] Both also knew the chiliast Paul Nagel. Rudolf von Gerßdorf (1598–1629) of Weichau (Wichów) was one of Boehme's correspondents and regularly received visits by Balthasar Walther and Boehme himself.[26] Abraham von Einsiedel, also a friend of Nagel's, not only supported Boehme in his battle against Esajas Stiefel but would later go on to experience a series of terrifying millennial visions in the 1630s.[27]

Not only did these friends and patrons advance and support Boehme's intellectual and spiritual interests, their lands also provided economic opportunities for the wandering theosopher, who spent much of his time selling his cloth and yarn wares along the *via regia*. During his travels, Boehme also encountered several other supporters, primarily among the professional classes. In addition to—among others—the Sprottau (Szprotawa) tanner Berend Nitsche[28] and Augustin Köppe, the manager of Fürstenau's Döbschutz property,[29] Boehme's foremost supporters were two copyists of his work: a Beuthen toll collector, Kaspar Lindner,[30] and the aforementioned Bernhard.[31] Both men were followers of the philosophy of Weigel, and Bernhard soon gave up his employment in order to devote himself to copying Boehme's works as well as other heterodox texts.

Boehme's reliance upon figures within his immediate network is emphasized by the fact that, when his works first came to the attention of alarmed Lutheran pastors outside Görlitz, such as Valentin Grießmann in 1623 and

Peter Widmann in 1624, these opponents were located in Wählitz (near Leipzig) and Lauban (Lubbin): cities well-known to Boehme and his supporters.[32] Furthermore, apart from the aforementioned Georg Rudolf and August von Anhalt-Plötzkau (1575–1653), his manuscripts appear not to have circulated more widely within contemporary heterodox epistolary and interpersonal networks whose participants were otherwise inclined towards mystical, chiliastic, alchemical, and Weigelian ideas.[33]

IV JURISTS, PHYSICIANS, AND CHYMISTS

While his patrons and professional contacts thus also shared Boehme's interests in heterodox thought, it appears that the greatest audience for his works were the educated classes, with a great deal of Boehme's initial friends and correspondents being university educated jurists, physicians, and chymists, who were based in Görlitz and further afield. Only the most significant of these figures will be listed below. Foremost among those after Walther was Tobias Kober (1587–1625), a correspondent and Boehme's personal physician, a convinced Paracelsian who attended the theosopher on his deathbed. Kober was said by Franckenberg to have supplied Boehme with Latin and Greek equivalents for several words and concepts in his writings.[34] The "exceptional alchemist and adept" Johann Rothe (ca. 1580–d. 1640) of Görlitz was another influential contact.[35] He was a keen reader of Tauler and Arndt, and, as the historian Ernst-Heinz Lemper speculates, may have brought earlier theosophical doctrines to Boehme's attention.[36] Two physicians and alchemists from Boehme's circle had direct familial contact with radical Paracelsian figures. Johann Hartig (1573–1632), who met Boehme in Zittau in May of 1624, had studied medicine in Basel and was the son-in-law of the famed Paracelsian Johann Montanus of Striegau (Strzegom, 1531–ca. 1604).[37] Johann Huser was master of the Glogau (Głogów) mint and a relation of the editor of the famous edition of Paracelsus's surgical and medical writings.[38]

Several further physicians from Boehme's circle also took part in the contemporary Rosicrucian debate, which was ignited by the printing of the *Fama Fraternitatis* (1614) and the *Confessio Fraternitatis* (1615) in Kassel. These millenarian tracts, which called for a "universal and general reformation of the whole wide world" were available in Görlitz through the town's major printer and bookseller, Johann Rhambau (1563–1634), and expressed an eschatology which, as we shall see, would be echoed in Boehme's final works. Adam Brux, city physician in Sprottau had, like Balthasar Walther, served as a personal physician to August of Anhalt-Plötzkau.[39] His *Helias Tertius* (1616) praised the Rosicrucian fraternity. Similarly, Valentin Tschirnes corresponded with Boehme about matters alchemical and issued two tracts addressed to the Rosicrucian fraternity, one of which was printed at Görlitz.

Some physicians were significant in building Boehme's readership through their own personal networks. Tschirnes, for example, was part of the influential circle of Boehme-adherents in Striegau, which centered around the figure of Johann Daniel Koschwitz.[40] Koschwitz knew the Brieg (Brzeg) jurist and mystic Johann Theodor von Tschesch (1595–1649).[41] Furthermore, his sister, or daughter, was married to Michael Ender von Sercha, one of Böhme's key patrons. Friedrich Krause, physician in Goldberg and Liegnitz,[42] was a correspondent of the Torgau chiliast Nagel, author of the manuscript devotional tract *Via Salutis*, and brother-in-law of the Schwenckfelder Balthasar Tilke.[43] A major influence on Boehme, on account of the many manuscripts he collected, may have also been Benedikt Hinckelmann (d. 1642), leader of Elector Johann Georg I's secret laboratory in Dresden.[44] Befriended by Balthasar Walther, Hinckelmann hosted Boehme when the theosopher visited the city in summer 1624.

V RELIGIOUS ENTHUSIASTS

However, if the "learned people," those "physicians, chymists and philosophers" with whom Boehme trafficked, provided him with "various Latin phrases and technical terms," as Franckenberg remarked, he must have taken something more from the overlapping associations of religious enthusiasts, chiliasts, prophets, astrologers, and visionaries, with whom he also interacted. Mentioned several times previously, the Torgau chiliast Paul Nagel—who predicted that a spiritual millennium would begin in 1624 in the wake of the grand conjunction of Jupiter and Saturn—was one of the foremost champions of Boehme's works in Saxony, as well as a correspondent who was visited at least once by Boehme. He authored some thirty prophetic works during his lifetime and excerpted Boehme's then unpublished *Aurora* in his *Prodromus astronomiae apocalypticae* (1620).[45] Like Balthasar Walther, Nagel was also initially a follower of the Thuringian antinomians Esajas Stiefel and Ezechiel Meth (d. 1640).[46] Among other things, Meth and Stiefel asserted that it was possible to embody the same heavenly substance of Christ if one truly interiorized his word. Compelled by Abraham von Einsiedel, Johann Rehefeldt, Nagel, and Walther, Boehme wrote two tracts against Stiefel and Meth in 1621 and 1622, in which he further honed his own theosophical doctrines. Although both men ultimately advocated an antinomianism that Boehme and his followers rejected, they sprung from the same intellectual tradition of disaffected Lutheranism as Boehme. Moreover, many of their immediate inspirations, such as Weigel, were shared by their Görlitz counterpart, as evidenced by Boehme's initially friendly approbation of their work.

Another member of the circle was the Sprottau clothier Christoph Kotter (1595–1647), who after 1616 experienced a series of ecstatic visions.[47]

Although unmentioned in Boehme's letters, he was one of the close friends who attended Boehme's deathbed. Another visionary was Paul Kaym (d. 1634), a Görlitz native employed as a revenue collector in Liegnitz.[48] He issued a response to the Rosicrucian brotherhood in 1616 and thereafter authored several unprinted millenarian works, some based on Paul Lautensack's (1478–1558) apocalyptic tracts, which he sent to Boehme for comment.

An intriguing member of Boehme's circle, albeit one not mentioned in his letters, was Gottfried Gloger von Schwanbach, a jurist and theosopher from Sprottischdorf (Henryków) and a close friend of Bernhard and Walther.[49] As we shall see, he collected works by a variety of heterodox figures and apocalyptically styled himself as "the least worthy of the sixth community in Philadelphia, who possess the sense of Christ in the Spirit of the Lord" (cf. Rev. 3:7–13), signing the copies he prepared "in God's wisdom of the time of the Holy Spirit."

Another figure with whom Boehme came into contact was Johann Staricius, an editor of Weigelian and Paracelsian works,[50] who held a disputation with Boehme at Liegnitz in 1622 concerning the election of Grace (*Gnadenwahl*). Staricius was among the learned elite of central Europe interested in theosophical and magical doctrines, and he was also acquainted with two of Boehme's most prominent followers, the Christian Kabbalist Abraham von Franckenberg, who met Boehme at the end of 1623, and the aforementioned Tschesch, whom Boehme encountered before 1622.[51] Franckenberg, in particular, emerged from an intellectual tradition similar to that of Boehme. In 1617 he experienced a mystical awakening (which he described as a *stillen Sabbath*) in which God informed him that the old Adam must die in order for Christ to live in the human heart. According to his own account, Franckenberg found this doctrine explicated in Tauler, the *Theologia Deutsch*, Weigel, Johann Arndt, Schwenckfeld, "and yet others."[52] Although both Franckenberg and Tschesch were apparently disinterested in the chiliasm that characterized the thought of Nagel, Kotter, Kaym, and Schwanbach, they nevertheless championed the idea of a School of the Holy Spirit, or "Pentecostal School" in which the true doctrine of God could be learned without worldly interference.

Boehme also corresponded with figures further afield through connections established by Walther, Franckenberg, Nagel, and others. In Lübeck and Lüneburg lived, for example, Joachim Morsius (1593–1643/4) and Leonhard Elver (1564–1631).[53] Both were converted to Boehme's theosophy in 1622 by Balthasar Walther and later corresponded with Boehme. Morsius and Elver possessed numerous magical, Rosicrucian, and chiliastic texts, and Elver was furthermore a patron of the aforementioned Nagel.[54] While their own potential impact on Boehme's thought was perhaps limited, Elver and Morsius nevertheless remain emblematic of the types of personalities that populated the margins of Boehme's networks.

VI CHRISTIAN KABBALAH AND CHILIASM: IMPACT OF THE HETERODOX MILIEU ON BOEHME'S WORKS

The preceding survey indicates that, between 1618 and 1624, Boehme dealt with numerous persons with experience in medicine, alchemy, astrology, prophecy, trade, politics, and education and was thereby probably exposed to a variety of intellectual, spiritual, and religious influences. But how, if at all, did these contacts influence the development or content of his theosophy? The most obvious way in which we can assess the impact of Boehme's networks on his writings is to look for direct influences within them. Yet this is no easy task. Boehme's output was voluminous, and the range of his probable and possible sources immense. Outside of the Bible, none are named directly. Complications also arise following the nature of many of Boehme's appropriations. As Will-Erich Peuckert and Arlene Miller-Guinsberg have pointed out with regard to alchemy and Paracelsian works, although informed by them, Boehme was certainly "no slave" to their content.[55] Furthermore, it appears that at least some of the material that he apparently applied in his works stemmed from oral communications and were no doubt transformed by Boehme, and his intermediaries, before they reached the page. Other apparent influences may not actually be influences at all. Although the title of Boehme's *De triplice vita hominis* (*On the Three-fold Life of Man*, 1620) evokes Marsilio Ficino's *De triplici vita* (1489), its content is representative of a very different intellectual tradition. Still, such influences *can* be found. In this section, I provide two examples. One, concerning Boehme's reception of Kabbalistic speculation, is an instance of specific borrowing through an oral source. The second, concerning Boehme's chiliastic eschatology, is indicative of a more general influence.

Within Boehme scholarship, there has long been debate about the precise impact of Jewish and Christian Kabbalah on his thought. While structural similarities to Kabbalistic concepts abound within Boehme's corpus, proof of direct knowledge of a single appropriate work has proven difficult to pinpoint. Skepticism is increased by the fact that Boehme knew no Latin, let alone Hebrew. However, in his lengthy explication of Exodus 34 in his *Mysterium Magnum* (1624), Boehme noted that, when receiving the Ten Commandments atop Mount Sinai, Moses had not received two tablets of stone from God, but instead a second covenant "written upon a globe."[56]

This strange declaration may have escaped notice were it not for Gottfried Richter (1594-aft. 1660), son of Boehme's chief antagonist Gregor Richter (1560–1624) and editor of the so-called *Thorner Ausgabe* (eight volumes, ca. 1653–1660) of Boehme's works.[57] Drawing on the benefit of direct contact with many people who knew Boehme and his friends personally, Richter wrote of this passage:

> What the author here writes appears to contradict the clear text of Moses (Exodus 34:1, Deuteronomy 10:1 and 1 Kings 8:9), which expressly

> speak of stone tablets. This may be explained thusly: the thoughts of Jacob Boehme of blessed memory concerning the two globes [*sic*! Boehme only mentioned one] upon which the law was recorded derived from a conversation with Dr. Balthasar Walther, who read it in Reuchlin, and lived with Boehme for an entire quarter-year.[58]

If we examine Reuchlin's *De arte cabalistica* (1517), we indeed find the statement that "at first, the Kabbalists assert, God wrote his Law onto a fiery globe, applying dark fire to white fire."[59] According to Reuchlin, the sources of this doctrine were Moses ben Maimon, or Ramban (1135–1204), and the writings of the thirteenth century Genoan rabbi Nachmanides, or Gerundensis. The globe of the covenant in the *Mysterium Magnum* is, therefore, an unambiguous demonstration that Boehme knew of, at third or fourth hand, Kabbalistic traditions, knowledge of which was mediated through members of his immediate circle.[60] A thorough investigation of Boehme's later works will undoubtedly reveal further similar influences, both specific and more general.

But where might we start such an investigation? Certainly, one beginning might be in comparing Boehme's works with books he was known to possess. Unfortunately, we have little idea of the content or extent of his personal library. We have, however, already seen that, after 1619, Boehme acquired Pseudo-Weigelian books for Kaspar Lindner and also read the alchemical tractate *Wasserstein der Weysen* (Frankfurt, 1619).[61] As there are few other leads at this time, I suggest that a useful starting point for further investigation of these influences might therefore be a comparison of Boehme's works with the contents of texts written, read, copied, collected, or circulated by individuals within his network. As I shall show with reference to Boehme's eschatological expectations, such a comparison can be very fruitful.

Fortunately, several collections of material—as well as inventories of further manuscript and book collections—which document the intellectual interests of several of Boehme's closest followers, are still extant. The most significant of these is undoubtedly the collection of magical and Kabbalistic manuscripts, copied in 1588 by Balthasar Walther and preserved today in Lübeck (mentioned above and discussed elsewhere).[62] Given Walther's demonstrable significance to the shape and character of Boehme's mature theosophy, any investigation of possible sources of influence should begin with these texts although there are also a handful of lesser-known collections that might prove equally interesting.

One of these is a four-volume set of copied works prepared between 1618 and 1628 by Gottfried Gloger von Schwanbach, preserved today in Leipzig.[63] In addition to copies of several of Boehme's works, the collection preserves texts by, among others, Paul Nagel, Christoph Kotter, Aegidus Guttmann, Paracelsus, Weigel (in an extract given Schwanbach by Walther), as well as extracts from Rosicrucian manifestos. In other words, these manuscripts preserve works not only dovetailing with the interests of Boehme's closest companions, but also works by members of the circle itself.

A second collector of heterodox manuscripts close to Boehme was the aforementioned Benedikt Hinckelmann, at whose Dresden residence Boehme composed one of his final tracts, the *Gebetbüchlein* (1624). As the inventory of his collection reveals, Hinckelmann possessed a selection of manuscript works by Boehme, Weigel, Friedrich Krause, Helisäus Röslin, Johann Valentin Andreae, Guillaume Postel, Johann Tauler, Christoph Kotter, Paul Linck, Christoph Weichart, Julius Sperber, Andreas Karlstadt, Abraham Behem, Eustachius Poyssel, and other contemporary prophets and theosophers, all of which may very well have been at Boehme's disposal.[64] In addition to these major collections, we might also add that several volumes from the libraries of Franckenberg, Tschesch, and Johann Sigismund von Schweinichen are today extant in Wrocław, covering ground similar to the works indicated above.[65] A further list of books belonging to Karl Ender von Sercha was discovered in May 1943, but unfortunately can no longer be traced.[66]

More distant members of Boehme's networks evidently held interests similar to those of Schwanbach and Hinckelmann. The manuscripts collected by Johann Rehefeldt (1590–1648), an Erfurt-based Stiefelian and reader of Boehme, contain works on magic, Kabbalah, chiliastic prophecy, and dissident religiosity.[67] A further relevant inventory is that of the Hamburg librarian Joachim Morsius (1593–1644), who, in addition to corresponding with Boehme, collected numerous prophetic and theosophical works by Adam Haslmayr, Helisäus Röslin, and others, the vast majority of which concerned a chiliastic final age.[68]

Of course, the mere fact that several of Boehme's friends and correspondents also authored or collected works by heterodox figures is no guarantee that Boehme himself was also interested in these same texts or that they influenced his work. However, I argue that there is clear evidence that Boehme *was* receptive to the ideas in several of these texts; in particular, the chiliastic notion of a forthcoming age of the Holy Spirit.

In 1621, in an incident long overlooked by researchers, Boehme experienced an ecstatic vision during which he learned that a new Reformation, as a prelude to what he called an *aureum seculum* (golden age), would soon dawn. In mid-1624, he announced that this "Reformation" was already in progress.[69] What did Boehme mean by this? Its fullest expression may be found in a letter which predates the vision of 1621 in a missive to Paul Kaym (August 14th, 1620):

> In this time a Zion shall indeed be discovered, and heaven will give its dew, and the earth its fat, but not to the extent that evil shall cease altogether. But that the Holy Spirit will be in the hearts of believers in Zion, I declare and know, for Zion will not come from outside, but inside the new man. It is already born. Who seeks it, he must seek only himself

> and depart the old Adam into a new life, and shall discover whether Jesus is born in him.[70]

While the emphasis on interiority and rebirth in the last days echoes the expectations of both Guillaume Postel (1510–1581) and Weigel, this declaration also mirrors the spiritual chiliasm of several of Boehme's contemporaries—including Paul Nagel. In 1624, for example, the same year that Boehme championed his new Reformation, Nagel wrote in strikingly similar terms of the *aureum seculum*:

> Thus shall follow and begin a new, short time, the anticipated period that we call a *secula aureum*, a right golden age . . . in which shall flourish a gilded freedom, love and fidelity, justice, understanding, wisdom and truth, virtue, holiness and the fear of God.Those who possess no divine riches (*aurum divinum*), but remain in the old birth and will persist in sin, they shall have no part of this golden age, and will be judged alongside the beasts.[71]

Irrespective of the question of who influenced whom, Boehme's expectations were therefore consistent with the eschatology contained in any number of the heterodox manuscript works copied or possessed by Schwanbach, Hinckelmann, Morsius, or Rehefeldt, many of which promised a new birth and were condemned by Lutheran theologians as constituting the heresy *chiliasmus subtilis*.[72] Indeed, if Boehme's expectations influenced Nagel—one of the most notorious chiliasts in contemporary Germany—then he is more crucial to the history of seventeenth-century heterodoxy than has heretofore been recognized.

But did Boehme himself see his doctrines in the same light as the expectations of persons like Nagel? It seems so. For, tellingly, he made several statements that explicitly compared his expectations with those contained in other contemporary books and manuscripts. In May 1624, for example, Boehme informed Tobias Kober that similar books to his, concerning the last days and the new birth, were available at the Leipzig Book Fair.[73] In a subsequent letter, he declared that these books were also openly available in Dresden bookshops.[74]

What books were these? Who were the authors? A search of the "Verzeichnis der im deutschen Sprachraum erschienen Drucke des 17. Jahrhunderts," the major bibliographical catalogue of German books of the seventeenth century, for texts that use terms adopted by Boehme to describe his expectations—*aureum seculum*, *güldene Zeit*, *neue Reformation*—printed between 1621 and 1625, provides some clues. It reveals a list of titles that conforms entirely with the expectations engendered by the manuscript inventories and works of members of Boehme's circle, including books alchemical, devotional, prophetic, Weigelian, and chiliastic.[75] Most fascinating of all is a text by Christoph Adolphi, evangelical pastor in Lauban, Upper Lusatia, whose

Reformation (1624), strongly influenced by Calvinist meliorism, closely mirrored not only Boehme's expectations about an imminent "universal and general Reformation" of the church, but also Boehme's language in predicting an "aurora" which would precede the Judgment Day.[76]

In an overlooked passage in yet another letter to Kober shortly after Pentecost 1624, however, Boehme himself provides us with an even more specific indication of the works he had in mind when speaking of books supporting his vision of the last days. There, he declared that "identical theological grounds" of the "great Reformation soon to come" were taught "entirely correctly" not only by himself, but also "by many others in Meißen, Saxony, Thuringia and the Hanseatic towns."[77] This is an explicit reference to the output, both printed and manuscript, of the likes of Nagel (Saxony), Kaspar von Fürstenau and Kaspar Lindner (Meißen), Johann

Figure 4.1 Paul Nagel, from the title page of his *Prognosticon astrologicum* (1619). Harvard University, Houghton Library, *GC6 N1317 619p Courtesy of Imaging Services, Harvard College Library.

Rehefeldt and the reformed Stiefelians (Thuringia), and Joachim Morsius and Balthasar Walther (Hamburg, Lübeck, and Lüneburg), with whom Boehme identified his intellectual mission and, directly or indirectly, informed his output.

Figure 4.2 Christoph Kotter, from Jan Amos Comenius's *Lux e Tenebris* (1667). Harvard University, Houghton Library, *ZCC6 C7345 657lc Courtesy of Imaging Services, Harvard College Library.

VII CONCLUSION

This chapter has endeavored to sketch the heterodox intellectual climate from which Boehme's works emerged and to demonstrate, concretely, Boehme's intellectual debt to this milieu. It shows, first, that Boehme's initial mystical experiences occurred in a town whose intellectual life was suffused with Paracelsian, Weigelian, Schwenckfeldian and other heterodox strains of thought. Second, it demonstrates that his early supporters, readers, and friends consisted of a surprising number of chymists and physicians with connections to Görlitz's Paracelsian milieu, and also, critically, a substantial number of visionaries, chiliasts, and religious enthusiasts who were supported by a small group of like-minded regional gentry. Third, it demonstrates, through the examples of Kabbalistic thought and chiliastic eschatology, that this constellation of figures made an impression on Boehme and influenced the content of his works in manners both specific and more general. Finally, as part of a demonstration of this influence, it has pointed out some tangible new avenues for researching further possible influences on Boehme's work, by bringing to light a series of overlooked inventories and collections of manuscript tracts that circulated or were preserved among Boehme's closest supporters.

Much work, however, remains to be done to elaborate on this background. An intellectual geography of Görlitz—concentrating particularly on the city's heterodox figures during the second-half of the sixteenth century and their relationship with similar figures in Silesia and elsewhere—remains to be undertaken. This will synthesize the scattered evidence concerning Schwenckfeldian, Paracelsian, and Weigelian presences in the city. A critical edition, or even in-depth study, of Boehme's *Sendbriefe* will allow greater insight into the geography, participants, and nature of his intellectual enterprise, smoothing the way for further studies of Boehme's networks. Finally, a systematic consideration of Boehme's complete works with regard to the books known within his networks will provide a new platform for the appreciation and analysis of his philosophy, its sources, and influences. Only then can the historical figure of Boehme and his work be rescued, definitively, from the specter of his own self-representations.

NOTES

1. See Bo Andersson, "*Du Solst wissen es ist aus keinem stein gesogen.*" *Studien zu Jacob Böhmes Aurora oder Morgen Röte im Auffgang* (Stockholm: Almqvist & Wiksell, 1986), 130–132.
2. Jacob Boehme, *Sämtliche Schriften*, eds. August Faust and Will-Erich Peuckert, (11 vols., Stuttgart: Bad-Canstatt: Frommann, 1955–1961), vol. 9, 50.1.
3. Boehme, *Schriften,* vol. 1, 10:27.
4. Boehme, *Schriften,* vol. 1, 25.60, 20.27; Andersson, *Du Solst wissen,* 130.

5. Some exceptions include Richard Jecht, "Die Lebensumstände Jakob Böhmes," in *Jakob Böhme. Gedenkgabe der Stadt Görlitz zu seinem 300jährigen Todestag* (Görlitz: Magistrat der Stadt Görlitz, 1924), 7–75; Ernst-Heinz Lemper, *Jakob Böhme. Leben und Werk* ([East] Berlin: Union Verlag, 1976); Ernst-Heinz Lemper, "Voraussetzungen zur Beurteilung des Erfahrungs- und Schaffensumfelds Jakob Böhmes," in *Gott, Natur und Mensch in der Sicht Jacob Böhmes und seiner Rezeption*, eds. Jan Garewicz and Alois Maria Haas, (Wiesbaden: Harassowitz, 1994), 41–69; Andrew Weeks, *Boehme: An Intellectual Biography of the Seventeenth-Century Philosopher and Mystic* (Albany: State University of New York Press, 1991).
6. Joachim Bahlcke, "Das Görlitzer *Gymnasium Augustum.* Entwicklung, Struktur und regionale Ausstrahlung einer höheren Schule im konfessionellen Zeitalter," in *Die Oberlausitz im frühneuzeitlichen Mitteleuropa*, ed. J. Bahlcke (Stuttgart: Franz Steiner Verlag, 2007), 123–143.
7. Joachim Telle and Wilhelm Kühlmann, eds., *Corpus Paracelsisticum* (Tübingen: Niemeyer, 2004), vol. 2, 705–728; Ernst-Heinz Lemper, "Görlitz und der Paracelsismus," *Deutsche Zeitschrift für Philosophie* 18 (1970): 347–360; Arlene Miller-Guinsburg, "Von Paracelsus zu Böhme: Auf dem Wege zu neuen Bestandsaufnahmen in der Beeinflussung Böhmes durch Paracelsus," in *Paracelsus in der Tradition. Vorträge Paracelsustag 1978* (Vienna: Verlag der Österreichischen wissenschaftlichen Gesselschaft, 1980), 96–118.
8. M. Reuther, "Der Görlitzer Burgermeister, Mathematiker, Astronom und Kartograph Bartholomäus Scultetus (1540–1614) und seine Zeit," *Wissenschaftliche Zeitschrift der Technische Hochschule Dresden 5* (1955/56): 1133–62.
9. Karl Sudhoff, *Versuch einer Kritik der Echtheit der Paracelsischen Schriften: II. Theil. Paracelsische Handschriften* (Berlin: G. Riemer, 1898), nos. 15, 83–85.
10. Lemper, "Görlitz und der Paracelsismus," 353.
11. Carlos Gilly, "Theophrastia Sancta. Der Paracelsimus als Religion im Streit mit den offiziellen Kirchen," in *Analecta Paracelsica. Studien zum Nachleben Theophrast von Hohenheims in deutschen Kulturgebiet der frühen Neuzeit*, eds. Wolf Müller-Jancke and Joachim Telle (Stuttgart: Franz Steiner Verlag, 1994), 425–488 at 432.
12. Winfried Zeller, "Naturmystik und spiritualistische Theologie bei Valentin Weigel," in *Epochen der Naturmystik. Hermetische Tradition im wissenschaftlichen Fortschritt*, eds. Antoine Faivre and Rolf Christian Zimmermann (Berlin: Erich Schmidt Verlag, 1979), 120–22.
13. Weeks, *Boehme*, 39; See "Theologica Manuscripta Summa diligentia multisque sumtibus, circa finem defluxi & principium currentis saeculi a N.N. hinc inde collecta," *Monatliche Unterredungen Einiger Guten Freunde von allerhand Büchern . . . Aprilis 1692* (Leipzig: Johann Friedrich Gleditsch, 1692): 258–74 at 264–5.
14. Leigh T.I. Penman, "Repulsive Blasphemies. Paul Nagel's Appropriation of Unprinted Works by Jakob Böhme and Valentin Weigel in his *Prodromus astronomiae apocalypticae* (1620)," *Daphnis* 38 (2009): 599–622; Boehme, *Schriften*, vol. 9, 9:10.
15. Boehme, *Schriften*, vol. 9, 12.60.
16. Horst Weigelt, *Spiritualistische Tradition im Protestantismus: die Geschichte des Schwenckfeldertums in Schlesien* (Berlin: Walter de Gruyter, 1973).
17. Lemper, "Voraussetzungen," 52–53.
18. Leigh T.I. Penman, "'Ein Liebhaber des Mysterii, und ein großer Verwandter desselben.' Toward the Life of Balthasar Walther, a Wandering

Paracelsian Physician," *Sudhoffs Archiv* 94/1 (2010): 73–99; Penman, "Walther, Balthasar," in *Killy Literaturlexikon,* 2nd edn., ed. Wilhelm Kühlmann et al. (Berlin: Walter de Gruyter, 2011), vol. 12, 129–31.

19. On Stiefel, see Ulman Weiß, *Die Lebenswelten des Esajas Stiefel oder Vom Umgang mit Dissidenten* (Stuttgart: Franz Steiner Verlag, 2007).
20. Elke Axmacher, *Praxis Evangelicorum. Theologie und Frömmigkeit bei Martin Moller (1547–1606)* (Göttingen: Vandenhoeck & Ruprecht, 1989).
21. Wrocław, Biblioteka Uniwersytecka, Akc. 1947/70 (iii), 430 (Christian Knauthe, 'Bibliotheca Böhmistica,' c. 1780).
22. On the Ender family, see Jecht, "Lebensumstände," 60–61; Carlos Gilly, "Biographisches Register," in *Jacob Böhmes Weg in die Welt,* ed. Theodor Harmsen (Amsterdam: In de Pelikaan, 2007), 457–84 at 462. Karl is the addressee of Sendbriefe 1, 2, 5, 6, 23, 37, 44, 52, 73, 74 and is mentioned in 3.2–3, 4.45, 40.10, 61.14, 62.11; Michael is mentioned in Sendbriefe 23.6, 60.3–6, 61.14, 62.11, 73.1–2.
23. Lemper, *Jakob Böhme*, 88; Jecht, "Lebensumstände," 43; Gilly, "Biographisches Register," 478; Addressee of Sendbriefe 18, 53; mentioned in Sendbriefe, 41.11, 44.3, 45.3, 54.10, 59.1, 61.14, 62.11.
24. Gilly, "Biographisches Register," 479; Mentioned in Sendbrief 10.1.
25. Jecht, "Lebensumstände," 61–62; Gilly, "Biographisches Register," 465; Mentioned in Sendbriefe 44.2–3, 64.19.
26. Gilly, "Biographisches Register," 465. Mentioned in Sendbriefe 21.4, 25.3, 29.1, 32.2–3, 38.17, 68.1, 69.3, 70.2, 72.1–7.
27. Daniel Colberg, *Das Platonisch-hermetische Christenthum,* 2nd edn., (2 vols., Leipzig, 1710) vol. 1, 264; V. König, *Genealogische Adels-Historie oder Geschlechts-Beschreibung*, (3 vols., Leipzig, 1727–36), vol. 1, 280–2; Gilly, "Biographisches Register," 461–462.
28. Gilly, "Biographisches Register,"474; Addressee of Sendbriefe 24, 36.
29. Gilly, "Biographisches Register," 470; Addressee of Sendbriefe 65, 66.
30. Gilly, "Biographisches Register,"472; Addressee of Sendbrief 12, mentioned in 21.3, 32.3, 72.2–3.
31. Gilly, "Biographisches Register," 458; Addressee of Sendbriefe II, III, IV, 4, 9, 13–14, 21, 25–27, 29, 32–33, 45, 48–49, 51, 57, 67–72, mentioned in 12.65–77, 38.17.
32. Valentin Griessmann, . . . *Getrewer Eckhart* . . . (Gera: Marmitzsch, 1623); Peter Widmann, *Christliche Warnung / Für einem new außgesprengeten Enthusiastischen Büchlein . . . Der Weg zu Christo* (Leipzig: Rehefeld, Grosse and Lamberg, 1624).
33. Carlos Gilly, "Zur Geschichte und Überlieferung der Handschriften Jacob Böhmes," in *Jacob Böhmes Weg in die Welt*, 39–55 at 51.
34. Jecht, "Lebensumstände," 57–58; Gilly, "Biographisches Register," 470; Addressee of Sendbriefe 61–64, mentioned in 31.1, 46.2, 65.3, 66.2–6.
35. Jecht, "Lebensumstände," 58; Gilly, "Biographisches Register," 477, mentioned in Sendbriefe 23.4–6, 61.14, 62.11, 63.12.
36. Jecht, "Lebensumstände," 58.
37. Jecht, "Lebensumstände," 62; Gilly, "Biographisches Register," 467, mentioned in Sendbrief 61.13.
38. Gilly, "Biographisches Register," 469. Addressee of Sendbrief 47, mentioned in 72.4–6.
39. Gilly, "Biographisches Register," 459, mentioned in Sendbriefe 25.5, 32.3.
40. Gilly, "Biographisches Register," 470; addressee of Sendbriefe 15, 19, mentioned in 17.6, 41.11, 53.18.
41. Gilly, "Biographisches Register," 480, mentioned in Sendbrief 15.4.

42. Gilly, "Biographisches Register," 470; addressee of Sendbriefe 30, 39–40, 60.
43. "Theologica Manuscripta," 259, 264; Concerning Tilke, see Gilly, "Biographisches Register," 481, mentioned in Sendbriefe 15.1–8, 18.2, 19.20, 40.2–18, 41.4.
44. Gilly, "Biographisches Register," 468, mentioned in Sendbriefe 57.3, 61.1–2, 62.2–12, 63.3.
45. Mentioned in Sendbriefe 23.7, 34.20, 71.6; See Leigh T.I. Penman, "Climbing Jacob's Ladder. Crisis and Transcendence in the Thought of Paul Nagel (†1624), a Lutheran Dissident during the Time of the Thirty Years' War," *Intellectual History Review* 20/2 (2010): 201–26; Gilly, "Wege der Verbreitung von Jacob Böhmes Schriften in Deutschland und den Niederlanden," in *Jacob Böhmes Weg in die Welt*, 71–98.
46. Weiß, *Lebenswelten*, passim, mentioned in Sendbriefe 12.77, 20.33, 32.3, 72.3.
47. Jana Hubková, "Comenius, Görlitz und der Prophet aus Sprottau," *Görlitzer Magazin* 22 (2009): 45–54.
48. Gilly, "Biographisches Register," 470; addressee of Sendbriefe 8, 11.
49. Gilly, "Biographisches Register," 478.
50. Helmut Möller, *Staricius und sein HeldenSchatz. Episoden eines Akademikerlebens* (Göttingen: Basta, 2003), mentioned in Sendbriefe 15.3–7, 41.1–11.
51. Sibylle Rusterholz, "Abraham von Franckenbergs Verhältnis zu Jacob Böhme: Versuch einer Neubestimmung der Textgrundlagen aufgrund kritische Sichtung," in *Kulturgeschichte Schlesiens in der Frühen Neuzeit*, 2 vols., ed. Klaus Garber (Tübingen: Niemeyer, 2005), vol. 1, 205–241, mentioned in Sendbriefe 22, 53.18.
52. Joachim Telle, ed., *Abraham von Franckenberg. Briefwechsel.* (Stuttgart-Bad Cannstatt: Frommann-Holzboog, 1995), 300–01.
53. Hermann Schneider, *Joachim Morsius und sein Kreis* (Lübeck: Quitzlow, 1923); addressee of Sendbrief 55, mentioned (by inference) in 57.2.
54. Gilly, "Biographisches Register," 462; Penman, "Towards Life of Balthasar Walther," 88.
55. Guinsberg, "Von Paracelsus zu Böhme," 113; Will-Erich Peuckert, "Das Leben Jacob Böhmes," in Boehme, *Schriften*, vol. 10, 81.
56. Boehme, *Schriften*, vol. 7, 121.
57. [Gottfried Richter, ed.] . . . *Alles aus J.B.T. Schriften gezogen* ([Thorn]: no printer, no date).
58. Richter's remark is reprinted in Boehme, *Schriften*, vol. 10, 91.
59. Johannes Reuchlin, *On the Art of the Kabbalah*, trans. Martin and Sarah Goodman (New York: Abaris Books, 1983), 293.
60. Cf. Sibylle Rusterholz, "Elemente der Kabbala bei Jacob Böhme," in *Mystik und Schriftkommentierung*, eds. Günther Bonheim and Petra Kattner (Berlin: Wießensee, 2007), 15–46, who suggests Franckenberg, and not Walther, may have passed this information on to Boehme.
61. For a discussion of this work's influence on Boehme, see Peuckert, "Leben," in Boehme, *Schriften*, vol. 10, 221–23.
62. Penman, "Towards Life of Balthasar Walther," 78–80.
63. Leipzig, Universitätsbibliothek, MS Rep. 106 IV, vols. 1–4.
64. "Theologica Manuscripta," 258–74.
65. János Bruckner, *Abraham von Franckenberg: A Bibliographical Catalogue with a Short-List of his Library* (Wiesbaden: Harrassowitz, 1988), 91–104.
66. Matthias Wenzel, "Das Schicksal des Linzer Böhme-Archivs von 1941 bis zur Gegenwart," in *Jacob Böhmes Weg in die Welt*, 383–98 at 392.

67. Leipzig, Universitätsbibliothek, MS 0 356, fols. 100r-01r (catalogue); Munich, Bayerische Staatsbibliothek, MS cgm. 4416 vols., 1–36.
68. Joachim Morsius, *Nuncius Olympicus* (Philadelphia [i.e., Amsterdam], 1626).
69. Boehme, *Schriften*, vol. 9, 58.13, 13.2.
70. Ibid., 8:24–25.
71. Paul Nagel, *Prognosticon Astrologicon, Auffs Jahr . . . 1625* (Halle: Bißmarck, [1624]), B3r.
72. Johannes Wallmann, "Reich Gottes und Chiliasmus in der lutherischen Orthodoxie," in Wallmann, *Theologie und Frömmigkeit im Zeitalter des Barock* (Tübingen: Mohr 1995), 105–23.
73. Boehme, *Schriften*, vol. 9, 61.8 (Letter to Kober, 15 May 1624).
74. Boehme, *Schriften*, vol. 9, 62.8 (Letter to Kober, "Sonntage nach Christi Himmelfahrt" 1624).
75. http://www.vd17.de. See nos. 3:603990R, 39:156674L, 3:602646H, 23:248133G, 23:280621R.
76. Christoph Adolphi, *Reformation . . . Was von der allgemeinen Reformation der Kirchen . . . zu halten seye?* ([Frankfurt/Main]: Unckel, 1624).
77. Boehme, *Schriften*, vol. 9, 63:9.

5 Jacob Boehme's Writings During the English Revolution and Afterwards

Their Publication, Dissemination, and Influence

Ariel Hessayon

On August 4th, 1653, Samuel Herring of Swan Alley in Coleman Street, London petitioned Barebone's Parliament to consider thirty propositions for the good of the nation. The second was that two colleges at Oxford and Cambridge should be devoted to the study of "attaining and enjoying the spirit of our Lord Jesus." Few books would be needed besides the Bible and English translations of "Jacob Behmen, and such like, who had true revelation from the true spirit."[1] This proposal was not adopted, nor is there evidence for how much support it attracted among Herring's fellow parishioners or in Parliament. Though he may have acted alone, it is equally possible that Herring represented the public face of a group promoting the dissemination of English versions of the German mystic's writings. Indeed, it is significant that between 1645 and 1662 most of Boehme's treatises and the majority of his letters were printed in English translation at London. Moreover, two shorter pieces were rendered from English into Welsh in 1655.

This chapter begins by examining the processes through which translations of Boehme's works were made and circulated within the wider context of the breakdown of prepublication censorship during the English Revolution. Locating these translations within the broader framework of the dissemination of continental alchemical, astrological, millenarian, and mystical writings during a turbulent period of English history, I will also look at the question of what happens when texts are circulated within contexts for which they were not intended. Boehme's principal English translator, the barrister and linguist John Sparrow, had hoped his efforts would be rewarded with the settlement of religious controversies and the disappearance of sects and heresies. But instead of doctrinal unanimity, there was discord. Indeed, Boehme's readers responded in largely unforeseen ways: sometimes with enthusiasm, but on other occasions with exasperation, ambivalence, and even revulsion.[2] A handful were convicted of blasphemy, others formed spiritual communities, while others still fulminated against what they regarded as Boehme's incomprehensible nonsense and vile falsehoods. All the same, I will suggest that engagement with Boehme's teachings was not only more extensive at this crucial moment in English history than has usually been recognized, but also that his influence was neither straightforward nor always easy to untangle from the wider tradition of continental mystical, prophetic, and visionary writing that he epitomized.

I THE TRANSLATIONS

Between 1641 and 1660, an estimated 32,238 titles were published in the British Isles or by English speakers elsewhere in the world; that is roughly 26% of the total amount of such publications between 1475 and 1700.[3] Although the number of English translations of continental European writings printed or reissued during this period has yet to be established, this heterogeneous corpus of material consisted of writings by more than 220 nonnative authors, including texts by or attributed to Greeks, Romans, and Church Fathers, as well as alchemists, anti-Trinitarians, astrologers, astronomers, cardinals, geographers, grammarians, heralds, herbalists, heresiographers, historians, lawyers, librarians, linguists, magicians, millenarians, monarchs, mystics, novelists, occultists, philosophers, physicians, physiognomists, poets, politicians, popes, prophets, satirists, soldiers, theologians, and travelers. Added to this were several untranslated works that appeared predominantly in the original Latin, but also in other languages.

Despite Christopher Hill's claim that the English Revolution was a short-lived age of "freedom" when relatively cheap and portable printing equipment may have made it easier than ever before for new and sometimes radical ideas to see the light of day, the desire to censor—as is widely recognized—remained in many quarters.[4] There were three effective ways in which this could be achieved: through prepublication, postpublication, or self-censorship. Prepublication censorship, particularly of religious literature, which had been used to increasing effect during the 1630s, became a lost cause after 1641. For in that year, the secular court of Star Chamber and the ecclesiastical court of High Commission were abolished by act of Parliament, leading to a disintegration of the London Stationers' Company monopoly. With the collapse of prepublication censorship, the licensing system upon which it had been built became increasingly used to protect the publisher's copyright rather than to indicate official approbation. Despite initial Parliamentary attempts at reasserting control by examining those considered responsible for committing abuses in printing and licensing, and subsequently through legislation, without an equivalent to the Papal Index of prohibited books, prepublication censorship appears to have been almost entirely at the licenser's discretion. As such, it was utterly ineffective. Indeed, during the later 1640s and much of the 1650s, licensing was characterized by inconsistent practice and the absence of a universally agreed upon strategy. By contrast, postpublication censorship proved most effective when implemented by those with intimate knowledge of the printing trade. And in exceptional circumstances, its outcome could be dramatic. For although no one had been burned at the stake for heresy in England since 1612, the published writings of blasphemers and seditionists were still consigned to the flames in public book burning rituals that resembled Protestant *Autos da Fé* by proxy.[5]

Besides these upheavals in the publishing world, the dissemination and early reception of Boehme's writings must also largely be set against a background of devastating Civil War and rebellion in the three kingdoms of England, Scotland, and Ireland; widespread poverty, harvest failure, desperate food shortages, economic decay, and outbreaks of plague; the abolition of episcopacy and emasculation of the Church of England; petitioning campaigns to introduce religious toleration and initiate ecclesiastical, educational, electoral, legal, medical, and taxation reforms; the associated emergence of political movements with radical demands such as the Levellers; impassioned apocalyptic speculation sometimes allied with anticlericalism, including clamoring to abolish the maintenance of ministers by tithes; the dramatic act of regicide, regarded by Royalists as the sinful shedding of innocent blood akin to the Jews' cruel crucifixion of Christ; and a brief period of oligarchic republican rule afterwards supplanted by an uncrowned Lord Protector (Oliver Cromwell) presiding with the aid of his council and successive Parliaments over a perpetual Reformation implemented by an unsteady alliance of magistracy, ministry, and military power.

Elsewhere I have discussed at greater length why Boehme's writings were translated into English and showed the mechanisms behind this process.[6] Among his followers there circulated a garbled story that Charles I had been the main patron of the venture before his execution in January 1649. Some, like Francis Lee (a founder of the Philadelphian Society), also maintained, probably correctly, that after the restoration of the monarchy in 1660, the remaining works were brought out under the auspices of Philip Herbert, fifth Earl of Pembroke. In their eyes, this tradition of royal and aristocratic support gave the undertaking prestige; yet it simplified developments, obscuring the involvement of a number of people with common aims. Actually, there were three overlapping phases. Initially, several individuals with knowledge of Latin or German received abstracts of Boehme's teachings or selected treatises from their associates in Amsterdam. Then manuscript translations were made from German and Latin versions of works published in Amsterdam, as well as from copies of the original texts. These circulated privately in much the same way as had the writings of the sixteenth-century mystic Hendrik Niclaes and other conspicuous members of his heretical sect known as the Family of Love. Finally, there was an organized scheme for publishing the extant corpus. While some of the cost was met by the translators themselves, it is clear that Samuel Hartlib, a Prussian émigré resident in London since 1628, and members of his circle acted as go-betweens by using agents to purchase books, subsequently shipping them to England.

Hartlib's circle, as is well known, promoted reconciliation between the Protestant churches and planned to establish a University in London with a College for Oriental Studies to assist with the conversion of the Jews to

Christianity. They also advocated educational and medical reform and disseminated the Moravian exile Johannes Amos Comenius's theories concerning universal knowledge (pansophy) and the importance of translation as a first step towards establishing communication through a common tongue.[7] Although it had gone unheeded by many of his compatriots, Boehme's announcement of the dawn of a new reformation thus chimed with their vision of universal reformation. Similarly, fearing the consequences of making such things known in his native language to "*so many various minds, as are now sprung up*," John Sparrow nonetheless contented himself with the knowledge that his public-spirited efforts might provide "*much comfort*" to "*troubled doubting*" souls, enabling them to attain that "*inward Peace which passeth all understanding*." It was, however, to prove a vain hope. Instead of the promised "Day of Pentecost," when the "*true sence and meaning of all Languages*" would be united into one tongue, there was a new Babel.[8]

All the same, the contributions of various intermediaries, patrons, translators, biographers, printers, publishers, and booksellers were crucial in facilitating the project through which Boehme's texts were copied, rendered into English, issued, and transmitted. Furthermore, uncovering the translators' social networks disclosed their ties through kinship and friendship as well as shared professional and commercial interests. Indeed, these extensive connections, which included sympathetic publishers, largely explains why Boehme's works were acquired so readily in printed English translations and later selectively rendered into Welsh. Moreover, it should be remembered that this was at a time when legislation empowered civil and military officials to fine or imprison the authors, printers, publishers, and booksellers of unlicensed material. This repressive element of postpublication censorship doubtless prompted strategies to avoid punishment: spurious imprints, anonymity, pseudonymity, and varying degrees of self-censorship. While Boehme's writings were not suppressed—the copyright of seven books was entered in the Stationers' Register—it is worth emphasizing that a few of his readers were punished by authority.[9] The most notable, both of whom we shall encounter later, were TheaurauJohn Tany (imprisoned for blasphemy) and Dr. John Pordage (ejected out of the rectory of Bradfield, Berkshire).[10]

II CRITICS AND ADMIRERS

Taken together, evidence from law suits, advertisements, auction catalogues, and commonplace books gives some indication of the sale price of Boehme's books, while marketability is indicated by their inclusion in *A Catalogue of The most vendible Books in England* (1658) under "Divinity."[11] Although it is not possible to determine every buyer, titles by Boehme are recorded in the libraries of a number of Englishmen. Among the most prominent were the antiquary Elias Ashmole; the Cambridge Platonist Ralph Cudworth; George Digby, second Earl of Bristol; Benjamin Furly, Quaker merchant of

Rotterdam; Samuel Jeake, nonconformist, lawyer, and political activist of Rye; Adam Littleton, chaplain to Charles II and headmaster of Westminster school; Henry Oldenburg, secretary of the Royal Society; John Owen, Cromwell's chaplain and afterwards Vice-Chancellor of Oxford University; the diarist Samuel Pepys; the English jurist and Oriental scholar John Selden; the Cambridge Platonist Peter Sterry; the educational reformer John Webster; the Irish alchemist and physician Benjamin Worsley; and John Worthington, Master of Jesus College, Cambridge. Moreover, correspondence, autograph inscriptions, and a variety of other sources enable us to add more names—including a handful of women such as Anne, Viscountess Conway and Elizabeth Foxcroft—to the list of people who owned printed works by Boehme in English. Ownership, of course, is not synonymous with readership, and in the case of some scholars and aristocrats who possessed thousands of books, having one or two Boehme titles listed in the auction catalogues of their libraries tells us very little. Nonetheless, more than one hundred seventeenth-century owners and readers have now been identified, ranging from the Civil War army officer John Lambert to the self-proclaimed High Priest of the Jews TheaurauJohn Tany and from the Cambridge Platonist Henry More to the Ranter Abiezer Coppe.[12]

In addition, according to a plausible story related after the Restoration by John Sparrow, it seems that Charles I was given an edition of *XL. Qvestions Concerning the Soule* during the period of his confinement by the army in 1647. When asked what he thought of it, the king supposedly replied

> that the Publisher in English seemed to say of the Author, that he was no Scholar, and if he were not, he did believe that the Holy Ghost was now in Men, but if he were a Scholar, it was one of the best Inventions that ever he read.[13]

If true, this was just one of a variety of responses, for as noted earlier, Boehme's readers reacted in a range of ways: from passionate engagement to being in two minds and from frustration to aversion. On the continent, the doctrines of "Teutonicus"—to borrow the code name used by some of Boehme's earliest followers—had been refuted by Gisbertius Voetius, professor at the University of Utrecht, and by the German Calvinist Christian Beckman in *Exercitationes theologicæ* (Amsterdam, 1644). These foreign critics exerted a degree of influence on the initial reaction to Boehme's writings in England. Thus, Beckman's work was cited with approval by both Meric Casaubon and the minister Richard Baxter, the latter maintaining that Boehme took his doctrine neither from Scripture nor from angels, but from that "drunken conjurer" Paracelsus. Baxter developed this judgment, later condemning Boehme's admirers for being duped by the "cloudy nonsense" and "willful obscurity" of Boehme's "enigmatical expressions," likening his "ridiculous" language to the "hideous bombardical" words used by ancient Gnostic heretics.[14] This censorious characterization of Boehme as a reincarnated Gnostic whose fanciful mysticism had, through Jesuitical cunning, spawned a hidden sect that helped prepare the way for the Quaker movement was adopted, at least in part, by several hostile commentators.

Another important association was the linkage between the "mysterious and divinely-inspired" Teutonic Philosopher's notion of signatures—that "signal and wonderful secret" to quote John Webster—and the "highly-illuminated fraternity" of the Rosy Cross's understanding of the "language of nature."[15] Others, however, associated Boehme, that "Father of Non-sense," with the Rosicrucians because, like the Quakers, he was perceived to conceal his unintelligible meaning behind newfangled barbarous expressions.[16] Significantly, Boehme was also studied by alchemists, such as Sir Kenelm Digby, and physicians eager to discover the secrets of nature and medicine. As the translator John Ellistone explained in his preface to *The Epistles of Jacob Behmen*, true knowledge of the "*Three Principles*" and the "Threefold" life in man

> must needs *advance* all Arts and Sciences, and conduces to the attainment of the Universall Tincture, and signature; whereby the different secret qualities, and vertues, that are hid in all visible and corporeall things, as Mettals, Minerals, Plants, and Hearbes, *& c.* may be drawne forth and applyed to their right naturall use for the curing, and healing of corrupt and decayed nature.[17]

Among medical practitioners, Boehme appealed to advocates of iatrochemistry—that is, physicians who favored cures manufactured in laboratories over those extracted from naturally occurring substances. They promoted the teachings of Paracelsus, often in conjunction with Hermetic philosophy and innovative modifications by Jean Baptiste van Helmont, as a challenge to traditional Galenic medicine. These readers included well-known Fellows of the College of Physicians like Luke Rugeley and Nathan Paget. Rugeley was regarded as a skillful, modest, and faithful man inclined to alchemy, while Paget was appointed physician to the Tower of London and afterwards delivered the Harveian oration as well as brokering the blind poet John Milton's marriage by license to his young cousin.[18]

Though he claimed not to have studied astrology, Boehme asserted that the "Starry Art" had a "*true* foundation."[19] So it is noteworthy that his publications were promoted in almanacs and read by the famous astrologer William Lilly, who was presented with a copy of Boehme's *The High and Deepe Searching out of The Threefold Life of Man* (1650) by his publisher Humphrey Blunden.[20] This approbation in turn provoked a denunciation of the "*diabolicall practises*" of "those subtill *Engineirs of Satan* the ASTROLOGERS, whose religion is the same with *Jacob Behmens*, the *German-Conjurer*." In the same vein, clergymen condemned the "*wild and ungodly studies of* Jacob Boehme, Astrology" and the like, one styling Boehme the "*Teutonick Wizard*."[21]

III THE CAMBRIDGE MEN AND THEIR ASSOCIATES

Turning to England's two universities, it was certain Cambridge-educated scholars rather than their Oxford counterparts who initially proved most willing to engage with Boehme's teachings.[22] Most of these readers can be considered as being part of a particular generation: they were largely born in the second decade of the seventeenth century and mainly admitted to Cambridge between 1625 and 1635. Some are also commonly regarded as having been Cambridge Platonists even though this anachronistic term is misleading: it came into usage during the nineteenth century, while those who read Plato alongside Plotinus and other ancient philosophers did not necessarily call themselves Platonists. Lacking formalized membership in the manner of Italian Academies, the so-called Cambridge Platonists formed a loosely configured intellectual circle in some measure because, as Sarah Hutton has pointed out, identification with this group was determined retrospectively.[23] Even so, there is a consensus as to who constituted the core—predominantly scholars connected with Emmanuel and Christ's Colleges—and who was on the periphery. The most familiar names are Benjamin Whichcote, Peter Sterry, John Worthington, Ralph Cudworth, Nathaniel Culverwell, and John Smith (all matriculated at Emmanuel) and Henry More (Christ's). Also included in recent studies are Nathaniel Ingelo (Queen's) and John Sadler (Emmanuel), while more attention has increasingly and rightly been paid to some of the Platonists' bluestocking family, friends, and patrons—notably Anne, Viscountess Conway and Elizabeth Foxcroft (Whichcote's sister).

We are not concerned here with the Cambridge Platonists as such, but with just a few of them together with their comparatively lesser-known friends and acquaintances. In several cases, the social networks formed when these young men entered University endured, occasionally even after profound disagreements, for the duration of a lifetime. Furthermore, it appears that the connections established during this period helped account for how Boehme's writings were disseminated and interpreted within these learned circles. Nor was there a uniform response to the Teutonic Philosopher's writings. While most of these readers bemoaned his lack of clarity, they were divided as to whether it was worth the effort attempting to discern Boehme's light shining within a sea of darkness. Some clearly had personal reasons for turning to Boehme. His translator Charles Hotham, for example, suffered a reversal of fortunes in academic politics and seems to have read him despondently for psychological comfort. Similarly, his biographer Durand Hotham witnessed the public decapitation of his half-brother and may have become attracted to Boehme because of the potential he perceived within his teachings for reforming and regenerating a divided, decaying society. At the same time, we must be careful not to examine Boehme's reception in isolation but to appreciate that he was read in conjunction with other works. These of course varied from reader to reader according to motive and taste. Nonetheless, it is clear that his writings can be located within broader currents: alchemy and alchemical medicine; apocalypticism and prophecy; astrology; heterodox writings; utopian literature; mystical theology, with a particular emphasis on Neoplatonic authors; and spiritual contemplation.

It is noteworthy that the Hotham brothers were educated at Christ's, as was their associate Luke Rugeley who amassed a considerable collection of Boehme's writings by the time of his death. All three along with John Milton—and around ninety others for that matter—shared the same tutor. Charles Hotham and Rugeley were also friends with Henry More. So it comes as no surprise to learn that titles by Boehme are recorded in the libraries of the well-known Platonists Ralph Cudworth, Peter Sterry, and John Worthington. Cudworth liked the "practical" parts of Boehme "very well" but did not approve of his "Revelations" unless they were to be explained by way of reason.[24] Sterry, for his part, could not decide whether Jesus had appeared to Boehme in a glorious vision or if Boehme had been tricked by a dark satanic minion in the guise of an angel of light. Yet he confessed to his correspondent Morgan Llwyd of Wrexham that he had profited from reading Boehme, meeting with "rich Depths, Sweet Heights" in these writings, which seemed to him to have an "Authority & Glory" in them beyond that of the "scribes & Pharisees." He therefore concluded:

> 1. The Lord gave him his Spirit by measure leaving much Darkeness mingled with his Light. 2. They y[t] reade him, had neede come to him well instructed in ye Mystery of Christ . . . Others will bee perverted by him.[25]

By contrast, Worthington believed that Boehme had been wrapped up in the "fooleries of enthusiasm" but still felt bound to praise his writings—along with those of his fellow mystics Thomas à Kempis and Johannes Tauler—for the "savoury truths" he discerned amongst "the stubble and wood and hay."[26]

It was Henry More, however, Fellow of Christ's College, who among the Cambridge Platonists engaged at greatest length with Boehme. Although it is not known when More began to read Boehme, he regarded him as a "holy and good" man whose imagination was so preoccupied with "*divine things*" that he could not (save for a miracle) avoid becoming an "*Enthusiast*" and receiving "divine truths."[27] Returning to this theme in *The Two Last Dialogues* (1668), More acknowledged that, although Boehme was a "*pious*" and "*well-meaning*" writer who had engendered sentiments of "*sincere Piety*" in others, he remained an enthusiast. As one of More's characters explained, the "invincible Obscurity" of the Teutonic Philosopher's writings would prevent him being "over-popular," while his "mistakes in his pretended Inspirations in matters of Philosophy ruin his Authority amongst the more knowing and sagacious sort of persons."[28] Similarly, in a letter dated September 15th, 1670, sent to Anne, Viscountess Conway at her country seat of Ragley, Warwickshire—where More had apparently had his "ears full of Behmenism"—he declared:

> Honest Jacob [Boehme] is wholsome at the bottome though a philosopher but at randome.[29]

About 1670, possibly at Lady Conway's behest, More wrote a lengthy private epistle, afterwards published in Latin translation as *Philosophiæ teutonicæ censura* (1679), in which he discussed questions such as whether Boehme was inspired, whether he was mad, and what his chief errors were. Despite reproving Boehme, like the Dutch philosopher Baruch Spinoza, for conceiving of God as corporeal, More admitted:

> I was not a little averse to reading such an obscure author; but truly, the rich veins of morality and divinity contained in them so invigorated and enraptured me that the aversion which I feared was turned to pure pleasure and delight.[30]

IV DIGGERS, RANTERS, AND MUGGLETONIANS

a Diggers

Given the justifiable claims made by the editors of the complete works of the Digger leader Gerrard Winstanley, that he was not just the "foremost radical of the English Revolution" but also one of the "finest writers" of a "glorious age of English non-fictional prose," his possible reading of Boehme deserves close attention.[31] For more than a century, various scholars encompassing a range of backgrounds and ideological commitments have, with varying degrees of caution, drawn a number of rarely convincing and, unfortunately, usually ill-informed parallels between the Teutonic Philosopher and Winstanley. Aspects of Winstanley's thought exhibiting suggested Behmenist resonances include his belief in human beings as microcosms or epitomes of the macrocosm; understanding of the nature of evil; conception of an inner light in conflict with darkness; conviction that the risen Christ would save all humanity and restore the creation to its former prelapsarian condition; identification of flesh with the feminine part of human nature, which is subordinate to and corrupted by evil masculine powers; usage of the Virgin as a figure representing mankind's plain heartedness; likening God the Father to a consuming fiery orb which burns up the dross within man and envisaging this spiritual purification as akin to an alchemical process; appeal to universally shared reason; preference for allegorical readings of Scripture; and the anticlericalism that imbued his reformist zeal.

All the same, it seems certain that Winstanley did not consult any of Boehme's works while writing his own. It also appears very probable that he never read Boehme. The disparities between them are far too great. Absent from Winstanley's writings is a vocabulary of technical alchemical, astrological, cosmological, and soteriological terms found in Boehme. Indeed, there is no analogue in the relevant texts by Boehme for a number of Winstanley's doctrines and exhortations. Furthermore, Winstanley never quotes, paraphrases, or alludes to Boehme. His prose style differs from the way in which Boehme's translators rendered him into English. Nor does Winstanley adopt any of the neologisms introduced by these translators. This is not surprising. Winstanley was not a university trained scholar or clergymen, nor a rich merchant, but rather a former bankrupt with a financially modest if settled existence when he began writing. So the likelihood is that, during the period of his literary activity from 1648 to 1652, he possessed only a handful of printed works, or at most a modest library intermittently supplemented with books borrowed from friends and relations. At the same time, in this particular case, greater consideration needs to be given to how ideas were transmitted not textually but orally since it is probable that some of the seeds that germinated into Winstanley's mature philosophy were sown in this manner. He heard Protestant clergymen preach sermons, for example, and seems to have discussed his doctrines privately in conversation and publicly during disputations.[32] Moreover, for all the inconsistencies and contradictions within his published writings, it must be recognized that Winstanley had a gift for original thought. Coupled with his undoubted literary achievement, this deserves our respect.

b Ranters

Since there is extensive literature on the Ranters, it is curious that little has been said about Boehme's possible influence on their ideas.[33] Concentrating on the printed texts rather than manuscript letters and reported speech, several scholars have drawn attention to the Ranters' understanding of the nature of God; good and evil; the significance of dualism in their thought; their use of paradox and combination of opposing properties such as light and dark, flesh and spirit; as well as their pantheistic speculation cum nature mysticism. Literary experts, moreover, have followed those contemporaries who remarked on the Ranters' elevated language by focusing on typography, genre, imagery, mimicry, parody, vocabulary, and modes of address. Together with these generally acute observations, there have been several intriguing though seldom adequately documented assertions concerning certain Ranters' unacknowledged debts to Boehme. What these commentators have highlighted is a problem not restricted to the Ranters: can Boehme's unmediated influence be distinguished from the wider tradition of theosophic and prophetic writing that he epitomized?

There is no mention of Boehme in the extant writings of those individuals whom sensible historians agree to have been onetime Ranters: Jacob

Bothumley, Lawrence Clarkson, Abiezer Coppe, Joseph Salmon, Thomas Webbe, Andrew Wyke, and the anonymous author of *A Justification of the Mad Crew* (1650). Nor did contemporaries connect the Ranters with Boehme. Regularly demonized as a lustful, ungodly crew given to all manner of wickedness, they were frequently perceived as a horrible, monstrous sect. Some condemnations were modeled upon and positioned within a long line of anti-heretical writing that stretched from Paul, Epiphanius, and Augustine to Luther and Calvin. Intemperate, alarmist, and often inaccurate, their purpose was to represent doctrinal and behavioral errors as inversions of truths so as to facilitate their extirpation. Constantly alert to precedents, several polemicists also provided the Ranters with a distinctive identity and genealogies that variously linked their blasphemous doctrines and abominable, filthy practices to a range of ancient and near-contemporary heresies. Yet unlike the Quakers, with whom they would be lumped together, there is a significant silence concerning the Ranters' alleged descent from the teachings of Paracelsus, Valentin Weigel, and Boehme. And for good reason, since with one notable exception, Boehme's influence on the Ranters was negligible. That exception, however, was significant. For Abiezer Coppe's "An Additional and Preambular Hint," which was written as a preface to Richard Coppin's *Divine Teachings* (1649), demonstrates in the marginal annotations a familiarity with Behmenist terms. Nonetheless, Coppe's interest in Boehme appears to have been brief, perhaps only extending to the duration of his known involvement with John Pordage, rector of Bradfield, Berkshire. For nothing Coppe wrote after September 1649 can be said to indicate deliberate use of expressions and ideas particular to Boehme.

Despite contemporaries not associating Boehme with the Ranters, one would have expected the Teutonic Philosopher to have had a greater influence on their writings, especially since there are traces of other mystical influences. There are, for example, fascinating resonances of Sebastian Franck's *The Forbidden Fruit* (1642) in one of Joseph Salmon's texts and possible hints of Nicholas of Cusa in Lawrence Clarkson. All the same, Boehme's unmediated influence on the Ranters was unimportant. There are several possible explanations. First, by the time of the Ranters' demise, the bulk of Boehme's writings had still to be published in English translation, though it is noteworthy that among the hundreds of works issued or sold either individually or in partnership by the radical London bookseller Giles Calvert were some by Clarkson, Coppe, Coppin, Salmon, and Boehme. Second, besides Coppe, the Ranters were not university trained scholars, so perhaps they found Boehme's writings inscrutable or unsuitable for their purpose.

c Muggletonians

It is not known when the heresiarch Lodowick Muggleton, an artisan who believed he was one of the two witnesses foretold in Revelation 11, first learned of Boehme. But there are no references to the Teutonic Philosopher in the writings of his fellow commissioned prophet John Reeve, who died in July 1658. Even so, this has not stopped some modern commentators from discerning supposed Behmenist overtones in certain aspects of Reeve's thought: notably, his conviction that God created the universe out of preexisting matter; his understanding of eternity; his belief that heaven would be populated entirely by males; his concept of Hell; and the notion that Satan was responsible for sin, that Cain and his offspring were descended from Eve and the evil one's sexual union, and the presence of two conflicting seeds—of Adam (elect, faith) and of the Serpent (reprobate, reason)—within human nature. Equally importantly, A. L. Morton and then Christopher Hill maintained that Reeve's central doctrine of the three commissions could be traced back through Boehme and the sixteenth-century Spiritual Reformers to the teachings of the twelfth-century abbot Joachim of Fiore.[34] On closer examination, however, these ostensible parallels are without foundation. Unfortunately, as I will show in greater detail elsewhere, they stem from ill-judged assumptions and a misreading of the evidence, thus partly undermining E. P. Thompson's overstated claim that "Muggletonianism was grafted upon Behmenist or Ranting stock."[35]

As for Muggleton, following his trial in 1677 on the charge of having published blasphemous books and subsequent imprisonment at Newgate, he reportedly declared with characteristic lack of modesty that:

> He knew *Behmen* and his works; but he was a fool, and talkt of things that he did not understand: and that in truth there had been no books printed these 1500 years worth reading but his own.[36]

The first mention of Boehme in Muggleton's writings comes after Reeve's death, in a letter dated March 29th, 1660, to Edward Fewterell, surgeon of Chesterfield.[37] In another letter of November 28th, 1661, responding to Ellen Sudbury of Nottingham, he claimed that Boehme was "utterly ignorant" of the doctrine of the six principles (the essential articles of Muggletonian faith). Boehme talked of God, the Devil, and angels but knew nothing of their true nature since he wrongly imagined them to be incorporeal beings. All the same, Muggleton conceded, perhaps in the spirit of conciliation to a prospective disciple, that Boehme's "philosophical light was above all men that doth profess religion, until this commission of the Spirit came forth."[38] Elsewhere, Muggleton indicated that the conception of God as an immortal, eternal being dwelling in spiritual form exercised a definitive influence in the formation of Quaker thought.[39] He even supposed that "*Jacob Behmont*'s Books were the chief Books that the Quakers bought," insisting that the "Principle or Foundation of their Religion" was to be found there. Although Muggleton's abhorrence of formless "Spirits without Bodies," whether divine or angelic, impaired his ability to observe subtle doctrinal distinctions, and although he seems to have associated Behmenism with a conception of God as immanent in direct opposition to his own view of him as corporeal, he was still right to emphasize Boehme's Quaker readership.[40]

V QUAKERS

The question of Boehme's influence on the early Quakers and the reasons why many Friends eventually repudiated his writings has been long debated. Thus on the one hand, it has been claimed that "the Quaker spirit and the spirit of Behmen were one," that no careful student could doubt that there were "so many" marks of the Teutonic Philosopher's influence apparent in George Fox's journal. On the other, however, it has been strongly argued by Geoffrey Nuttall in particular that Quakerism grew out of "the soil and climate of the time;" that while much in radical Puritanism was in sympathy with Quaker practice, there was something in Quakerism contrary even to the radical Puritans' beliefs. Quakerism, for Nuttall, was therefore explained as the product of English contexts—a "spiritual climate"—and studies of Quaker origins against a largely continental background of Anabaptism, spiritualism, and mysticism dismissed as primarily of academic interest. Consequently, within the framework of this greater debate, Boehme's influence upon the Quakers was pronounced specious.[41]

In reexamining the early Quakers' attitude towards Boehme, I have shown elsewhere how polemicists provided Quakers with a genealogy linking them to Paracelsians, Behmenists, and Familists and then outlined the manner in which Boehme's Quaker readers responded.[42] I suggested that both their engagement with his writings and their association in contemporaries' minds with his teachings was more extensive than has hitherto usually been acknowledged. Although it is clear that only a minority of early Quaker printed texts and extant manuscripts show familiarity with Boehme's terms or doctrines, nonetheless, among those that were influenced by Boehme were several important figures in the British Isles, Europe, the West Indies, and North America at a time when Quakerism was taking shape. It is also significant that some of Boehme's Quaker readers became schismatics: Rice Jones, John Perrot, Robert Rich, William Bradford, and Daniel Leeds. A few were also active outside England: Ralph Fretwell, Benjamin Furly, and John Crabb. Others were foreigners: Jan Claus, Jacob Claus, Hilary Prache, and Johann Georg Matern. Moreover, I have argued that we need to reopen the larger debate on the origins of Quakerism as well as reassess the extent to which several Quaker leaders were able to transform their followers into an organized, disciplined, doctrinally coherent group. Indeed, as with problematic sectarian labels such as Seeker and Ranter, there was an initial lack of consensus—whether through ignorance, confusion, misinformation, or deliberate distortion—as to what was understood by the pejorative name "Quaker" beyond the notion that adherents trembled before the presence of God. The early Quakers' relationship with Boehme's writings is therefore a crucial aspect in understanding the formation of their individual identities and that of the movement as a whole.

Doctrinal uniformity, silent meetings, and a preference for Friends' plain style over Boehme's abstruse notions accounts for why many who became convinced of Quakerism turned away from the Teutonic Philosopher—as they did from other authors too. But the crucial sticking point in this instance was that, unlike the Behmenists, Quakers denied the validity of the sacraments of Baptism and the Lord's Supper as well as the Lord's Prayer[43] — so much so that in a couple of undated treatises John Pordage attacked certain "errors of the Quakers" as a way of accentuating the doctrinal differences between Friends and Behmenists.[44] Accordingly, it is to Pordage and his spiritual community that we now turn.

VI JOHN PORDAGE AND HIS "FAMILY"

John Pordage and his "family," who lived together in "community," were denounced by Richard Baxter as the "chiefest" Behmenists in England. Established at Bradfield, Berkshire before September 1650, they were said to have abhorred "flesh & carnal Relations" and appear to have objected to the lawfulness of marriage as well. Moreover, theirs was a Behmenist universe, consisting of a dark world ("Mundus tenebrosus") and light world ("Mundus Luminosus") and a cosmos populated by good and evil angels visible to the "inward eye." Members adopted biblical names; thus Pordage was "Father *Abraham*," his wife Mary, "*Deborah*," while a follower named Mary Pocock was "*Rahab*." This community was to be joined by Thomas Bromley and Edmund Brice, two members of Oxford University, who heard Pordage preach a sermon at St. Mary's, the University church. Another who became convinced of the "Extraordinary Power & operation of y[e] Spirit" and joined himself and waited with them was Philip Herbert, fifth Earl of Pembroke. In his last years, Pordage wrote a number of treatises influenced by Boehme. Though none of the original texts appear to have survived, manuscript copies of some of these works circulated both during and after his lifetime. Shortly after his death and apparently at his behest, an abbreviated version of Pordage's untitled work on "The Archetypal Globe" (no date) together with his treatise "Of Eternal Nature" (1671) were published under the title *Theologia Mystica* (1683). Pordage, moreover, appears to have collaborated with his son Samuel in writing the Behmenist "sacred" poem *Mundorum Explicatio* (1661).[45]

Thomas Bromley of Upton upon Severn, Worcestershire, favored communal ownership of property and possessions (community of goods) but not polygamy (community of women) since he advocated celibacy; indeed, he died unmarried and childless. In 1655, after Pordage was ejected, he published *The Way to the Sabbath of Rest*, a mystical treatise influenced by Boehme, which Baxter judged a "most clean and moderate piece" of doctrine. Bromley was also a correspondent of Anne, Viscountess Conway through whom he became acquainted with Henry More and Francis Mercurius van Helmont. His library contained works on the apocalypse, Socinianism, atheism, and heresy as well as the Latin version of Charles Hotham's introduction to the Teutonic philosophy.[46] For his part, Edmund Brice was "a Lover of the *Hermetick Science*" and translated alchemical works. He owned a copy of Boehme's *Aurora* (1656) that passed into the hands of a founding member of the Philadelphian Society.[47] As for Pembroke, he received Bromley and Pordage at Wilton, Wiltshire, his country seat. About 1661 John Sparrow loaned him English translations of four treatises by Boehme. Two were either manuscripts or printed copies taken from *The remainder of the books written by Jacob Behme* (1662) and two were printed copies from *Several Treatises: of Jacob Behme* (1661). According to the physician and non-juror Francis Lee, both publications were brought out "under the auspices" of the Earl of Pembroke.[48] Also noteworthy is that Edward Phillips, Milton's "sober, silent" elder nephew and "industrious" multi-lingual biographer, was employed by Pembroke both as tutor to his son and—because of his "incredible patience"—to assist with interpreting "some of the Late Teutonic philosophers, to whose Mystic Theology his Lordship" was "not a little addicted."[49]

As Pordage's enemies charged, however, these were not the only visitors to Bradfield. One alleged guest was Richard Coppin, to whose "erroneous and blasphemous" book *Divine Teachings* (1649) Pordage "gave his approbation." Another man Pordage was said to have "entertained" was Abiezer Coppe, notorious for "blasphemy, and *rantisme*," whom we encountered earlier. Other callers at Bradfield included the prophetess Elizabeth Poole, the former Digger leader William Everard, and TheaurauJohn Tany, who allegedly styled himself King of the Jews. Tany's debts to Boehme were numerous; most strikingly was his heterodox adaptation of Boehme's teachings on cosmogony and soteriology. But as I have written on him extensively elsewhere, it is best now to conclude.[50]

VII CONCLUSION

The essential narrative of the English Revolution would have been the same whether or not Boehme's writings had been translated. His texts made no significant contribution to debates about the political and religious settlement, or to electoral and legal reform, liberty of conscience, the readmission and conversion of the Jews, even the timing of the anticipated apocalypse. More surprising was his muted impact among many religious radicals and heterodox thinkers: Diggers, all bar one of the Ranters, most Muggletonians, and the majority of—though by no means all—Quaker authors. Initially, he seems to have mainly been read by continental Protestant exiles, university-educated ministers, scholars, lawyers, physicians, alchemists, army officers, and a handful of artisans turned lay preachers. Even then their responses ranged, as we have seen, from condemnation, exasperation, and ambivalence to qualified approbation and unbridled enthusiasm. Consequently, one could be forgiven for asking the question why bother with Boehme?

The answer lies in the contribution his writings made to debates in several spheres and the ways in which particular individuals, learned circles, and spiritual communities appropriated and reworked his central teachings for their own ends. Thus Boehme's influence can be seen in alchemical experimentation and attempts to create universal medicines within the laboratory; in almanacs and astrological predictions; in mystical thought, notably speculation about the creation of the universe, the nature of angels, and the fall of Adam; in the literary expression of prophetic experience; in the development of heterodox doctrines about God's presence within all living things, the nature of the soul, and the denial of an external heaven and hell; in spiritual contemplation and psychological comfort from melancholic temptations such as suicide; in utopian literature through his vision of a new age; in the enrichment of the English language through neologisms; in the evolution of semiotics with his notion of signatures; and in attempts to regulate sexual conduct through the imposition of celibacy. Taken together, I would suggest this adds considerably to our knowledge of how potentially powerful albeit somewhat strange and incomprehensible ideas were disseminated, received, and adapted at this crucial moment in early modern English history.

VIII EPILOGUE: JANE LEAD AND THE PHILADELPHIAN SOCIETY

Sarah Apetrei

The peculiar fascination with Boehme among seventeenth-century English readers persisted, and a vital link in the chain between the translations of 1644–62 and the mysticism of William Law can be found in the writings of Jane Lead (1624–1704) and her circle known as the "Philadelphian Society" at the turn of the eighteenth century. Lead's works were published in English between 1681 and 1702 and have enjoyed a remarkably wide and enduring circulation, disseminating his thought as successfully as any more learned assessment of Boehme. An elderly, impoverished widow with failing eyesight at the high point of her prophetic activity, Lead seems an unlikely conduit of Boehme's dense theosophy. Yet each generation of English-speaking readers has rediscovered Lead alongside Boehme. Jane Lead (*née* Ward) embodied in herself the paradoxes of Boehme's own intellectual profile. She was an example both of what Andrew Weeks characterizes as "folk piety" or popular spiritualism, but also of that distinctive species of omnivorous early modern autodidacticism.[51]

Ward experienced her earliest spiritual breakthrough in the early 1640s shortly before her marriage to William Lead, when she heard the controversial preacher Tobias Crisp on "the New Covenant of Free Grace."[52] A later landmark in her biography was the association with John Pordage, which began in around 1673.[53] An almost monastic society directed by Lead,

Pordage and their friend Thomas Bromley eventually started "to wait together & Exercise ye Gifts of Prayer Exhortation Singing & under a Living P[owe]r & Operation of ye Holy Spirit." Privately, members kept visionary journals, some of which were published in the 1690s. After Pordage's death in 1681, Lead struggled to continue his work, publishing her first tract *A Heavenly Cloud Now Breaking* in that year, and Pordage's *Theologia Mystica* together with her second book *Revelation of Revelations* shortly afterwards. *A Heavenly Cloud* eventually found an audience in Germany and by 1694 had won Lead a wealthy German patron.[54] From 1694 onwards, prophetic gatherings in London venues started to grow.[55] Based on a contemporary prophecy that a new spiritual epoch was to be inaugurated in August 1697, Lead's group consciously sought a public platform and began a promotional campaign. They called themselves the "Philadelphian Society," denoting both the sixth church of Revelation which would replace the "Sardic" age of institutional churches and an era of brotherly love bringing to a glorious end the confessional infighting of preceding decades.[56]

The Philadelphians elaborated on Boehme's eschatological emphasis on a coming "age of the spirit." The third age of the Spirit would be distinguished by the operation of Sophia in a generation of holy women: "constituting Female Representatives & commissioning them to Joyn in ye Preparation work of ye K[ing]dom of X[hrist] in Spirit."[57] This female-centered vision of Sophia's work in the last days would inspire feminist ecological and Jungian theorists.[58] In Lead's visions, Virgin Wisdom appears as the mother of the second birth: through a sacrificial death to the body of sin, the spirit would break through to a new virgin life akin to that enjoyed by paradisiacal Adam (a clear development of Boehme's anthropology). This process of regeneration was the preparation for bridal union with Christ in his heavenly flesh, for "he will match himself only to a Virgin Spirit, incorporating, and thereby changing into his own pure Humanity: and this is a Begetting into a Living Substance."[59] In Lead's visions, she describes this new incarnation of Christ through Sophia's maternal agency in the flesh of the saints. Lead envisioned a regenerate existence "not in gross Corporality, but rather like a Seraphick, or as a flaming Body," that "in nothing I might be inferior to the Glorified and Angelical Spirits, who have not such a gross Animal Nature to deal withal as I have."[60] Lead herself was regarded as one of those who had attained a "Seraphick" body.

Her intellectual passivity aligned Lead with Boehme's maternal Sophia, the divine mirror or image, the fertile ground in which the seed of divine life was sown. For the Philadelphians, rooted in the writings of Boehme, Wisdom understood as passive imagination was the precise converse of the critical, probing ratiocination that prevailed in scholastic approaches to theology. Revelation came through the *via negativa*, the shedding of all acquired knowledge. Though William Law might have described Boehme, memorably, as the "the mother of Pordage and Lead," it was Boehme's own dynamic conception of Sophianic revelation that liberated Lead from a slavish dependence.[61] Her insights, like those of Boehme himself, had "not been taught me by men, or books, but by following the Lamb whethersoever he hath guided me."[62] They were "discovered from the Central Light, and Original Copy, wherein the mind of God was made known unto me, in these things; which are now no longer to be concealed, or shut up, but are to have their use and service throughout the whole Creation."[63] Indeed, her German translator Loth Fischer wrote tentatively to her in June of 1701 on the subject of eschatology, pointing out rather nervously that her views were "diametrically opposed" to those of the "the highly illuminated Jac. Behme."[64]

NOTES

1. Society of Antiquaries of London, MS 138 fol. 155v, printed in John Nickolls, ed., *Original Letters and Papers of State, Addressed to Oliver Cromwell* (London: William Bowyer, 1743), 99.
2. Ariel Hessayon, "Jacob Boehme's theology and the reception of his writings in the English-speaking world: the seventeenth century" (forthcoming).
3. John Barnard, D.F. McKenzie and Maureen Bell, eds., *Cambridge History of the Book. Vol. IV. 1557–1695* (Cambridge: Cambridge University Press, 2002), 781–83, 789.
4. C. Hill, "Censorship and English Literature," in *The Collected Essays of Christopher Hill. Volume One. Writing and Revolution in 17th Century England* (Brighton: Harvester Press, 1985), 34, 40, 51.
5. A. Hessayon, "Incendiary texts: book burning in England, *c.*1640–*c.*1660," *Cromohs—Cyber Review of Modern Historiography* 12 (2007): 1–25, accessed July 25, 2012, http://www.cromohs.unifi.it/12_2007/hessayon_incendtexts.html.
6. A. Hessayon, " 'The Teutonicks writings': translating Jacob Boehme into English and Welsh," *Esoterica* 9 (2007): 129–65, accessed July 25, 2012, http://www.esoteric.msu.edu/VolumeIX/EsotericaIX.pdf.
7. Mark Greengrass, Michael Leslie, and Timothy Raylor, eds., *Samuel Hartlib & Universal Reformation: Studies in Intellectual Communication* (Cambridge: Cambridge University Press, 1994).
8. Jacob Boehme, *XL. Qvestions Concerning the Soule*, trans. J[ohn] S[parrow] (London: Humphrey Blunden, 1647), "To the Reader"; Jacob Boehme, *Signatura Rerum*, trans. J[ohn] Ellistone (London: Giles Calvert, 1651), A3^{r-2}.
9. G.E. Briscoe Eyre, H.R. Plomer and C.R. Rivington, eds., *A Transcript of the Registers of the worshipful Company of Stationers from 1640 to 1708* (3 vols., London: privately printed, 1913–14), vol. 1, 248, 268, 281, 309, 459; vol. 2, 91.
10. Ariel Hessayon, "Totney, Thomas (bap. 1608, d. 1659?)," *ODNB*; Ariel Hessayon, "Pordage, John (*bap*. 1607, *d*. 1681)," *ODNB*.
11. William London, *A Catalogue of The most vendible Books* (London, 1658), L.
12. A. Hessayon and L. Penman, "Seventeenth-century editions of Jacob Boehme's works in English and Welsh: a census of extant copies, their owners and their readers" (forthcoming).
13. Jacob Boehme, *Forty Questions of the Soul*, trans. John Sparrow (London: Lodowick Lloyd, 1665), "Preface."
14. Dr. Williams's Library, MS Baxter: Treatises, III 67 fol. 302v; Richard Baxter, *The Vnreasonableness of Infidelity* (London: Thomas Underhill, 1655), iii, 147, 155; Richard Baxter, *The Quakers Catchism* (London: Thomas

Underhill, 1655), C3v; Richard Baxter, *A Key for Catholics* (London: Nevil Simmons, 1659), 331, 342; Richard Baxter, *Reliquiae Baxterianiæ*, ed. Matthew Sylvester (London: T. Parkhurst et al., 1696), i, 116.

15. John Webster, *Academiarum Examen* (London: Giles Calvert, 1654), 26.
16. S[amuel] R[olle], *An Impartial Vindication of the Clergy of England* (London: Randal Taylor, 1680), 25.
17. Jacob Boehme, *The Epistles of Jacob Behmen*, trans. J[ohn] E[llistone] (London: Giles Calvert, 1649), "Preface."
18. Ariel Hessayon, "*Gold Tried in the Fire.*" *The Prophet TheaurauJohn Tany and the English Revolution* (Aldershot: Ashgate, 2007), 309.
19. Jacob Boehme, *Aurora*, trans. John Sparrow (London: Giles Calvert, 1656), 22.9–14, 25.1–3 (at 512–13, 583–84).
20. Henry Huntington Library, shelf-mark 88271, title page.
21. William Rowland, *Judiciall Astrologie* (London: Joseph Blaiklocke, 1651), "To the Reader"; Thomas White, *The Practice of Christian Perfection* (London: Thomas Vere, 1651), A2v; Thomas Gataker, *Thomas Gataker His Vindication* (London: Philemon Stephens, 1653), 32.
22. A. Hessayon, "'Honest Jacob' Boehme, the Cambridge men and their associates" (forthcoming).
23. S. Hutton, "A Radical Review of the Cambridge Platonists," in *Varieties of Seventeenth- and Early Eighteenth-century English Radicalism in Context*, eds. Ariel Hessayon and David Finnegan (Aldershot: Ashgate, 2011), 161–82.
24. Sheffield University Library, HP 31/22/1B.
25. National Library of Wales, MS 11438 D, letter 68, partly printed in N.I. Matar, "Peter Sterry and Jacob Boehme," *Notes & Queries* 33 (1986): 34.
26. Richard Christie, ed., *The Diary and Correspondence of Dr. John Worthington*, Chetham Society, 114 (1886), vol. 2, ii, 291–93, 294, 302, 305, 307, 322.
27. Henry More, *Enthusiasmus Triumphatus* (London: J. Flesher, 1656), "Contents," 42, 289, 294–95.
28. Henry More, *The Two Last Dialogues* (London: J. Flesher, 1668), a2v–a3, 336, 351.
29. Marjorie Hope Nicolson, ed., *The Conway Letters* (1930; revised Sarah Hutton, Oxford: Clarendon Press, 1992), 297, 381, 512; Christie, ed., *Diary and Correspondence of Worthington*, vol. 2, ii, 287.
30. Henry More, *H. Mori Cantabrigiensis Opera omnia* (3 vols., London: J. Martyn and Walter Kettilby, 1675–79), vol. 2, 536, translated in S. Hutton, "Henry More and Jacob Boehme," in Sarah Hutton, ed., *Henry More (1614–1687). Tercentenary Studies* (Dordrecht: Kluwer, 1990), 160.
31. Thomas Corns, Ann Hughes, and David Loewenstein, eds., *The Complete Works of Gerrard Winstanley* (2 vols., Oxford: Oxford University Press, 2009), vol. 1, 65; A. Hessayon, "Gerrard Winstanley and Jacob Boehme," *Cromohs* 18 (forthcoming).
32. *Complete Works of Winstanley*, vol. 1, 99, 285, 313–14, 316, 317, 318, 513, 526, 542, 558, 567; vol. 2, 80, 91, 287.
33. A. Hessayon, "The Ranters and their sources: the question of Jacob Boehme's supposed influence," in Vittoria Feola, ed., *Antiquarianism and Science in Urban Networks, c. 1580–1700* (forthcoming).
34. A.L. Morton, *The World of the Ranters: Religious Radicalism in the English Revolution* (London: Lawrence & Wishart, 1970), 127, 138; C. Hill, "John Reeve and the origins of Muggletonianism," in Christopher Hill, Barry Reay, and William Lamont, *The World of the Muggletonians* (London: Temple Smith, 1983), 83, 85, 87, 88; Christopher Hill, *The English Bible and the Seventeenth-Century Revolution* (Harmondsworth: Penguin, 1994), 239.

35. E.P. Thompson, *Witness Against the Beast. William Blake and the Moral Law* (Cambridge; Cambridge University Press, 1994), 66; A. Hessayon, "Two Witnesses. Reviewing Muggletonian History, 1652–1979" (forthcoming); cf. Brian Gibbons, *Gender in Mystical and Occult Thought: Behmenism and its Development in England* (Cambridge: Cambridge University Press, 1996), 121–22.
36. Anon., *Muggleton Reviv'd* (London: D.M., 1677), 6.
37. John Reeve and Lodowick Muggleton, *A Stream from the Tree of Life* ([London], 1758), 31, 33.
38. John Reeve and Lodowick Muggleton, *Veræ Fidei Gloria est Corona Vitæ. A Volume of Spiritual Epistles* (ed. Tobiah Terry, 1755; London: W. Smith, 1820 edn.), 45–46.
39. Lodowick Muggleton, *A True Interpretation of the Eleventh Chapter of the Revelation of St. John* (London: L. Muggleton, 1662), 158; Lodowick Muggleton, *The Neck of the Quakers Broken* (['Amsterdam' = London], 1663), 16; Lodowick Muggleton, *A Looking-Glass for George Fox* (London, 1668), 85–86.
40. Reeve and Muggleton, *Stream from Tree of Life*, 33; Muggleton, *Looking-Glass for Fox*, 5.
41. A. Gordon, "The origin of the Muggletonians," *Proceedings of the Literary and Philosophical Society of Liverpool* 23 (1869): 257; Rufus Jones, *Spiritual Reformers in the 16th and 17th Centuries* (1914; reprinted, Gloucester, MA: Peter Smith, 1971), 220; Geoffrey Nuttall, *The Holy Spirit in Puritan Faith and Experience* (2nd edn., 1947; reprinted, Chicago: University of Chicago Press, 1992), xxvi, xxviii, 13–14, 16–18, 150–51, 155.
42. A. Hessayon, "Jacob Boehme and the early Quakers," *Journal of the Friends Historical Society,* 60 (2005): 191–223.
43. Friends House Library, Portfolio MS 15/90, transcribed in FHL, Minutes of the Morning Meeting 1673–1692, vol. 1, 1–2; John Anderdon, *One Blow at Babel In those of the Pepole called Behmenites* (London, 1662).
44. Christopher Walton, *Notes and Materials for an adequate Biography of . . . William Law* (London: privately printed, 1854), 203; John Pordage, *Göttliche und Wahre Metaphysica* (3 vols., Frankfurt and Leipzig: Joh. Martin Hagen, 1715), iii, 596–97, 669–73.
45. Hessayon, "*Gold*," 317–18; Hessayon, "Pordage, John," *ODNB*.
46. Hessayon, "*Gold*," 318–19; Ariel Hessayon, "Bromley, Thomas (bap. 1630, d. 1691)," *ODNB*.
47. Hessayon, "*Gold*," 319–20; Ariel Hessayon, "Brice, Edmund (fl. 1648–1696)," *ODNB*.
48. Hessayon, "*Gold*," 320–23.
49. BL, Add. MS 78,298 fol. 166r, printed (with differences) in William Bray, ed., *Diary and Correspondence of John Evelyn, F.R.S.* (4 vols., London: Henry Bohn, 1859), vol. 3, 196–98.
50. Hessayon, "*Gold*," 194–200, 323–24; Ariel Hessayon, "Coppe, Abiezer (1619–1672?)," *ODNB*; Ariel Hessayon, "Everard, William (bap. 1602?, d. in or after 1651)," *ODNB*; Hessayon, "Totney, Thomas," *ODNB*.
51. Andrew Weeks, *Boehme: An Intellectual Biography of the Seventeenth-Century* (New York: SUNY Press, 1991), 173–74.
52. Julie Hirst, *Jane Leade: A Biography of a Seventeenth-Century Mystic* (Aldershot: Ashgate, 2005), 18–19.
53. Walton, *Notes and Materials*, 203.
54. Nils Thune, *The Behmenists and the Philadelphians: A Contribution to the Study of English Mysticism in the 17th and 18th Centuries* (Uppsala: Almquist & Wiksells, 1948), 81–90; Thomas Haywood, "An Essay towards the

Life or rather some account of the late Learned and Pious Francis Lee, MD," Gonville and Caius College Cambridge, Add. MS 725/752, 52.

55. Ibid., 65.
56. See also Warren Johnston on Thomas Beverley's interpretation of the "Philadelphian ideal of reformation," in *Revelation Restored: The Apocalypse in Later Seventeenth-Century England* (Woodbridge: Boydell Press, 2011), 194, 216–17.
57. Bodleian Library, Oxford, MS Rawlinson D. 832, fol. 82r. See Sarah Apetrei, *Women, Feminism and Religion in Early Enlightenment England* (Cambridge: Cambridge University Press, 2010), chapter 6.
58. On Lead's ecological feminism, see Sylvia Bowerbank, *Speaking for Nature: Women and Ecologies of Early Modern England* (Baltimore, MD: John Hopkins University Press, 2004), chapter 4.
59. Jane Lead, *A Fountain of Gardens* (London: J. Bradford, 1696), vol. 1, 70.
60. Ibid., 293; 78.
61. Ibid., 207.
62. Diary fragment dated "November 12th 1679," in Bodl. MS Rawlinson C. 266, fol. 19r. This fragment has been attributed to Lead by Sarah Apetrei.
63. Jane Lead, *The ascent to the Mount of Vision* (London, 1699), preface.
64. Bodl. MS Rawlinson D. 832, fol. 47.

6 Did Anyone Understand Boehme?

Nigel Smith

> Only let not the Non or Misunderstanding of the most rational Reader (if not a little sublimed above the Sphere of common Reason) be imputed as a fault to this Elevated Philosopher, no more than 'twas to the Divine *Plotine*, whose highest Notions many, even of his own School, after much Study were not able to reach.
>
> The Publishers Preface to the Reader Edward Taylor, *Jacob Behmen's Theosophick Philosophy Unfolded*[1]

> 'Boehme is difficult'
>
> Northrop Frye

In the entrance hall of Victoria College in the University of Toronto is a portrait of one of its former masters, Northrop Frye. It is famous, in Canada at least. In it, Frye, older in years, is portrayed by Barbara Braunohler sitting, but to my eye almost floating, in a brightly colored academic gown, no doubt doctorate of divinity robes (there is another portrait of Frye, more soberly dressed, in which he does float).[2] The picture is startling; it symbolizes to me not just Frye's huge array of learning all directed at interrogating the imaginative in literature, but also his encounter with Jacob Boehme.

Famously he proclaimed, repeating an observation he had heard that referred to the notorious density of Boehme's prose, "It has been said of Boehme that his books are like a picnic to which the author brings the words and the reader the meaning."[3] I always thought that was a splendid recommendation to the student, since it meant that you could say what you liked about Boehme's text with no fear of ever being wrong. For Frye, Boehme is a "psychopomp," or Hermes figure who engages in a descent into the dark night of the soul, the *Urgrund*.[4] The descent constitutes a "deification of the void," the darkness in us or in the cosmos, but it worried Frye because, in Boehme's version, this descent does not involve the redemptive personality of Jesus.[5] In his first encounter with Boehme, Frye found the theosophist impenetrable and difficult. "I've never got much out of Boehme" he said, although this impenetrability, which focused for Frye on the "abyss-fire-wrath" world, was worthy of description as one big visionary poem.[6] This changed for Frye in his later years: during the 1980s he wrote in a notebook that Boehme's writing made a link between the Bible and the creative imagination for which he had always been searching. For Frye, it was a writing of visionary revelation typified by its ecstatic metaphors and where, crucially, the inner properties of things are manifested in outer forms—an approach that he sees as typically Paracelsian. In other words, Boehme's writing was a confession or an unrepressing of that which Biblical fundamentalism did not and does not want to hear:

> Of all those in the Christian theological tradition, perhaps Boehme is the most thoroughgoing in showing that the conception of God is essentially connected with nothingness, that the presence of God appears in an *Urgrund* from which all conditions and attributes of being have been withdrawn. Boehme's vision of creation anticipates Hegel in speaking of a negation of negation, a transforming of God from a nothingness to an infinite something, which left the nothingness behind as a kind of vacuum suction, drawing everything within its reach into nonbeing. The abandoned nothingness is the principle of evil, the Lucifer or light-bearer which turns into the adversary of light, or Satan, after the light, or Word, has freed itself. This may sound difficult but Boehme is difficult.[7]

The point of my invocation of Frye is to return to the conclusion he reaches in this last quotation: "Boehme is difficult." Indeed. Much contemporary Boehme commentary seeks to show that he connected things that orthodox theology very rarely connected or did not connect: God as abyss and abyss extending into outspoken world (our world) through the membrane, so to speak, of the light and dark spiritual worlds; cosmic existence, the passing of time in the phenomenal universe, as a permanent and ongoing act of creation, and, significantly, the Godhead in some sense involved in this process of change through time and hence subject to change; and action and stasis, light and dark, good and evil, as interconnected and inter-involved. The addition or recovery of the figure of Wisdom or Sophia, seen by some as a fourth person of the Trinity, is also notable, as is the originally androgynous Adam, who falls into sexual difference through self-desire (although sexual desire has a positive aspect elsewhere). Then there is the use of complex occult terms in ways at once both literal and symbolic, such as the "tincture," the joyous energy that suffuses all things, that transforms them, and which, because it comes from the "light," is always evident in visible aspects of creation—reflected gleams of sunlight or the growth of plants.[8] Many of these themes had been addressed in earlier writing in the longer esoteric and occult traditions, much of it Gnostic in nature. No one managed to offer quite such a rich synthesis as Boehme did—one that escaped from the trammels of strict alchemy in a richer form of reflection: what we know as theosophy. Only Paracelsus's writings come close to Boehme's in this respect, but much of the former's more theological work was unknown until very recently.[9] Paracelsus it was with whom contemporaries compared Boehme.[10] For some, Boehme, like Paracelsus, was to be regarded as an alternative medical authority.[11]

The fact is that many people, like the younger Northrop Frye, found Boehme so difficult that they either avoided him or remained confused and put him down. But others did not, and among all the readers and appreciators of Boehme in the century after his first publication, two remarkable phenomena stand out. First is the publishing of his works in Amsterdam, safe from the power of German Lutherans, and the acquisition of his manuscripts by an Amsterdam merchant, Abraham van Beyerland, followed by the appearance of many of these works from 1634–5 in Dutch translation by van Beyerland and Michel Le Blon.[12] Second, it was the German and Latin Amsterdam editions of Boehme's works that provided the sources for the translation of all of Boehme's writings into English between 1644 and 1661, although there is occasionally the presence of Dutch intermediaries and other Dutch materials in some of the translations.[13]

Yet, as I argued in my first monograph, few, if any, early English readers of Boehme were able to understand him in as full a sense as we now do today, or as I think became the case increasingly from the early to mid-eighteenth century onwards.[14] That is partly why we have had so many illuminating modern studies of Boehme and why, for some, that process of understanding is ongoing in an as yet unfinished progressive revelation.[15] The citations and allusions to Boehme's writings are widespread in mid-seventeenth-century English publications. But what they said of Boehme and how they used him is, in the written and printed world, seemingly far short of how we think of him today. Why were people so interested in an author they could not seemingly comprehend? Is it precisely because they could not understand him, or only very partially understand him, so that the attractiveness lay in his very mysteriousness?

I

We are likely to find more interest today in the fact that two of the earliest translators of Boehme into English, John Sparrow and John Ellistone, were either involved in or related by kin to Commonwealth figures investing in a project to settle the Bahamas in 1649 as a utopian society called "Eleutheria" ("Liberty"), or that in Interregnum England Boehme was recommended to be established on university syllabuses by act of Parliament, rather than in the understanding of Boehme's writings themselves.[16] These are fascinating facts that come nowhere near the complexity of understanding demanded by Boehme in his writings. There is very little in the prefaces by the translators that points to a grasp of what we now consider to be the crucial parts of Boehme's theosophy. In his preface to his translation of *Signatura Rerum,* John Ellistone professes himself unable to understand Boehme's sense with any informed expertise, despite being impelled to do so by that "*little spark of breathing desire which is in me after true knowledge.*"[17] But he is "*an unlearned A.B.C. Scholler in Sophia's School, that would fain learn to read her Christs Cross line.*" Then comes a series of commonplace, scripture-based invocations to follow wisdom—not, at first glance, very exciting. There might be a conventional expression of humility here and a sense that full revelation will only come on the "Day of Pentecost," but there is also something more. First of all, Ellistone sees Reason as a useless tool in this pursuit:

> *Herein lieth that simple child-like way to the Highest Wisdome, which no sharp Reason, or worldly learning can reach unto; nay it is foolishness unto Reason, and therefore so few go the way to finde it: The proud Sophisters, and wiselings of this world, have alwaies trampled it under foot with scorn and contempt, and have called it Enthusiasm, madness, melancholy, whimsey, phancy, &c.*[18]

Only the adept will understand it: "*none can understand their obscurely-clear writings, but those that have had admittance into the same School, and have tasted of the Feast of* Pentecost."[19] And so, for the sake of purity of doctrine: "*a parabolical or Magical Phrase, or Dialect is the best, and plainest habit, and dress that Mysteries can have.*"[20] You do not just have to be educated as an adept; you also have to be reborn into these mysteries. Those who use Reason will soon find themselves in "*a maze of doubtful Notions, wherein he will bewilder himself, and think the Authors tedious, irkesom, and strange.*"[21] For another early translator, Charles Hotham, Boehme was undoubtedly using "imagination" (imagination, which translates in German as *Einbildnis,* is a distinctive part of Boehme's theology) against reason. To trust to reason is to miss the point, says Ellistone, as he quotes his own translation of Boehme: "It is a very clear Gate of the Great Mystery of all Beings; by Glosses, Comments, Curiosity and Self-wit, none shall be able to reach or apprehend it in his own ground."[22] Indeed, said John Sparrow, Boehme was a short-cut because he provided remedies that would otherwise take much exegetical machinery to compass, "without neede of having any reference to the vast Commentaries of Authours."[23] As Ariel Hessayon shows, Sparrow regarded Boehme as superseding all previous commentaries on the Bible and enabling readers to reconcile their differences.[24] The [Holy] Spirit guides the interpreter, an idea that was deeply fashionable with the Puritan establishment as well as with the enthusiasts of these years.[25] For Ellistone, Boehme spoke of the deepest mysteries in God and nature, and in accordance with experimental theology, another key aspect of Puritan piety, each person who read him would be affected according to their own capacities.[26] Ellistone's cousin and fellow Boehme translator Sparrow came to understand that such access to the inner word was equivalent to a meeting with the uncreated mind of God, and so he maintained that Boehme pointed to truths present but not explicitly explained in the Bible.[27]

Despite Ellistone's protestations to the contrary, he did in fact have some sense of what he understood in Boehme. He saw the texts as curative, part of a quest to make a universal medicine: "how the outward Life may be freed from sickness by its likeness or Assimulate, and be again introduced into its first Essence,"[28] because Boehme understood how the light may be transmuted from the dark and how its inward state emanates to outward qualities—how the cosmos redeems.[29] It is a cure that addresses the soul as well as the body. That which is part of the dark principle will be turned light and quite without taint, but the explanation is only made with the help of an astrological jargon:

> *thy doubtful, unsetled* Jupiter *will be turned into a Plerophory, or most full assurance of true joy, and saving comfort in thy Religion; thy earthly* Venus *into heavenly Love, and thy eclipsed mutable* Luna *into the pure, perfect, and cristalline streams of Light, Life and Glory.*[30]

Ellistone gives no evidence that he can analytically and extensively discuss Boehme's theosophy (he tends to name parts of the theosophy but stops there: "Virgin Sophia" and "Three Principles"), yet as a translator at least, he claims to know exactly what it does. And in his preface to Boehme's *Epistles* (1649), he describes its focus as the work of Sophia, that is, wisdom. Their teaching is a revelation of the "abyss" (i.e., ground or foundation) of philosophy that must be encountered so that it can be restored to its "original purity" in the reader's mind. This description imitates Boehme's idea of God as a negation and is about as insightful as anything you will find in English on Boehme in this half of the seventeenth century. Note that it is a comment on philosophy rather than the actual abyss that is so important to Boehme. Boehme's notion of evil inter-involved with good is not present in Ellistone's formulation, but the definition of an essential and deep inner being is there, a manifestation of a personal self-knowledge coterminous with the idea that creation is God's own coming to self-knowledge:

> the Centre of all Beings (of which his Writings speake) we come rightly to understand what Time and Eternity is; and therein the Science of the Nothing, Something and All things; whereby we may come to find out whence the inward radicall *Ens*, working essence, true subsistence, and full existence of every thing proceedeth; and also to what end every thing hath such an Essence, life, power, vertue, forme, colour; and then whither it goeth, and what it shall be hereafter in Eternity.[31]

Ellistone understands that this knowledge leads to the true understanding of the order of nature so that it may be cured and healed, divorced from its corruption and decay. Sparrow saw Boehme's insights into "inwardness" as a completion of theology, without which we are endlessly lost in intra-confessional disputes and worse still, religious wars. It is within this context that we should note Sparrow's readiness to lend his works of Boehme to various people, including the relatively influential fifth Earl of Pembroke.[32]

Like Ellistone, a more contextually attuned Sparrow relates Boehme to very current 1650s debates, asserting Boehme's Christ as unified, inner and outer, against the alleged Quaker view that Christ was merely an inner divine being, distinct from the historical Jesus. This seems to be a position that he was to state with an increasingly sure grasp in the later 1650s, but it was one that remained within the same conceptual boundaries. Sparrow argues that Boehme helps us understand what earthly perfection might be, an issue that was part of the debate concerning Antinomianism in these years. "How could anything be more useful?" he says, locating Boehme firmly within English theological disputes, demonstrating the relevance of Boehme to his contemporaries and justifying the effort involved in translating him. The same goes for his discussion of salvation, where he carefully skirts the predestination/free will issue and makes Boehme sound uncontroversial, whereas Calvinists took offence at Boehme's belief in free will. Where Sparrow lacks Ellistone's facility with occult concepts, he makes up for it in intellectual history, placing Boehme at the end of a line of renovators that includes the politician and philosopher Francis Bacon (1561–1626); the lawyer and scholar John Selden (1584–1654); the proponent of universal education Jan Amos Comenius (1592–1670); the mathematician John Pell (1611–85); the poet Edward Herbert (1583–1648), first baron Cherbury; and the French philosopher René Descartes (1596–1650)—all of whom have, he says, plumbed the depths of nature.[33] Boehme has exceeded them in looking into the spiritual world and therefore belongs with "Hermes Trismegistus, Zoroaster, Pythagoras, Plato, and other deep Men, conversant in the Operative Mysteries of Nature, and the Modern, Trevisanus, Raymundus Lullius, Paracelsus, Sendivogius, and others:[34] by which men will be satisfied, that not only they have gotten, but that we also may get that Lapis Philosophorum, the Philosophers Stone, indeed," and is headed for the *prisca theologia* itself, which can reconcile the differences between discrete knowledge systems.[35] There is a big hint of Rosicrucian utopianism in these sections.[36] This is undoubtedly a distinctive lineage: Bacon would not have enjoyed keeping company with Comenius. Sparrow was pushing hard to cross the divide between the natural philosophers and the occultists, and his syncretism bears comparison with that of the sometime Antinomian or Seeker minister, educational reformer, and natural philosopher John Webster.[37] Ellistone is also well attuned to the religious atmosphere and reading tastes of his time. He objects to those who refuse to read other books through the certainty of their own position and those who read voraciously but nonetheless refuse to be sympathetic to an unusual author. He favors the genuine "seeker," the open-minded, unprejudiced, selfless, experientially directed Christian and argues that Boehme is the way out of the confusion that typifies commonwealth religious disputes:

> The true way and meanes for a man to free himselfe from all blind contentions, disputes, doubts, errours, and controversies in Religion; and to *get out* of that tedious Maze, and wearisome laborinth of perplexing thoughts, wayes, and opinions concerning God, Christ, Faith, Election; the Ordinances, or the way of worship, wherein the World doth trace it selfe, is faithfully set downe, and declared according to *the ground of the Scripture*, and *true experience* in this Authour.[38]

So Boehme's writings represent a new kind of discourse, an elevation into the world of the spirit.

Sparrow agrees with Ellistone that obscurity is a problem but one that Boehme himself tried to resolve:

> *And because this Author could not so deepely and fundamentally disclose these mysteries, but in such significant though* hard *Termes of expression as he* * [* *See the preface to* Jacob Behmes *clavis, vers.* 10. 11.] *useth; he wrote therefore for the satisfaction of his loving friends, some explanatory Tables, and a Clavis, which are already printed in English: yet still for all that, they are accompted very difficult to be understood.*[39]

The anonymous author of a prefatory address, possibly the publisher Humphrey Blunden, acknowledged that Boehme's language could even seem "monstrous" but that the writings reward, "far exceeding in recompence" the effort that goes into confronting their difficulty. At first it seems unsettling, just as when children learn their alphabet. This person describes understanding Boehme as a gradual enlightenment, requiring frequent consultation, which he calls a "conversation." The reader will be bewildered at first but will then return again and again with a growing understanding, on a certain path to self-knowledge: "to free his minde from those mentall Idolls of hypocrisie and opinion."[40] What is at first dark will finally become exceedingly clear; if the reader consults the *Three Principles of the Divine Essence*, "though hard at first, easie at last, and then all his other Bookes easie and full of Deep Understanding."[41]

Boehme cannot be translated in a regular way, accommodating his German to the idioms of English: fidelity to his text requires verbatim translation, which makes him read unusually in English.[42] There is no space here to discuss the extensive marginal annotations in several of the English translations, most of them supplied by Sparrow, in which English terms for the German (and a little Latin), and alternative renderings in English, are explained.[43] Sparrow goes so far as to begin to provide literal descriptions of Boehme's symbols. These annotations suggest the challenges that Boehme's rich and polyvalent German presented to his translators, and it is surely here, in the act of translation, that much of the early thinking about Boehme took place. The text Blunden finds most illuminating is the *Morgenröthe*, the ABC for the later more complicated books. Elsewhere, Sparrow makes the point that, if Boehme was misunderstood in Germany, it is no surprise he is hard-going in English translation, "*wherein much of the accurateness, and apt expression of an Author is* lost," but no one in Germany ever said he was incomprehensible, or, as some English have claimed, just "not *to be* understood."[44]

There is even a sense of humor in the prefaces with regard to difficulty. The short Boehme treatise has advantages over the longer one, claims Charles Hotham: "this Paradise of usefull truths stands not guarded by a fiery Cherubim hindring the Readers access, and dazling his eyes with a flaming sword of obscurities."[45] If, says Hotham, philosophers and various technical adepts are to be allowed hard specialist words and phrases, why not a man "rapt up in the third heaven" of mystical illumination.[46] Because Boehme is so difficult, English translators are in fact on an equal footing with German editors. And in any case, it is necessary to speak Angel as well as "Dutch" (Hotham might mean German here) to translate Boehme. If you do not have the Spirit, you certainly cannot translate Boehme with any assurance of accuracy, he claimed. Daniel Foote translated into English Charles Hotham's Latin dispute on the transmission of the soul, which was indebted to Boehme, who is described throughout as the "Teutonic Philosopher." The sense of humor here comes from the thought of reading and then translating this obscure writing:

> As to the matter of the matter and Authour of the Teutonick Philosophy, which you here abbreviate, though you know I always affected it and him, yet durst never saile into the Ocean of his vast Conceits with my little Scull; methought the reading of him was like the standing upon a precipice, or by a Canon shot off, the waft of them lickt up all my brains.[47]

Others were more evidently reverential. Humphrey Blunden (again, probably) regarded Boehme not merely as an author but as virtually a saint: miracles are the only things that do not accompany the life of someone who can write in such a holy way. Boehme writes by affirmation because he is directly in touch with the Spirit, not needing logic and not needing to have been so trained. His words here sound like Milton's definition of true faith in *Paradise Regained*: "having not received his Knowledge from men, or from the imperfect fallible Principles of the Schools, but from the true Fountain of Wisdom and Knowledg."[48] And indeed, it is claimed that Boehme has been led by God to recuperate the "language of Nature" lost by Adam at the Fall.[49]

Similarly, writing on Christmas Day 1658, Sparrow seems to understand the extraordinary dimensions of that which contemporaries called the "inward" or "inner" Word, that it is an aspect of the uncreated being of God. Sparrow amplifies in a distinct way the call for believers to listen to an inner light, and, as we have seen, marries it indissolubly with the Puritan idea of experimental religion, a message he persistently pushes in his prefaces. In this respect, Boehme seems to exemplify the most optimistic dimension of Interregnum religion and utopianism (perhaps a religious counterpart to Harringtonian republicanism). Nothing could be clearer, although it is undoubtedly a sanitizing of Boehme that other figures—not translators, but prophets or the associates of prophets like John Pordage and Jane Lead—could simply not accept. Finally, some time after Ellistone, Sparrow informs us that Boehme is a guide to perfection in this life. Here, to be sure, there is a glimpse in Sparrow's own writing by 1661 of the Behmenist idea of the dark elements in the individual soul being purged, in imitation of Boehme's notion of creation, and of the presence and powers of desire ("the eternal Magia" that "maketh, frameth and imageth") in both light and dark worlds.[50] We should submit in this life, Sparrow claims Boehme teaches, to a fiery consumption of our self-love, so that we may escape the fires of hell.[51] By the time he is finished, Sparrow begins to sound more like a Philadelphian, from the later seventeenth and early eighteenth centuries, despite the marginal notes that do everything to dress the text as a piece of Puritan morality:

> *if we suffer vices and* Evill thoughts *to possess our Hearts, our Image will be darke, and that will forme us into ugly deformed Beasts or Devills, and we shall* no more appeare *in the right Colours, figures, formes, beauty and brightness, but be as the Blackness of Darkness in anguish and Torment thence forth and for Evermore: As when we have a Sickness, our beauty decayeth, the Blood is Corrupt, lookes pale, yellow and sometimes Black, by the distemper of the Feaver, which disturbes the whole constitution of a Man, so that the Light of the* Sun, Garden, Pictures, Musick, *or any thing that delights us most in health, is Irksom to us, then Darkness, the Night and Sleepe doth most affect us, but then also the Fire of the Disease in the Corruption of our Mortall Body of Flesh, troubles us within, and the most pleasing Thoughts we have had, doe much molest us, which shewes that the inward Corruption and the wrath of God, hath gotten a life in Our Bodyes.*[52]

This is undoubtedly Behmenist, although it still does not sound or read quite like Boehme himself. Let us look at the English translation of Boehme himself in the example here from the *Three Principles of the Divine Essence*:

> *Now seeing Man knoweth that he is such a twofold Man, in the* [s] [[s] *Or,* Potentiality of being good or evill.] *Capacity of Good and Evill, and that they are both his own, and that he himselfe is that Onely Man which is both good and evill, and that he shall have the reward of either*

> *of them, and to which of them he inclineth in this life, to that his soule goeth when he dieth: and that he shall arise at the Last Day in power, in his Labour* [*and Works*] *which he exercised heere, and live therein Eternally, and also be Glorified therein: and that shall be his Eternall foode and* [t] [[t] Source or sustenance.] *subsistence: therefore it is very necessary for him to learne to know himselfe, how it is with him, and whence the impulsion to Good and to Evill cometh, and what, indeed the Good and Evill meerly are in himselfe, and whence they are stirred, and what properly is the Originall of all the Good, and of all the Evill, from whence, and by what* [*means*] *Evill is come to be in the Devills, and in Men, and in all Creatures: seeing the Devill was a holy Angel, and Man also Created Good, and that also such* [u] [[u] *Or*, Evill disposition.] *untowardnesse is found to be in all Creatures, biting, tearing, worrying, and hurting one another, and such Enmity, strife, and hatred in all Creatures: and that every* [x] [[x] *Corpus* or body or naturall substance.] *thing is so at oddes with it selfe, as wee see it to be not onely in the Living Creatures, but also in the Starres, Elements, Earth, Stones, Mettalls, in Wood, Leaves, and Grasse, there is a Poyson and Malignity in all things: and it is found that it must be so, or else there would be no life nor mobility, nor would there be any colour or vertue, neither thicknesse nor thinnesse, nor any perceptibility or sensibility, but all would be as Nothing.*[53]

The repetition, whereby the words embody the concepts Boehme is trying to impart, is missing in the earlier quotation. It rhetorically enacts the mystery Boehme is seeking to convey. This is part of what Andrew Weeks correctly identifies as Boehme's "word magic."[54] It is only later, by the 1680s, that we have a perceptible English way of writing Boehme that is faithful to Boehme's own expressive universe. Before then, it is fair to say that if Boehme was understood in a profound way, that profundity was not reflected in English expression, with a very few exceptions to which I will come. His texts were read. They mystified some, repelled some, and convinced others that they were so "deep" they should be revered. Yet talking about them in extensive depth remained a challenge.

Neither is the earliest, to my knowledge, piece of Boehme-influenced printed discourse in England anything less than Boehme mastered. It is Charles Hotham's Cambridge dispute of 1647 concerning the birth of the soul, published first in Latin in 1648 and then in an English translation almost certainly by Daniel Foote in 1650.[55] Here, Boehme's style has been mastered by the rigors of Cambridge Platonism. None other than Henry More provides a commendatory poem to the volume, together with a verse reply from Hotham in which he asserts that fruitful matter may be gleaned from the obscure genius.[56] Hotham borrows from Boehme on 32 ff. in the English translation in respect of the definition of God as an abyss. The abyss or deep (so named in the biblical Hebrew מוהת) is the body of God, a space from which creation is made. מוהת is translated as "creation." In the abyss is a force of creating, or coagulation, and a force against it, the fire of the abyss. Hotham (who was also, at least later in life, a practicing chemist) likens this to the interaction of metals and acids, which he saw as part of the same chemical process. Within this abyss is hell, not actualized until Lucifer's fall. Hotham uses a faithful rendering of Boehme's three principles to argue that the soul is engendered by God, and by God through someone's parents, the position known as traduction.[57] He does this by showing how creation is a permanent replication, in the natural world, of the divine processes that occurred in the creation of the original three regions from the abyss and in the creation of earth and mankind after the fall of the angels—exactly as Boehme describes it. But it was an academic dispute. The publication of the translation was an attempt to reach out to a broader audience. Since the original occasion was a Latin disputation in front of the Vice-Chancellor, we may suppose that Hotham, recently intruded by the Earl of Manchester as a Fellow of Peterhouse, was trying to convert the University with a refined type of Platonism, and it is in this tradition that he presents Boehme.

II

The efforts of the English translators made possible an encounter with Boehme for a far greater and more diverse number of people than would otherwise have been possible. Writing in February 1678 to Francis Mercurius van Helmont, then resident at Ragley Hall with Lady Conway, the Quaker Charles Lloyd confessed that he had been glad to meet "one [i.e., either Lady Conway or Helmont], who had trodden some of mine unusual paths—amongst the Seekers, Levellers, Familists Behmenists & them above ordinances."[58] One can see why some Quakers, with their stress on the "inner light" as a manifestation of Jesus, were interested in Boehme, even as others saw him a threat (initial limited interest was followed by official disapproval).[59] The reading of Boehme among this widespread group, some learned, some decidedly not, has been the subject of considerable attention.[60] Like much of this kind of evidence, Lloyd merely mentions Boehme by name. Matters change with the confession of John Pordage, published in 1683 (but written earlier; Pordage died in December 1681):

> I acknowledge that none could lay a deeper ground, as to this Subject, than divine Behme hath done; yet I find withal that he hath brought it forth something obscurely, so that he is understood by few, and misunderstood by most: This hath moved me to search into the Nature of this Subject for my own private satisfaction, according to the innate light of my own intellect, and the inward discoveries of the Triune Deity to the Spirit of my Soul. . . . for reason with all its Academical knowledge cannot comprehend it, it being only to be discerned by an intellectual sight.[61]

Pordage perceived in Boehme a way to view God's complexity in nature:

> This Divine *Behme* well understood, therefore he saith, *If the Spirit of the Soul could sink down into this Eternal Nothing and Abyssal still Essence, then he would come into that ground, where God was when he brought forth Eternal Nature and Creatures, and from which he brought forth Eternal Nature.* And thus I have led you to the original ground of Eternal Nature, even the *Abyssal still Essence of Eternity*.[62]

But, says Pordage:

> me thinks I hear some body object against what hath been said, that I seem clearly to contradict *Behme*, who place's [*sic*] Darkness and Light back to back, as opposite to one another, and makes the Fire, a distinct center from the Light; speaking of a *Cross birth in Eternal Nature*, which divides the fourth form of the Fire, from the fifth of the Light?
>
> To which I answer, that what *Behme* saith is most true, but it must be noted that *he speaks this of Eternal Nature in its fallen and degenerate state*, whereas *I speak of it, in its original spotless purity. Behme* speaks *of God in Nature*, but *I* speak *of Eternal Nature's birth in order to God's introducing himself into Nature's Essence*. So that it appears that I do not in the least contradict *Behme's* writings.[63]

This stated desire to be close to Boehme is one piece of evidence that could be used to make the case for Pordage as the first genuine English Behmenist, someone who wrote within a paradigm defined by Boehme's understanding and expression.

Pordage was an educated and, by all accounts, deeply contemplative man. It would seem that his familiarity with "teutonic" philosophy resulted in an early, very significant cultural achievement: the publication in 1661 of his son Samuel's creation epic *Mundorum Explicatio*, five years before Milton's *Paradise Lost*, the first extensive and serious poetic application of Boehme in English letters, and over a hundred years before William Blake's Behmenist prophetic books. It has been argued that Milton is in fact disagreeing with Boehme in his own presentation of the creation.[64] It is not insignificant in this respect that Daniel Foote says in his translation of Hotham's treatise that Milton is the only author who writes great English prose because this gives further evidence of a connection between the serious Behmenists and Milton's text, if not his person.[65] While the epic contains prefatory epideictic of Boehme, and while it undoubtedly harbors many aspects of Boehme's thought within its occult mix (light and dark spiritual worlds preceding the "outspoken" world, first principle as dark, a second as light; evil angels having bodies made up of sulphur, mercury, and salt; Adam as androgyne; and a fall into sexual difference), the narrative structure of the poem, its act of mimesis, and its engagement with allegory works at one remove from the discovery of the processes that in Boehme's own discourse are part of the very act of writing.[66]

Moreover, writing poetry mostly takes place in the domain of the study. It is philosophical. Either Samuel Pordage was himself at a greater remove from Boehme's thought than was his father, or the very process of writing a creation epic put Boehme's ideas at a further distance from the way in which John Pordage encounters the "Teutonic philosophy" in his prose. Moreover, Pordage had also been working with his communities, first at Bradfield and then in London, to experience being in the world according to Boehme's description of the cosmos. You cannot just read Boehme as if he were but a philosopher, you have to go and see the outspoken word as it permanently manifested itself in nature. This is what brought charges of blasphemy and immorality to Pordage's community in Bradfield in the 1650s, involving allegations that angels (or demons) were present in the rectory, in a practice of evidently sometimes ecstatic household worship that the local Puritan divines regarded as disordered, heretical, and Satanic, and where Pordage was eventually ejected from his position.[67] Twenty-four years ago I argued that it is in the fragmentary evidence of this community that we see the first evidence in England of a lay, non-academic understanding of Boehme in the writings of one MP, Mary Pocock or perhaps Mary Pordage, in a treatise of 1649 (just one year after Charles Hotham's use of Boehme in his Latin treatise), where the ongoing fall of man is regarded as an alienation of human reason (Kingliness or Adam is alienated from divine reason, Eve); the reconciliation of the two, and therefore of Boehme's inner and outer worlds, connecting emanating abyssal godhead to "outspoken" world, was interpreted as a solution to the country's damaged churches: "true Independants indeed."[68] We might agree with Cyril O'Regan that the functioning of this community amounted to a return of the Gnostic within English reformed religion.[69]

It is only when a prophetic lifestyle is adopted that Boehme's peculiar mode of writing is answered. The rhetorical invocation of cosmic activity is to be borne out not in the realm of applied reason, but through an affective and visionary demonstration of its truth. This explains the extraordinary activities and writings of Thomas Tany, as demonstrated by Ariel Hessayon, where Tany is shown to derive from Boehme, among others, a distinctive cosmogony, anthropology, and soteriology, and the growth of the Philadelphian Society, in which Pordage played a founding role.[70] There is sharp disagreement about the depth of Tany's knowledge of Boehme, but no doubt that his prophecies embody an autochthonous, dynamically transforming response to the experience of God in nature. The Philadelphian Society found its fullest realization after Pordage's death when its figurehead, Jane Lead, now blind, began to prophesy. In 1670, Lead had been left destitute by her husband's death (she lived at that point in Lady Mico's College, a refuge for widows): her visions of the Virgin Wisdom, exhorting her to follow a virgin life, begin in this period. In 1674, she began to share a house with Pordage, and in 1697, she was given a house in London by a German baron; in these dwellings, the Philadelphians received Lead's visions, written down daily, sibyl-like, on single sheets of paper, and organized the dissemination of their views, not least through the publication of books and a serial journal.

There has been a welcome revival of interest in Jane Lead, and her voluminous writing has been the subject of several recent readings.[71] What is said here is therefore of the briefest nature. The heart of Lead's vision is believers being saved as Lead imagines them reborn in her dreams. She is the mother of redemption, bringing on an age of new spiritual revelation and universal salvation. This is undoubtedly Paracelsian, Hermetic, and alchemical material, and we learn that Lead's words are indeed the "pure language of nature" that had been lost at the Fall (elsewhere, the original language is also discussed), fused with an optimism in the powers of medical science: "there will also be outward Medicines discovered that have not yet been, that will have a wonderful Efficacy for the preserving and fortifying Nature, and recovering the lost Paradisal Body."[72]

Boehme's figure of Sophia or Wisdom plays a bigger role in Lead's world than she does in Boehme's. In a further vision, the union between prophet and Wisdom is described as an erotic coming together of two females, androgynous in its mixture of categories:

> lustrous Presentation of her [Wisdom's] perfect Comeliness and Beauty into one Spirit I was all inflamed, making complaint, bemoaning our selves, how we might possibly compass the obtaining this matchless Virgin-Dove for our Spouse and Bride, who with her piercing fiery Arrow of Love, had wounded us so deep, as no Cure throughout the Circumference of this lower Sphere could be found.[73]

Even at a relatively early stage, Sophia had become in Lead's imagination a "goddess," reconciling the light and dark elements of the Godhead: "The Divine Wisdom kept all in their place and station inviolated in himself."[74] There is even a claim that Wisdom will excel the witness of Jesus (in effect, she becomes a feminine incarnation of Christ), which parallels the claims made for the birth in the dreams of a new generation of spirits.

I have discussed elsewhere the argument recently made by Phyllis Mack that eighteenth-century religious enthusiasm is characterized as a quest through experience for transcendence of bodily limitations, rather than the decidedly in-the-body experiences and behavior of their seventeenth-century predecessors.[75] In this context, I contended that Jane Lead's dreams and visions might be seen as a middle state in which the dream remakes the body in ideal imaginary terms, beyond the limits of its mortal constraints and the orthodox modes of defining it. That Wisdom after her third appearance said she would no longer appear as a visible figure but would be a presence in Lead's mind is also important evidence of a kind of turning of visionary prophecy and ecstasy to conscience. What it also suggests is a prophetic voice of no little originality, where Boehme has undoubtedly been learned from in a very fundamental way but also quite distinctly left behind, despite the notable investment by Lead in further obscurity. Her prophecies were explicitly conceived by Lead as an attack on the rationalists, both philosophers and new scientists.

Lead was widely read, and the English Philadelphians may be understood as a precursor of the German Pietist movement for whom her writings remained important, as the autobiographies of some early Pietists attest.[76] Lead's visionary writing connects with a Germanic tradition of piety and expression that, at least at first glance, has little to do with English traditions. In this context, it would be unforgiveable not to mention the writing of another favorite of the Pietists, Quirinus Kuhlmann (1651–1689), poet and millenarian, famously burned in Moscow for heresy, a profound follower of Boehme, and a visitor to England among many other places. Kuhlmann's discovery of both the combinatory arts of the Jesuit Athanasius Kircher (*Ars Magna Sciendi*, 1669) and the *Mysterium Magnum* (1640) of Jacob Boehme in Leiden in 1673, where he was finishing his legal studies, dramatically changed his life.[77] Before then, Kuhlmann was immersed in classical and patristic authorities, but Kircher and Boehme opened up prophetic possibilities. As he put it in one of the handful of his works translated into English:

> In my three and twentieth year, I was very powerfully stirred up, driven, and compell'd, until all of a sudden the *Paradisick Light-world* visibly in the Inward, surrounded me with thousand-thousand-thousands with *Powers, Colours, Splendors, Glances, Changes, Wonders*, and *Aspects*, being all unexpressibly surrounded with Light, from the most Holy Triangle of the *Lightest-Lightest-Lightest Lights-Light-Light.*[78]

This turns out to be near the time he first encountered theosophy:

> After that *Jehovah*, beyond my expectation, had snatched me out of the Accademical *Babel*, and Mediately excited by Immediate Knowledge, by the Writings of the most highly Illuminated *Jacob Behmen*, and that I was immediately called, forced and pressed with great Power to the Purging of the Learned *Babel.*[79]

By the late 1670s, Kuhlmann wanted to establish an interim 1000-apocalyptic-year realm before the second coming of Christ in his own name as "Kuhlmannsreich" (Kuhlmann's Empire), led by the "Kühlmonarch" in the city of Kuhlmannopolis. This is the time of the "Coolman" (a literal translation of the meaning of Kuhlmann's name), when all will be refreshingly cooled down.

In many ways, Boehme remained alive and well in Kuhlmann's ongoing work. The *Kühlpsalter* (1684–87), his poetic record of his prophetic mission, has prefatory engravings that imitate quite precisely engravings found in Boehme's commentary on Genesis, *Mysterium Magnum* (1623). The symbols relate to the biblical Henoch (i.e., Enoch), whom Boehme interpreted as "divine breath," the symbol of the last, sixth period of the world; Kuhlmann himself is a re-realization of Henoch; with Henoch's arrival comes the fall of Babylon and the furious fire that will consume sword and rod.[80] The lilies and roses are Behmenist emblems for eternal blessed life. Not the quietist mystic that some have made of him, Kuhlmann's reading of Boehme identified him as a prophet of the great renovation that was to come and tied him directly to the ideals of the Rosicrucians and in response to other prophecies that related to the Thirty Years' War. Indeed, Boehme's original prophecies had found ready application in the revolutionary England of 1649.[81] Kuhlmann called for an alliance of Protestant princes, the Tzar, and the Ottomans against the Holy Roman Emperor and the Pope: one reason why he was regarded as subversive in Moscow.

Philology—"speculative philology"—is at the heart of Kuhlmann's later poetry. "Kuhl" comes from the Vulgate text of Acts 3:20, referring to a cooling down of the world after the new coming, which the *Kühlpsalter* was designed to bring on. Like Boehme, Kuhlmann is interested in the kinetic and creating power of the Word. Language is important because it commands, not because it denotes. Like Boehme, who believed that German was close to God's creating language, Kuhlmann made German as like as possible to the original creative language, the *Ursprache*.[82] Thus, he verbalized nouns to underline the effect of kinesis. In this respect, Kuhlmann became a Messiah in poetry, using the name "Jesuel," where "E" is a divine name, "an hypostatic person, an angel," according to Dionysius the Areopagite. Here, the essence of God's primordial ideas is named:

The dark, how deep it darkens me
For essence begins secretly,
O fortune rare, o fortune's gem.
Inside me rises the high stream
Which outside hardly ever seems
A brook to normal men
An ocean groe[w]s and swells and fills
Though only trifling slender rills
Provide its fundament.

Then light is visible on earth, visible for the first time because Kuhlmann has seen it:

3.13 Ach Nacht! Und nacht, di taget!	Oh night! And night, that dawns
O Tag, der nacht vernünftger Vernnunfft!	O day, the night reason of reasons
Ach Licht, das Kaine plaget,	O light, that torments Cain,

Unde helle strahlt der Abelszunfft!	And the light illuminates Abel's tribe!
Ich freue mich ob deiner finstern Kunfft.[83]	I rejoice at your dark future.

As these poems push against the boundaries of intelligibility, they feel indeed like those of William Blake before his time: a fusion of the primitive Behmenism seen in some parts of Henry Vaughan's verse with the geographical particularizing of mystical experience that we see later in Blake.[84] Blake subsumed Boehme into his own particular visionary system; over a hundred years earlier, Kuhlmann sees himself poetically as the re-articulation of Boehme's original vision: not merely echoing Boehme's language and concepts but possessing his spirit, presenting obscurity as a profoundly significant divine code. With militant prophetic edge, Kuhlmann endows both London and himself with the power of delivery, according to the presence of Boehme's "Lilirose":

1. London, Ort der Lichteswunder,	1. London, city of miraculous delight
In dem Gott mein leid versüsst!	Where God sweetened my suffering!
Du wirst neu von mir gegrüsst,	You will be greeted anew by me,
Weil du gibest flamm und zunder!	Because you give flame and tinder!
Schau, wi Gott dich angethan,	Look, how God clothed you,
Das kein Rom dir schaden kan	So that Rome cannot harm you
Um der *Lilirose* bahn!	In the presence of the Lilirose!
2. Von dir bin ich ausgegangen	2. From you I came out
Durch den Ost und Mitternacht!	Through the East and midnight!
Zu dir ward auch hergebracht.	What you became was also brought to you.
Was in Ost und Nord empfangen!	What was received in the East and North!
Was so rings dort Rom unringt,	What so around there vexes Rome,
Und ihm seine Macht verdringt,	And pressed his power
Weil di *Lilirose* singt.	Because the Lilirose sings.
3. Wiclef is aus dir enstanden	3. Wycliff is Created out of you
Der das stoltze Rom verschrekkt:	Who scared proud Rome:
Wiclef wird erst recht geschmekkt,	Wycliff is only tasted right
Nun das falsche Rom wird landen.	Now false Rome will arrive.
Wiclef, der erst Rom anwiest,	Wycliff, who first warned Rome
Ist nun, der den zirkel schleust,	Is now scattered to the compass,
Weil di *Liliros* aufscheust![85]	Because the Lilirose awes!

Perhaps it was status and some influential connections that kept Kuhlmann out of trouble in England, even though he was associated with the Fifth-Monarchist platform. In England, he defended Boehme against several academic adversaries, including among Lady Conway's circle, and in doing so may have been responsible for perpetuating some rumors concerning Charles I's admiration for Boehme.[86]

It is significant that John Pordage, Lead, and Kuhlmann were unqualified admirers of Boehme and that the latter two saw themselves as genuine prophets in their own right, retransmitting his message. Many others who read and then wrote about Boehme chose to engage often sympathetically with him, like the thoughtful Lady Conway and her companion Elizabeth Foxcroft. Henry More was polite about Boehme, if ultimately critical, claiming that, despite his piety, he had been unable to overcome his embodied state and enter in this life a sufficiently purified state; others, like Richard Baxter, were less respectful.[87] But those who followed him to the degree of Pordage, Lead, and Kuhlmann created the first authentically "Behemenist" literature, truthful to the full range of Boehme's interests and modes of expression, not least in expounding the dual nature, light and dark, of divinity, and in perceiving the principles of androgyny that reach out into the physical universe. In doing so, they also perpetuated that obscurity or "difficulty" and made it part and parcel of the Pietist and spiritualist literature of the eighteenth and nineteenth centuries, and beyond. As the first English translators of Boehme began to see, you cannot engage with Boehme with earthly reason: you have to be open to what they regarded as extra- or supra-rational perception. That would lead to the extraordinary verbal performances that we know from the writings of Tany, Lead, and Kuhlmann. Did those first translators understand this? Yes, finally, I think they did. Not only did they acknowledge that Boehme would not play well with rationalists, they also proposed an engagement with Boehme based on intuition: "it [Boehme's *Three Principles*] will rise in the Minde of it selfe, with a ravishing sweetness and content; and he will finde that the Threefold Life is tenfold deeper than this, and the fourty Questions to be tenfold deeper than that."[88] They could not precisely tell you what was in Boehme beyond starting points (although Sparrow's competence clearly grew over time), but they knew it would reach out automatically once it was published. Do not think too hard about this material; just read it; once experienced, you will know how to use it. Did this matter? Yes it did. Boehme answered an old quest for the integration of imagination and the perceived operations of the cosmos, including the "darkness" in God's universe. The history of theology, philosophy, and ultimately literature owes a lot to Boehme.

NOTES

1. Edward Taylor, *Jacob Behmen's theosophick philosophy unfolded* (London: Thomas Salusbury, 1691), b2^{v}.
2. This is the "Frye in the Sky" painting that hangs in the E.J. Pratt Library, University of Toronto.
3. Northrop Frye, *Fearful Symmetry: A Study of William Blake* (Princeton NJ: Princeton University Press, 1947; repr. 1969), 427–28.

4. Northrop Frye, *Notebooks and Lectures on the Bible and Other Religious Texts*, ed. Robert D. Denham (Toronto: University of Toronto Press, 2003), 228.
5. Northrop Frye, *The "Third Book" Notebooks of Northrop Frye, 1964–1972: The Critical Comedy*, ed. Michael Dolzani (Toronto: University of Toronto Press, 2002), 214.
6. Northrop Frye, *Late Notebooks, 1982–1990: Architecture of the Spiritual World*. 2 vols. *Collected Works of Northrop Frye*, vol. 5 (Toronto: University of Toronto Press, 2000), 2.480.
7. Northrop Frye, *Words With Power: Being a Second Study of "The Bible and Literature"* (Toronto: University of Toronto Press, 2008), 289.
8. Andrew Weeks, *Boehme. An intellectual Biography of the Seventeenth-Century Philosopher and Mystic* (Albany, NY: SUNY Press, 1991), 122–3.
9. Charles Webster, *Paracelsus: Medicine, Magic and Mission at the End of Time* (New Haven and London: Yale University Press, 2008).
10. And for good reason since, as other contributors to this volume show, Boehme was influenced by him.
11. Hence the Latin translation of half of *Signatura Rerum* from Boehme's German made in 1631 for the physician Richard Napier: Bodl. MS Ashmole 756. See, W. Poole, "Theodoricus Gravius (fl. 1600–1661): Some Biographical Notes on a German Chymist and Scribe Working in Seventeenth-Century England," *Ambix* 56 (2009): 239–52.
12. A. Hessayon, "'The Teutonicks writings': translating Jacob Boehme into English and Welsh," *Esoterica* 9 (2007): 129–65. http://www.esoteric.msu.edu/VolumeIX/EsotericaIX.pdf; Frank van Lamoen, *Abraham Willemsz van Beyerlanden het Nederlandse hermetisme in de 17e eeuw* (Amsterdam: In de Pelikaan, 1986).
13. Jacob Boehme, *A Consideration of the Divine Revelation* in *Several Treatises of Jacob Behme*, trans. John Sparrow (London: L[odowick] Lloyd, 1661), 72–3.
14. Nigel Smith, *Perfection Proclaimed: Language and Literature in English Radical Religion, 1640–1660* (Oxford: Clarendon Press, 1989), chap. 6.
15. Gerhard Wehr, *Jakob Böhme. Ursprung, Wikrung, Textauswahl* (Wiesbaden: marixverlag, 2010).
16. Ariel Hessayon, "*Gold Tried in the Fire.*" *The Prophet TheaurauJohn Tany and the English Revolution* (Aldershot: Ashgate, 2007), 310–11; John Nickolls, ed., *Original Letters and Papers of State* (1743), 99.
17. Jacob Boehme, *Signatura Rerum*, trans. John Ellistone (London: Giles Calvert, 1651), A2^{r}.
18. Boehme, *Signatura Rerum*, trans. Ellistone, A2^{v}.
19. Boehme, *Signatura Rerum*, trans. Ellistone, A3^{r}.
20. Boehme, *Signatura Rerum*, trans. Ellistone, A3^{r}.
21. Boehme, *Signatura Rerum*, trans. Ellistone, [A4^{r}].
22. Boehme, *Signatura Rerum*, trans. Ellistone, [A4^{v}].
23. Jacob Boehme, *Aurora*, trans. John Sparrow (London: Giles Calvert, 1656), A1^{v}.
24. Hessayon, "Teutonicks Writings," 148.
25. Boehme, *Epistles*, trans. Ellistone, [A3^{r}].
26. Boehme, *Epistles*, trans. Ellistone, [A4^{r}]. See also Jacob Boehme, *Of Christs Testaments*, trans. John Sparrow (London: Humphrey Blunden, 1652), B4^{v}.
27. Jacob Boehme, *The Fifth Book of the Authour* (London: Lodowick Lloyd, 1659), trans. John Sparrow, a7$^{r\text{-}v}$.
28. Boehme, *Signatura Rerum*, trans. Ellistone, A3^{v}–4^{r}.
29. Jacob Boehme, *Several treatises of Jacob Behme not printed in English before*, trans. John Sparrow (London: Lodowick Lloyd, 1661), A2^{v}–3^{r}.

30. Boehme, *Signatura Rerum*, trans. Ellistone, [A4^{r-v}].
31. Boehme, *Epistles*, trans. Ellistone, a2^{v}.
32. As recorded in Sparrow's diary, Bodleian Library, MS Rawl., Essex 23. I am most grateful to Ariel Hessayon for showing me his forthcoming edition of this diary.
33. John Sparrow, "*To the Earnest Lovers of Wisdom*," in Boehme, *Forty questions of the soul concerning its original, essence, substance, nature or quality and property, what it is from eternity to eternity*, trans. Sparrow (London: Lodowick Lloyd, 1665), A3^{r}–A5^{v}.
34. Hermes Trismegistus, purported author of the *Corpus Hermeticum*; Zoroaster, ancient Persian founder of Zoroastrianism; Pythagoras of Samos (580?–c.500 BC), Greek philosopher and mathematician; Plato (424/423–348/347 BC), Greek philosopher; Bernard Trevisan (1406?–1490), Italian alchemist; Ramon Lull (*d.*1315), philosopher; Michael Sendivogius / Michał Sedziwój (1566–1636), Polish alchemist.
35. *Prisca theologia*: notion of an ancient, God-given, true theology which threads through all religions; regarded as embodied in Hermetic philosophy and popular with Italian Neoplatonists such as Marsilio Ficino and Giovanni Pico della Mirandola.
36. Susanna Åkerman, *Rose Cross over the Baltic: The Spread of Rosicrucianism in Northern Europe* (Leiden and Boston: Brill, 1998).
37. See John Webster, *Academiarum Examen* (London: Giles Calvert, 1654); *ODNB*. Further comparison with the related but not identical intellectual genealogies of Henry More, Henry Vaughan, and Thomas Traherne would be appropriate.
38. Boehme, *Epistles*, trans. Ellistone, A2^{v-3}.
39. Boehme, *Aurora*, trans. Sparrow, B^{v}-(a)2^{r}. The text referred to is Boehme's *The Clavis, or Key*, trans. John Sparrow (1647).
40. Jacob Boehme, *Mercurius Teutonicus* (London: Humphrey Blunden, 1649), A2^{v}.
41. Jacob Boehme, *Four Tables of Divine Revelation*, trans. H[umphrey] B[lunden?] (London: Humphrey Blunden, 1654), H4^{v}; Jacob Boehme, *The Second Booke. Concerning the Three Principles of the Divine Essence*, trans. John Sparrow (London: Humphrey Blunden, 1648), A2^{r}.
42. Boehme, *Four Tables*, trans. B[lunden?], [A3^{r}].
43. Boehme, *Second Booke*, trans. Sparrow.
44. Jacob Boehme, *The Remainder of Books written by Jacob Behme*, trans. John Sparrow (London: Giles Calvert, 1662), A2^{r}.
45. Jacob Boehme, *A Consolatory Treatise of the Four Complexions*, trans. Charles Hotham (London: Humphrey Blunden, 1654), A2^{r}.
46. Boehme, *Consolatory Treatise*, trans. Hotham, A2^{v}.
47. Charles Hotham, *An Introduction to the Teutonick Philosophie*, trans. D[aniel] F[oote?] (London: Nathaniel Brooks, 1650), A3^{v}.
48. Boehme, *Four Tables*, trans. B[lunden?], [H4^{r}].
49. Boehme, *Four Tables*, trans. B[lunden?], H4^{v}; cf. Boehme, *Second Booke*, trans. Sparrow, A3^{r}.
50. Boehme, *Several treatises*, trans. Sparrow, A3^{v}.
51. Boehme, *Remainder of Books*, trans. Sparrow, 10–11.
52. Ibid., 12–13.
53. Boehme, *Second Booke*, trans. Sparrow, [a3^{r-v}].
54. Weeks, *Boehme*, 86, 151, 193.
55. For the attribution (as opposed to Hotham's brother Durand) and Foote's career as a translator and associate of Francis Mercurius Van Helmont, see R. Lewis, "Of 'Origenian Platonisme': Joseph Glanvill on the Pre-existence of Souls," *Huntington Library Quarterly* 69, No. 2 (June 2006): 272, n. 21.

56. For More's objections to as well as respect for Boehme, see below.
57. For the full context, see Lewis, "Of 'Origenian Platonisme.'" Henry More himself believed in the soul's pre-existence.
58. BL, MS Add. 23217, f. 25^{r}.
59. Hessayon, "*Gold*," 311–15.
60. G.F. Nuttall, *James Nayler: A Fresh Approach* (London: Friends' Historical Society, 1954); Smith, *Perfection Proclaimed,* chap. 5; Hessayon, "*Gold*," 294–317.
61. John Pordage, *Theologia Mystica* (London [s.n.]), 108–9.
62. Pordage, *Theologia Mystica*, 112.
63. Ibid., 127.
64. James Grantham Turner, *One Flesh: Paradisal Marriage and Sexual Relations in the Age of Milton* (Oxford: Clarendon Press, 1987), 154–55, 164, 171.
65. Hotham, *Introduction to Teutonick Philosophy*, trans. F[oote?], A3^{v}. For Foote's authorship of the preface, see above n. 55.
66. Samuel Pordage, *Mundorum Explicatio*, ed. Harriet Spanierman Blumenthal (New York: Garland Publishing Inc. 1991); note, for instance, the Behmenist explanations at 145, 178, 187–8, 317.
67. As documented in Pordage's defense: *Innocencie appearing, through the dark mists of pretended guilt* (1655). The events are the subject of many interpretations; for the most recent, see Joad Raymond, *Milton's Angels: The Early-Modern Imagination* (Oxford: Oxford University Press, 2010), 125–61.
68. M[ary] P[ocock?], *The Mystery of the Deity in the Humanity* (1649), 33–35; Nigel Smith, *Perfection Proclaimed*, 190, 210–2. The Behmenist language of this treatise is matched by that of Pordage and his followers as they appear in *Innocencie appearing*.
69. Cyril O'Regan, *Gnostic Apocalypse: Jacob's Boehme's Haunted Narrative* (Albany, NY: SUNY Press, 2002), 1–2.
70. Hessayon, "*Gold*," 16, chap. 12.
71. In the light of Sarah Apetrei's work in particular, the claim that "after Pordage's death, . . . the spiritual leadership of Jane Lead and Francis Lee, is less vibrant with experimental theology, visionary communication and the occult" is unwarranted: Raymond, *Milton's Angels*, 161.
72. Jane Lead, *The Ascent to the Mount of Visions* (London: [s.n.,] 1699), 27.
73. Jane Lead, *A Fountain of Gardens* (London: [s.n.], 1697), II, 106.
74. Jane Lead, *The Revelation of Revelations* (London: A. Sowle and J. Lead, 1683), 35.
75. P. Mack, "Religious Dissenters in Enlightenment England," *HWJ*, 49 (2000): 1–23; Nigel Smith, "Pregnant Dreams in Early Modern Europe: The Philadelphian Example," in Johanna Harris and Elizabeth Scott-Baumann, eds., *The Intellectual Culture of Puritan Women, 1558–1680* (Palgrave MacMillan, 2011), 190–201.
76. Johanna Eleonora Petersen, *The Life of Lady Johanna Eleonora Petersen, Written by Herself*, ed. and trans. Barbara Becker-Cantarino (Chicago: University of Chicago Press, 2005), 15–17, 22, 93.
77. Quirinus Kuhlmann, *Der Neubegeisterte Boehme* (1674), ed. Jonathan Clark, (2 vols., Stuttgart, 1995).
78. Quirinus Kuhlmann, *A. Z! Quirin Kuhlman a Christian Jesuelit his Quinary of slingstones* (London and Oxford: Printed for the Author, 1683), 6.
79. Kuhlmann, *Christian Jesuelit*, 12–13; cf. 26.
80. Wilhelm Schmidt-Biggemann, "Salvation Through Philology: The Poetical Messianism of Quirinus Kuhlmann (1651–1689)," in Peter Schäfer and Mark R. Cohen, eds., *Toward the Millennium: Messianic Expectations from the Bible to Waco* (Leiden and Boston: Brill, 1998), 262.

81. Boehme, *Mercurius Teutonicus*; Smith, *Perfection Proclaimed*, chap. 3.
82. For a comprehensive treatment of this tradition in seventeenth-century German thought and Kuhlmann's place in it, see Arno Borst, *Der Turmbau von Babel: Geschichte der Meinungen über Ursprung und Vielfalt der Sprachen und Völker*, Band III Umbau, Teil I (Munich: Deutscher Tashcenbuch Verlag, 1995), 1342–76 (1362).
83. Quirinus Kuhlmann, "Der 2. (62.) Kühlpsalm," Weiter Theil, "*Des Kühlpsalters Fünfftes Buch*," *Der Kühlpsalter*, ed. Robert L. Beare, (2 vols., Tübingen: M. Niemeyer, 1971), vol. 2, 12.
84. Blake's fullest vision of London is contained in *Jerusalem: The Emanation of the Giant Albion* (1804–1823).
85. Kuhlmann, "Der 7. (52.) Kühlpsalm," "*Des Kühlpsalters Virdtes Buch*," *Der Kühlpsalter*, vol. 1, 227–8. The "Lillyrose" is Boehme's adaptation of the Rosicrucian use of the rose as a symbol of reformation.
86. Hessayon, "*Gold*," 293.
87. Sarah Hutton, *The Conway Letters*, rev. ed. (Oxford: Oxford University Press, 1992), 297, 306, 381–2, 512; Sarah Hutton, *Anne Conway. A Woman Philosopher* (Cambridge: Cambridge University Press, 2004), 56, 61, 64–6, 79, 178, 195 n., 236; Robert Crocker, *Henry More, 1614–1687: A Biography of the Cambridge Platonist* (Dordrecht: Kluwer Academic Publishers, 2003), 54–5, 58.
88. Boehme, *Second Booke*, trans. Sparrow, A2.

7 Jacob Boehme and the Anthropology of German Pietism

Lucinda Martin

I INTRODUCTION

Pietism ranks second in importance only to the Reformation in the history of Protestantism.[1] The movement swept through the German-speaking territories in the mid- to late seventeenth century and continued for much of the eighteenth century.[2] It was closely related to reform efforts throughout Europe and the North American colonies, so some historians conceive of a "transatlantic evangelical revival movement," of which German Pietism was but one part.[3] Pietism included movements in the Lutheran and Reformed churches as well as separatist groups. Yet all of these factions, despite holding a range of beliefs, shared certain core concerns: a desire for a more heart-felt religion, more lay participation in church matters, the use of conventicles, and the experience of "rebirth."

The treaty ending the Thirty Years' War in 1648 had made three confessions possible in the German states of the Holy Roman Empire: Catholicism, Lutheranism, and Calvinism, with the ruler of each principality determining the faith for his subjects. New "sects" were expressly forbidden and punishments were severe. This situation defined the shape of Pietism since participants, wishing to avoid legal trouble, had to claim that their meetings were merely private gatherings of friends and in no way an alternative to the official church. Those who rejected these limitations stayed underground or emigrated.

Yet Pietism, especially before 1700, encompassed a whole spectrum of reformers who were in dialogue with one another about how to improve church and society. Only in the late seventeenth century did the lines harden between those who wanted to improve the state churches and those who thought they were beyond reform and advocated separatism. From the role of sacraments to the toleration of other faiths, the central debates in early Pietism owed much to Jacob Boehme.

Boehme's profound influence on Pietism has not received as much scholarly attention as it deserves. Boehme was long uninteresting to church historians who were more concerned with clerical figures in their own confessional histories than with lay thinkers such as Boehme. Another problem is that Boehme's thought mingled with other traditions, so it is difficult to tease out precisely which ideas owe their genesis to Boehme.

Some historians categorize Boehme as a "spiritualist," although many of those who took up his teachings in the late seventeenth century have been designated "radical Pietists."[4] In this chapter, I outline the reception and transformation of Boehme's thought among German Pietists, as well as sketch his impact in three key areas: Pietists' ecclesiology, language, and anthropology.[5] I then flesh out in more detail Pietist transformations of Boehme's anthropological thought. In a final step, I show how Pietist women relied on Boehme's anthropology to claim the authority to write and speak in the public sphere.

II "LIKE TOADS CRAWLING FROM A BOG": THE EARLY CIRCULATION OF BOEHME'S WRITINGS

The ideas of the "Teutonicus Philosophus" often reached his fellow Germans through circuitous routes. Boehme's writings spread from underground communities in German territories—where his texts were almost always censored—to German religious exiles in the Netherlands, to English sectarians, and finally back to the German lands in the translated works of English authors inspired by Boehme.

During his lifetime and afterwards, hand-written copies of Boehme's writings—as well as a few early publications—circulated secretly among German speakers.[6] German polemical literature of the seventeenth century mentions "Böhmisten" and the "Jakob Böhme sect" as if they constituted a cohesive group, but these were actually disparate groups and individuals who adhered to selected aspects of Boehme's thought.[7] As Leigh Penman discusses in his chapter on Boehme's networks, they included Rosicrucians, pansophists, alchemists, Kabbalists, and natural philosophers. Furthermore, German poets and religious writers such as Daniel Czepko, Quirinus Kuhlmann, and Angelus Silesius (that is, Johann Scheffler) took much from Boehme's creative use of language, as did the Dutch poet, Jan Luyken.[8]

Following Boehme's death, Abraham von Franckenberg had several of Boehme's writings published at Amsterdam from 1631.[9] Policies regarding publishing and religious freedom were much more liberal in the Netherlands than in the German states.[10] Indeed, in the history of Boehme reception on the continent, two places bordering the German territories are central—the Netherlands, especially Amsterdam, and Altona (then ruled by Denmark). Both Amsterdam and Altona offered religious nonconformists refuge, and both cities were leading hubs of publishing. Amsterdam in particular played a key role in the publication and dissemination of Boehme's writings.

Anti-Boehme literature of the period took note of the Dutch role in the spread of Boehme's thought. The author of one such polemical work, Erasmus Francisci, wrote, "The writings of Boehme, which for some time now have been coming out of Holland like toads crawling from a bog, are nothing but a misuse of the holy Scriptures." Francisci blamed Boehme's popularity on "profiteering Dutch accountants" who sought financial gain from the sale of sectarian literature, but in fact it was most often German-owned presses in the Netherlands publishing works that would have been censored in the German states.[11]

In the 1630s, the Dutch businessman Abraham Willemszon van Beyerlandt (1587–1648) collected Boehme manuscripts, had them translated into Dutch, and even had some texts published in the original German.[12] In his essay in this volume, Ariel Hessayon details how, by the 1630s, German and Latin editions of Boehme's works also reached English shores, so that by the 1640s the writings of "Jacob Behmen" were being translated into English.

Furthermore, it was not only the writings of Boehme himself that were traveling strange roads. From the 1620s on, a number of German-language disciples of Boehme were publishing in Amsterdam, including Paul Felgenhauer, Johannes Theodorus von Tschesch, and Ludwig Friedrich Gifftheil. Sketching the complete network of Boehme descendents who influenced Pietism would go beyond the bounds of this essay, but if there is one common denominator, it is Friedrich Breckling (1629–1711).

Breckling had been a Lutheran pastor in North German Flensburg. He first ran into trouble with authorities when he published a text criticizing corruption in the German Lutheran church and especially the church's entanglement in war.[13] Fleeing impending imprisonment, Breckling went to Amsterdam and soon became pastor of a German-speaking congregation in nearby Zwolle. Breckling's home in Zwolle quickly developed into a magnet for spiritualists such as Joachim Betke, Christian Hoburg, and Johann Georg Gichtel. Scholars sometimes classify these men as "radical Arndtians" because they took much from the ecclesiastical and social criticism of Johann Arndt (1555–1621).[14] However, the men were just as concerned with the writings of Jacob Boehme.

Through his prolific publications and extensive web of correspondents all over the continent, Breckling constituted an important conduit of Boehme's thought. He compiled lists of the "witnesses to Truth" throughout history and believed that Boehme was one of the greatest of these. Breckling's lists fed into Gottfried Arnold's infamous *Impartial History of Church and Heresy,* which portrayed so-called heretics throughout the ages as the "true church" and the official churches as "Babylon." Arnold's book would become one of the most popular and influential in German Pietism and beyond, going into multiple editions.[15]

Breckling also facilitated the career of Johann Georg Gichtel (1638–1710), perhaps the most flamboyant promoter of Boehme's thought. Although Gichtel held radical views long before his association with Breckling, his interest in Boehme intensified after meeting Breckling. Gichtel hailed from the southern German city of Regensburg, but because of his repeated anti-church polemics was driven into exile in the Netherlands. Like other German critics of the state church, Gichtel found refuge in Breckling's home.

In 1672, Breckling moved to Amsterdam where he eked out a living through writing and editing. In 1688 he published his defense of Jacob Boehme and spiritualism, "Anti-Calovius," part of a public dispute with the theologian Abraham Calov (1612–1686). From 1690 until his death, Breckling lived in poverty in The Hague and was only able to survive due to meager financial support from Princess Elisabeth of the Palatinate, Mary of England, and William III of Orange. Later, the so-called father of "church" Pietism, Philipp Jacob Spener (1635–1705), arranged for Breckling to receive a pension from Princess Anna Sophia of Saxony, a constellation that raises the question of a Boehme/Breckling influence even in the most conservative branches of Pietism.

III BOEHME'S "GRAIL KEEPER": JOHANN GEORG GICHTEL

By the late seventeenth century, there were pockets of Boehme enthusiasts across Europe, and many were connected through correspondence networks. Yet Boehme's wider reception was only possible because of the life's work of Johann Georg Gichtel, sometimes called by historians the "self-appointed Grail Keeper of Boehme's legacy."[16]

When Gichtel's views forced him to flee the German territories, Friedrich Breckling offered him refuge, but their friendship did not last long. When Breckling decided in 1667 to marry, Gichtel was outraged since he interpreted Boehme's writings as advocating chastity. Around the same time, Gichtel undertook to "defend" Breckling in a disagreement with church officials in the Netherlands. Gichtel's anonymously written letter to the authorities was so incendiary that Gichtel was jailed for a time and Breckling lost his post.

Gichtel soon left for Amsterdam, where he drew his own followers, becoming the head of a celibate household. Outsiders referred to them as "Gichtelianer," but they called themselves the "Angel Brothers" because they strove to achieve the purity of angels (Matthew 22:30).[17] Although Jacob Boehme had seen no harm in marriage, the Angel Brothers rejected it, believing that the born-again must await spiritual marriage with the divine Sophia. Convinced that they could count on God to provide for them, Gichtel's followers rejected paid work. Nonetheless they lived a fairly luxurious life since Gichtel proved to be adept at winning patrons. The Angel Brothers could thus devote themselves full-time to what they saw as their holy duty: the preservation and distribution of Boehme's writings.

Gichtel's accomplishment was nothing less than monumental. He edited all of Boehme's theosophical works and published them in 1682–1683 in a 15-volume edition in Amsterdam.[18] Gichtel's followers put out subsequent expanded editions: Johann Otto Glüsing, who led a cell of Angel Brothers in Altona, published an edition in 1715, and Johann Wilhelm Überfeld, who led the network from Leiden in the Netherlands after Gichtel died, released another edition in 1730.[19] These texts stirred great interest in German Pietist circles and beyond; leading figures had to take a stand on Boehme, and his most important tenets were hotly debated in literary battles.[20]

From 1668 on, Gichtel and Breckling increasingly saw one another as rivals, and as Gichtel built up his own network of followers, he became increasingly critical of other religious activists of the day as well: Antoinette Bourignon was too rich; the Labadists allowed marriage; the Mennonites worked; Philipp Jacob Spener was too bound to the churches; August Hermann Francke was too interested in "reason"; the Quakers did not respect hierarchies, and so forth.[21] For his part, Breckling was especially critical of the English Philadelphians since he saw them as corruptors of Boehme's legacy. Of course, all of these factions were competing for funding and members from the same limited pool of people interested in religion outside the bounds of the state church.

Competition may also help explain some of the in-fighting in Gichtel's own household. Two men in particular helped Gichtel to edit Boehme's texts, the theologian and Hebrew scholar Alhart de Raedt and the wealthy politician Coenraad van Beunigen. The three fell out over Beuningen's patronage of the Boehme-inspired prophet Johannes Rothe, who preached that a "Fifth Monarchy" would replace "Babylon"—that is, the state-church complex—in 1674.[22] According to Rothe, Amsterdam was the "city of God" where the new order would come into being.[23] Rothe was one of the most theatrical of the era's radical prophets, and he attracted many advocates of Boehme's thought, such as the poet Quirinus Kuhlmann, who saw in Rothe's chiliastic writings a confirmation of Boehme.[24]

Yet, as in so many other instances, Gichtel revealed his shrewdness by choosing the most politically advantageous position. Rothe agitated against the aristocracy and especially against the Prince of Orange, despite the prince's toleration and financial support of religious nonconformists. In 1676, officials in The Hague imprisoned Rothe, and by the end of the affair they declared his sponsor, Coenraad van Beuningen, insane and institutionalized him, his wealth and connections notwithstanding. In contrast, Gichtel confirmed that God had established traditional social hierarchies. Far from condemning the aristocracy, Gichtel flattered them whenever possible since he depended on noble benefactors for his livelihood. In letters to one of his most important patrons, Princess Elisabeth of the Palatinate, Gichtel argues that the Quakers' leveling of social rank undermines her God-given authority. The clear message was that Elisabeth should support Gichtel and his followers, portrayed as peaceful subjects, rather than rabble-rousing Quakers.[25]

This episode reveals Gichtel's practical side. He was charismatic, able to draw followers and to persuade donors to give generously. Yet he was eccentric and difficult company. A contemporary biography written by one of his supporters was printed with Gichtel's *Theosophica Practica* in 1722.[26] Among other things, the work describes how Gichtel suffered for years from a threatening hallucination: a great wheel that he interpreted as a symbol of the world's temptation. Over the years, Gichtel experienced many visions induced by fasting and especially by sleep deprivation. Since, according to Boehme, the Fall into sin was brought about by sleep, Gichtel believed that sleep was sinful.

Beyond describing his religious development, Gichtel's biography especially emphasizes his "shyness" around women and his success in avoiding falling into their clutches. A number of episodes recount how Gichtel was chased by passionate female admirers, but always managed to escape.[27] In one case, Gichtel was in such panic that he fled home on foot through the snow, leaving his horse and carriage behind.[28] In other texts, Gichtel boasts of marriage proposals from wealthy women who offered him high dowries, as if to prove that he could have married if he had wished to do so.[29] Gichtel justified his celibacy by pointing to the New Testament (1 Corinthians 6:19) as well as to Boehme's writings on Sophia, although sources reveal that Gichtel's revulsion at the opposite sex predated his exposure to Boehme.[30] This has led some researchers to suggest he may have been homosexual, a speculation that might help to explain the attraction of a celibate community like the Angel Brothers.[31]

Small communities of Gichtel's Angel Brothers—some of which existed into the nineteenth century—sprung up in Prussia, the Netherlands, Lithuania, Denmark, and Switzerland, but more significantly, dozens of cohorts participated in a correspondence network.[32] Gichtel even corresponded with Anna Magdalena Francke, the wife of August Hermann Francke, the founder of the most important Pietist center, the Francke Institutes in Halle. Gichtel's ideas about celibacy led to a crisis in the Francke marriage and may have been a factor in August Hermann Francke's turn away from more radical forms of Pietism.[33] Gichtel corresponded with ordinary believers as well as the wealthy and powerful, always seeking not only spiritual exchange, but also donations for his community. Hundreds of these letters were printed in Gichtel's *Theosophische Sendschreiben*, but many others survive only in manuscript.[34]

Gichtel himself produced only one independent theological treatise.[35] The work, based on Boehme's cosmology, discusses the "three principles" and deals primarily with the ideal of celibacy to enable the born-again individual to achieve spiritual marriage with Sophia. Jacob Boehme taught that marriage with Sophia and the subsequent restored androgyny would come only in the afterlife, but Gichtel believed that these things could be accomplished by the righteous in this life.

IV "PHILADELPHIAN YEAST" IN GERMANY

Even after Gichtel published his edition of Boehme's writings, the texts remained censored and scarce in German territories. Many Germans first came into contact with Boehme's thought through the translated writings of Jane Lead (1623–1704) and John Pordage (1607–1681), who had read English versions of Boehme's texts. Near the end of the seventeenth century, Lead was at the center of a circle known as the Philadelphian Society. The group combined Boehme's thought with their own chiliastic expectations to conceive of "Philadelphia," a union of true believers in all confessions (Revelations 2 and 3:1–13). Although not explicitly part of Boehme's system, the notion of a "Philadelphian" community had already been present among German followers of Boehme in the first generation after his death.[36] Yet the idea gained traction only when the writings of English Philadelphians reached German Pietists.

In 1694, Jane Lead's *Heavenly Cloud* was translated into German and many other texts soon followed.[37] These works found resonance among radical Pietists, such as the couple Johanna Eleonora Merlau Petersen (1644–1724) and Johann Wilhelm Petersen (1649–1727), who adopted many of the Boehme-inspired tenets of the Philadelphians and spread them further in their own writings. By 1703, Johann Wilhelm Petersen was one of about 70 people listed in a *Catalogus amicorum in Germania* of the Philadelphian Society, a list of prominent continental nonconformists that the group planned to contact, some of whom actually opposed the Philadelphians.[38] In the same year that he appeared in the catalog, Petersen wrote that he had "recognized that dear truth" as early as three years before, referring in this context to the writings of Gottfried Arnold and John Pordage on Sophia.[39] As early as 1695, the Petersens had possessed a copy of Lead's *Eight Worlds*, and Johanna describes in her autobiography how she absorbed Lead's ideas but then "corrected and completed" them.[40] She believed that Lead had miscalculated the order of events for the coming apocalypse and establishment of God's kingdom on earth: Satan would be redeemed after 50,000 years, not after only 8,000 years. She also criticized Lead for relying too much on her own revelations instead of seeking confirmation of them in Scripture. Yet, with the exception of such technicalities, the Petersens did not reject Lead's revelations. Rather, they were convinced that they had found proof of them in the Bible.[41]

The English Philadelphians sent a German missionary, Johann Dithmar, to spread their message on the continent. In particular, the group targeted Pietists, believing that they would be most receptive. Indeed, a Philadelphian correspondence network thrived and German enthusiasts even donated money to the English group. The Philadelphians employed a translator in Amsterdam, and their German works also met with success among Pietists.

In terms of spreading their tenets, the Philadelphian Society was extremely successful. Hans Schneider has written that, "Nearly all of eighteenth-century radical Pietism was leavened with the yeast of Philadelphian thought."[42] Yet Dithmar's efforts to persuade Germans to pledge allegiance to the Philadelphians' official creed failed dismally. Although many Pietists adopted the general goal of "Philadelphia," few were willing to become formal members of the group. Joining a "sect" could have serious legal consequences. Beyond that, many Pietists believed in the ideal of an "invisible spiritual church" but did not see the need for yet another "walled church."

Although "Philadelphia" did not take root in the form the English group had hoped, the most socially significant radical Pietist groups were all trying to realize a supra-confessional Philadelphian "flock" (John 10:16). This includes the *Herrnhuter*, later called in English the Moravian Church, as well as numerous small circles that believed they were preparing for the "time of Philadelphia." These groups were careful to label themselves "societies" or "clubs" to underscore that they were not separatist sects.

In a few cases, sympathetic rulers enabled "Philadelphia" to thrive. Under the rule of Count Casimir (1687–1741), the town of Berleburg became a haven for Philadelphians and other nonconformists in the first quarter of the eighteenth century. Berleburg would influence German culture for decades due to its prolific publishing program.[43] The physician Johann Samuel Carl (1676–1757) edited a periodical, the *Geistliche Fama*, which spread radical Pietist and Philadelphian thought in thirty issues between 1730 and 1744. Even more significant was the *Berleburg Bibel* (1726–1742).[44] Under the leadership of the theologian Johann Friedrich Haug (1680–1753), the eight-volume work re-translated the Bible and included extensive scriptural interpretations. In keeping with the Philadelphian ideal, the annotations drew on a wide range of international religious thinkers, including not just Philadelphians but also Pietists, Quietists, Catholic mystics, and others.

V BOEHME'S CONTRIBUTIONS TO GERMAN PIETISM: CHURCH, LANGUAGE, AND ANTHROPOLOGY

From early underground followers in the German territories, to German exiles in the Netherlands, to the English Philadelphians, Boehme's ideas entered Pietism through multiple channels. His thought thus saturates German Pietism, especially in three crucial aspects: Pietists' understanding of "church," their use of language, and their ideas about anthropology—all of which were conditioned by chiliasm. While Boehme never specified a date for the end of mortal time, many of the Pietists who picked up his ideas did try to predict the date when God would establish his kingdom on earth. For this reason, Pietists' apocalyptic speculations were often associated with Boehme, even if their utopian plans bore little resemblance to anything Boehme had conceived.

Yet Boehme's influence went beyond chiliasm. Boehme had contrasted "walled churches" to an "invisible spiritual church" of the godly in all faiths. His view, that the individual had to find God on his own, challenged the authority of the church to mediate between God and parishioner and undermined the necessity of sacraments.

In Pietist circles, Boehme's ideas merged with those of others, especially Johann Arndt in his writings on "true Christianity." Yet Pietists took "true Christianity" further than anything Boehme or Arndt had in mind. Pietists styled themselves as a supra-confessional, spiritual elite, which they contrasted with a superficial, "worldly" Christianity practiced by their orthodox neighbors. To distinguish themselves from the "worldly," Pietists displayed outer signs of their supposed superiority: a plain (although uncodified) mode of dress, a rejection of "frivolous" entertainment, and the use of a unique sociolect, the so-called "Language of Canaan," an idiom that drew extensively on Boehme's language. In fact, theosophical terms came to stand for Pietist speech in general, especially for critics of Pietism.[45]

Perhaps the most lasting artifact of the Pietist Language of Canaan stems from Boehme's text, "On the new Birth" (*Von der neuen Geburt*). For Boehme, the central Lutheran doctrine of grace did not suffice to justify sinners; the individual had to make a conscious choice to slough off the "old Adam" and be "born again" free of sin. In Boehme's system, rebirth occurs through the divine Sophia in a way analogous to the birth of a child or the Creation itself. More than any other trait, being "born-again" became the litmus test for who counted as a "true Christian," that is, a member of the elite Pietist community. Indeed, Martin Brecht wrote, "Whenever Pietism replaces justification with rebirth, it usually goes back to the tradition of Boehme."[46] Although the concept of spiritual renewal has many sources, it was in particular the German Pietist understanding of rebirth that accompanied Boehme-inspired Pietist sects to North America to become a core criterion of modern, "born-again" Protestant Evangelicalism.

Pietists gave Boehme's theological concept of "rebirth" a new social significance. They believed that God would endow the born-again with a different—divine—nature. According to Pietists, rebirth actually produced a new kind of human being, one stripped of the consequences of sin. Bearing a divine semiotic, "true Christians" would be recognizable in their speech, behavior, and even in their physical appearance.

The idea of a God-given "natural language" permeating the cosmos has many sources but came into Pietism particularly through the writings of Boehme and Arndt. Significantly, both men were deeply indebted to Paracelsus, the great sixteenth-century physician, botanist, and alchemist.[47] Paracelsus had theorized that medicinal plants contain the iconic "signature" of the body part or disease that they treat.

In his *Signatura Rerum* (1621), Boehme further developed Paracelsus's idea of signatures. Boehme recounts how he learned through visions that the relationship between God and humanity is signified in all things. A concealed kernel of truth, God's "signature," lies beneath the surfaces of words, of things, and of the soul itself. The fact that each person, animal, or substance exhibits innate, specific properties proves this "signature."

The notion of underlying signatures was central for many Pietists' Biblical interpretations. Pietists applied Kabbalah and other esoteric systems to the Bible with the aim of revealing hidden meanings. "Signatures" were also one motivation behind some Pietists' attempts to separate themselves from their "worldly" contemporaries. In dressing, speaking, and behaving differently, they wanted to bear a holy signature. The idea of a "signature of the soul" went through many permutations in Pietism, most famously in the writings of Johann Caspar Lavater. The late eighteenth-century theologian is best known for his physiognomic studies in which he correlated the outer, physical characteristics of a person to inner, moral ones. For many Pietists, exhibiting their "born-again" status through outer appearances proved that they had achieved an inner marriage with the divine Sophia.

VI SOPHIA BETWEEN JACOB BOEHME AND GOTTFRIED ARNOLD

The doctrine of "Sophia" or a personification of "divine Wisdom" has ancient roots going back to the Bible and early church fathers.[48] German Pietists, however, knew of Sophia primarily through Boehme's writings or through the texts of others who transformed Boehme's ideas. In fact, scholars regard the theosophist as the "Father of Western Sophiology."[49] Through his writings and those of his adherents, the Sophia doctrine spread throughout Western Europe in the seventeenth and eighteenth centuries. Boehme understood his insights as a "divine science," revealed to him through "eternal Wisdom" or Sophia.[50] For Boehme, Sophia is an integral part of the cosmos and the godhead. Indeed, Sophia is the mechanism through which God creates himself out of the *Ungrund*. Literally the "un-ground," the *Ungrund* is God's lack of knowledge or certainty, a primal state in which matter is still unfixed in any definite form. According to Boehme, the forms of plants, animals, and minerals only become fixed when the divine Will "births itself" out of the divine Sophia. In the act of self-reflection through Sophia, God creates the entire cosmos so that all the things of creation emerge with a firm identity. Sophia is God's "tool for creation" and for revelation.[51]

God, according to Boehme, encompasses everything in the cosmos and simultaneously reconciles opposites such as hot/cold, life/death, or male/female—all principles that, Boehme underscores, are important and necessary in nature. Since Boehme claims that God possesses both male and female characteristics, he also believes that the first human being, created in God's image, had both masculine and feminine qualities: this *Urmensch*, or original human, had the "tincture of all being" within himself. As a microcosm of the universe, the original human shared a measure of all the substances and principles of the cosmos, including the male and female.

In Boehme's model, the *Urmensch* destroyed the integrity of humanity with God and the cosmos when he fell asleep, thus directing his attention away from God. Through this sinful act, the original human being lost his God-like powers. His body became mortal, susceptible to illness and the forces of nature. He would have had the ability to reproduce through Sophia, who had been united with him, but through sin, he lost Sophia and the power of regeneration. God thus created out of the *Urmensch*, or first, "angelic Adam," a new, mortal Adam and a mortal companion for him, Eve. According to Boehme, it was not Eve's eating of the "forbidden fruit," but the first Adam's egoistic turn away from God—his sleep—that led to the Fall. Boehme insists that it is the goal of all human love to gain back this original unity with God and the universe: men and women seek in the opposite sex that which they lack, but no matter how hard they try, mortals cannot overcome the separation into two irreconcilable sexes. Boehme emphasizes that it is only in heaven that human beings will regain their lost "paradisiacal" form, that is, their androgynous bodies.

Pietists read and debated Boehme's writings, as well as Boehme-inspired texts by English Philadelphians, Gichtel, the Petersens, and others. Yet it was primarily through the publication of Gottfried Arnold's *The Secret of the Divine Sophia* in 1700 that the Sophia doctrine reached a large readership in Germany.[52] Among German Pietists, Arnold was probably the most important proponent of a radical understanding of church since he was able to spread his thought in academic literature that also appealed to a lay public.

In 1693, Arnold took up a private teaching post in Quedlinburg in central Germany, where he lodged in the home of Susanna Margaretha Sprögel and Johann Heinrich Sprögel. The couple's home was a stopover for traveling nonconformists, the conventicle they hosted was an incubator for radical Pietism, and they distributed Philadelphian and other sectarian literature. In September 1697, Arnold began a position as professor of history at the University of Giessen, but in March of the following year, he resigned to escape the state-church and all its trappings. He then returned to Quedlinburg. It was during this period that Arnold began to study mystical authors, and—even more important for his subsequent work—Boehme and the English Philadelphians.

Although most Pietists would learn of "Sophia" through Arnold, his account in *The Secret of the Divine Sophia* was very much informed by life in the Sprögel household. Since at least 1699, Arnold corresponded with Gichtel about their mutual interests. Yet Arnold's host, Susanna Margaretha Sprögel, had been writing to Gichtel much longer, since at least 1696, and was an ardent supporter of the Sophia doctrine.[53] In 1701, Arnold married the Sprögel's daughter, Anna Maria, and the couple would later name one of their children Sophia. Obviously, "Sophia" was discussed at length in the Sprögels' home, which raises interesting questions about the origin and genesis of Arnold's thought.

Certainly, Arnold's Sophia owes much to John Pordage, whose own Sophia text had appeared two years previously.[54] Like Pordage, Arnold draws on Boehme, but transforms the Sophia concept. Arnold's Sophia does not play the same central role in creation and is much less complex than Boehme's Sophia. Arnold also does not rely on Boehme's dense, metaphorical language, and he circumvents the discussion about biological androgyny, thereby avoiding many of the criticisms aimed at Boehme. Like Boehme, he conceives of the first human, the *Urmensch,* as having both male and female characteristics; but, for Arnold, these are only in spirit and not in body.[55] Boehme and Arnold see Sophia differently because they understand the workings of the natural world differently. Arnold conceives of a purely spiritual plane and contends that spirits have no body.

Boehme maintains, however, that all spirit must have some kind of physical existence, a "body," and that conversely, all bodies, that is, all physical things, must possess some kind of spirit, regardless whether those things be human, animal, or mineral. For Boehme, the fact that substances exhibit unique chemical and physical properties is proof of what he calls "spirit." Boehme thus differentiates between the "fleshly bodies" of living creatures and the "light bodies" of angels, of the original human, or of Sophia. Arnold, too, conceives of a "spiritual power" or a "light body" made up of a "heavenly spiritual substance."[56] Yet in contrast to Boehme, Arnold believes that angels have no materiality and stones have no spirit.

Like Boehme, Arnold claims that his knowledge about Sophia derives from divine revelation. Yet Arnold's *Secret of the Divine Sophia* relies not on revelation, but on his training as a theologian. Arnold cites Scripture and supports his claims with quotes from church fathers to show that Sophia was widely accepted in the early Church.[57] Arnold devotes much of his argumentation to explaining Sophia's relationship to the Trinity. Christ and Sophia are different aspects of the same spirit, but Sophia is also the "essence" of all three persons of the Trinity and therefore not an independent entity in the same way as Christ.[58] Although he legitimizes Sophia with canonical sources, Arnold states that such divine mysteries exceed human understanding.[59]

Despite their different conceptions of Sophia, both Boehme and Arnold agree that she is passive. Boehme stresses that God "births himself" through Sophia, as opposed to her birthing him. Similarly, Arnold makes her only a "mirror." In seeing himself reflected, God becomes self-aware and wills himself into being.[60] This passive role of the Sophia stands in contrast to the very active and creative role that she came to play in radical Pietist experiments.

VII BOEHME AND SOCIAL EXPERIMENTS IN PIETISM

Despite Boehme's insistence that "Zion" is to be found in the human soul, many Pietists saw in his writings a justification for building "Zion" or the "New Jerusalem" on earth. Since Pietists wanted to reform not just the churches but also the world, their interest in Boehme soon inspired a variety of experiments with gender roles, sexuality, and social structures. In much of Pietism, Boehme's Sophia obliterated the traditional reading of Genesis in which Eve is responsible for the woes of humanity. The conventional interpretation had always argued that women were unfit for "male" endeavors requiring leadership, strength, or moral character. But with God having both masculine and feminine attributes, the "female" gained a new respectability at the same time as the "male" took on a new burden of sin.

Based on Sophia, Pietists drew conclusions about the organization of social life that Boehme himself had not imagined. When Arnold wrote that the Christian becomes increasingly like God while on earth (the process is completed only in heaven) and that God is androgynous, he implied that women should become more like men, and men should become more like women. To some extent, this is what happened in Pietist circles: Pietist women moved into the previously male realms of religious leadership, biblical interpretation, and theological writing. At the same time, male Pietists such as Zinzendorf touted and strove after "female" traits like spiritual empathy and the ability to nurture.

Pietists' experiments with gender roles and family structures did not simply result from religion; rather, theology offered solutions for contemporary problems. Because of changes in economic structures, many people were unable to attain the financial basis required to establish a family (these matters were strictly governed by law). This was true for a variety of people: the lower nobility was crumbling and many women, in particular, from poor aristocratic families could not marry. At the same time, new methods of production displaced whole classes of craftsmen.

In fact, historians refer to the seventeenth century as a time of "general crisis," which included wars, economic shifts, natural disasters, famines, and plagues. The "crisis" was especially acute in the German territories, which had been devastated by the Thirty Years' War (1618–1648). Pietists, many of whom expected the Final Judgment in the immediate future, certainly felt an urgent sense of crisis. It would go too far to analyze all of these factors here, but it is clear that Pietists had many motivations for trying to shape their lives "differently." Boehme's Sophia doctrine justified such experiments in the social fabric.

Many of the Pietists' experiments with marriage, sex, and living arrangements found an ideological basis in the notion of Sophia and the androgynous *Urmensch*. Some Pietist groups, such as the Herrnhuter, conceived of the relationship between men and women in a new way. Instead of seeing women as subservient "helpers" to men, they viewed both men and women as servants of God. As a result, the Herrnhuter developed a system in which both men and women worked in parallel ecclesiastical and community structures. There was even a child-care program to enable women to pursue careers, including as church administrators, alongside their male counterparts. The criteria for success in this system were individual ability and religiosity, not education or social status. Men and women lived in separate but comparable houses. Marriage existed within the community, but was subordinated to the needs of the church, with elders arranging marriages between members as they saw fit.[61] The Herrnhuter viewed marital relations positively, since sex within marriage constituted a "sacrament," but one that served God and not individuals.

Some of the continental groups inspired by Boehme understood the religious community as a new kind of "family." This was the case for the Labadists, who were active in Germany and the Netherlands and formed a settlement in Maryland in 1683. The Labadists' two most important leaders were Jean de Labadie and Anna Maria van Schurmann, whom members referred to as "Papa" and "Mama," while other group members were "brothers" and "sisters." The Labadists initially rejected marriage, preferring spiritual marriage with Sophia, but after an unmarried woman in the group became pregnant, they decided to allow marriage between members.[62] The public was incensed that the Labadists, like many other Pietist groups, ignored social boundaries and that aristocratic ladies like van Schurmann lived and worshiped side by side with rustic craftsmen. Members of such groups increased their numbers not through childbirth but by gathering the "children of God" through conversion. In this way, Pietists who could not marry for economic reasons or who did not wish to marry could nonetheless have a "family."

Other Pietists understood the existence of the male and female sexes as nothing more than evidence of sin, a result of the division of the *Urmensch* into two sinful halves. These Pietists rejected sexuality completely and tried out various forms of celibacy, including chaste "spiritual marriages." They wanted to await their "true" or "spiritual" marriage in heaven, where the sinful mortal body would be restored to its perfect androgynous state. Both men and women were seen as "stained" and incomplete. Many German Pietists took the same attitude as Jane Lead, who, although her marriage had apparently been a happy one, later commented that it had delayed her "true marriage of the soul with the Heavenly Sophia."[63]

The leading Pietist proponents of celibacy based on Sophia were Gichtel and, for a time, Arnold. Only a year after writing his *Secret of the Divine Sophia* and two years after distancing himself from the state church, Arnold softened his views, taking a wife and an official church post to support his family. Upon hearing the news, Gichtel expressed the hope that Arnold "wanted not a wife, but a sister for a wife," but later had to note in disappointment that Arnold had "lapsed" into having children.[64]

While there were small communities of Gichtel's "Angel Brothers" network all over the continent, many other small celibate households existed independently. In such homes, a handful of like-minded believers structured the day with prayer, worship, study, and work. One such community was led by Gerhard Tersteegen, often considered the greatest Pietist poet. Tersteegen, who first turned to radical religion after reading Boehme, preached before groups of hundreds of seekers and traveled extensively, advising other "spiritual households."

This kind of private Pietist monasticism developed furthest in North America, where many of the most socially radical Pietists congregated having fled persecution in Europe. A group consisting mostly of scientists and mathematicians made the first attempt to create a celibate utopia in the colonies. They lived as hermits in the woods of Pennsylvania and kept astronomic watch of the night sky with their telescopes, since they expected "heavenly signs" such as comets to announce the return of Christ (Matthew 24: 29–30). The group rejected all names as smacking of sectarianism, but locals called them the "Woman in the Wilderness" community, because they awaited the woman prophesied in Revelations 12:1–6, whom the group interpreted as the divine Sophia.

This group combined with other Pietists influenced by Boehme and eventually formed the Ephrata Cloister near Lancaster, Pennsylvania, a large-scale Protestant institution that accommodated male and female inhabitants.[65] As in the settlements of the Herrnhuter, men and women lived in separate but parallel structures—an architectural expression of the androgyny principle. Furthermore, Boehme's writings on Sophia inspired yet other Pietist communities in North America, such as the so-called "Rappists" who settled in Pennsylvania and Indiana and persisted into the nineteenth century.

Doubtless the most infamous Sophia-inspired sect on the German religious scene was the Mother Eva Society or "Buttlar gang," named after their leader, Eva Margaretha von Buttlar.[66] The group tried to rise above the sinful mortal body by enacting sexual rituals as sacraments, aiming to reconcile the male and female. Through their "cleansing" ceremonies, they believed that they could cancel out the sexual differences that sin had imposed on humanity. For men, purification essentially consisted of intercourse with Eva von Buttlar. The procedure that female members underwent was much more grisly: a manual crushing of the uterus that was extremely painful and led to years of health problems for some group members. The group thought that this gruesome ritual—carried out by a member who was a medical student—was necessary in order to kill "the beast," that is, Satan, whom they believed to reside in the uterus.

VIII SOPHIA AND PIETIST WOMEN'S WRITING

Boehme's anthropology led many Pietists to believe that sexuality held the key to salvation, whether through celibacy or through the elevation of intercourse to a sacrament. Yet Pietist experiments based on Boehme's anthropology were not limited to separatist sects. The Sophia doctrine also inspired Pietist women to take up the pen and to argue for an expansion of women's sphere of activity. Thus Johanna Eleonora Merlau Petersen explains that Sophia is really just another name for the Holy Ghost.[67]

Gottfried Arnold had declared that it is unimportant that the term, "der Geist" (spirit), has a neuter or feminine gender in other languages, but this question is central for Petersen.[68] She points out that the Hebrew word for "spirit" (*rûah*) is feminine.[69] For Petersen, the original gender of the word proves that God encompasses female as well as male elements. Indeed, she asserts that it is the female "fertile mother or breeding dove" which makes the "invisible in God visible," that is, the Holy Spirit is the medium of God's revelation. Without her, there is no *Logos*, no word.

Petersen thus takes up a very old discussion in Christianity, that between "word" and "spirit." Pietist women writers like Petersen gave "spirit" primacy over "word" because "word" was forbidden to them. Women were allowed neither to study at universities, nor to hold clerical positions, and the texts that women were forbidden to study were the very texts used to justify women's exclusion. "Spirit," on the other hand, cannot be regulated by institutions. Although Johanna Eleonora Merlau Petersen relies on extensive theological and philological knowledge in her writings, she always appeals in the end to "spirit" to justify her activity.

While Petersen refers to Sophia in veiled terms as the "great secret" behind her writings, another woman writer, Susanna Margaretha Sprögel, is more forthright in her assertion of the doctrine. In 1705, a new book in which the Sophia doctrine played a central role arrived on the German book market, written by an anonymous author but with a preface by Arnold.[70] Scholars have attributed *Consilia und Responsa Theologica* to Susanna Margaretha Sprögel, Arnolds' mother-in-law.[71] The fact that she issued the work anonymously attests to the controversial nature of women's publishing, especially on questions of theology. In the preface, Arnold avoids mentioning the author's sex by referring only to a "person taught by God."[72] He also calls the book's author a "Theologus" (a designation meant either to mislead or provoke), and describes the book as the "inner biography of this soul," indicating its origin as a Pietist spiritual journal.[73] Much of the work consists of dialogues between the author's soul and God as well as various theological questions to which God "replies." The book also contains prayers, poems, and the dreams and visions of the author.

Boehme and Arnold both imagined Sophia as a passive "tool" of God, but according to Sprögel, Sophia is an active agent of redemption. It is Sophia who works change in the soul and leads erring humans back to God. In *Consilia*, Sophia "speaks" forcefully in the first person in a way reminiscent of the scriptural Sophia.[74] For Arnold, Sophia is a "spirit," but not a "person," and Boehme writes confusingly that Sophia is not a "person," but nonetheless a "personality." Yet for Sprögel, Sophia is the person within the godhead who creates all that is good in the universe and who has dominion over life and death.[75] Sprögel also makes clear that it is Sophia who will restore a state of androgynous perfection to the born-again.[76]

Furthermore, Sprögel maintains that Sophia shares her mysteries not with ordained theologians, but with the "voiceless" in society. The notion that God reveals himself through the meek and not the proud was one of the most widespread ideas in Pietism. Women and lay Pietists countered the argument that only ordained theologians had the authority to speak publicly on religious issues by claiming that the "chosen" were not the privileged of this world, but rather often those with the least influence in human affairs.

Similarly, Pietists looked to doctrines like Sophia and an androgynous "first Adam" to argue for social alternatives. Arnold saw in Christ's birth through Mary a fusion and thus reunification of the male and female elements in the divine. According to Arnold, when mortals answered the call of Sophia, they could thus become "new creatures." Sprögel and Arnold thus agree that Jesus and Sophia are united as different aspects of God, but Sprögel adds a social dimension. She sees in the union of Jesus and Sophia a theological solution for a real-world problem: that of "unclean" marriage.

Like many Pietists, Sprögel subscribed to the belief that the end of mortal time was at hand. She argued that God was already setting up his kingdom on earth and that as it progressed, worldly differences between men and women would melt away. Not only would born-again Christians take on new, androgynous bodies, but God, or rather, "Jesus-Sophia," would also initiate a new kind of marriage in which man and woman are "one in Christ" and in which neither dominates the other.[77]

Sprögel melds Jesus and Sophia into one person as Arnold does, but instead of writing in the theological idiom of Arnold, she writes in an alchemical language reminiscent of Boehme or her correspondent, Gichtel. Sprögel identifies the "godly-masculine" and the "godly-feminine" "tinctures." According to Sprögel, the "manly tincture" is strength, and the "feminine tincture" is wisdom. She writes that the enemy, Satan, wants to divide the powers of female wisdom and male strength, and that believers must unite the "perfect virginal man and the manly maiden in one undivided guise" in order to achieve "the right true new birth."[78]

Sprögel makes wisdom itself a feminine quality, a clear elevation of the female. Yet she argues that wisdom and strength are available to both men and women because they are *inner* characteristics of the soul, not physical attributes. Rules and customs regulating the behavior of the sexes should thus be applied to the "inner human" and not to the "outer creature." Sprögel therefore interprets Paul's prohibition on women's speaking in the church to mean that the weak and cowardly had to remain silent, that is, those who were "female" on the *inside*. She writes of male and female "dispositions." The author advises her readers to seek within themselves to discover whether they are "male" or "female" and thus whether or not the apostle's injunctions apply to them:

> **The women should stay silent in the congregation** / says Paul / and this is also true according to the **correct meaning of the spirit.** Because all **weak womanly and lazy dispositions** should stay silent [. . .] So let each look into his heart / and seek what the **womanly silence** consists of [. . .] since in Christ there is neither man nor woman / but rather all are one in him [. . .].[79]

Sprögel's advice includes men as well as women. According to her anthropology, nature determines what one is on the outside—be it man, woman, or child—but spiritual maturity defines what one is on the inside. She thus argues, "[. . .] **many men still have to learn to stay silent** / who may be called men / but who have not even become converted **little children** in Jesus / [. . .] let alone **able to teach others**. They [. . .] should learn to stay silent / as the Spirit commands them."[80]

According to Sprögel, the female represents that which is weak and should therefore remain silent. Yet she claimed the right of religious speech, reserved by the apostle Paul for men. Embedded in a world in which "female" had few positive connotations, this author relied on Boehme's anthropology to redefine herself. Based upon her understanding of male and female as inner attributes, she clearly saw herself as a man.

IX CONCLUSION

The belief that God created human beings in *his* image is a central tenet of Christianity—one that had long justified the male domination of women, from "house fathers," to "church fathers," to the king as "father of the land." Boehme's Sophia doctrine encouraged men and women to see their world with new eyes. The doctrine taught that God had not created the female sex to serve the male, but instead that the female was an intrinsic part of the divine with an important role to play in God's plan for the cosmos. The androgynous "first Adam," not Eve, was culpable for humanity's Fall into sin. The notion that God charged men to master over women thus lost its foundation in many Pietist circles. In this environment, women could take on roles previously reserved for men. Some Pietist groups enabled women to hold leadership positions that went far beyond anything offered by the secular Enlightenment.

Based on Boehme's writings, Pietists not only challenged religious hierarchies but also opened up new debates about the possible shape of society. They experimented with gender roles, social structures, and even the forms a family could take, yet many of their ideas did not survive the eighteenth century. Pietist cloisters and celibate "spiritual marriages" could not compete with other ways of organizing life. After 1760 most radical Pietist experiments petered out, including expanded opportunities for women. Protestant women would not regain such prospects until the twentieth century.

Yet the promotion of women's writing did take hold. The Pietist emphasis on individual spiritual development led Pietists to observe the inner workings of the soul and to record these in spiritual journals. Sophia, or "divine Wisdom," inspired many women Pietists to take up the pen. As women increasingly wrote and published their own insights, traditional notions that such activities were unfitting for women gradually subsided, and clichés about the supposed inability of women lost ground. This expansion of opportunities for women (and lay men) to write and publish is one of Pietism's enduring contributions to the modern world. What is more, through their writings, the radical Pietist idea that the inner essence of a person is more important than outer, "worldly" attributes like gender, race, or social standing lived on to inspire radicals in epochs to come.

NOTES

1. Carter Lindberg, ed., *The Pietist Theologians* (Malden, MA: Blackwell, 2005), 3, 28. In the following, all translations are mine unless otherwise noted. I am grateful to the Fritz Thyssen Stiftung for awarding me a Herzog Ernst grant for study at the Forschungsbibliothek Gotha.
2. This was the "classical" period of Pietism, which continues in other forms to the present. Historians have not been able to agree on Pietism's parameters: Jonathan Strom, "Problems and Promises of Pietist Research," *Church History* 71 (2002:3): 536–554.
3. W.R. Ward, *Early Evangelicalism: A Global Intellectual History* (Cambridge: Cambridge University Press, 2006).
4. Martin Brecht, "Die deutschen Spiritualisten des 17. Jahrhunderts" in *Geschichte des Pietismus,* vol. 1, ed. Martin Brecht (Göttingen: Vandenhoeck & Ruprecht, 1993), 205–240: 205; Hans Schneider, *German Radical Pietism* (Lanham, Md: Scarecrow Press, 2007), 1–10.
5. Developments pertaining to Friedrich Christoph Oetinger and his milieu go beyond the bounds of this essay.
6. Brecht, "Spiritualisten," 212; and Leigh Penman's chapter in this volume.
7. For example, Abraham Calovius, *Anti-Böhmius [. . .] Qvuid Habendum de Secta Böhmen* (Wittenberg: Schrödter, 1684).
8. Brecht, "Spiritualisten," 216–217. Hans-Georg Kemper, *Deutsche Lyrik der frühen Neuzeit,* vol. 3 (Tübingen: Niemeyer, 1988).
9. Hans Schneider, "Böhmisten" in *Enzyklopädie der Neuzeit.* Vol. 2. (Stuttgart: Metzler, 2005), 335–37.
10. Ferdinand van Ingen, *Böhme und Böhmisten in den Niederlanden im 17. Jahrhundert* (Bonn: Presse- und Kulturabteilung der Kgl. Niederländischen Botschaft, [1984]).
11. Ingen, *Böhme,* 5–6; 30–31. Generally, see John Bruckner, *A Bibliographical Catalogue of Seventeenth-Century German Books Published in Holland* (The Hague and Paris: de Gruyter, 1971). The quote is in: Erasmus Francisci, *Gegen = Stral Der Morgenröte* (Nürnberg: Endter, 1685), 755.
12. A diplomat, M. le Blon, and the publisher H. Beets continued this work (Schneider, "Böhmisten," 336). Beyerland paved the way for—and helped finance—Gichtel's 1682 edition of Boehme's theosophical works. W. Heijting, "Hendrick Beets (1625?-1708), publisher to the German adherents of Jacob Bohme in Amsterdam" *Quaerendo* 3 (1973): 250–80.
13. Friedrich Breckling, *Speculum Repurgatum* ([Amsterdam]: [Breckling], 1661).
14. Brecht, "Spiritualisten," 221–237.
15. Gottfried Arnold, *Unparteyische Kirchen- und Ketzer-Historie,* (2 vols., Frankfurt a.M.: Fritsch, 1699–1700).
16. Hans Schneider, "Der radikale Pietismus im 17. Jahrhundert," in Brecht, ed., *Geschichte des Pietismus,* vol. 1., 391–437 at 415.
17. J. Jürgen Seidel, "Gichtelianer," in *Enyzklopädie der Neuzeit*, vol. 4, (Stuttgart: Metzler, 2006), 894–96.

18. *Des Gottseeligen Hoch-Erleuchteten Jacob Böhmens Teutonici Philosophi Alle Theosophische Wercke* (Amsterdam: [n. pub.], 1682–83).
19. Glüsing, ed., *Theosophia Revelata* ([Hamburg]: [Holle], 1715). Überfeld, ed., [same title], ([n. pub.], 1730).
20. Schneider, "Der radikale Pietismus im 17. Jahrhundert," 394.
21. See Gichtel's letters, Archives of the *Franckesche Stiftung* (hereafter: AFSt) in Halle, Germany: AFSt D 60. Cf. also: Gertraud Zaepernick, "Johann Georg Gichtels und seiner Nachfolger Briefwechsel mit den hallischen Pietisten, besonders mit A. M. Francke," in *Pietismus und Neuzeit* 8 (1982): 74–118 at 93.
22. Ingen, *Böhme,* 21–27.
23. Rothe, *Een nieuwe Hemel en Aerde,* 2nd ed. (Amsterdam: Pieter Arentsz, 1673), 40.
24. Kuhlmann, *Neubegeisterter Böhme* (Leiden: de Haes, 1674).
25. AFSt D 60, 101ff., esp. 107r-08v.
26. [Gichtel], *Theosophia practica.* 7 vols., vol VII ([Leyden], n.pub. 1722). Zaepernick gives the author as Johann Georg Pronner, but Võsa attributes it to Jakob Michelmann: Zaepernick, "Briefwechsel," 79; A. Võsa, "Johann Georg Gichtels Verhältnis zum anderen Geschlecht in Leben und Lehre," in *Der radikale Pietismus,* Breul et al., eds., (Göttingen: Vandenhoeck & Ruprecht, 2010): 361–68 at 362.
27. [Gichtel], *Theosophia practica,* vol. VII, 20. Cf. Võsa, "Johann Georg Gichtels Verhältnis."
28. [Gichtel], *Theosophia practica*, vol. VII, 22.
29. Ibid., vol. I, 532.
30. Võsa, "Johann Georg Gichtels Verhältnis," 362–65.
31. This was the consensus of the conference, "Radikaler Pietismus—eine Zwischenbilanz der Forschung," March 28–31, 2007, Marburg, Germany.
32. The successor of these communities is a German club that still exists, the "Vereinigung der Freunde von Jakob Böhme" (Seidel, "Gichtelianer," 895–96).
33. Zaepernick, "Briefwechsel."
34. *Erbauliche Theosophische Sendschreiben* ([n. pl.]: [n. pub.], 1700, 1701, 1710).
35. *Eine kürze Eröffnung und Anweisung der dreyen Principien* ([n. pl.]: [n. pub.], 1696).
36. Boehme's friend and biographer, Abraham von Franckenberg (1593–1652), included the ideal of "Philadelphia" in his own writings. Paul Felgenhauer (1593–c. 1677) also tried to gather a Philadelphian community near Bremen. Cf. Hans-Jürgen Schrader, *Literaturproduktion und Büchermarkt des radikalen Pietismus: Johann Henrich Reitz', Historie der Wiedergebohrnen' und ihr geschichtlicher Kontext* (Göttingen, Vandenhoeck & Ruprecht, 1989), 375–76.
37. Cf. Nils Thune, *The Behmenists and the Philadelphians: A Contribution to the Study of English Mysticism in the 17th and 18th Centuries* (Uppsala: Almquist & Wiksells, 1948), 110–14.
38. Forschungsbibliothek Erfurt/Gotha A 297: 5–8; Thune, *Behmenists*, 125–27.
39. Johann Wilhelm Petersen, *Mysterion Apokatastaseos panton* ([Offenbach]: [Brede], 1703), vol. 2: 170; John Pordage, *Sophia* (Amsterdam: n.pub., 1699).
40. Johanna Eleonora Petersen, *Leben Frauen Joh. Eleonora Petersen* (n.p.: n. pub., 1718), 56. See also: Martin, "Women's Religious Speech and Activism in German Pietism," (PhD diss., University of Texas, 2002), 197ff. and Ruth Albrecht, *Johanna Eleonora Petersen: Theologische Schriftstellerin des frühen Pietismus* (Göttingen: Vandenhoeck & Ruprecht, 2005), 112ff. and 277ff.

41. Johann Wilhelm Petersen, *Das Leben Jo. WILHELMI PETERSEN* (Halle: Renger, 1717), 297.
42. Hans Schneider, "Der radikale Pietismus im 18. Jahrhundert," in *Geschichte des Pietismus*. vol. 2., eds. Klaus Deppermann and Martin Brecht (Göttingen: Vandenhoeck & Ruprecht, 1995), 107–197 (at 112).
43. Schrader, *Literaturproduktion*; Schneider, "Der radikale Pietismus im 18. Jahrhundert," 160–66.
44. *Die Heilige Schrift Altes und Neues Testaments*, (8 vols., Berleburg: Johann Heinrich Haug, 1726–42).
45. Lucinda Martin, "The Language of Canaan: Pietism's Esoteric Sociolect," *Aries: Journal for the Study of Western Esotericism* 12 (2012): 237–53.
46. Brecht, "Spiritualisten," 212.
47. Arndt had studied Paracelsian medicine, not theology. Hermann Geyer, *Verborgene Weisheit*, (3 vols., Berlin: Walter de Gruyter, 2001).
48. Cf. the Book of Proverbs (esp. chapters 1, 2, and 8), Ecclesiastes 7–8, and the apocryphal books, Wisdom of Solomon (1, 6, 7, 8, 9), and Jesus Sirach 24.
49. Lucinda Martin, "Jakob Böhmes göttliche Sophia und Emanzipationsansätze bei pietistischen Autorinnen," in *Offenbarung und Episteme. Zur europäischen Wirkung Jakob Böhmes im 17. und 18. Jahrhundert*. eds. Friedrich Vollhardt and Wilhelm Kühlmann (De Gruyter: Tübingen, 2012), 241–57: 242.
50. *Mysterium Magnum*, 67 (13) and *Von der neuen Wiedergeburt*, 8 (13), in Jakob Böhme, *Sämtliche Schriften*, eds. August Faust and Will-Erich Peuckert, (11 vols., Stuttgart: Bad Canstat: Frommann, 1955–61). Here, the first number refers to the chapter, the second in parentheses to the paragraph.
51. Boehme, *Beschreibung der Drey Principien Göttliches Wesens* (1619), 139 (38–142); 56; *Von der Gnaden-Wahl* (1623), 4 (1–9); 22; *Mysterium Magnum* (1623), 190 (14); *Schutz-Schriften wieder Balthasar Tilken* (1621), 119 (64–121), 85.
52. Gottfried Arnold, *Das Geheimniß der göttlichen Sophia* (Leipzig: Thomas Fritsch, 1700). In citing Arnold's *Sophia*, the first number refers to the page and the second in parentheses refers to the paragraph.
53. Only Gichtel's letters from the exchange have survived. Forschungsbibliothek Erfurt /Gotha A 297, 217–33; Zaepernick, "Briefwechsel," 118.
54. Pordage, *Sophia*.
55. Arnold, *Sophia*, 40 (2).
56. Ibid., 102–103 (25–26).
57. Ibid., 37–39 (11–17); 40–42 (2–10); 44–45 (16–19); 51–52 (3–8); 54–57 (17–25); 99ff (14ff); 114–115 (16–17); 125ff (10ff).
58. Ibid., 35 (3); 38 (13).
59. Ibid., 39 (17).
60. Ibid., 45 (19).
61. Choices were subject to the lot and the consent of individuals. Martin, "Women's Religious Speech," 277–282.
62. Trevor John Saxby, *The Quest for the New Jerusalem: Jean de Labadie and the Labadists, 1610–1744* (Dordrecht: Nijhoff, 1987). On Boehme's influence on Schurmann, see Ingen, *Böhme*, 11–12.
63. Donald F. Durnbaugh, "Jane Ward Lead (1624–1704) and the Philadelphians," in Lindberg, *The Pietist Theologians*, 128–147 at 130.
64. Gichtel, *Theosophia practica*, vol. V, no. 62; vol. I, 425, 572; vol. VI, 1416; Schneider, "Der radikale Pietismus im 18. Jahrhundert," 116–17.
65. Jeff Bach, *Voices of the Turtledoves: The Sacred World of Ephrata* (Penn State UP: University Park, PA, 2003).

66. Willi Temme, *Krise der Leiblichkeit. Die Sozietät der Mutter Eva (Buttlarsche Rotte) und der Radikale Pietismus um 1700* (Göttingen: Vandenhoeck & Ruprecht, 1998); Martin, "Women's Religious Speech," 97–103; 124–30.
67. *Leben Fr. Joh. Eleonora Petersen*, 68; Martin, "Women's Religious Speech," 157–225.
68. Arnold, *Sophia*, 41 (6 and 7).
69. Like Petersen, early Christian scholars interpreted *rûah* to mean that God is androgynous—a fact of which she may have been aware. Helen Schüngel-Straumann, "Ruah (Geistin)," in *Feministische Theologie: Perspektiven zur Orientierung*, ed. Maria Kassel (Stuttgart: Kreuz Verlag, 1988) 59–75.
70. *Consilia und Responsa Theologica [. . .] gemein gemacht von Gottfried Arnold* (Frankfurt: Thomas Fritsch, 1705).
71. On the attribution, see Martin, "Jakob Böhmes göttliche Sophia," 252–53.
72. Arnold in *Consilia und Responsa*, unpag. introduction, paragraph 3.
73. Ibid., paragraph 5.
74. Cf., for example, Wisdom of Solomon 1:6; Sirach 24:1–3.
75. [Sprögel], *Consilia und Responsa*, 138–139.
76. Ibid., 231–232.
77. Ibid., 231–232.
78. Ibid., 253–254.
79. Ibid., 328–329. The boldface type in quotes appears in the original.
80. Ibid., 329–330.

8 "No New Truths of Religion"

William Law's Appropriation of Jacob Boehme

Alan Gregory

In 1737, William Law (1686–1761) published *A Demonstration of the Gross and Fundamental Errors of a late Book, called "A Plain Account of the Nature and End of the Sacrament of the Lord's Supper.*" This was the first of his books to reflect the influence of Jacob Boehme, albeit less thoroughly than *The Grounds and Reasons for Christian Regeneration*, which followed it two years later. Exactly when Law started to read Boehme is unclear, but his adoption of a Behmenist vocabulary is quite sudden and, once adopted, dominates all the major works of the last twenty years of his life.[1] At some point between 1733 and 1737, Law was introduced to Boehme's writing through an anonymous treatise, *Faith and Reason Compared,* recommended to him by the physician George Cheyne.[2] Following this up, though, proved strenuous. Law's first reading of one of Boehme's works put him "into a *perfect sweat.*" Boehme's terms shaping his recollections, Law explained his persistence as due to finding "glimmerings of a deep ground and sense." The work was worth the sweat: "[I] perceived that my heart felt well and my understanding kept gradually opening."[3] By the early 1740s, Law was teaching himself the "High German language" necessary for a direct engagement with Boehme's books.

By the time Law picked up *Faith and Reason Compared,* he was respected, and also denounced by some, as the author of two widely-read treatises on Christian life and devotion, *A Treatise upon Christian Perfection* (1726) and *A Serious Call to a Devout and Holy Life* (1729). Both works exhort a thoroughgoing renewal of Christian practice involving the return to a rigorous life of self-denial, generosity, and prayer inspired by an apostolic urgency and integrity. The "highest Degree of Christian Perfection," Law reminded the spiritually half-hearted, "is also the lowest Degree of Holiness which the Gospel alloweth."[4] What is striking, especially about the *Serious Call,* is the combination of demanding strictness with a measured, reasonable tone and considerable charm. Law's style, however, changed markedly under the influence of Boehme: forceful and clear, almost syllogistic argument, illustrated by well-observed, memorable vignettes, disappears in favor of meditative expositions, some in dialogue form, that gradually unfold their themes, turning around key symbols and events in an overarching narrative of creation, and fall and redemption. Though Law writes very differently under Boehme's inspiration, there is still a profound stylistic contrast between the two writers. It is not simply that Law is a far clearer, more orderly writer, but that he deploys Behmenist ideas as elements in a largely settled and stable doctrinal presentation. Whereas Boehme struggles for expression, revising and developing terms and theological structures as he proceeds, groping under the pressure of creativity, Law handles Behmenist language as an established discourse with which he is familiar and that he has mastered.

In addition to his fame as the author of *A Serious Call*, Law was known as a sharp theological controversialist who had tackled, with sober argument as opposed to pious fulmination, both Bishop Hoadly (1676–1761), whose views on Church and State we shall discuss below, and the Deist Matthew Tindal (1657–1733). Law's first "Behmenist" work was also a contribution to theological dispute, not Christian spirituality, and, once again, the target was Bishop Hoadly. That said, all Law's later works include a polemical dimension, as indicated by dialogue characters such as the Deist Humanus and the scholarly but spiritually obtuse Academicus. When he entered the row provoked by Bishop Hoadly's "plain account" of the Lord's Supper, which had appeared anonymously in 1735, Law defended a sacramental theology of Holy Communion from a position suggested by his recent grappling with Boehme. Since his use of Boehme here is quite modest compared with later works, the *Demonstration* indicates the original inspiration for Law's use of the "Teutonic Philosopher."

According to Hoadly's eucharistic theology, the relationship of Christians to Christ, in connection with the Lord's Supper, is external, historical, and mediated by a clear understanding as to what is involved. Christians, therefore, must participate in the communion with a correct grasp of its meaning and recognize that it is not a way to receive the benefits of Christ's death but rather an act of remembrance whereby communicants are to gird up their loins for the "actual Amendment and Reformation" of their lives, that being the truly necessary condition of enjoying any benefits from God. The supper is a "memorial," and nothing but a memorial, therefore it cannot involve the presence of Christ. We remember, do we not, only someone who is absent? So important is this that Hoadly instructs us to tell ourselves, when we receive the elements, that Christ is not there. Should we momentarily imagine him present in some particular way, we disobey him. Christ has taught us the moral conditions for salvation, and, in his death, given us the pledge that, assuming we have done our best, God will reward us when our eschatological due date pops up. That done, Christ absents himself to heaven, leaving us the *aide memoire* of the Lord's Supper. Rejecting this hyper-Zwinglian doctrine, Law draws on Boehme to provide a language for the present working of Christ—the formative energies of grace—within the believer. Boehme, therefore, funds Law's account of interior change as a transforming of the Christian through the active presence of God in Christ, a continuous divine working of which moral improvement, Hoadly's

"Amendment and Reformation" of life, is a fruit, not the cause and substance of grace. Taking up Boehme's vocabulary, Law insists that Christ is a present and "real Principle of Life to us,"[5] and so His work can never be a past or "transient" act but "something that is always doing, and never will be done." At each reception of the sacrament, at each approach and feeding in faith, we receive all of that vivifying principle "that we are then at that time capable of."[6] Christian life, therefore, is a process of continual growth, an infusing of divine life that overcomes the turbulence of selfhood and issues in the "fruit of the Spirit." However different the style and mode of argument from *A Serious Call*, Law's concern, in both his early and late works, is the spiritual renewal of the individual Christian.

Given his wide reading in pre-Reformation as well as early modern Catholic and Protestant mysticism, Law might have found a vocabulary for interior change without putting himself into the "perfect sweat" of reading Boehme. Law, however, wanted a doctrine of spiritual renewal in which the divine sources of that renewal were continuous with, and exemplified at, another level, the formative powers of God in nature. Law needed Boehme for theological work at the level of ontology. Specifically, Boehme enabled him to develop what he considered to be a thoroughgoing alternative system to the "mechanical philosophy." Since the mechanical philosophy was synonymous with Newtonianism, Law could hardly have barked at a more prestigious target. He did, however, try to excuse Newton himself, claiming, if not exactly arguing, that Newton had "plowed with Boehme's heifer," and failure to appreciate this meant that Newton's work suffered from hopelessly reductive misunderstanding.[7] In Law's reading, the mechanical model of nature severed the Creator from creation and posited a dualism between nature and spirit that fostered the kind of resolution proposed by Hoadly: an essentially mechanistic reduction, which emptied any doctrine of believers' participation in divine grace and flattened the relationship between God and humanity to a species of moral contract. Law found in Boehme a doctrine of creation animated by divine activity, open to a continuous divine expression and fulfillment, and unified through the divine working.

Though Law's later writings were never as popular as his "practical treatises," he achieved a considerable reputation as a "disciple" of Boehme. Shortly after his death, the English translations of Boehme were republished, trading on Law's reputation by including, with prominent advertisement, "Figures, illustrating [Boehme's] Principles, left by the Reverend William Law, M.A."[8] The "figures" were lifted from the work of the early Behmenist scholar Dionysius Andreas Freher (1649–1728), whom Law had certainly read but without being inspired to diagrammatize. John Byrom (1692–1763), diarist and inventor of a form of shorthand, lovingly versified sections of Law's later books, including *Way to Divine Knowledge* and *Spirit of Prayer*, so as to extend his friend's readership to those who "averse to res'ning may be taught by rimes."[9] Much of the reaction, though, was hostile. Law's readers liked being told that "the incomprehensible Trinity" is "eternally breaking forth" in "Eternal Nature" even less than they liked exhortations to avoid the theater and knock off swearing. So, if Law had earlier been castigated for casting "a noxious and baleful shade o'er all the comforts of life," now the Bishop of Oxford accused him of having "without explanation, or proof, thrown together such a heap of monstrous enthusiastical absurdities, and impieties, unintelligible jargon, and raving dreams, as in my life I never saw before. I appeal to the world; let any man *in his wits* read, and judge."[10] Holding a very different theological position from the Latitudinarian Joseph Trapp, John Wesley also wrote a strong condemnation of Law's dependence on Boehme, denouncing the heretical waywardness of a man he had once regarded as a spiritual mentor.[11]

There is some irony in all this, since, without referring to it in any way, Law abandons all the most obviously heterodox elements in Boehme's theology. Holding by the injunction to "put away all needless curiosity in Divine matters," Law is confident that he has brought Boehme's teaching to the aid of "practical Christianity," demonstrating, against "Deists, Arians, and Socinians," the accordance of Nicene Trinitarian Christianity with the truth of "Nature" and the way of human redemption. Consequently, the most striking thing about Law's Behemism is the absence of almost everything that the Romantics and German Idealists were to admire in Boehme, most specifically his exposition of the "living God" in developmental, narrative terms. We shall now look at that deed of radical excision a little more closely, after which we shall return to the apologetic side of Law's writing before concluding with a brief discussion of his "orthodox" purpose.

I RECASTING BOEHME'S NARRATIVE

In Boehme's narrative, God himself changes and develops, attaining his own nature as creative love and grace. This, therefore, is a "theogony": there is a history of both becoming and overcoming in the divine being. In the "Unground," Boehme tells us, the "unnatural, uncreaturely Deity," "there is nothing more than a single will . . . ; and he wills in himself nothing more than just to seize and find himself, go out from himself, and with the outgoing bring himself into an intuition."[12] Law, by contrast, follows the classical Christian tradition in which only created reality is capable of formation and, therefore, of being told as a story. Removing Boehme's theogonic narrative is not as straightforward as "excision" may suggest, though. If he wished to achieve any theological and narrative coherence, Law could not simply ignore those beginnings within the Divine being and start with "Eternal Nature" and the creation of the angels, even though, superficially, that appears to be just what he does do. The appearance of naive bowdlerization contributed, at least in part, to Louis Bouyer's famous judgment that Law revised Boehme into "a very British kind of mild dottiness."[13] Boehme's narrative, however, proceeds from stage to stage through anticipations and repetitions distinctive to each level. Also, though Boehme does make a clear distinction between God and the material creation, it is still the case that the temporal creation has a role in divine self-constitution. Recasting the narrative, therefore, so that change, becoming, and conflict begin with creation demands considerable reworking both as to logic and the arguments deployed to justify the telling—and with respect to content. Before outlining Law's reworking of Boehme's narrative, we shall look at two examples: Law's interpretation of God's "wrath," which mainly illustrates a new argumentative basis for a claim inspired by Boehme, and his description of "Eternal Nature," in which there is a decisive change as to doctrinal content.

Cyril O'Regan has argued that, whilst Boehme is greatly indebted to the tradition of "negative theology," especially by way of Eckhartian mysticism, his use of the "apophatic," the language of negation, is subversive.[14] Led by God's transcendence of all naming, negative theology privileges unknowing over knowing and speechlessness over speech. God is "beyond all being and knowledge"; the mysteries of "God's Word lie simple, absolute, and unchangeable in the brilliant darkness of a hidden silence."[15] The being of God, though, precisely as beyond all naming, is an inexhaustible plenitude, the perfect fullness named "apophatically" by such negative terms as "unknowable," "beyond being," "immaterial," "nameless," "infinite," and so on. The language of "kenosis" or self-emptying, as applied to the incarnation, for instance, derives its force from the originating perfection of God (cf. Philippians 2:6–11). Boehme, however, reverses this association of the apophatic with fullness. Thus, the divine "Unground," the God "beyond" and "behind" the God who finds himself as light and love, and who creates, is "natureless, passionless, creatureless . . . as it were an eternal nothing."[16] This reality beyond being, however, is not the divine plenitude but, as yet, only the potential for self-consciousness: the potential for God's subjectivity, both as internally self-related and as related "externally" to creatures.[17] The quiescence of the Unground, therefore, is disturbed and set in developmental motion by the agency of the "unfathomable will," which, in itself, undergoes becoming and change in its realization as the will of the creative and communicative God.

Abandoning the theogonic narrative, Law reasserts the plentitude and, with it, the incomprehensibility of God. More than anything, God is to be enjoyed as:

> an Infinity of mere Love, an unbeginning, never-ceasing, and forever overflowing Ocean of Meekness, Sweetness, Delight, Blessing, Goodness, Patience, and Mercy, and all this as so many blessed Streams breaking out of the Abyss of universal Love, Father, Son, and Holy Ghost, a Triune Infinity of Love and Goodness, for ever and ever giving forth nothing but the same Gifts of Light and Love, of Blessing and Joy, whether before or after the Fall, either of Angels or Men.[18]

That "Infinity of mere Love," Law tells us, means that God is "absolutely free" of wrath, which is "as inconsistent with and as impossible to have any existence in the Deity, as lumps of ice, or the hardness of intolerable frosts."[19] Law can hardly just abandon such a prominent biblical symbol as "divine wrath," however, so he projects it outwards, into the creation, insofar as the creation resists God's love. Turning from God is self-destruction, and that self-destruction is experienced as "wrath," as nature putting itself to the rack. All biblical talk of wrath leads to "two infallible truths": that wrath "worketh nowhere but in the wrathful, disordered elements and properties of fallen nature," and that God uses even this self-torment for the purposes of love.[20] Here, Law follows a similar move by Boehme. God "dwells in the abyss of the godless soul; but He is not recognizable to her in any other way than as a wrath."[21] Wrath itself, though, does "not penetrate the heart of God; but His benevolent love issues from His heart, penetrating into the most external generation of wrath, and extinguishing the latter."[22] In Boehme's case, though, the unqualified character of divine love is an outcome, an overcoming. On the way to love and light, the "First Principle" is generated from the divine being, not directly from the "Unground" but from the fourfold structure of immanent Trinity together with Wisdom. Boehme identifies the "First Principle" with desire, darkness, and wrath, and God the Father with the "fire" that overcomes this dark chaos and mediates the Son, who is light, love, and life. Law abandons this—whilst maintaining the opposition between "love," which is divine, and wrath, which does not belong to a fully divine life—he is forced to find new argument for the opposition. He does so, first by appealing to God as an eternal plenitude and identifying as love the expression of that plenitude. God's love, therefore, is his "eternal immutable Will to all Goodness."[23] Wrath, on the other hand, can only be understood as a passion, "storms of rage and resentment" that are manifested in the will to do harm. This allows Law to make the required hermeneutical move that interprets biblical assertions of God's wrath in terms of subjective—but more than merely subjective—experience and the internal contradictions of a fallen nature. Wrath is the "natural" outworking of the unnatural; it is, so to speak, coded into creation. We should, therefore, still speak of *God's* wrath:

> the Psalmist . . . saith of God, 'He giveth forth his ice like morsels, and who is able to abide his frosts'. Now, Sir, if you know how to explain this scripture and can show how ice and frost can truly be ascribed to God, though absolutely impossible to have any existence in Him, then you have an easy and unerring key.[24]

Law's transformation of "Eternal Nature" may be described more briefly since we have already referred to Boehme's version by another name. Boehme associates "Eternal Nature" with the "First Principle." Eternal Nature introduces opposition into the divine itself, a "virulent realm of anti-divine activity."[25] That said, Eternal Nature also teems with life, a boiling chaos of potential essence and entity, and, as such, is necessary for the emergence of real essence and freedom. Eternal nature is formless, but it provokes further the "theogonic struggle [which] is to get form."[26] Thus the "wrath of the Eternal Nature" is "mortified" and "does as it were die to its self-good, and is taken into the *Only-Spirit.*" "The Wrathfulness and painful source is the Root of Joy, and the Joy is the Root of the Enmity of the dark Wrathfulness; so that there is a *Contrarium*, whereby the good is made manifest, and known that it is good."[27] Love overcomes wrath and issues in eternal freedom, but "God's love would not have been made manifest without the eternal nature, that is, because the fire of love would not have been manifested without the fire of wrath."[28]

Excising the element of divine progress, Law transforms Boehme's Eternal Nature from a threatening chaos, which he relocates, as part of the consequence of angelic and human falls, to a community of blissful Platonic forms. Again, plenitude is recovered as primordial. "Eternal Nature" is "an Infinity, or boundless opening of the properties, powers, wonders, and glories of the hidden Deity."[29] God knows his own wisdom, his own goodness, his own beauty, and "Eternal Nature" is the "opening," the infinite and eternal expression in which He knows it. In this exposition of the ideal forms of every creative possibility, God enjoys all the ways in which He might give finite form to His wisdom, goodness, and beauty. "And this is not *once done*, but ever doing . . . for ever and ever breaking forth and springing up in new Forms and Openings of the abyssal Deity, in the Powers of Nature."[30] The elements of Boehme's "three principles" persist—Law even acknowledges their dynamic connection—but their relationship of conflict and struggle is reserved for the fallen world. In Eternal Nature, their harmony is without shadow of any overcoming. "Fire, Light, and Spirit" image the Trinity, as they do for Boehme, but they do so in their plenitude, not in terms of the movement of their becoming. Law's Eternal Nature is not a chaos but form, and its forms are the "first Workings of the *inconceivable God*" in which "the Trinity appears in an outward State of Glory in the Splendour of united Fire, Light, and Spirit, all kindled and distinguished, all united and beatified by the *hidden Three.*"

How, then, does Law develop his Behmenist inspirations into a soteriological narrative, a narrative in which creation and salvation are intimately related, but one without Boehme's stages of divine self-constitution? Law's later meditations and dialogues repeat, expound, and expand on a story of two falls and a continuous work of redemption. The narrative begins with the creation of the angels and their angelic kingdoms. The latter is important. Law picks up Boehme's connection between creation and imagination, a link that was to be very important in Romanticism. Both angels and, in their turn, human beings exist in worlds the forms of which proceeds from their creative, collective imagination. The resistance of "world" to imagination, or its capacity to engender dark and poisonous imaginings, is a tragedy of fallenness. The angels, therefore, have their "angelic kingdoms" in which "all the *Powers* of Eternity, treasured up in their *glassy Sea*, unfolded themselves, and broke forth in ravishing Forms of Wonder and Delight, merely in Obedience to [the angels'] Call."[31] Imagination, however, is both glory and temptation; it is ready to turn sinister. So, the angels become enamored with this power and, considering it as their own, begin "to fancy that there was *some Infinity of Power hidden* in themselves." With this "proud Imagination," they strove to take "their Kingdom, with all its Glories, to themselves, by eternally abjuring all Meekness and Submission to God."[32] They suffer a twofold self-contradiction, seizing that which they already possess as a gift, and seeking to hold that which exists only in a generous communication. Disaster follows; instead of "rising up above God (as they hoped) by breaking off from Him, there was no End of their eternal Sinking into new Depths of Slavery, under their own self-tormenting Natures."[33]

Those "angelic kingdoms" now implode into the chaos spoken of in Genesis 1:2. The angels are trapped in this ontological broil which is the outward form of their furious and desperate desire, the true formless form of "their own Nature," as they had sought it, "without God."[34] That once heavenly environment falls to "a horrible Chaos of Fire and Wrath, Thickness and Darkness, a Height and Depth of the confused, divided, fighting Properties of Nature." The counter-point of redemption, however, begins with God's halting of this otherwise eternal implosion and use of these fiery ruins of a heavenly realm as the material for a new creation. The darkness and harshness, the destructive force, is taken up and put to service in this second world. The demonic forces are thus held, bound within the order of what will be the environment for Adam. Adam's condition recapitulates that of the angels, albeit in the particular material mode proper to him. Thus, the joyful imagination reappears again, this time as a force for sustaining peace, the world being "a mixture of heaven and hell." Adam is "an heavenly artist, that had power and skill to open the wonders of God in every power of outward nature."[35] His subsequent fall proceeds, at least in the version Law provides in *Way to Divine Knowledge*, in analogy with the angels. Law follows Boehme, though, in adopting a more differentiated account of Adam's ruin, expanding upon Genesis 3.

Adam, Law tells us, is also captured by the workings of his own imagination, and he begins to love the creation rather than God, desiring to know this Paradise as his *own* world, a world apart from God. Once again, the redemptive counter-point appears. In mercy, God splits this androgynous creature by creating Eve out of Adam himself. Since Adam has turned toward the creaturely, God gives him a companion, a fellow-creature whom he may love wholeheartedly, and yet, in doing so, be referred constantly back to God through His image. A second and final fall comes quickly upon the pair, however. Adam and Eve make the disobedient choice of the "knowledge of good and evil," a choice that opens them to the darkness and the misery of insatiable desire. The narrative has already shown, though, the principle of divine working, the dialectic of opposition and its overcoming that Law found in Boehme. Redemption begins at the same moment as the pair fall since God does not leave Adam and Eve in their ruin but implants in them an "inspoken Word," "a seed of Christ," an "*Immanuel* or *God with them*, [that] should be born in all their Posterity, and be their Power of becoming again such Sons of God."[36]

The "inspoken Word" makes God's salvific action continuous with the time and space of creation. "Christ within" is always drawing the orientation of human wills towards God, a persistent counterforce to the prevailing and self-consuming curve of the heart towards itself. Law inherits the centrality of the "Will," theologically, anthropologically, and also cosmologically, from Boehme. "The Will," he insists, "whether in God or the creature, is the Ground and Seed of every Thing; is the generating working Power."[37] The fallen will, however, as Law had learned also from Paul and Augustine, is set in self-referential patterns, distracted and discordant loves. Those loves are excited and reinforced by our environment, in which the violence of hatred and conflict has broken out and shattered the peace of Eden. Not only this, our environment is imaginatively invested, as we render it "godless," absent of hope, or "secular." "Wherever, and in whatever," Law warns, "the *working* Will chooseth to *dwell* and *delight*, that becomes the Soul's *Food*, its *Condition*, its *Body*, its *Clothing*, and *Habitation*: For all these are the true and certain Effects and Powers of the working Will." The "inspoken Word" strives against the working will of fallen humanity, without which such good as there is might have long since been smothered. What is needed, however, is a new beginning, which must be "truly only a Growth of Life, or magical Birth from the Powers of Father, Son, and Holy Ghost, upon the working Will in the Soul."[38] Law opposes the doctrines of Christ as the Word "inspoken" from the beginning, and of a necessary new birth for the will, to Hoadly's elimination of grace as an interior work of God. Also, in response to the Deist flattening of soteriology and creation into a universal "religion of nature," Law mounts his own "universalist" coordination of nature and salvation, grounded in God's continually active presence within nature and humanity, and having its culmination in the Incarnate Word, the Christ without.

The importance of the incarnate, as opposed to the "inspoken" Word, was not obvious to some of Law's sympathetic readers, among whom were Quakers and others influenced by Boehme. Law, however, is very definite on the subject:

> Let no one here think to charge me with Disregard to the Holy Jesus, who was born of the *Virgin Mary*, or with setting up an *inward* Saviour in Opposition to the outward *Christ*, whose History is recorded in the Gospel. . . . [I] will assert no inward Redemption but what wholly proceeds from, and is effected by that Life-giving Redeemer, who died on the Cross for our Redemption.[39]

On the other hand, Law rejects not only the historicizing reductionism of the extreme Latitudinarians, and the Socinian emphasis on Jesus as our teacher, but also the much more normative account of justification as "imputed righteousness," based upon a forensic understanding of atonement. Boehme, whose criticism of Lutheran orthodoxy on the matter of "imputed," rather than actual, righteousness, was furious, confirmed Law in interpreting "justification" as a "regeneration" that made the believer actually righteous, if not finally so. Christians, then, are not merely recipients of the imputed righteousness of Christ: Christ works within them a righteousness that is their own. If salvation is regeneration, and regeneration a new working of the will, Christ's own righteousness must be the originating power of the believer's own "devout and holy life." Jesus thus possesses a twofold significance. In his life and death, as the Incarnate Word, the "wrath and hell that sin had brought forth" was extinguished. By this overcoming within himself of the wrathful and destructive will, Christ "became a fountain of the first heavenly life to the whole of mankind."[40] Here, incarnate Christ and inspoken Word become correlative, via Law's other term for the Christ within, the metaphor "seed of Christ." Law takes up the Pauline identification of Christ as the "Second Adam," who has become "a life-giving spirit" and, as such, a formative environment for the "seed of Christ" within human beings. "As in Adam all die, so in Christ shall all be made alive," as Christ works upon and within believers through the outwardness that is his bodily presence in Scripture, sacrament, and Church.[41] Crucially, for Law, there is nothing "arbitrary" or "unnatural" about this, arbitrariness and contradiction with nature being accusations that Deists routinely leveled at Christianity's narrative of revelation and salvation. On the contrary, Law argues, the dynamic of desiring and adapting, flourishing, and growth enjoyed by creatures within their proper environments is found throughout nature and cannot possibly be opposed to spiritual renewal, which is simply the highest instance of it. Inward and Outward, universal seed and historical, and incarnate Christ are brought together in an analogy that holds throughout creation:

> Inwardly Man has a *Seed* of the Divine Life given into the Birth of his Soul. . . . Outwardly he has *Jesus Christ*, who as a *Sun* of Righteousness, is always casting forth his enlivening Beams on this *inward Seed*, to kindle and call it forth to the Birth, doing that to this Seed of Heaven in Man, which the Sun in the Firmament is always doing to the vegetable Seeds in the Earth.[42]

Christ is thus "naturally" the "quickener" of life in us. God does nothing except "in a *natural* Way, or according to the Nature of Things." It takes the poverty-stricken rationalism of a Deist to miss the point that God's working "in a *natural* way," a way that, according to His nature and that of His creation, "must be *mysterious* to Man, because it is doing something *more* and *higher* than his Senses or Reason ever saw done."[43]

II BOEHME CONTRA DEISM

All is done "in a *natural* way, or according to the Nature of Things." Having explained Boehme's doctrine of the "seven properties," Law's spokesman, Theophilus, reiterates his warning that these weighty teachings should not merely serve intellectual satisfactions. They are not for the building up of opinions about the world, a storehouse of knowledge to be held in the mind, possessed like the angels wanted to seize their heaven, and Adam his Eden. Instead, their sole purpose is "to compel you, *by every Truth of Nature*, to turn to Christ . . . not as notionally apprehended, or historically known; but as experimentally found, living, speaking, and working, in your Soul." This alone is the purpose of "all that *Jacob Behmen* has written."[44] Law's claim for Boehme's teaching is that it opens creation, so that we recognize in "every Truth of Nature" the single working of God. "For this is the Will and Working of Heaven; it has but one Will, and one Work; and that is, to change all the Wrath, Evil, and Disorder of Nature, into a Kingdom of God."[45] Believers are those who allow this Will to be born in them, for the regeneration of the human will and the peaceful ordering of Nature's forces now contending within them. Put differently, Law read Boehme as offering an account of nature and grace that is neither dualistic nor monist, one that reads all creation as the expressive and formative field of divine Spirit without compromising the distinction between Creator and creature.[46] The narrative that we have outlined, therefore, unifies soteriology and the doctrine of creation; it is an ontologically freighted narrative that discloses the "one Work" that operates diversely, but to a single end, at all times and at all levels of created existence.

Arguing that Christianity is "according to Nature" is the marker of Law's continuing apologetic concern. His Behmenist writings contend, as had his practical treatises, for an "authentic Christianity," in an age Law judged as astray in Christian practice and lacking an understanding that revealed the necessity of that practice—its ground in our humanity and our world. "According to the Nature of Things," then, is a polemically loaded phrase. It challenged Deism in general and, specifically, the notorious writing of Matthew Tindal, "*Christianity as old as the Creation: or the Gospel a Republication of the Religion of Nature.*"[47] Law had already written against Tindal a few years before he got into that Behmenist sweat. His principle argument against the Deist anticipated the later books in that Law recognized the circular relationship between one's understanding of "Nature" and the theological wisdom drawn from it. He tried to break that circle with the sharp observation that, if God acts according to the "Nature of Things," then He most certainly acts according to His own nature, which is essentially mysterious and beyond the coordinates of finite reason. Tindal's rationalist reductionism was self-defeating. Law's continuing critique of Deism, a theme in almost all his Behmenist books, might seem excessive. As a movement, Deism was a minority affair, and the arguments of Tindal and others struck too deeply at the orthodox assumptions of Anglican clergy.[48] Also, they were not particularly persuasive. Law, however, understood Deism as an extreme version of a more widespread theological decay. Like that much less orthodox reader of Boehme, William Blake, Deism stood for a spiritual condition. It is the distillation of worldly faith: an absent God derived from a mechanical nature who dispenses eschatological rewards for an outward obedience.

Not all Christian apologists who appealed to the book of Nature as an apologetic prolegomena to Christian practice were narrowly rationalist. In the same year that Law published the *Appeal*, Edward Young began work on the 10,000 lines of his poem *Night Thoughts, on Life, Death, and Immortality*, later printed in nine books between 1742 and 1746. Much of the poem is apologetic. Young seeks to persuade the dissolute and free-thinking Lorenzo to attend to his soul and return to orthodox Christianity. Young appeals primarily, though, not to the story of Israel, Christ, and the Church, but to the sublimities of the night sky as a testament to God's power. Young, who had the ability to yell in blank verse and never wrote a line not aspiring to the momentous, tries to overwhelm Lorenzo with theologically suggestive immensities:

> An undevout astronomer is mad.
> True, all things speak a GOD;
> but, in the small, Men trace out Him;
> in great, He seizes man;
> Seizes, and elevates, and wraps, and fills
> With new inquiries.

Young's stargazers are rationally complacent; the night sky takes reason to new heights, quite beyond its quotidian self. Our souls, "wither'd, shrunk,/ Blighted by Earth's unwholesome air,/ Will blossom here; spread all her faculties/ To these bright ardours."[49] "How glorious then appears the mind of Man . . . great objects make/ Great minds enlarging as their views enlarge;/ Those still more godlike, as these more Divine."[50] Young's apologetic, though scarcely Deist, remains fundamentally, and for similar reasons, at odds with those "Truths of Nature" that Law presents "to compel you to turn to Christ." Young leaves intact the dualism between the books of "Nature" and "Revelation," and even hints that the advantage lies with the former since the night sky is "Scripture authentic! Uncorrupt by man." Most seriously from Law's perspective, though, Young, like the Deists, perverts the structure of humanity's belonging in nature and, therefore, the unity and form of God's "one Work." The poet ushers Lorenzo into Nature as a cosmic theater, a display of wonders for his admiration and intellectual enlargement. Emotional excitements follow, too, but they do not dissolve the structural distance between spectator and play. "O let me gaze!—Of gazing there's no end. . . . An eye of awe and wonder let me roll,/ And roll for ever; who can satiate sight?"[51] The soteriological metaphor here is not regeneration but elevation. Awe before "Nature's system of divinity," an expression that turns Law's "working Nature" inside out, forces us, Young promises, to "think of more than man." Such thinking, though, turns back to glorify the human: "boundless mind that affects a boundless space: That vast surveys, and the Sublime of things, / The soul assimilate, and make her great."[52] From where Law stands, though, this is a grotesque self-complacency.

Nature, in Law's reading of Boehme, is not theater but environment. Humanity finds itself within nature. There is no opposition of nature and spirit here and so no dividing as spectacle and spectator. After Adam, nature is the truncated nature of the fallen imagination, our desires and actions disordered from within by the civil strife that troubles the whole creation. In Christ, however, nature is opened to its origins in "Eternal Nature," becoming the medium of grace, the one working of Christ within and without. Creation is thus returning to its purpose, as "the *Infinity* of Height and Depth" within which "boundless Love" forms expressions of divine glory. "All the striving and working Properties of Nature are only to give *Essence* and *Substance*, Life and Strength, to the *invisible hidden Spirit of Love*, that it may come forth into outward Activity."[53] The believer does not conclude to the workings of God from the evidence of her gazing upon the world. Rather, the believer suffers an inward recognition, the awakening of desire for that active, embracing context through which an inner transformation, the regeneration of the will, begins. Law's critique of Deism applies also to apologetics of orthodox intent like Young's *Night Thoughts*, as well as to the more sober physico-theologies of design. All objectify nature, whether teeming with wonders or intricate in mechanical detail, as an evidential source that stands over against the human mind. Thus, humanity is divided from nature, nature from revelation and grace, and the spirit from participation in God's single and "universal Remedy of all Evil broken forth in Nature and Creature."[54] Early in the following century, Coleridge would launch much the same attack on William Paley and the still lively trade in "evidences" for Christianity.

III BOEHME WITHIN THE LIMITS OF ORTHODOXY?

Joseph Trapp's dismissal of Boehme as an "illiterate enthusiast," from whom one could only expect "falsehood and frenzy," stung Law to especially fulsome praise of the "Teutonic Philosopher." Jacob Boehme "may be placed among those who had received the highest Measures of Light, Wisdom, and Knowledge *from Above*. He was no more a *human writer*, spoke no more from *Opinion*, *Conjecture*, or *Reason*, in what he published to the world, than St. *John* did, when he put his *Revelation* into writing." Unsurprisingly, Law is quick to qualify the comparison with the New Testament, and he does so with a hermeneutic claim that places Boehme in relation to orthodox Christianity. The shoemaker's distinctive mission was to "open" up the "deepest Ground," and reveal the innermost necessity of Christianity, as witnessed to in Scripture and taught by the Church. In no sense had Boehme anything "to alter, or add, either in the *Form*, or Doctrine of Religion." He neither innovated nor completed because he "had no new Truths of Religion to Propose to the World."[55]

If the distinction between "adding" and "opening" is one prong of Law's defense of Boehme's orthodox credentials, the other is his stress on the performative character of Boehme's writing against any appearance of encouraging theological or philosophical speculation. *Academicus*, the intellectual fall-guy in Law's dialogues, exemplifies this distinction. His excitement at understanding something of Theophilus's expositions is routinely slapped down as a desire for intellectual satisfaction and control. Boehme, Law argues, never sought to satisfy any speculative urge, nor to inform or build up knowledge. All his writings intend is to provoke the reader to open herself to "the Birth of . . . Light and Love." Intellectual wrangling, or even the simple desire for explanation, misses the entire purpose and character of these books: "to help anyone to work with his Brain for clear Notions, and rational Conceptions, of what he has written, is helping him to do and be that, which all his Works, from the beginning to the End, absolutely declare against, as contrary to the whole Nature and End of them."[56]

At one level, Law wants to head off in advance an assessment of Boehme from the perspective of theological controversy. He is also, though, returning to his critique of dualism—in this case, that of reason and desire or, in characteristically eighteenth-century terms, rationality and enthusiasm. There is a more subtle point than his critics would allow behind Law's sometimes vigorous and deliberately provocative dismissal of the productions of reason. Theology seen as a body of truths that may be entertained, considered, and argued about, theology as the product of "reason," is only possible because the desire to know has fallen apart from the desire for the good. Thus, in the internal war between desire and desire, of the divided will, knowing can insulate against loving, and intellectual stimulation can be mistaken for spiritual renewal. The truth of Boehme's writings, according to Law, lies in that transformation that is the new birth of the will, but the working of that will reconciles knowing and willing as the believer now recognizes, working within her, the divine power active throughout nature. A merely intellectual apprehension of truth, a "notional Christianity," is, therefore, a symptom of estrangement from God because the will to the good is severed from the will to truth, which results in, among other things, arguments over Boehme's orthodoxy and accusations of frenzied enthusiasm. The "deep manifestations of the Grounds and Reasons" that Law finds in Boehme, effect, therefore, a transcending of the oppositional pairing of "rationality and enthusiasm," and cannot be understood from within it.

Law's primary defense, then, against charges that Boehme had led him into heresy, charges made by Bishop Warburton and John Wesley among others, was to insist that Boehme was not an innovator of new doctrines, and that reading him for the purposes of doctrinal assessment was to misread him at the most fundamental level. Law was also prepared, as we have seen, to dispute quite directly accusations of pantheism and of privileging the "Christ within" above the "Christ without."[57] All that said, Law was also willing, under Boehme's leading, to challenge some doctrinal elements considered normative in Anglicanism and creedal Protestantism. It is unfair, therefore, to dismiss him as a theological bowdlerizer. The most notorious instance in this regard is Law's rejection of the almost universally accepted teaching that God created the world "out of nothing."

Creation *ex nihilo* denied that God created either an eternal and divine world out of his own "substance," an essentially pantheist solution, or that he created out of some preexisting matter, a possibility that denied God as the sole ground of all being. The classical Christian position is that creation is an absolute gift. God did not have to create. He filled no lack in doing so, needed no help in doing so. Moreover, the creation has, thereby, its own integrity and relative independence: it is not illusion or mere appearance but real with all the reality and integrity needed to be the object of divine love. Nothing of this, however, would Law have rejected. Law's version of "Eternal Nature" might have encouraged a verbal dispute with creation out of nothing, along the lines that creation is, in truth, not from nothing but from "Eternal Nature." That, though, would be a rather weak motivation. *Ex nihilo* in the classic sense did not—except in nominalist versions—challenge the affirmation that all the perfections of creation were contained beforehand in the divine Word. Claiming that creation manifests the Divine glory and eternal Wisdom does not contradict creation *ex nihilo*. Boehme's rejection of the doctrine was strongly motivated through his account of divine self-constitution, which gives a theogonic background to "all qualities in nature are one in another as one *quality*, in that manner as God is all, and as all things descend and come forth from him . . . the *heart* or fountain of nature."[58] Law abandons the intra-divine story, however, and so seems left with only weak grounds to abandon such a familiar Christian position on creation. Yet, he is hardly moderate in rejecting it: "it is a *Fiction*, big with the grossest Absurdities."[59]

The force behind Law's view takes us back to that dualism of nature and revelation, the book of creation and the text of Scripture. Law regards "from nothing" as implicitly denying that God in any way gives himself or manifests himself in creation:

> ["Out of nothing"] *separates* every thing from God, it leaves *no Relation* between God and the Creature, nor any *Possibility* for any *Power, Virtue, Quality*, or *Perfection* of God, to be in the Creature: for if it is created *out of nothing*, it cannot have *something* of God in it.[60]

If the world comes "from nothing," Law reasons, then it reflects nothing, manifests nothing beyond its own appearance.

> If that which begins to be comes out of Nothing, it can only have the Nature of that out of which it comes; and therefore can have no more said about it, why it is this or that, than can be said of that Nothing, from whence it comes.[61]

A creation "from nothing" can "bear no testimony of God." In other words, if this creation has no precedent within the life of God, such as is given through "Eternal Nature," then the character of the world, that it is this world rather than another, is entirely *arbitrary*. That is the key term. In debates over the rationalist theology of the Deists, "natural" and "arbitrary" were fundamental and opposing categories. The God who calls a particular people, sends his Son, and demands faith in Jesus' saving work is an "arbitrary" God, whereas the God who demands only that we act according to what we can reason out for ourselves is behaving "according to nature," and his religion is "natural." This reasoning was not limited to Deists; Hoadly deploys it in eliminating Christ's presence from the Lord's Supper. Law read back into *creatio ex nihilo* the mechanical philosophy that the Deists assumed, along with all Newtonians: that creation is a self-contained rational system of matter in motion.[62] He is determined to expose and undermine the opposition natural/arbitrary as a rationalist rending of the Spirit's "one working," the fissure at the root of all "notional Christianity." It is not, therefore, revelation that is arbitrary but the Deists' distinction itself and, with it, their account of nature. Creation "out of nothing" must go since it favors this understanding of nature, which is arbitrary both in the sense of being a groundless fancy of the fallen imagination and also, in itself, a world flattering to human reason, not a nature revelatory all the way down. The mechanical philosophy, Law argued, gives us only "*Facts* and *Appearances*" and leaves humanity in a world that is, for all the appearance of intelligibility, an enigma that refers only back to itself. In such a creation, the soul must either be absorbed into the mechanism or be left without its true environment—a stranger among the cogs and wheels.

For many who have learned from Jacob Boehme, especially those of philosophical or theosophical interests, Law's interpretations of this "wonderful treasure" are underwhelming; he simply leaves out "all the best bits." He also invites a graver conclusion. Comparing Law's work with Freher's studies of Boehme, Charles Muses concludes that Law simply did not understand either Boehme or his German expositor.[63] Some of Law's appropriations give substance to this. Our restoration to Adamic glory, he claims, requires that Jesus not only take on our fallen flesh but also have "veiled" under that flesh "an holy humanity of heavenly flesh and blood." "Our common faith, therefore, obliges us to hold, that our Lord had the perfection of the first Adam's flesh and blood united with, and veiled under that fallen nature, which he took upon him from the blessed virgin Mary." The genealogy of this probably goes back, via Boehme, to the sixteenth-century mystic Valentin Weigel (1533–1588), as well as to the "radical" reformer Caspar Schwenckfeld (1489–1561).[64] Law seems not to notice that this undermines the integrity of Christ's humanity and so threatens his recapitulatory doctrine of Christ's work. Owing as much to Irenaeus as Boehme, that doctrine required a robust account of Jesus's full humanity as that in which he reversed Adam's disobedience and overcame the domination of "wrath and hell." Stephen Hobhouse has noted, too, Law's unsatisfactory adoption of the "seven properties," which, though the first three provide opportunity for arresting images of interior conflict, remains truncated and poorly integrated.[65] Nevertheless, as his rebuffs to poor Academicus suggest, Law is not an exegete of Boehme, unlike the insightful and painstaking Freher. Law was inspired by Boehme and inspired to a theological and apologetic purpose of his own. To use a Coleridgean term, his reading of Boehme was "oceanic;" it spread widely, picking up, by and large with fair consistency, only what served its purpose. Law's contribution and importance is more justly regarded if he is placed within an English tradition, critical of modernity, and especially of its dualisms and its rationalist reductions of humanity and nature. This tradition provides a "radically conservative celebration of the mystical significance of the cosmos, the human body, human sexuality and human language," which, in its later representatives, has also strenuously opposed any reductive metaphysics generated out of the natural sciences.[66] Traherne, Burke, Coleridge, Keble, Ruskin, and Chesterton all belong in this line. William Law is one point, and not the only one, at which Boehme entered and informed that tradition, one otherwise so theologically at variance with his teaching.

NOTES

1. The "Behmenist" works include *A Demonstration of the Gross and Fundamental Errors of a late Book, called 'A Plain Account of the Nature and End of the Sacrament of the Lord's Supper'* (1737); *The Grounds and Reasons for Christian Regeneration* (1739); *An Appeal to All who Doubt the Truths of the Gospel* (1740); *An Earnest and Serious Answer to Dr. Trapp's Discourse* and *Some Animadversions on Dr. Trapp's Reply* (1740); *The Spirit of Prayer* (1749); *The Way to Divine Knowledge* (1752); *The Spirit of Love* (1752–54).
2. For discussions of Law's use of Boehme, see S. Hobhouse, "Fides et Ratio. The book which introduced Jacob Boehme to William Law," *Journal of Theological Studies* 37 (1936): 350–68; A. Wormhoudt, "Newton's natural philosophy in the Behmenistic works of William Law," *Journal of the History of Ideas* 10 (1949): 411–29; P. Malekin, "Jacob Boehme's Influence on William Law," *Studia Neophilologica* 36 (1964): 245–60; P. Grant, "William Law's *Spirit of Love*: Rationalistic Argument and Behmenist Myth," in Patrick Grant, *Literature and the Discovery of Method in the English*

Renaissance (Athens, GA: University of Georgia Press, 1985), 124–45; C. D. A. Leighton, "William Law, Behmenism and Counter Enlightenment," *Harvard Theological Review* 91 (1998): 301–20.

3. Recalled from a conversation with Francis Okely, shortly before Law's death; see, Christopher Walton, *Notes and Materials for an Adequate Biography of . . . William Law* (London: privately printed, 1854), n. 426.
4. William Law, *A Practical Treatise Upon Christian Perfection (Works of William Law, Vol. 3)* (Wipf & Stock Publishers, 2001), 6.
5. William Law, *A Demonstration of the Errors of a Late Book and the Grounds and Reasons of the Christian Regeneration (Works of William Law, Vol. 5)*, (Wipf & Stock Publishers, 2001), 39.
6. Ibid., 5:47.
7. William Law, *William Law: Serious Call to a Devout and Holy Life, and the Spirit of Love* (Mahwah, NJ: Paulist Press, 1978), 375; Henri Talon, ed., *Selections from the Journals & Papers of John Byrom, Poet, Diarist, Short-hand Writer, 1691–1763* (London: Rockliff, 1951), 221–22. Law's claim was robustly rejected, see; Stephen Hobhouse, ed., *Selected Mystical Writings of William Law* (Kessinger, 2010), 344–47.
8. William Law, ed. *The Works of Jacob Behmen, the Teutonic Theosopher*, (4 vols., London: M. Richardson, 1764–81).
9. Talon ed., *Selections from Byrom*, 21.
10. *A Letter to Mr. Law; Occasion'd by reading his Treatise on Christian Perfection* (London: 1728), 22; Joseph Trapp, *A Reply to Mr. Law's Earnest and Serious Answer* (London: L. Gilliver, 1741), 41.
11. *The Works of John Wesley* (3rd edn., 14 vols., London, 1831; reprinted, Grand Rapids, MI, no date), vol. 9, 466–509.
12. Jacob Boehme, *On the Election of Grace and Theosophic Questions* (Kessinger Publishing, 1992), 1.9.
13. Cited in Law, *Serious Call; Spirit of Love*, 22.
14. Cyril O'Regan, *Gnostic Apocalypse: Jacob's Boehme's Haunted Narrative* (State University of New York Press, 2002), 69–82.
15. Colm Luibheid, trans., *Pseudo-Dionysius: The Complete Works* (New York: Paulist Press International, 1993), 135.
16. Boehme, *Election of Grace and Theosophic Questions*, 1.3.
17. O'Regan, *Gnostic Apocalypse*, 71–75. To expound God's self-relatedness, Boehme's deploys Trinitarian language, though not in the classical Christian sense of three persons or "subsistent relations," who are co-eternal and co-equal with respect to the divine nature and whose relations are revealed in their salvific work.
18. Law, *Serious Call; Spirit of Love*, 391.
19. Ibid., 422, 425.
20. Ibid., 425.
21. Jacob Boehme, *Mysterium Magnum*, 3rd ed. (Sophia Perennis, 2007), 60.31.
22. Jacob Boehme, *Aurora* (London: John Watkins/John Clarke, 1960), 85.
23. Law, *Serious Call; Spirit of Love*, 394.
24. Ibid., 423–24.
25. O'Regan, *Gnostic Apocalypse*, 37.
26. John Joseph Stoudt, *Jacob Boehme: His Life and Thought* (Wipf and Stock Publishers, 2004), 231.
27. Boehme, *Mysterium Magnum*, 28.4.
28. Boehme, *Election of Grace and Theosophic Questions*, 7.29.
29. Law, *Serious Call; Spirit of Love*, 418.
30. Ibid., 46.

31. William Law, *The Spirit of Prayer (The Works of William Law, Vol. 7)* (Wipf & Stock Publishers, 2001), 8.
32. Ibid.
33. Ibid.
34. William Law, *The Way to Divine Knowledge* (Kessinger, 2010), 76.
35. Law, *Spirit of Prayer*, 7.
36. Ibid., 95.
37. Law, *Way to Divine Knowledge*, 149.
38. Ibid., 162.
39. Law, *Spirit of Prayer*, 23.
40. William Law, *An Earnest and Serious Answer to Dr. Trapp's Discourse; An Appeal to All Who Doubt the Truths of the Gospel (Works of William Law Vol. 6)* (Wipf & Stock, 2001), 65.
41. 1 Corinthians 15:22.
42. Law, *Spirit of Prayer*, 32.
43. Law, *Way to Divine Knowledge*, 262, italics added.
44. Ibid., 252.
45. Ibid., 251.
46. Law summarizes both aspects in a letter: "whereas the operation of God, in its whole kind and nature, is as different from anything that can be done by creatures, as the work and manner of creation, is different, in power, nature, and manner, from that which creatures can do to one another. . . . This, and this alone is the working of the deity in heaven and on earth; nothing comes from him, or is done by him through all the eternity of his creatures, but that essential manifestation of himself in them, which began the glory and perfection of their first existence," William Law, *A Humble, Earnest, and Affectionate Address to the Clergy; A Collection of Letters; Letters to a Lady Inclined to Enter the Romish Church (The Works of William Law, Vol. 9)* (Wipf & Stock Publishers, 2001), Letter XXV.
47. Matthew Tindal, *Christianity as Old as Creation or the Gospel: A Republication of the Religion of Nature (British Philosophers and Theologians of the 17th and 18th Centuries Series)* (Garland, 1978).
48. Though the number of those who identified themselves as Deists is small, the influence of Deism was considerable and enduring; see Margaret Jacob, *Newtonians and the English Revolution 1689–1720*, 1st ed. (Cornell University Press, 1976), 201–50.
49. Edward Young, *Young's Night Thoughts, or Thoughts on Life, Death, and Immortality* (New York: Worthington Co., 1889), 240.
50. Ibid., 252.
51. Ibid., 256.
52. Ibid., 250.
53. Law, *Serious Call; Spirit of Love*, 366.
54. Law, *Spirit of Prayer*, 108.
55. Law, *An Earnest and Serious Answer to Dr. Trapp's Discourse; An Appeal to All Who Doubt the Truths of the Gospel (Works of William Law Vol. 6)*, 201, 205.
56. Law, *Way to Divine Knowledge*, 222–23.
57. An accusation of Spinozism came from Bishop Warburton; see, B. W Young, *Religion and Enlightenment in Eighteenth-Century England: Theological Debate from Locke to Burke* (Oxford University Press, 1998), 133.
58. Boehme, *Aurora*, 41.
59. Law, *Spirit of Prayer*, 75.
60. Ibid, 76.

61. Law, *Way to Divine Knowledge*, 248.
62. Strictly speaking, of course, Newton's universe was not wholly self-contained as it required preservation from gravitational collapse.
63. Charles A. Muses, *Illumination on Jacob Boehme: The Work of Dionysius Andreas Freher* (New York: King's Crown Press, 1951), 137.
64. O'Regan, *Gnostic Apocalypse*, 96–97.
65. Stephen Hobhouse, ed., *Selected Mystical Writings of William Law* (Kessinger, 2010), 344–47.
66. John Milbank, "After Rowan: The Coherence and Future of Anglicanism," item, April 4, 2012, http://www.abc.net.au/religion/articles/2012/04/04/3470498.htm.

9 Boehme and German Romanticism

Kristine Hannak

Du wirst das letzte Reich verkünden, Was tausend Jahre soll bestehn; Wirst überschwenglich Wesen finden, Und Jakob Böhmen wiedersehn.[1]	You will proclaim the last kingdom Which will last a thousand years; You will find the abundance of being And meet Jacob Boehme again.

These lines, taken from the poem *An Tieck* [*To Tieck*] (1800) by Novalis (Friedrich von Hardenberg), explicitly linked the Romantic hope for universal renewal with Jacob Boehme's name. Indeed, Boehme's writings played an important role in the literature of German Romanticism around 1800. It was Novalis's friend Ludwig Tieck who had introduced Boehme's works to the literary and philosophical circle of the young Romantics in Jena, thus preparing the ground for the texts' revival and assigning them a key role in Romantic reflections on new concepts of art, religion, and nature.

I HISTORICAL CONTEXT AND PATHS OF TRANSMISSION OF BOEHME'S WORKS IN THE EIGHTEENTH CENTURY

Although Boehme's writings had been part of a Spiritualist and Pietist subculture throughout the seventeenth and eighteenth centuries, they had, for over a century, been marginalized from the major philosophical and literary discourses as the outpourings of a "shoemaker-prophet." Around 1800, however, a young generation of poets born in the 1770s, who lived at a time of profound social and economic change, rediscovered these texts. These poets and writers included, besides Ludwig Tieck (1773–1853) and Novalis (1772–1801), the famous brothers Friedrich (1772–1829) and August Wilhelm Schlegel (1767–1845), their friends/wives Dorothea Veit (Schlegel) (1763–1839) and Caroline Böhmer (Schlegel, later Schelling) (1763–1809), Wilhelm Heinrich Wackenroder (1773–1798), the philosopher Friedrich Joseph Wilhelm Schelling (1775–1854), and the painter Philipp Otto Runge (1777–1810).

Around 1800, burgeoning industrialization accelerated the pace of life and shaped an understanding of nature and society that was increasingly technical, secular, and profane.[2] There was a concern that technical progress would deprive nature of its mystique and human experience of a deeper meaning beyond the constraints of economic necessities. The French Revolution, which had inspired high hopes for personal and political freedom in the early 1790s, had turned increasingly violent from 1792 onwards. The German states were quick to implement strict social and political measures to counter the spread of revolution and, where necessary, to restore the old order.[3] Yet despite relative political stability, the late eighteenth century saw profound philosophical and social challenges that were perceived as an increasing disintegration of the early modern worldview. The traditional order of knowledge and art, the social hierarchies, and the entire Christian outlook were profoundly challenged by changes that unfolded during the eighteenth century, triggered and accompanied by philosophical criticism of the Enlightenment.

The young Romantics had grown up studying the philosophy of Kant, Fichte, Hemsterhuis, Leibniz, Spinoza, and Plato.[4] But while they were in many respects children of the Enlightenment, these young intellectuals distanced themselves from previous generations when it came to demands for rationality and utilitarianism, based on a Protestantism that rejected inner visions or the idea of a divine spark in the human soul. The sacralization of art and the fascination with the world of Catholicism and the Middle Ages, as depicted in Wackenroder's and Tieck's *Herzensergießungen eines kunstliebenden Klosterbruders* [*Confessions of the Heart by an art-loving Friar*] (1797) or in Novalis's *Die Christenheit oder Europa* [*Christianity or Europe*] (1799), reflect the search for a more emotional, intuitive approach to reality that might surpass the faculty of reason. In the intellectual circles of early Romanticism, the world of art became the idealized contrast to the world of rationality. Today's theories about the autonomy of art, independent from all demands of utility and from any kind of rules, can be seen as an outgrowth of this conflict in the Romantic era.

To these thinkers and artists, however, the world of art not only offered an alternative realm where individuals might find new wholeness and deeper meaning, but also promised to be a medium that might lead to a spiritual renewal of society generally. In this respect, the Romantics' hopes matched the aspirations of some of Boehme's more notable readers during the first phase of his reception. After the hopes of the French Revolution were shattered in the German territories, the Romantics believed—just as Friedrich Schiller did—that a transformation of people's consciousness would have to precede real political and social change. This historical context helps explain the Romantics' belief in the power of art and also their rediscovery of Boehme's works. Just as the seventeenth-century mystic had challenged church doctrines and had tried to inspire a theological completion of the Reformation, so too did the Romantic artists consider the philosophical rationalism of the Enlightenment as the first and still-to-be-overcome step of an emergent new era. And just as Boehme had predicted the dawn of a Golden Age, which he had called the time of lilies, so too did the Romantics long for the dawn of a Golden Age, one brought about by art.

While Boehme's works had not been forgotten during the eighteenth century, they were certainly not included in dominant discourses. Leading Enlightenment thinkers such as Johann Christoph Gottsched (1700–1766) had considered Boehme and his readers to be part of a culture of "superstition," one that they hoped their generation would overcome.[5] Yet Boehme's texts circulated in a strong subculture of Hermetic, mystic, and Paracelsian thought, kept alive largely by Pietist readers.[6] In fact, the novel *Theobald oder die Schwärmer* [*Theobald, or: The Enthusiasts*] (1784) by Johann Heinrich Jung-Stilling (1740–1817), a leading voice of the Pietist Awakening Movement, outlines the traditions of late eighteenth-century "enthusiasm" from a contemporary perspective and highlights three major sources: Jacob Boehme; the English Behmenists John Pordage (1607–1681) and Jane Lead (1624–1704); and the French-Flemish mystics Antoinette Bourignon (1616–1680), Madame Guyon (1648–1717), and Pierre Poiret (1646–1719). Jung-Stilling also mentions a variety of Pietist authors influenced by these sources, such as the couple Johann Wilhelm Petersen (1649–1727) and Johanna Eleonora Petersen (1644–1724), Johann Conrad Dippel (1673–1734), and Ernst Christoph Hochmann von Hochenau (1760–1721).[7]

In the second half of the eighteenth century, Friedrich Christoph Oetinger (1702–1782) acted as Pietist mediator between Boehme's writings and Friedrich Wilhelm Joseph Schelling's philosophy. Oetinger read Boehme as an alternative to the rationalistic philosophy of Gottfried Wilhelm Leibniz (1646–1716), Christian Wolff (1679–1754), and to the occasionalism of Nicolas de Malebranche (1638–1715). Inspired by Boehme's concept of a non-dualistic relationship between matter and spirit, Oetinger developed the idea of bodily forms as the "end" and completion of God's creative paths, thus preparing the ground for Schelling's philosophy of nature, which is again set against the rationalistic transcendentalism of Immanuel Kant.[8]

Thus, through the conduit of Pietism, leading philosophers and poets drew on an undercurrent of theosophical and Hermetic writings, although they often distanced themselves publicly from authors such as Boehme. The most famous example is certainly Johann Wolfgang Goethe (1749–1832). The young Goethe came into contact with Hermetic undercurrents in Pietist circles while convalescing in Frankfurt in 1768–69. Johann Friedrich Metz (1720–1782), an alchemist doctor, and Susanna Katharina von Klettenberg (1723–1774), a member of the pietistic Herrnhut sect, introduced him to alchemical and mystical literature. Furthermore, Goethe's account of his reading list in *Dichtung und Wahrheit* reveals that he read Paracelsus and

Basilius Valentinus as well as Gottfried Arnold's *Unpartheiische Kirchen- und Ketzerhistorie* [*Impartial History of Heretics*] (1699–1700).[9] When, in *Dichtung und Wahrheit*, Goethe explains his so-called private religion by referring to the myth of Lucifer, he stresses the Hermetic idea of universal contraction and expansion, which resembles Boehme's doctrine of the light and dark principle in all things.[10]

Yet, despite a certain mediated influence, Boehme's writings had no major impact on the leading discourses of the late Enlightenment. To the contrary: the term "Boehmenist" could even be used by late Enlightenment authors such as the literary critic Friedrich Nicolai (1733–1811) to make fun of opponents—"Boehme" had become a synonym for someone who wrote in a bizarre and incomprehensible style. In Nicolai's case in particular, this epithet was directed against the *Athenäum*, the leading journal of the Romantics, and its editor, Friedrich Schlegel.[11]

II BOEHME AND THE POETIC IMAGINATION IN ROMANTIC POETICS AND LITERATURE

It was Ludwig Tieck, author of the novels *Geschichte des Herrn William Lovell* [*The History of Mr. William Lovell*] (1795–96) and *Franz Sternbalds Wanderungen* [*The Wanderings of Franz Sternbald*] (1798), who bought an edition of Boehme's *Aurora* in 1797. Tieck became a passionate reader of Boehme from 1799, introducing Boehme's writings to his friend Novalis and thus to the circle that became known as the early "Romantics" in Germany.[12] Inspired by Tieck, Novalis checked out nine volumes of the Amsterdam edition of Boehme's works from the Dresden library in November 1800,[13] confessing that he had found a profound poetic inspiration in Boehme. In 1801, Tieck introduced Boehme's writings to the painter Philipp Otto Runge, who used them to flesh out what he called a "new art."[14] In order to understand the fascination with Boehme among young poets and artists alike, it is helpful to reconstruct their reflections on these disciplines together with their envisioned relationship to nature and religion. Letters and theoretical treatises will illustrate the Romantics' perspectives on Boehme.

"Read J. Boehme," Tieck wrote to his sister Sophie in 1800, "there is abundance of life, there is the eternal spring that no longer blooms anywhere else. Boehme is the great authority on language. I convert everybody to him here, and I am his preacher."[15] As a boy, Tieck had suffered from the sober and rational stance towards religion in his environment, and in Boehme he found what he longed for: a deep spirituality and a vivid poetic language. In a letter dated February 23rd, 1800, Novalis shared his first impressions of Boehme with his friend Tieck, using metaphors similar to those that Tieck had chosen to describe his experience of Boehme:

> Now I am reading Jacob Boehme in context, and I begin to understand him as he has to be understood. You see perfectly in him the overwhelming spring with its swelling, budding, creative forces mixing, to give birth to the world—a real chaos full of dark desires and wonderful life—a true, expanding microcosmos. I am delighted to have got to know him through you.[16]

Novalis, who was himself the son of a Pietist pastor, read Boehme while working on his novel *Heinrich von Ofterdingen* (1802), which was composed as an homage to poetry.[17] He saw the seventeenth-century mystic as a poet and even planned to include him as a character in his novel, which remained a fragment, however, due to Novalis's early death.[18]

The most important transformation in the Romantic perception of Boehme is the understanding of Boehme as a poet. By perceiving Boehme no longer primarily as a shoemaker-prophet but rather as a poet, and in particular as a poet of nature,[19] Tieck and Novalis overcame the Enlightenment dismissal of Boehme as an obscure theosophist. In the winter of 1799–1800, Tieck defended Boehme against the criticism of the philosopher Johann Gottlieb Fichte (1762–1814) by pointing out that Boehme combined philosophy and poetic vision, thus bridging the gap between rational analysis and imagination.[20] Friedrich Schlegel, the leading theorist of the early Romantics, argued along the same lines when he contextualized Boehme in the age-old opposition between poetry and philosophy, as it was introduced by Plato and still upheld by Fichte. In his reflections on Boehme in the *Philosophische Vorlesungen* [*Lectures on Philosophy*] (1804–05), Schlegel even called Boehme's work the greatest, deepest, and best philosophy of Idealism because it already merges the oldest and newest aspects of "true" philosophy, the speculative thoughts of Plato and Fichte, in its own words.[21] But in contrast to Plato's and Fichte's philosophical systems, Boehme's theosophy is rich in allegories and offers profound interpretations of Christian symbols and metaphors. Thus, Schlegel understood Boehme's theosophy as a synthesis of philosophy and religion with strong affinities to poetry: "In short, the philosophy of Jacob Böhme can best be characterized as follows: Its form is religious, its content philosophical and its spirit poetic."[22]

When the Romantics read Boehme as a poet, it is worth examining their concept of poetry with regard to its philosophical references in the history of ideas. In his *Gespräch über die Poesie* [*Dialogue on Poetry*] (1800), Schlegel mentions Boehme together with Spinoza in the context of his reflections on art. Schlegel envisions art, in its truest sense, as a work of nature. Physics, Schlegel wrote, as long as it is not reduced to a technical science, is in its true nature Theosophy, a mystical science of the whole. True art, which Schlegel contrasts to the mere results of intellectual studies, therefore grows out of the mysteries of realism, as a revelation of the All in One in nature.[23]

Physics and metaphysics, nature and religion, are hereby closely linked and contrasted, not only with a mechanistic view of nature as well as the doctrines of the church, but also with traditional poetics. According to Schlegel, poetry may not be confined to a tradition or a set of rules, mastered only by a *poeta doctus*. Humans have ignored the fact that all of creation was God's "poetry," of which human beings, too, were not only a part, but also a "blossom." Schlegel lamented the fact that the divine spark in the human soul had been almost suffocated by humanity's self-made state of alienation in the present time. Dissociated from a numinous quality of reality and blind to the depth of their own being, humans have to be reminded that their true and deepest purpose in life was to be a conscious part of God's cosmic poem—creation itself.[24] The motif of God expressing himself in all of creation harks back to the vision of the seventeenth-century mystic. In Schlegel's view, it is essentially the poet's task to make the beauty, abundance, and mystery of the spirit visible in the world. He quoted the popular motif of the dualism between the (dead) letter and the (living) spirit (2 Corinthians 3:6) from early modern Spiritualism when he insists that the magical quality of true art escapes all calculating attempts to grasp, quantify, or explain it. On the contrary, to the true poet, the sacred spirit of true art always transcends the mortal beauty in which it veils itself and points to the Infinite. It thus turns all mortal beauty into a hieroglyph of the one eternal love in abundant and creative nature.[25] Schlegel's concept of art was based on a vision of nature as the All in One, so that nature and the work of art reflect each other as two "expressions" of the creative spirit. Schlegel discusses this particular vision of nature, which is the cornerstone of his concept of art, in reference to Spinoza. But he observed that Spinoza was just one representative of this philosophy. With more time, he would have also traced its origin to "the great Jacob Boehme."[26]

The new interest in Boehme's texts around 1800 thus arose in the context of a highly ambitious artistic program with spiritual and political implications. Since their own times appeared to the Romantics to be utterly devoid of a numinous quality, Schlegel and Novalis developed a program of "romanticizing" and "poeticizing" the world through art. This meant nothing less than making the visible world transparent for the invisible one and linking the realm of the mystical to everyday life. In contrast to the great contemporary philosophical systems of Kant and Fichte conceived by scholars, the Romantic poets attempted to overcome the chasm between a purely rational world of the mind and reality with its living and material forms. Thus, they stated that the task of true art was a "trivialization of the divine and an apotheosis of the ordinary".[27] In his famous explanation of Romantic poetry as a "progressive universal poetry" (*Athenäums-Fragmente,* 1798), Friedrich Schlegel envisioned poetry as the medium through which to overcome the fragmentation in all the arts, thus even making life and society "poetic."[28] In his collection of fragments, Novalis even called the ideal state "poetic." This "poetic" quality, however, which is to be revealed and integrated in humans, nature, society and even the state, is a spiritual quality, one with the power to overcome the contemporary experience of living in a time of dissociation and fragmentation: "The spirit is always poetic," Novalis wrote, "the poetic state is the true ideal state."[29]

In their search for a deeper dimension of being not beyond but rather within reality itself, the Romantics were fascinated by Hermetic, Neoplatonic, and Kabbalistic texts as well as by contemporary Mesmerism. These interests prepared the ground for their reading of Boehme. Novalis borrowed the idea from Paracelsus that all creatures were fragments of the absolute that bridged the dualism between spirit and matter, God and creation.[30] In Novalis's *Lehrlinge zu Sais* [*Apprentices of Sais*] (1798–99)—written before he had read Boehme—he already dwells on the mystery of nature "speaking" in sacred "signatures" to those who have the intuition and poetic understanding to grasp it. Novalis sketched a vision of a healed relationship between humans, nature, and the divine in his metaphor of the soon-to-be-restored Golden Age.[31] In the *Lehrlinge zu Sais,* it is the artist who, after a long journey, finds the veiled statue in Sais, and Isis, the "mother of all things," reveals herself to him in the shape of his own bride who embraces him lovingly.[32] In this image, Novalis blends divine and human love, emphasizing the sacredness of human love as well as the mystery of nature. In contrast to contemporary rationalism, Novalis's image of the mystery of nature does not exclude nature's material forms. Nor is the absolute envisioned as a purely transcendent (male) God. In the artist's vision, the material forms of nature are turned into symbols that not only represent, but also manifest, the living presence. Spirit and matter, God and nature, are not separate entities in this vision, neither are they mere objects of philosophical speculation. On the contrary, the material forms of nature reveal the living presence in the present moment to the artist's eyes. The artist is neither a *poeta doctus* nor a dreamer, but instead resembles a priest able to decipher the sacred language of nature. In this priest-like role, the artist acts in humanity's service and is thus seen to perform a deeply meaningful task.

Although the idea of sacred semiotics may also be found in Jewish Mysticism and Florentine Neoplatonism, it is linked to a concept of rebirth in Boehme's writings that proved consonant with the Romantics' interests. According to the seventeenth-century mystic, his first-hand experience of the divine mystery had enabled him to develop a deeper understanding of a number of things, including those that became central to the concepts of art and nature around 1800: a theory of imagination as a world-creating, God-like power; the idea of the world as the body of God; the concept of rebirth as the discovery of the paradise within; and last but not least, the motif of androgyny in God and in the primordial Adam, who had lost his androgyny during his fall but had to restore it through rebirth.

First, Boehme's account of his mystical experience seemed to prove the Romantic concept of a spiritual realm in this reality. Boehme had described his own mystical experiences as a profound breakthrough that utterly transcended his rational faculties, allowing him to see into the depth of infinity within himself and in nature:

> I knew and saw in my selfe all the three Worlds; Namely, the Divine, Angelicall, and Paradisicall [World] and then the darke World; being the originall of Nature to the Fire: And then thirdly, the eternall, and visible World, being a procreation, or extern birth; or as a substance expressed, or spoken forth, from both the internall, and spirituall Worlds; and I saw, and knew the whole Being [or working Essence] in the Evill, and in the Good; and the mutuall originall, and existence of each of them.[33]
>
> In this light my mind could see through everything and recognized God in all creatures, in the weeds and in the grass, and I saw who He was and how He was and what His will was.[34]

In fact, the Romantic concepts of the artist and nature strongly resemble Boehme's understanding of the spiritually-reborn individual and of a language of nature. Additionally, Boehme's account of his own transforming experience proved to be an inspiration to those who hoped to work on a spiritual and "poetic" renewal of their age.

In Boehme's *De signatura rerum,* this concept of an individual breakthrough was linked to the notion of a language of nature. According to Boehme, the prerequisite for speaking the language of nature is nothing less than a rebirth, a substantial transformation of the individual. This transformation does not consist in positive knowledge that can be studied or taught. Only after an essential change in their entire being are humans granted the faculty to "see magically," as Boehme puts it.[35] Boehme describes reading the book of nature in oral and musical metaphors. The signatures are mute to those who try to understand them through reason. The reborn individual, however, is able to "tune himself" to the divine spirit speaking the language of nature. Boehme even goes so far as to compare nature to a lute concert played by the spirit.[36] This is rooted in the Kabbalistic idea of the language of Adam, who in his primordial state was able to see into the heart of things and to name them according to their true nature—a faculty lost with the Fall. According to Boehme, the language of Adam was not lost forever but could be regained by the spiritually reborn individual who had become one with Christ, the second Adam. Only then could the reborn gain the magical (in)sight into the heart of things that would enable them to "read" nature. In Boehme's writings, the book of nature is more than just a popular metaphor of the early modern era: for him, it becomes a simile, a mirror of the spirit world.[37] God's motif for the creation was to know himself.[38] Therefore, the entire creation becomes a revelation. Boehme talks about the world as the body of God: in order to know itself, the creative word has to become visible in creation.[39]

Parallel to the debate among Boehme's contemporaries about the relationship between the letter and spirit of scripture, Boehme claimed that the letters of nature appear dead to those dissociated from the living spirit within them. Only through rebirth is man able to overcome his fallen state, enabling him not only to "decode" the spirit lying dormant in nature, but also to participate in God's ever-creative word, the logos. Rebirth therefore enables man to perform the ultimate task of human existence in Christ's succession: to help regain the paradise within. It is noteworthy that Boehme's synonyms for the spiritually reborn individual are not only "the magus" as in Florentine Neoplatonism,[40] but also "the artist":

> The artist searches for paradise. If he finds it, he has found a great treasure on earth. But a dead person does not awaken another dead one. The artist has to be alive to say to a mountain: 'rise and throw yourself into the sea' [Mark 11:23].[41]

Boehme's account of the spiritually reborn individual bears not only traces of the Renaissance concept of the magus, who is able to decipher God's language in nature, but also appears like the religious blueprint of the Romantic concept of the artist as sketched out in Novalis's most famous novel *Heinrich von Ofterdingen.*

III NOVALIS'S *HEINRICH VON OFTERDINGEN* (1802)

One of the classical texts of German Romanticism, Novalis's *Heinrich von Ofterdingen* (1802), now serves as a case study for how Boehme's ideas were picked up, transformed, and incorporated into a novel that traces the unfolding of the poetic spirit in the artist. First, it is important to note that Novalis wrote this in reaction to another recently published "classic": volume one of Goethe's *Wilhelm Meister* (1795–96), a text that still remains the template for a *Bildungsroman.*[42] Novalis had been a great admirer and an avid reader of Goethe. Yet the above-quoted letter to Tieck from February 1800 reveals his utter disappointment with Goethe's novel and relief at finding in Boehme what he believed lacked in Goethe.

In Goethe's novel, the protagonist Wilhelm Meister experiences a series of events that foster his development as a character. He spends some time as an actor with a traveling troupe of artists, where he meets the girl Mignon and an old harp-player, both prototypical artist figures. In the end, however, the artists prove to be of little importance to him, and instead of pursuing an artist's life, Wilhelm settles down and decides to limit his aspirations to the practical life of a medical doctor. Novalis labeled the pragmatic end of the book "artistic atheism," seeing it not as a work of art, but of reason.[43] He wrote to Tieck:

> I don't understand how I could have been blind for such a long time. Reason is in it [Goethe's novel] like a naive devil. The book is infinitely strange—but you are quite happy when you are released from the fearful embarrassment of the fourth part and have reached the end. What a serene merriment you find by contrast in Boehme, and in this alone we live like a fish in water.[44]

Novalis cites Boehme as a remedy to Goethe's novel and thus contrasts Goethe's pragmatic stance with issues he considered crucial: the necessity of a humane sense for the divine, the striving for the infinite, and the indisputable and transforming value of art.

Novalis's own novel, *Heinrich von Ofterdingen,* is also the story of a young man finding his way in the world, but with an important difference: in Novalis's novel, the protagonist Heinrich follows a distinctive calling to become a poet. The novel itself, which integrates elements from traditional narrative, allegories, fairy tales, and poems, is a celebration of the magical power of poetry.[45] The protagonist's path begins with an intense dream of a blue flower. While his father mocks Heinrich's belief in dreams as glimpses into a world beyond ordinary consciousness, Heinrich takes the prophetic quality of his vision seriously. In the course of the novel, his calling to become a poet becomes clearer as do the magical, theosophical, and mystical implications of being a poet. Novalis thus compares the work of a poet to a secret art, linked to the inner realm of existence.[46] Unsurprisingly, Heinrich learns that, "in the old days," nature was much more alive than in the present. Furthermore, the poet's work was intimately linked to nature's secret life. Thus, the poet was not only a poet, but also a priest, a prophet, and a healer. As an artist, he could tune himself to the hidden sympathies of living creatures and decipher the signatures in the language of nature. The artist could even work magic—transforming the world with his words and songs.[47] Just as in Boehme's understanding of the language of Adam, the poetic language of the "old days" is conceived of as being able literally to "create" worlds by (be)speaking a cosmic mystery in melodies and conjuring the depths of reality by the power of words. Since Heinrich's path follows a series of trials to be mastered, obviously the poet must regain this state of being in harmony with nature. He must live through profound transformations of his whole being; just the kind of transformation Boehme envisioned for the reborn Christian.

An important encounter on Heinrich's path is the poet Klingsohr. He is not only the father of the woman Heinrich falls in love with, but also the narrator of a highly sophisticated fairy tale in the center of the first part of the novel (*Das Klingsohrmärchen*). In the fairy tale, certain allegorical characters represent the faculties of the human mind. Among them are Eros, representing love; Fable, representing the "spirit" of poetry; the mother, representing the heart; the father, representing the inner sense; the priestess, Sophie, representing divine wisdom; and a grim and scheming writer, representing the petrifying forces of reason that Novalis saw in the technical side of the Enlightenment.[48] After the mother falls victim to an intrigue and is burned at the stake, the young Fable collects her ashes and brings them to Sophie, who puts the ashes in a chalice on the altar and performs a ceremony. Following the ceremony, she asks everybody to drink the transformed liquid. After all have drunk from the chalice, they become aware of the mystical, but very real, presence of the mother within their own hearts.[49]

It is helpful to compare this scene with Boehme's account of Adam's fall and redemption, which is simultaneously the story of androgyny lost and regained. In contrast to traditional interpretations of Genesis 1:1–3, Boehme describes the loss of Adam's pristine, prelapsarian state in the metaphor of his lost union with the divine Sophia, which precedes the creation of Eve and the cosmic fall. The soul, however, is not bereft of comfort after the fall.[50] Boehme's *Von wahrer Buße* [*Of true Repentance*] contains a remarkable dialogue between the soul and divine Sophia, which is staged as an inner dialogue between the soul and Sophia's voice, who speaks from the soul's own hidden depths. The divine Sophia reminds the soul that it was the soul who broke their union during the fall and now exists in two rather ambiguous realms: in the spiritual realm of the dark principle and in the material world.[51] She, in contrast, is still the loving bride awaiting her husband, although he is not able to perceive her presence during this earthly existence. She also keeps the longed-for "little pearl"—a metaphor for the kingdom of heaven (Matthew 13:46)—while the soul dwells in its earthly existence. She does so because the soul will not be able to touch the heavenly gift without spoiling it while it still lives under the dark principle's dominion. But Sophia comforts the soul with remarkable and, in that context, heretical words: she certainly may not descend into his earthly existence since she is the "queen of heaven" and her kingdom is "not of this world."[52] But she dwells with the pearl in the hidden depths of the heart, and the more the soul gives its will to her, the more she will guide it, her beloved bridegroom, to overcome the postlapsarian state of being. In tender and loving words, she assures him that she will stay with and within him until the end of time and that she will let him drink the water of eternal life from her fountain. Together, they will fulfill the purpose of existence, namely to serve God in the temple, which is the soul itself.[53] This remarkable dialogue is based on the Spiritualists' premise of heaven as a ubiquitous, secret realm within the visible world and therefore also within the depths of the soul as sketched out in Valentin Weigel's works, which Boehme knew.[54] But while the Spiritualists tried to overcome the traditional separation between God and the world by referring to Jesus's words of the kingdom within (Luke 17:21), Boehme took this concept one step further by assigning the role of a divine presence in the hidden depths of the soul to the female voice of Sophia, who encourages the soul to surrender to her in order to become aware of her loving guidance.

Just as Boehme had claimed that once Adam had overcome his fallen, separated state, he would regain his lost virgin bride, the divine Sophia, so too do the protagonists in Novalis's novel—among them Fable itself, the "spirit" of poetry—experience a new state of being that is associated with the motif of androgyny regained. Significantly, the priestess Sophie performs the ceremony and causes the others to drink the water of life that makes them aware of the mystical presence of the mother within. The gift of alchemical transformation in death, rebirth, and spiritualization does not entirely overcome the fallen state of being just as Boehme had envisioned it in the myth of Adam and Sophia, but it does lie in a new wholeness of existence, which integrates the female quality in the soul. In Novalis's novel, the priestess Sophie comments on the transformation:

> The great secret is revealed to all and yet remains eternally unfathomable. The new world will be born of pain, and the ashes will be dissolved in tears to be transformed into the drink of eternal life. The heavenly mother lives in everyone of us to eternally give birth to each child.[55]

Novalis's striking image of "the heavenly mother" in his Romantic fairy tale has no parallels with traditional Christian dogma or the myths of antiquity. It does, however, recall Boehme's account of the "queen of heaven," Sophia, whose divine presence reveals itself in the depth of each soul that awakens.

Shortly before the novel breaks off, Heinrich meets the hermit Sylvester who teaches him to listen to his conscience as an inner guiding voice. In Enlightenment discourse, the motif of an inner, moral sense was linked to the writings of the Dutch philosopher Franz Hemsterhuis (1721–1790), and Novalis was well acquainted with this motif.[56] Yet the hermit's choice of words in the novel shows that the notion of an inner sense was not simply taken from a contemporary philosophical discourse but rather resembles Boehme's concept of the inner Christ: "conscience is the inborn mediator in every human being," Sylvester teaches Heinrich, explicitly ascribing the role of Christ to conscience, "it represents God on earth. [. . .] The conscience is the most inherent essence of the human being in his full glory. It is the primordial Adam."[57] Anthropologically speaking, the parallel between conscience, a Christ-like inborn mediator, and the primordial Adam indicates the presence of a prelapsarian quality that has not been entirely lost with the fall. Moreover, Sylvester identifies conscience, not the intellectual faculties of reason, with the role of this "inborn mediator." Heinrich has to learn to trust his inner, intuitive sense absolutely. In contrast to the faculties of reason, the inner sense has never lost its connection with the divine realm at a deeper level of reality. Sylvester's words echo Boehme's, who had envisioned the new Adam in his virgin state as lying hidden deep within the old Adam, so that he had to be "grown out" of the fallen state of being.[58] Boehme had been very clear that the primordial Adam and Adam in the fallen state were not ontologically separate beings, but "that the new reborn individual, who lies hidden in the old one like gold in stone, is made of a heavenly tincture, of divine, celestial flesh and blood; and that this flesh's spirit was no foreign spirit, but its own, born out of its own essence."[59]

Since in Boehme's cosmology the fall and the loss of paradise were caused not by God's curse but by a misdirection of Adam's imagination, the process of rebirth and of regaining paradise is also a matter of the right use of imagination's creative power.[60] In Novalis's novel, Sylvester's anthropology draws not only a parallel between the voice of conscience—virtue—and the "primordial Adam" that evokes Boehme's concept of the inner Christ lying deep within human existence, but it also explicitly links this concept to the essence of art itself: "So the true spirit of the fable is the spirit of virtue in a friendly disguise."[61] For Novalis, art is Spirit, packaged in a "friendly" form. The Christ-like, primordial quality of virtue as the voice of conscience is thereby associated with the quality of poetic vision. Thus, the "true" spirit of the fable—as a work of imagination—is characterized by the transformative power Boehme had ascribed to the imagination as the faculty that not only had caused the fall, but could also help regain paradise.

Poetry and art are thereby associated with the sacred in a way that recalls Boehme's anthropology and his concept of nature. The young poet Heinrich has to learn that the "true" spirit of his deepest self is simultaneously the true spirit of the cosmos. To the poet who has developed the sense to listen to it, this spirit transforms everything in nature into the so-called Holy Scriptures of sacred poetry, which the poet in turn may express through his art. In Sylvester's words:

> You will now understand that all of nature exists only through the spirit of virtue [. . .] It is the all-kindling, life-giving light within its earthly veil. [. . .] The innocence of your heart makes you a prophet. [. . .] Everything will become comprehensible to you; the world and its history transforms itself for you into the Holy Scriptures.[62]

While Boehme still had to justify himself when he talked about rebirth and the sacred semiotics in nature,[63] Sylvester's words reflect the impact of this idea during the next century. According to Novalis's novel, being a poet amounts to a divine call to act as prophet and therefore to work toward regaining the lost abundance for humanity in the face of an increasingly cold and technical world. The poet's authority derives from his participation in nothing less than a work of redemption: "The higher voice of the cosmos speaks in the poet as well, and it calls with enchanting words in more beautiful and better known worlds."[64]

The high hopes and daring speculations of the Romantic poets did not come to fulfillment. Novalis died in 1801, aged 29, before he could even finish his novel that would inspire the classical symbol of German Romanticism: the blue flower that Heinrich saw in his dream. He did not live to see the conservative turn of Romanticism during the Restoration period after the Napoleonic wars, nor the accelerated industrialization in the nineteenth century. However, both his novel and poems are remembered not only as some of the "classical" texts of German Romanticism, but they also show the impact of Boehme's writings around 1800. The same can be said about Friedrich Schlegel's theoretical reflections on art and nature or about Ludwig Tieck's novels. The literature and theory of art of early Romanticism stand next to Schelling's and Hegel's contemporary philosophies of Idealism as substantial contributions to European intellectual history, which are indebted to the writings of the seventeenth-century mystic.

IV CONCLUSION

Boehme's texts mattered to this generation of young artists because they provided a blueprint for the hoped-for spiritual and "poetic" revolution that was thought to succeed where the French Revolution had failed. They provided a model to stress the sacredness of creation in the face of an accelerating industrialization and increasing rationalization of all aspects of society. And they provided in many aspects important inspiration for the Romantic sacralization of art. In contrast to Immanuel Kant's transcendental philosophy (the most prominent philosophy in the last decade of the eighteenth century), the Romantics' ideas of art insisted on the necessity to strive for the infinite. They also dismissed the rationalistic notion that reason alone could count as the mind's highest capacity. Drawing on—among other sources—Boehme's concept of the primordial Adam, they stressed intuition, moral feeling, and imagination as humanity's divine heritage. The artist, who is connected with his inner voice, may be creative out of himself like God. The central role of the (poetic) imagination as a world-creating power in Romantic treatises echoes Boehme's theosophy where not only God created the world by imagination, but Adam's fall and redemption are also seen as the result of his wrong or right use of it.

Boehme's texts also mattered to this generation because they helped to transfer the concept of speaking "truth"—a privilege still ascribed to theology and philosophy and administered by clergy and academics—to the metaphorical language of poetry. The turn of the century saw the emergence of the modern concept of autonomous art. In Romantic portraits of the artist, he performs his role not as a student of tradition, but as a student of nature and his own inner guidance. The artist's path becomes a way of listening intimately to the inner nature of things and calling them forth in language, thus building a bridge between the visible world and the invisible one for his fellow human beings. Boehme's vision of the unity of God, nature, and humanity became an important means by which to counterbalance Cartesian dualism and its implied split between matter and spirit, nature and God, senses and ratio, body and mind. The Romantic program of "romanticizing" the soul and "poeticizing" the world would be unthinkable without the premise of a ubiquitous secret realm within this reality that Boehme had called "heaven," the "paradise within" or the "inner Christ." Just as Boehme had envisioned the transformation in rebirth as necessary to overcome the fallen state of man, so too did the Romantics suggest that humanity's full potential was still to be realized. While Boehme had set his hopes on the transformative process of rebirth that would restore the reborn to his lost wholeness, unveil the spiritual qualities of nature, and complete the *Renovatio Christianismi* begun in the Reformation, so did the Romantics set their hopes on the artist as a pioneer on the way to a spiritual renewal of society. Their metaphor of androgyny to describe this state of wholeness was indebted to Boehme's interpretation of the creation myth as a story of androgyny lost and regained. In 1800, his texts still inspired a young generation to imagine the poet as the one who, in a time of rapid change, awakes to testify to the holy, to that which helps to make the soul whole.

NOTES

1. Novalis, *Das dichterische Werk,* eds. Paul Kluckhohn and Richard Samuel, vol. 1 of Novalis, *Schriften: Die Werke Friedrich von Hardenbergs,* eds. Paul Kluckhohn and Richard Samuel (Darmstadt: Wissenschaftliche Buchgesellschaft, 1977), 413. The translations, unless otherwise noted, are my own.
2. Cf. Lothar Pikulik, *Frühromantik: Epoche—Werk—Wirkung*, 2nd ed. (Munich: Beck, 2000), 20–25; Detlef Kremer, *Romantik* (Stuttgart: Metzler, 2001), 1–7.
3. Kremer, *Romantik*, 8–11, 22–27.
4. Pikulik, *Frühromantik*, 33–45.
5. Gottsched quotes Boehme and Pordage several times as examples of religious, literary, and linguistic "enthusiasm." He points out the supposed parallels between Boehme's "obscure" language and his "irrational," "enthusiastic" ideas. Johann Christoph Gottsched, "Versuch einer Critischen Dichtkunst," in *Johann Christoph Gottsched: Schriften zur Literatur,* ed. Horst Steinmetz (Stuttgart: Reclam, 1972), 35, 153.
6. Heinrich Bornkamm, "Pietistische Mittler zwischen Jakob Böhme und dem deutschen Idealismus," in *Der Pietismus in Gestalten und Wirkungen,* ed. Heinrich Bornkamm et al. (Bielefeld: Luther Verlag, 1975), 139–154. A satirical portrait of Boehme's presence in Pietist culture appears in the comedy *Die Pietisterey im Fischbein-Rocke* (1736), written by Gottsched's wife. Luise Adelgunde Victorie Gottsched, *Die Pietisterey im Fischbein-Rocke*, ed. Wolfgang Martens (Stuttgart: Reclam, 1968), 86.
7. Johann Heinrich Jung-Stilling, *Theobald oder die Schwärmer. Eine wahre Geschichte,* vol. 6 of Johann Heinrich Jung-Stilling, *Sämtliche Schriften* (Stuttgart: J. Scheible's Buchhandlung, 1837), 9–40. Frustrated by the

Enlightenment criticism of religion, Jung-Stilling even composed his own theosophical explanation of creation based on Boehme as late as 1776: *Theosophischer Versuch vom Wesen Gottes und vom Ursprung aller Dinge.*

8. Gerhard Wehr, "Aspekte der Wirkungsgeschichte Jakob Böhmes," in *Gott, Natur und Mensch in der Sicht Jakob Böhmes und seiner Rezeption,* eds. Jan Garewicz and Alois Maria Haas (Wiesbaden: Harrassowitz Verlag, 1994), 175–96; Friedemann Stengel, *Aufklärung bis zum Himmel. Emanuel Swedenborg im Kontext der Theologie und Philosophie des 18. Jahrhunderts.* (Tübingen: Mohr Siebeck, 2011).
9. Johann Wolfgang Goethe, *Autobiographische Schriften.* Textkritisch durchgesehen von Lieselotte Blumenthal, vol. 9 of Johann Wolfgang Goethe, *Werke: Hamburger Ausgabe in 14 Bänden,* ed. Erich Trunz (Munich: Deutscher Taschenbuch Verlag 2000), 338–50. Cf. Rolf-Christian Zimmermann, *Das Weltbild des jungen Goethe: Elemente und Fundamente,* (2 vols., Munich: Wilhelm Fink Verlag, 1969); Hans-Jürgen Schrader und Katharine Weder, *Von der Pansophie zur Weltweisheit: Goethes analogisch-philosophische Konzepte* (Tübingen: Niemeyer Verlag, 2004).
10. Goethe, *Autobiographische Schriften,* 350–53.
11. Friedrich Nicolai, "Vertraute Brief von Adelheid B** an ihre Freundin Julie S**" in Friedrich Nicolai, "*Kritik ist überall, zumal in Deutschland, nötig*": *Satiren und Schriften zur Literatur,* ed. Wolfgang Albrecht (Leipzig: Gustav Kiepenheuer Verlag, 1987), 86.
12. Edwin Lüer, *Aurum und Aurora: Ludwig Tiecks 'Runenberg' und Jakob Böhme* (Heidelberg: Universitätsverlag C. Winter, 1997), 34.
13. Novalis, *Das dichterische Werk,* 690.
14. Melanie Öhlenbach, "Lilie, Licht und Gottes Weisheit: Philipp Otto Runge und Jakob Böhme," *Aries* vol. 5, no. 2 (2005): 159.
15. Quoted in Lüer, *Aurum und Aurora,* 40.
16. Novalis, *Tagebücher, Briefwechsel, Zeitgenössische Zeugnisse,* ed. Richard Samuel, vol. 4 of Novalis, *Schriften* (Darmstadt: Wissenschaftliche Buchgesellschaft, 1975), 322. Cf. Carl Paschek, *Der Einfluß Jacob Böhmes auf das Werk Friedrich von Hardenbergs (Novalis)* (Bonn: Rheinische Friedrich Wilhelms Universität, 1967), 73.
17. Dennis Mahoney, *Friedrich von Hardenberg (Novalis)* (Stuttgart: Metzler Verlag, 2001).
18. In the drafts for the second half of the novel, Novalis sketches the idea that the protagonist Heinrich would live through a series of transformations along the chain of being, and he would even meet Jacob Boehme in the end of the book: "Heinrich von After[dingen] becomes flower—animal—stone—star. And Jacob Böhm in the end of the book," Novalis, *Das dichterische Werk,* 341.
19. A contemporary comment on Novalis by a local official (the Kreisamtmann Just) underlines the intimate connection between Novalis's perception of Boehme and poetry: "His [Novalis's] imagination has quite an expanded understanding of poetry. The whole of nature seemed him to be poetic, and in Boehme he found sublime poetry." Quoted in Paschek, *Der Einfluß Jacob Böhmes,* 90.
20. Lüer, *Aurum und Aurora,* 40.
21. Friedrich Schlegel, "Die Entwicklung der Philosophie in zwölf Büchern (Cologne, 1804–05)," in Friedrich Schlegel, *Erster Teil: Philosophische Vorlesungen (1800–1807),* ed. Jean-Jacques Anstett, vol. 12 of *Kritische Friedrich Schlegel-Ausgabe,* ed. Ernst Behler unter Mitwirkung von Hans Eichner and Jean-Jacques Anstett (Munich: Schöningh Verlag, 1964), 259. Schlegel sees

an intimate relationship between Boehme's Theosophy and the philosophy of Idealism when he writes: "Just as Theosophy is on the one hand necessarily Idealism, so does Idealism always lead to Theosophy as the highest principle of the spirit."

22. Schlegel, "Die Entwickung der Philosophie," 260; cf. Paschek, *Der Einfluß Jacob Böhmes*, 89.
23. Schlegel, "Gespräch über die Poesie," in Friedrich Schlegel, *Erster Teil: Charakteristiken und Kritiken I (1796–1801)*, ed. Hans Eichner, vol. 2 of *Kritische Friedrich-Schlegel-Ausgabe*, (Munich: Schöningh Verlag, 1967), 325–26.
24. "Yes, we as human beings are and have no other subject of all activity and joy in eternity than this one poem of God, of which we are a part and a blossom as well—the earth. We are able to hear the music of the infinite music box, we are able to understand the beauty of a poem because a part of the Poet, a spark of his creative spirit, lives in us as well and never ceases to glow with secret power deep under the ashes of our self-created irrationality." Schlegel, "Gespräch über die Poesie," 285.
25. Schlegel, "Gespräch über die Poesie," 334.
26. Ibid., 326.
27. Pikulik, *Frühromantik*, 220.
28. Schlegel, "Athenäums-Fragmente," in Friedrich Schlegel, *Erster Teil: Charakteristiken und Kritiken I (1796–1801)*, ed. Hans Eichner, vol. 2 of *Kritische Friedrich-Schlegel-Ausgabe*, 182.
29. Novalis, *Das philosophische Werk I*, ed. Richard Samuel, vol. 2 of Novalis, *Schriften* (Darmstadt: Wissenschaftliche Buchgesellschaft 1965), 468.
30. Paschek, *Der Einfluß Jacob Böhmes*, 123.
31. Novalis, "Die Lehrlinge zu Sais," in Novalis, *Das dichterische Werk,* 79, 86.
32. Novalis, "Die Lehrlinge zu Sais," 95.
33. Jacob Boehme, *The Epistles of Jacob Behmen*, trans. J[ohn] E[llistone] (London, 1649), 2.7–8 (19–20). Cf. Alois Maria Haas, "Erfahrung und Sprache in Böhmes *Aurora*," in *Gott, Natur und Mensch in der Sicht Jacob Böhmes und seiner Rezeption,* eds. Jan Garewicz and Alois Maria Haas (Wiesbaden: Harrassowitz Verlag, 1994), 7.
34. Böhme, *Aurora*, in *Jakob Böhmes Sämtliche Schriften*, Faksimile-Neudruck der Ausgabe von 1730 in elf Bänden, begonnen von August Faust, neu herausgegeben von Will-Erich Peuckert (Stuttgart 1955–61), 19:13 (the first number here refers to the chapter and the second to the paragraph). Cf. Sibylle Rusterholz, "Zum Verhältnis von *Liber Naturae* und *Liber Scripturae* bei Jacob Böhme," in *Gott, Natur und Mensch*, 133.
35. Jacob Böhme, *De signatura rerum*, in Jacob Böhme, *Werke*, ed. Ferdinand von Ingen (Frankfurt: Deutscher Klassiker Verlag, 1997), 600.
36. Böhme, *Signatura rerum*, 515.
37. Ibid., 621.
38. Ibid., 521.
39. Cf. Pierre Deghaye, "Die Natur als Leib Gottes in Böhmes Theosophie," in *Gott, Natur und Mensch*, 72.
40. Böhme, *Signatura rerum*, 595.
41. Ibid., 598.
42. Pikulik, *Frühromantik*, 217; Kremer, *Romantik,* 126.
43. Pikulik, *Frühromantik*, 218.
44. Novalis, *Tagebücher, Briefzeugnisse,* 323; cf. Paschek, *Der Einfluß Jacob Böhmes,* 74.
45. Cf. Johannes Mahr, *Übergang zum Endlichen. Der Weg des Dichters in Novalis' "Heinrich von Ofterdingen"* (Munich: Fink Verlag, 1970).

46. Novalis, "Heinrich von Ofterdingen," in Novalis, *Das dichterische Werk,* 210.
47. Novalis, "Heinrich von Ofterdingen," 211. Cf. Mahr, *Übergang zum Endlichen*, 72.
48. Pikulik, *Frühromantik,* 232.
49. Novalis, "Heinrich von Ofterdingen," 312. Cf. Regula Frankhauser, *Des Dichters Sophia. Weiblichkeitsentwürfe im Werk von Novalis* (Cologne: Böhlau Verlag, 1997), 105–13, 166–72.
50. Cf. Roland Pietsch, "Jacob Böhmes Lehre von der göttlichen Weisheit und von der himmlischen Jungfrau Sophia," in *Erkenntnis und Wissenschaft. Jacob Böhme (1575–1624): Internationales Jacob- Böhme-Symposion Görlitz 2000,* ed. Oberlausitzische Gesellschaft der Wissenschaften e.V. (Görlitz: Oettel, 2001), 45–47.
51. Böhme, *Christosophia, das ist: Der Weg zu Christo I Von wahrer Buße*, 49.
52. Böhme, *Christosophia,* 49.
53. Ibid., 49–51.
54. Valentin Weigel, *Sämtliche Schriften*, ed. Horst Pfefferl, vol. 11 (Stuttgart-Bad Cannstatt: Fromman Holzboog Verlag, 2007), 228. Valentin Weigel, *Ausgewählte Werke*, ed. Siegfried Wollgast (Stuttgart: Kohlhammer Verlag, 1977), 264, 297, 303–05; Boehme, *Theosophische Sendbriefe*, 12:59–60. Cf. Andrew Weeks, *Valentin Weigel (1533–1588): German Religious Dissenter, Speculative Theorist and Advocate of Tolerance* (New York, 2000), 112.
55. Novalis, "Heinrich von Ofterdingen," 312.
56. Pikulik, *Frühromantik,* 41; Manfred Dick, *Die Entwicklung des Gedankens der Poesie in den Fragmenten des Novalis* (Bonn: H. Bouvier u. Co. Verlag, 1967), 207.
57. Novalis, "Heinrich von Ofterdingen," 332.
58. Böhme, *Von der Menschwerdung Jesu Christi* I, 12: 22.
59. Ibid., 14:12.
60. Ibid, 11:8.
61. Novalis, "Heinrich von Ofterdingen," 332.
62. Ibid., 333.
63. Böhme, *Aurora*, 23:9–10.
64. Novalis, "Heinrich von Ofterdingen," 333.

10 Boehme and the Early English Romantics

Elisabeth Engell Jessen

Amongst the early English Romantics, two writers in particular were influenced by Boehme: William Blake (1757–1827) and Samuel Taylor Coleridge (1772–1834). Along with William Wordsworth (1770–1850), these men are often listed together as avatars of the early Romantic movement in English poetry. Although Wordsworth owned copies of Boehme and occasionally paraphrased him, it was Blake and Coleridge who displayed the deeper affinity with his theosophy.[1] In this chapter, I examine first how Blake's reading of Boehme influenced his works, and conclude by contextualizing Blake's engagement with Boehme within English Romanticism at the turn of the eighteenth century, with particular reference to Coleridge's response to Boehme.[2]

I BLAKE AND BOEHME

We do not know when Blake first read Boehme, and no edition of Boehme owned by him is known today.[3] Blake nowhere discusses Boehme critically. We have no annotated copy belonging to him, and there are only two *direct* references to Boehme in all of Blake's works and known letters.[4] A note made by the journalist and diarist Henry Crabb Robinson in 1825, two years before Blake's death, indicates that Blake, like his contemporary Coleridge, knew the Law edition: Crabb Robinson here notes that Blake praised "the figures in Law's transl.n as being very beautiful," thought that "Mich:Angelo co[d] not have done better," and called Boehme "a divinely inspired man."[5] This, however, is the only known contemporary source directly quoting Blake on Boehme.[6] We do not know exactly which of Boehme's works Blake knew, although there are indications that he owned more than one edition: in a letter from 1864, Frederick Tatham (who inherited many of Blake's books from Blake's wife Catherine) notes that Blake owned "a large collection of works of the mystical writers, Jacob Behmen, Swedenborg, and others," but no specific titles are mentioned.[7] Given the availability of Boehme's works in English, it is not hard to imagine that Blake would have owned other Boehme editions than the "huge quartos" of the Law edition[8]—perhaps some of the cheap, readily available collections of mystical or prophetic texts in which Boehme was often included.[9]

What we can discern, however, is an original and imaginative appropriation of Behmenist motifs in Blake's texts and images, a reception of Boehme through creative engagement with his writings. It seems that Blake—like Coleridge, as we shall see—engaged with Boehme from early on. In one of the two direct references to Boehme in the Blake corpus, Blake mentions him in a letter to his friend, the artist John Flaxman (1755–1826). Flaxman was, as Blake himself had briefly been, connected with the Swedenborgian New Jerusalem Church in London, and in a poem that is included in the letter and intended to praise Flaxman, Blake lists some of his poetic-prophetic influences:

> Milton lovd me in childhood & shewd me his face
> Ezra came with Isaiah the Prophet, but Shakespeare in riper years gave me his hand
> Paracelsus & Behmen appeard to me.
> [. . .]
> The American War began[.][10]

We note here that Blake mentions Boehme together with Paracelsus and that the two are placed in the company of the poets Milton and Shakespeare as well as the prophets Ezra and Isaiah (all of whom Blake admired) as sources of inspiration—early sources, that is, since he appears to have been familiar with them from before "The American War" began in 1775, when he was seventeen.[11]

Further indications that Blake engaged with Boehme at an early age are found in the Behmenist complexion of Blake's first two illustrated books *All Religions are One* and *There is No Natural Religion* (both 1788).[12] In *All Religions are One*—the title alone is quite a statement—Blake proposes that "As all men are alike (tho' infinitely various) So all Religions & as all similars have one source/ The true Man is the source he being the Poetic Genius" (E2). These lines may be understood as echoing the ecumenical, inclusive outlook of Boehme and the Behmenists.[13] But they have also been argued to refer to Boehme's concept of *der rechte Mensch* in the phrase "the true Man."[14] Furthermore, there might be visual connections between the Behmenist tradition and *All Religions are One*, in that this is where Blake—probably for the first time—uses the visual trope of a centrally placed hovering bird with extended wings.[15] This bird is similar to the dove shown, for example, on the title page of Boehme's *Three Principles of the Divine Essence* in *Theosophia Revelata* (1730) and later seems to become partly translated into one of the central figures in Blake's visual language: namely the hovering figure with extended arms, which denotes (divine) creativity.[16]

Blake's early engagement with Boehme is also evident a few years later, when Blake produces his first illuminated book, *The Marriage of Heaven and Hell* (1790–93). Here we find the second of Blake's two direct references to Boehme. Blake once again puts Boehme in distinguished company, mentioning him (as in the letter to Flaxman) together with Paracelsus and Shakespeare. As before, this occurs within a Swedenborgian context. Indeed, one of the central themes in *The Marriage* is Blake's critique of Swedenborg, whom Blake accuses of having degenerated from an original living religious *vision* to a hardened and unimaginative religious *system*. Blake's critique comes immediately after his own period of involvement with the New Jerusalem Church in London and represents Blake's break with Swedenborg.[17] "Any man of mechanical talents," Blake writes,

> may from the writings of Paracelsus or Jacob Behmen, produce ten thousand volumes of equal value with Swedenborg's. and from those of Dante or Shakespear, an infinite number. But when he has done this, let him not say that he knows better than his master, for he only holds a candle in sunshine.
>
> (*The Marriage* 22, E43)

Although the reference has been understood by some as a denigration of Boehme—placing him as a lesser poet than Dante and Shakespeare and claiming that any person of "mechanical talents" could produce works of "equal value" with him[18]—the point seems to be rather the opposite: namely, that even if a person of "mechanical talents" had produced these works, they would still only be of inferior value to the originals. As in the rest of *The Marriage*, the joke is on Swedenborg.[19]

II BEHMENIST PATTERNS IN BLAKE: THE PRESENT

Apart from these few direct references, however, where do we find echoes of Boehme in Blake's works, and how might Boehme have inspired Blake? One place to start would be to observe that the center of both Boehme's writings, unpublished during his lifetime (except for *The Way to Christ*), and Blake's home-printed illuminated books is *the present*. This is the present of the reader, or Blake's "Eternal Now" (*Annotations to Lavater* 407, E592), in which the reader appropriates the transforming message of the book, opens his or her "Center" (*The Four Zoas* 98.11, E370) and is spiritually and intellectually changed. Even though the vision that Blake poses in his works is more loosely connected with what we might call traditional Christian thought than that presented by Boehme, more radically critical of institutional Christianity and less specific with regards to directing the reader spiritually and intellectually, the underlying premise and theological anthropology in both Blake and Boehme is the same: the way of the human subject back to God proceeds via the continual seeking of God within, the opening of the divine senses, the annihilation of the selfhood, and the use of the divine imagination to navigate in a universe of moving, energy-creating opposites. Thus in both Blake's and Boehme's works, Paradise and the Last Judgment are always present and available: as Boehme writes, Paradise "is only withdrawn from our Sight and our Source; for if our Eyes were opened, we should see it" (*Aurora* 10.98).[20] Placed between these two available locations, the subject's turning to the divine is based on a choice of direction that he or she must make continually. For, according to Blake, "whenever any Individual Rejects Error & Embraces Truth a Last Judgment passes upon that Individual" (*A Vision of The Last Judgment* 84, E562). This choice of the believer—and reader—is also clearly staged in the treatises that appear in Boehme's *Way to Christ*. Here the reader is positioned "at this Hour and Instant . . . before the Face of the *holy Trinity*" and must "firmly know and believe" and "resolve that he will this very Hour turn the Eyes and Desire of his Soul towards God again, and with the poor, *lost*, and *returning Son*, come to the Father" (*Of True Repentance*).[21] It is in this undecided state, where the reading subject feels "a *Hunger*, or *Desire* to *repent*, and yet feeleth no true *Sorrow* in himself for his *Sins*" (*Of True Repentance*),[22] that the text has its place, urging the reader to come forward and walk the "narrow bridge" (*Aurora* 19.22)[23] with the narrator and follow his (spiritual) example. And although Blake does not share Boehme's focus on sin and repentance, a thread runs through Blake's works that asks the reader to turn from "Single vision & Newtons sleep"[24] to life in "the Imagination. that is God himself" (*Laocoön*, E273); "England! awake! awake! awake!," Blake urges in *Jerusalem* (77, E233).

III THE OPENING CENTER

The trope of the opening of the center, which, as Kathleen Raine first showed, Blake may well have inherited from Boehme, is central for both of them and represents the transforming event in the life of the reader that their respective works attempt to realize.[25] This opening is the moment and place in which eternity breaks through temporal and spatial boundaries and opens up an experience of divine being. The center is at the same time eternal and present, visible even in the smallest part of created being, and when it is opened, the subject is likewise opened to perceiving eternity and the divine as being present everywhere. As Blake puts it, "in your own Bosom you bear your Heaven/ And Earth, & all you behold, tho it appears Without it is Within" (*Jerusalem* 71.17–18, E225). As with Paradise and the Last Judgment, the opening of the center is an always-available event; or, to quote Bryan Aubrey, human life is always "pregnant with divinity" in Boehme's works.[26] This event is latent in the smallest part of being—as Blake writes on the sweet smell of flowers, "none can tell how from so small a center comes such sweets/ Forgetting that within that Center Eternity expands" (*Milton* 31.47–48, E131). Similarly, Boehme writes that "If thou conceivest a small *minute* Circle, as small as a Grain of Mustard-seed, yet the Heart of God is wholly and perfectly therein" (*Threefold Life of Man* 6.71).[27] And Blake responds:

> To see a World in a Grain of Sand
> And a Heaven in a Wild Flower
> Hold Infinity in the palm of your hand
> And Eternity in an hour[.]
>
> *(Auguries of Innocence 1–4, E490)*

IV NATURE

Despite the sentiment expressed here, Blake—uncharacteristically for a Romantic poet—is not generally inclined to pick up on the tendency in Boehme to see the divine as revealed in nature without qualification; nature is not in itself inherently good or bad, but can appear to us differently according to how we see it.[28] Whereas Boehme gladly represents nature as a means through which to understand the divine mysteries, Blake ultimately values (human) form over nature's formlessness: "Where man is not nature is barren," he posits in *The Marriage* (10, E38). Although the divine is not absent from nature as such, it is not in nature per se that we meet, recognize, and perceive the divine reality (just as it is not in rational or abstract thought, or "cloudy vapour," *Descriptive Catalogue* 37, E541). Instead, we perceive the divine in human form, imagination, outline, and "minute particulars"—as Blake writes in *Jerusalem*, "General Forms have their vitality in Particulars: & every/ Particular is a Man; a Divine Member of the Divine Jesus" (91.29–30, E251). Thus:

> the Sanctuary of Eden. is in the Camp: in the Outline,
> In the Circumference: & every Minute Particular is Holy:
> Embraces are Cominglings: from the Head even to the Feet;
> And not a pompous High Priest entering by a Secret Place.
>
> *(69.41–44, E223)*

In order to perceive the divine reality, we therefore need to expand our senses and see every minute particular in the world (be it in nature or culture) with the eyes of the imagination that give form to everything they see: "As a man is So he Sees. As the Eye is formed such are its Powers."[29] Only by seeing with the "Imaginative Eye" (*A Vision of The Last Judgment* 70, E554) are we able to understand the world, or being, in its divine form.

V GOD, CHRIST, AND FORM

This philosophy of form and minute particulars also informs Blake's views on God and Christ. Whilst he is often ambivalent towards God the Father as distant, authoritative, and judgmental,[30] Blake's main positive focus, like Boehme's, is on the figure of Christ, who comes to us as the "human form divine" (*Songs of Innocence*, "The Divine Image" 11, E13). It is in Christ that we, according to Blake, experience being "mutual in love divine" (*Jerusalem* 4.7, E146), entering into a close relation with Christ that is different from the potentially abstract and distant relation with God the Father. As Blake has Christ proclaim in the beginning of *Jerusalem*: "I am not a God afar off, I am a brother and friend" (4.18, E146). Without the intervention of Christ, God remains unapproachable and potentially oppressive: "God out of Christ is a Consuming Fire" (*Epitome Hervey*, E691), Blake notes, echoing both Hebrews 12:29 as well as Boehme's God in the first principle, who is also "a consuming fire" (*Treatise of the Incarnation* 1.40).[31] Christ's incarnate form is not experienced and appropriated through reasoning ("Rational Truth is not the Truth of Christ but of Pilate," *Annotations to Bacon* 1, E621), but through affect and experience:

> Think of a white cloud. as being holy you cannot love it but think of a holy man within the cloud love springs up in your thought. for to think of holiness distinct from man is impossible to the affections. Thought alone can make monsters, but the affections cannot[.]
>
> *(Annotations to Swedenborg 11, E603)*

Ultimately, nature is also enclosed in this grand divine form (an echo, perhaps, of Freher's three "Tables" in the third volume of the Law edition). To speak in Pauline terms, everything created is a member of the body of Christ (1 Corinthians 12:12–14). Blake's "One Man" is the divine form that holds everything together—and outside it there is only formlessness and void (as in Genesis 1), which is similar to Boehme's still formless *Ungrund*. As "the Divine Family" articulates it in *Jerusalem*:

> Mutual in one anothers love and wrath all renewing
> We live as One Man; for contracting our infinite senses
> We behold multitude; or expanding: we behold as one,
> As One Man all the Universal Family; and that One Man
> We call Jesus the Christ: and he in us, and we in him,
> Live in perfect harmony in Eden the land of life,
> Giving, receiving, and forgiving each others trespasses.
>
> *(34.16–22, E180)*

The central components of Blake's theology are all present here: his focus on mutual human-divine love, on brotherhood in Christ, and on the forgiveness of sins above all. As Blake writes elsewhere, "The Gospel is Forgiveness of Sins & has No Moral Precepts" (*Annotations to Watson* 108, E619), and as Boehme writes, "Christ himself is the Forgiveness of Sins" (*Of the Election of Grace* 13.37–38).[32] Thus, in Blake's works (which, we must remember, are dialectical and demanding works of fiction, not doctrinal tracts), we often note the absence of any moral implications of the divine-human relationship or any particular notion of sin in itself—apart from its forgiveness, which is central: "Mutual Forgiveness of each Vice/ Such are the Gates of Paradise" (*For The Sexes: The Gates of Paradise* 1–2, E259). As Blake plays down the moral side of Christianity, he conversely emphasizes the antinomian, energetic, human, and revolutionary side of Christ. This is seen, for example, in *The Everlasting Gospel* (ca. 1818), where he conjures up an image of a radical, anti-establishment Christ.[33] "The Vision of Christ that thou dost see/ Is my Visions Greatest Enemy," Blake writes, continuing:

> Thine has a great hook nose like thine
> Mine has a snub nose like to mine
> Thine is the Friend of All Mankind
> Mine speaks in parables to the Blind
> Thine loves the same world that mine hates
> Thy Heaven doors are my Hell Gates
> [. . .]
> [. . .] thou readst black where I read white[.]
>
> *([e]1–14, E524)*

Blake also experimented visually and textually with tropes connected with Jesus's death and crucifixion, which also occur in Boehme's works, for example in *The Way to Christ*. In the first two decades of the 1800s, Blake explored ways of representing Jesus's wounded, open body, before shifting in around 1822 to portraying visions of the crucifixion that focus on the glorified (not wounded) body of Jesus.[34] This development, however, does not so much represent a change in Blake's Christology as a continuing exploration of the body (or form) of Christ as a salvific space—a salvific space that we recognize also from Boehme, who in *Of True Repentance* urges his reader to follow the narrator into the death of Jesus: "I sink myself down into the *Death* of my *Redeemer* Jesus Christ, and wait for thee, whose Word is Truth and Life. *Amen.*"[35]

VI SELFHOOD AND SELF-ANNIHILATION

This period of more intense preoccupation with the cross and death of Jesus seems connected with Blake's increased use of the tropes of selfhood and self-annihilation, which he may very well have derived from Boehme.[36] In fact, despite having known Boehme's work for a long time, it is not until the two long, illuminated books *Milton* and *Jerusalem* (both initiated in 1804) that these concepts begin to play a key role. It is unclear why Blake did not explore them earlier, but it remains the case that the two spiritual portraits of the characters Milton and Albion provided a setting in which Blake could explore the concept of selfhood and its annihilation in all its complexity. Both of these illuminated books describe the journey of a divided protagonist towards restoration and unity—in *Milton*, it is the journey of an individual, the poet "Milton" as recast in Blake's imagination; in *Jerusalem*, it is the journey of a collective body personalized as "Albion." In both works, Blake's new emphasis on the death of Jesus,[37] the self, and self-annihilation underscores a possible Behmenist influence. This Behmenist influence is further emphasized by the fact that *Milton* in particular indicates that Blake probably took visual inspiration from Freher.[38] In the text of *Milton*, the spiritual, intellectual, and emotional development that the character undergoes leads him from acknowledging his inner division, to his experience of self-annihilation, and finally to restoration to a united existence. Just after Milton has realized the way he has to go, he lays out a spiritual route that will take him through a self-annihilation similar to that yearned for by the narrator in Boehme's *Of True Repentance* ("cast my whole *Self-hood* down to the Ground in thy Death"):[39]

> I go to Eternal Death!
> [. . .]
> When will the Resurrection come; to deliver the sleeping body
> From corruptibility: O when Lord Jesus wilt thou come?
> Tarry no longer; for my soul lies at the gates of death.
> I will arise and look forth for the morning of the grave.
> I will go down to the sepulcher to see if morning breaks!
> I will go down to self annihilation and eternal death,
> Lest the Last Judgment come & find me unannihilate
> And I be siez'd & giv'n into the hands of my own Selfhood
> The Lamb of God is seen thro' mists & shadows, hov'ring
> Over the sepulchers in clouds of Jehovah & winds of Elohim
> A disk of blood, distant; & heav'ns & earth's roll dark between
> What do I here before the Judgment?
> [. . .]
> I in my Selfhood am that Satan: I am that Evil One!
> He is my Spectre! in my obedience to loose him from my Hells
> To claim the Hells, my Furnaces, I go to Eternal Death.
>
> *(Milton 14.14–32, E108)*

This moment of self-annihilation or temporary destruction before an experience of restoration or rebirth recurs frequently in Blake, and in particular in those works that seem to refer most directly to a Behmenist universe, namely *The Marriage*, *Milton*, and *Jerusalem* (and to some extent, *The Four Zoas*). In these works, a series of transformations or conversions within each book, crafted as moments similar to the progress taking place through

Boehme's fourth property, leads to a final moment of transformation towards the end. This often, like the fourth property, consists of an annihilation in fire[40] (both *The Marriage* and *Jerusalem* end with the protagonist throwing himself into flames or furnaces) followed by an individual and/or collective rebirth—in *Jerusalem* even, unusually for Blake, a longer vision of life in the restored world. In *Jerusalem*'s restored reality, self-annihilation now becomes identified with the crucial forgiveness of sins as the "covenant of Jehovah," as everything is

> rejoicing in Unity
> In the Four Senses in the Outline the Circumference & Form, for ever
> In Forgiveness of Sins which is Self Annihilation. it is the Covenant of Jehovah[.]
>
> *(Jerusalem 98.21–23, E257)*

These final moments of transformation in Blake's works, however, read not as ultimate conclusions to the narrative of each book, but as openings towards a new existence or, indeed, another narrative (as evident, for example, in the very last lines of *Milton*).[41]

Milton's restoration in Blake's work consists of two main interconnected components: his annihilation of his selfhood and his restoration to unity with his female counterpart, Ololon. According to Blake, part of the problem with the historical figure of Milton was that he insisted on keeping separate what ought not to be separated: man and woman, earthly and divine.[42] The transformation that Blake proposes in his works is thus more explicitly sensually grounded than in Boehme's.[43] He develops Boehme's concept of the separation of the sexes after the fall into a thought system in which the subject's way to restoration is explicitly manifested in images focusing on the body, the relationship between genders, and the senses. Perhaps this functions for Blake as a substitute for the positive and sense-based understanding of nature that Boehme shows to a larger degree—or perhaps it is as an echo of Blake's familiarity with Moravian spirituality, in which the senses, physical experience, and joy played a central part. In either case, physical pleasure and engagement with the (naked) "human form divine," as seen in both Blake's texts and designs, are not morally suspicious activities, but rather represent involvement with divine reality as it is manifested in the minute particulars of the human body: "ourselves in whom God dwells" (*Jerusalem* 38.13, E184). Joy and delight, in other words, are not sinful and should not be avoided: "every thing that lives is holy, life delights in life" (*America a Prophecy* 8.13, E54). Following on from this, self-annihilation in Blake's works does not consist in annihilating a sinful or morally corrupted self, but in annihilating the "spectre" as the rational power in the subject—a position similar to Boehme's distrust of any hegemony of "blind reason, which sitteth in the dark, and seeketh God in the Darkness" (*Threefold Life of Man* 3.32).[44] As Blake puts it in *Milton*:

> The Negation is the Spectre; the Reasoning Power in Man
> This is a false Body: an Incrustation over my Immortal
> Spirit; a Selfhood, which must be put off & annihilated alway[.]
> *(40.34–36, E142)*

The annihilation of the spectre in Blake's works brings the human subject closer to communal life in Christ and further away from divided, isolated existence in selfhood. Furthermore, it must be experienced continually: "All Life consists of these Two Throwing off Error [. . .] continually & receiving Truth [. . .] Continually" (*A Vision of The Last Judgment* 84, E562).[45] In other words, in Blake, as in Boehme, the turning towards God (conversion) is continual, and experienced, it seems, as an oscillating movement between poles. And, as in Boehme, the reader of Blake's works is addressed and inserted into the very center, which can be opened, and in which the turning or transformation might happen: "There is a Moment in each Day that Satan cannot find" (*Milton* 35.42, E136). In these moments of continual turning towards God—who is both "within, & without" (*Jerusalem* 12.15, E155)—life in the divine imagination, or Paradise, is realized: "our own Imaginations, those Worlds of Eternity in which we shall live for ever; in Jesus our Lord" (*Milton* 1, Preface, E95).[46]

There are many more specific points in Blake's works where he might have been inspired by Boehme. Several have previously been pointed out. There is, for example, Blake's devaluation of the importance of formal education; his insistence on the spiritual capacity of children; his use of fire and light as markers of divinity; his exploration of monism and rejection of theological dualism; his insistence on his works as anti-elitist and accessible to any reader (a point which both Boehme and Blake stubbornly insist on, despite their convoluted style and complex narrative universes); a certain anticlerical or anti-establishment tendency; his concept of a fallen divine language which will one day be restored; his idea of the prelapsarian subject as androgynous, a state which is to be required again after the resurrection (as indeed illustrated by Milton's journey towards unity with Ololon in *Milton*); his idea of different spheres of the universe relating energetically to each other as illustrated in the concept of necessary "opposites" or "contraries," and so on.

But more important than these minute particulars is the sense that the actual focal point of both Blake's and Boehme's works is not the elaborate and complicated narrative systems that they describe. The representation of these systems or universes in texts and images (described in alchemical, religious, philosophic, and psychological terms) is not meant as an end in itself, to be fully understood in the intellectual sense only by the uttermost stretching of one's rational power. Instead, they are intended as ways in which to stir the reader towards a more immediate spiritual or affective engagement with the divine existence they point towards. Thus, the works of both Blake and Boehme might seriously challenge their readers' interpretative powers and need intellectually to apprehend a text—but more importantly, they both address the reader exactly at that moment of reading and engaging imaginatively with the text. In doing so, they attempt to insert the reader directly into that center in the fourth principle where transformation is possible and facilitate this transformation precisely through both their content and their demanding, but also curiously open, form. This is the moment where eternity breaks through, where the reader, through the act of reading, is opened up towards communal life in the divine body—and indeed, where the poet's work is done:

> For in this Period the Poets Work is Done: and all the Great
> Events of Time start forth & are concievd in such a Period
> Within a Moment: a Pulsation of the Artery.
>
> *(Milton 29.1–3, E127)*

VII COLERIDGE, BLAKE, AND BOEHME

Samuel Taylor Coleridge was one of the few illustrious contemporaries of Blake to have admired his work during his lifetime. In a letter dated February 1818, Coleridge described his reading of *Songs of Innocence and of Experience*, and concluded that Blake was "a man of genius", or rather "a mystic, *emphatically*." He continued:

> You perhaps smile at *my* calling another poet, a *Mystic*, but verily I am in the very mire of commonplace common-sense compared with Mr Blake, apo- or rather anacalyptic Poet, and Painter![47]

This comment hints at Coleridge's slightly detached and complacent attitude towards Blake, but also at a kinship between them. They would later meet, by early 1826, introduced by a mutual friend, Charles Augustus Tulk, who was probably, fittingly, a Swedenborgian.[48] An article published in 1830, soon after Blake's death, reported that "Blake and Coleridge, when in company, seemed like congenial beings of another sphere, breathing for a while on our earth; which may easily be perceived from the similarity of thought pervading their works."[49]

Boehme's work was one of the places where the mystical interests of Blake and Coleridge converged. Coleridge engaged critically but sympathetically with Boehme over a long period. He owned and annotated the Law edition of Boehme's works, which Thomas De Quincey (1785–1859) had given him in 1808,[50] but he claimed to have read Boehme as early as his schooldays: in a letter to Ludwig Tieck from 1817, he mentions "Behmen's Aurora, which I had *conjured over* at School".[51] Boehme's influence on Coleridge can be detected in particular passages in his poetic works, such as the line "A light in sound, a sound-like power in light" from "The Eolian Harp," which, it has been suggested, referred to Boehme's *Aurora*, chapter 10.[52] But Boehme's influence can also be detected in the more general development of Coleridge's thought. In particular, Boehme might have informed such crucial themes in Coleridge's religious writings as his concept of the will, his views on the Trinity, the positive value he placed on self-annihilation and the imagination, and his ideas about dynamic relations being based on the energy arising from "opposites."[53] What Coleridge perceived as Boehme's pantheism, on the other hand, remained a problem for him. Thus, in a marginal note to *Mysterium Magnum* from 1819, Coleridge expressed his "great delight [. . .] that Behmen guided by the light of a sincere love of truth, worked himself out of the Pantheism (God = Chaos) of his earlier writings: and seems in this Tract to have emerged into the full Day."[54] As early as the following day, however, a disappointed Coleridge had to conclude that "as I read on, I [. . .] found that this first Chapter is a deceptive Promise: that Behmen soon deviates into his original error [. . .] and places the polarities *in* the Deity. [. . .] In short, Behmen remains, I fear and as far as I have hitherto read, a Cabiric Physiotheist."[55]

But beyond the particulars of Boehme's "system," of which Coleridge remained at least partly critical, he seems to have valued what he considered Boehme's curious combination of visionary power and philosophical clarity, and being "a poor unlearned man."[56] "What wonder then," asks Coleridge,

> if in some places the Mist condenses into a thick smoke with a few wandering rays darting across it [. . .] The true wonder is, that in so many places it thins away almost into a transparent Medium, and Jacob Behmen, *the Philosopher*, surprizes us in proportion as Behmen, the Visionary, had astounded or perplexed us.[57]

Likewise in a letter from 1810, Coleridge may well disparagingly comment on Boehme's "ridiculous Analysis of the word, Mercurius, with the separate meanings of Mer, Cu, Ri, and Us"[58] and tell the recipient of the letter, Lady Beaumont, that he does "not think, you will derive any advantage from [Boehme's] works—the worst and most suspicious circumstance in them is that they dwell so much in *shapes* & *fancies* & things which if true would delight the *curiosity.*"[59] But in the same letter, Coleridge calls Boehme "an extraordinary man" and notes that even though he thought Boehme to be "ignorant of Logic & not versed in the Laws of the Imagination, he rendered many *Intuitions* in his own mind, perhaps of very profound Truths, and, as it were, *translated* them into such *Images* and *bodily* feelings as *by accident* were co-present with his Intuitions."[60] Despite Coleridge's impression of Boehme's lack of formal learning—or perhaps even because of it—he seems to have been struck by Boehme's ability to propose a written vision that addressed the "head" as well as the "heart" of the reader (even though he found Boehme to have had "but a scanty store of Words," so that he was "obliged to repeat the same word with various predicates where more learned men would have established distinct Terms").[61] Thus in the autobiographical *Biographia Literaria* (1817), Coleridge notes with reference to Boehme, William Law, and the Quaker leader George Fox (1624–91) that

> the writings of these Mystics acted in no slight degree to prevent my mind from being imprisoned within any single dogmatic system. They contributed to keep alive the *heart* in the *head*; gave me an indistinct, yet stirring and working presentment, that all the products of the mere *reflective* faculty partook of DEATH.[62]

The two features of Boehme's work that Coleridge notes above—his translation of "truths" into "images and bodily feelings" and his equal addressing of the "heart" and the "head" of the reader (a sometimes infuriating authorial choice when trying to understand Boehme's works)—seem also to have been picked up by Blake some years earlier. Indeed, one could say that Blake (in a way which few other Boehme readers have done) reacts precisely to the pictorial quality in Boehme's works. This pictorial quality, which is also reflected in Dionysius Andreas Freher's illustrations,[63] manifests itself in the way that Boehme's concepts are given form in his writings; Sophia, for example, is not an abstract concept, but a woman, as is Blake's figure *Jerusalem*.[64] Blake, unlike Coleridge, refuses to resort to abstractions to interpret Boehme. For Coleridge, there is always an intellectual and coherency test, the test of orthodoxy, which he must pass: his ignorance of logic and of "Laws of the Imagination" are his weakness rather than his strength. It is Blake's instinctive understanding of Boehme's three-dimensional world that, arguably, makes him the more faithful, and potentially the more radical, reader of the Teutonic philosopher.

NOTES

1. On Wordsworth's reading of Boehme, see the *Catalogue of the Varied and Valuable Historical, Poetical, Theological, and Miscellaneous Library of the Late Venerated Poet-Laureate, William Wordsworth* (Preston: Charles Ambler, 1859), 20; Newton P. Stallknecht, *Strange Seas of Thought* (Bloomington: Indiana University Press, 1958).
2. For further reading, see A. D. Snyder, "Coleridge and Boehme," *Publications of the Modern Language Association* 45 (1930): 616–18; Bryan Aubrey, *Watchmen for Eternity: Blake's Debt to Jacob Boehme* (Lanham, MD, University Press of America, 1986); D. Stewart, "Blake, Boehme and the human or prophetic character" (DPhil. diss., University of Oxford, 1990); T. Fulford, "Coleridge, Bohme, and the Language of Nature," *Modern Language Quarterly* 52 (1991): 37–52; E. P. Thompson, *Witness against the Beast: William Blake and the Moral Law* (Cambridge: Cambridge University Press, 1993); Kevin Fischer, *Converse in the Spirit: William Blake, Jacob Boehme and the Creative Spirit* (Madison, NJ: Fairleigh Dickinson University Press, 2004); M. Newman, " 'Milton's Track' revisited: Visual Analogues to Blake's

Vortex in the 'Law Edition' of Boehme," *Interdisciplinary Literary Studies* 5, no. 2 (2004): 73–93.

3. Blake's library was not kept together after his death, and many of his books (including, for example, his Bible) are untraced. Books that we know he owned are listed in G. E. Bentley Jr., *Blake Books* (Oxford: Clarendon Press, 1977), 681–702, and G.E. Bentley Jr., *Blake Books Supplement* (Oxford: Clarendon Press, 1995), 313–25.
4. As noted above, the influence of Boehme on Blake has been discussed extensively in various studies.
5. G.E. Bentley Jr., *Blake Records* (New Haven; London: Yale University Press, 2004), 423–24. Visual connections between Blake and Freher (whose illustrations were used for the Law edition), or between Blake and other Boehme illustrators, have been suggested, but not yet been sufficiently studied.
6. At least according to Bentley's *Blake Records*.
7. Bentley Jr., *Blake Records*, 57. These were probably Boehme's works in English translation, although Tatham in the same letter claims that Blake had "a most consummate knowledge of all the great writers in all languages" (ibid.).
8. Thomas De Quincey, "Coleridge and Opium-Eating," *Blackwood's Edinburgh Magazine* 58, no. 357 (1845): 118.
9. Jon Mee, "Behmenism," in *An Oxford Companion to the Romantic Age: British Culture 1776–1832*, ed. Iain McCalman (Oxford: Oxford University Press, 1999), 420.
10. *The Complete Poetry and Prose of William Blake*, ed. David V. Erdman, Newly Revised edn. (New York: Anchor Books, 1988), 707–8. Hereafter E.
11. Blake seems to have engaged with these early sources of inspiration on his own initiative; he had no formal education but appears to have read widely and eclectically from an early age; see G.E. Bentley Jr., *The Stranger from Paradise: A Biography of William Blake* (New Haven; London: Yale University Press, 2001), chapter 1; Alexander Gilchrist, *The Life of William Blake*, ed. W. Graham Robertson (London; New York: John Lane The Bodley Head; John Lane Company, 1907), 16.
12. Mona Wilson, *The Life of William Blake*, ed. Geoffrey Keynes (Oxford: Oxford University Press, 1971), 57; Robert Rix, *William Blake and the Cultures of Radical Christianity* (Aldershot: Ashgate, 2007), 14–15.
13. William Law, ed. *The Works of Jacob Behmen, the Teutonic Theosopher*, (4 vols., London: M. Richardson, 1764–81), vol. 2, 60. Blake's ecumenical tendencies might also be connected with his assumed familiarity with the Moravian tradition through his mother, who was a member of the Moravian community in Fetter Lane from 1750–51; see, Keri Davies and Marsha Keith Schuchard, "Recovering the Lost Moravian History of William Blake's Family," *Blake / An Illustrated Quarterly* 38, no. 1 (2004): 36–43.
14. Rix, *Blake*, 15.
15. *All Religions*, copy A, pl. 10, in William Blake, *The Early Illuminated Books: All Religions are One, There is No Natural Religion, The Book of Thel, The Marriage of Heaven and Hell, Visions of the Daughters of Albion*, eds. Morris Eaves, Robert N. Essick, and Joseph Viscomi (Princeton: The William Blake Trust / Princeton University Press, 1993).
16. Janet A. Warner, *Blake and the Language of Art* (Kingston; Montreal: McGill-Queen's University Press, 1984), chapter 3.
17. Although he later seems to nuance these views: in *Milton a Poem* (1804–11), for example, Blake refers to 'Swedenborg! strongest of men, the Samson shorn by the Churches!' (22.50, E117).

18. Samuel Foster Damon, *A Blake Dictionary: The Ideas and Symbols of William Blake* (London: Thames and Hudson, 1973), 40.
19. References to Swedenborg in *The Marriage* are obvious—even the title, *The Marriage of Heaven and Hell*, refers to Swedenborg's *A Treatise concerning Heaven and Hell*, which Blake annotated (E601–9). See Robert Rix, "'In Infernal Love and Faith': William Blake's *The Marriage of Heaven and Hell*," *Literature and Theology* 20, no. 2 (2006): 107–25.
20. Quoted in Fischer, *Converse in Spirit*, 64.
21. Law, ed. *Works of Behmen*, vol. 4, 10.
22. Ibid., 9.
23. Quoted in Fischer, *Converse in Spirit*, 63.
24. Blake to Thomas Butts (22 November 1802), l. 88, in E722.
25. Kathleen Raine, *Blake and Tradition*, (2 vols., Princeton: Princeton University Press, 1969), vol. 2, 151–71; Aubrey, *Watchmen*, 131–34.
26. Aubrey, *Watchmen*, 30.
27. Law, ed. *Works of Behmen*, vol. 2, 66.
28. Jonathan Roberts, *William Blake's Poetry: A Reader's Guide* (London: Continuum, 2007), 64–67.
29. Blake to Revd Dr Trusler (August 23, 1799), in E702.
30. In "To Nobodaddy," for example, the narrator asks: "Why art thou silent & invisible/ Father of Jealousy/ Why dost thou hide thyself in clouds/ From every searching Eye" (1–4, E471). The father figure usually represents a problematic presence in Blake's works.
31. Law, ed. *Works of Behmen*, vol. 2, 16.
32. Quoted in Fischer, *Converse in the Spirit*, 206.
33. Cf. Thompson, *Witness against Beast*; Christopher Rowland, *Blake and the Bible* (New Haven; London: Yale University Press, 2010).
34. Elisabeth Engell Jessen, "Conversion as a Narrative, Visual, and Stylistic Mode in William Blake's Works" (DPhil. diss., University of Oxford, 2012), chapter 2. Blake's inspiration for experimenting with representations of the wounded or open(ed) Christ might be connected with his familiarity with mid-eighteenth-century Moravian spirituality, in which Christ's wounds—particularly his side-wound—played a central role.
35. Law, ed. *Works of Behmen*, vol. 4, 13.
36. Although it has been argued that Blake (and Coleridge) did not get the term "self-annihilation" directly from Boehme, but rather from David Hartley, who was also a Boehme reader; see, John Howard, *Blake's "Milton": A Study in the Selfhood* (Rutherford: Fairleigh Dickinson University Press, 1976), 177–78.
37. This had also played a role in late revisions of the unfinished illuminated manuscript *The Four Zoas* (ca. 1797–1807).
38. Aubrey, *Watchmen*, chapter 4; Newman, "'Milton's Track,'" 73–93.
39. Law, ed. *Works of Behmen*, vol. 4, 19.
40. Boehme's fourth property is defined in *The Clavis* as "the Fire, in which the Unity appears, and is seen in the Light, that is, in a burning Love; and the wrath in the Essence of Fire"; see, Law, ed. *Works of Behmen*, vol. 2, 10; Fischer, *Converse in Spirit*, 110–19.
41. 42.36–43.1, E144.
42. David Riede, "Blake's Milton: On Membership in the Church Paul," in *Re-Membering Milton: Essays on the Texts and Traditions*, eds. Mary Nyquist and Margaret W. Ferguson (New York; London: Methuen, 1987), 257–77.
43. Although Boehme was, as Aubrey observes (*Watchmen*, 30), "far less world-negating than many of the medieval mystics."

44. Law, ed. *Works of Behmen*, vol. 2, 24.
45. "Error" is perhaps the closest Blake comes to a concept of sin; see, Jeanne Moskal, *Blake, Ethics, and Forgiveness* (Tuscaloosa; London: University of Alabama Press, 1994).
46. Although imagination in Boehme's works appears to be a neutral faculty, which can be employed in a good as well as a corrupted way, it still plays an important role in his thought: "Understand through *Imagination*," he writes in *Signatura Rerum*, "for the *Eternal* is *Magical*" (2.20); see, Law, ed. *Works of Behmen*, vol. 4, 14; Brian Gibbons, *Gender in Mystical and Occult Thought: Behmenism and its Development in England* (Cambridge: Cambridge University Press, 1996), 125. In Blake's works, on the other hand, imagination is identical with the body of Christ, which we can all partake in: "O Human Imagination O Divine Body" (*Jerusalem* 24.23, E169).
47. *Collected Letters of Samuel Taylor Coleridge*, ed. Earl Leslie Griggs, (6 vols., Oxford: Clarendon Press, 1959), vol. 4, 833–34.
48. Morton D. Paley, *Samuel Taylor Coleridge and the Fine Arts* (Oxford: Oxford University Press, 2008), 191–92.
49. "The Inventions of William Blake, Painter and Poet", in *London University Magazine* (March, 1830), cited in ibid., 192.
50. Samuel Taylor Coleridge, *Marginalia 1: Abbt to Byfield*, ed. George Whalley, vol. 12, *The Collected Works of Samuel Taylor Coleridge* (Princeton: Princeton University Press, 1980), 553.
51. *Collected Letters*, vol. 4, 751. Coleridge's annotated Law edition is now in the British Library (C.126.k.1), and the annotations (which refer in particular to *Aurora* and *The Three Principles of the Divine Essence* and were probably made between 1808 and 1826) appear in print in Coleridge, *Marginalia 1*, 553–696.
52. M.H. Abrams, "Coleridge's "A Light in Sound": Science, Metascience, and Poetic Imagination," *Proceedings of the American Philosophical Society* 116, no. 6 (1972): 458–76; John B. Beer, *Coleridge the Visionary* (London: Chatto & Windus, 1959), 163–64; Duane B. Schneider, "Coleridge's Light-Sound Theory," *Notes and Queries*, no. 208 (1963): 182–83; John B. Beer, "Coleridge and Boehme's "Aurora," *Notes and Queries*, no. 208 (1963): 183–87. Coleridge himself established the connection between his light-sound image and Boehme—and more specifically *Aurora*—in the 1817 letter to Tieck quoted above.
53. For additional literature on Coleridge and Boehme, see note 2 above.
54. Coleridge, *Marginalia 1*, 677.
55. Ibid., 678.
56. Inserted leaf, in ibid., 558.
57. Ibid., 558.
58. *Three Principles of the Divine Essence* 1.12.
59. Coleridge, *Collected Letters*, vol. 3, 279.
60. Ibid, 278.
61. Marginal note to *Aurora*, in Coleridge, *Marginalia 1*, 561.
62. Samuel Taylor Coleridge, *Biographia Literaria or Biographical Sketches of My Literary Life and Opinions*, eds. James Engell and W. Jackson Bate, (2 vols., Princeton: Princeton University Press, 1983), vol. 1, 152.
63. Charles A. Muses, *Illumination on Jacob Boehme. The Work of Dionysius Andreas Freher* (New York: King's Crown Press, 1951).
64. Susanne M. Sklar, *Blake's Jerusalem as Visionary Theatre: Entering the Divine Body* (Oxford: Oxford University Press, 2011), 72–75.

11 The Russian Boehme

Oliver Smith

The colossal influence of Jacob Boehme on Russian culture has been acknowledged for some time.[1] While there are names that feature more regularly in the largely one-sided conversation in which Russian thinkers began to engage their Western peers and forebears from the end of the seventeenth century, the relative unanimity of adulation that characterizes Boehme's reception is striking. Hegel and Schelling are by turns exalted and denounced in the fickle world of the Russian intellectual, yet Boehme can be ignored but almost never reviled. The exceptions to this rule include certain "official" parties in state and church, although both spheres contained sympathizers.[2] His writings, as well as his life and personality, form one of the most consistent backdrops to the birth of the Russian literary tradition as well as Russian religious philosophy, from the early mason-mystics to consummate philosophers such as Vladimir Soloviev (1853–1900) and Nikolai Berdyaev (1874–1948) and from early Gothic novelists such as Vladimir Odoevsky (1803–69) to symbolist experimenters like Fyodor Sologub (1863–1927). Many of these figures, unlike in the West where readers of the German mystic tended to belong to heterodox communities outside the mainstream churches, were Orthodox Christians who regularly attended the divine liturgy, a fact that lends a particular temper to the Russian reception of Boehme and which points toward a certain inner resonance between the cobbler-mystic and Orthodox liturgical culture. Indeed, Boehme's texts often appear to perform a function not dissimilar to the ceremonial absorption of the individual believer within liturgical space, enfolding not only the mind and will of their Russian reader but also his very sensual being. In this context, Boehme's writings not only take on properties of sacred utterances;[3] they themselves are treated as instruments of transformation which, in the right hands, can lead their reader to an experience of the authentically divine. For this reason, the account that follows necessarily involves recognizing the dynamic relationship between the text and its readers as well as simple source analysis.

I

The beginning of Boehme's influence in Russia dates to the 1670s, when there existed a Behmenist circle in Moscow under the leadership of Kondratii Norderman (d.1689), who appears to have translated some of Boehme's writings into Russian and even sent a letter to Tsar Alexei Mikhailovich in 1669 replete with his own prognostications as to the future of humanity.[4] This circle was for a short time invigorated by the arrival of the prominent Behmenist Quirinus Kuhlmann (1651–89) who, convinced that "the light will arise from the East" and that there "a new kingdom and a new people shall be formed," arrived in Moscow to preach his message of the "Fifth Monarchy" to co-regents Ivan and Peter. Kuhlmann and Nordermann were, after a desultory investigation, executed by burning, having been accused of the distribution of "certain prophetic books,"[5] which were duly incinerated alongside them. Although these books, besides Kuhlmann's own works, may have included translations of Boehme, it was most likely the challenge to political authority that the group represented rather than any inherent distaste for German mysticism that motivated the authorities to act.[6]

Indeed, the ability of highly positioned figures within the state apparatus to engage in esoteric activities with seeming impunity is illustrated by one James Daniel Bruce (1669–1735), an early scientist of Scottish descent and an influential statesman under Peter the Great. While it is difficult to separate truth from myth in the case of Bruce, whose name had already in his lifetime become synonymous with sorcery and the occult, it is known that his library, alongside numerous other esoteric writings, contained at least four German volumes of Boehme.[7] Given the paucity of evidence surrounding Bruce's final years spent on his beloved estate Glinki, as well as the insufficiency of his written legacy in forming an opinion as to his worldview, it is difficult to ascertain the extent of Boehme's influence on him. Nevertheless, the connection between the writings of Boehme and the birth of Russian freemasonry, of which Bruce was a notable representative, seems to be borne out by developments in and around his estate from the mid-eighteenth century. Glinki was the first stone estate in Russia (outside the imperial complexes of the tsars), and has been called the first "nest of masonry" in Muscovy. It included a pavilion, which may have been used as a lodge, and masonic symbols proliferated in the architectural details of the house as well as in the sculptural ensembles that lined the grand pathways of its gardens. At the same time that Russia was busily absorbing centuries of Western religious, philosophical, and scientific thought—a process if not initiated then certainly given added urgency by Peter—its managed landscapes were undergoing a similar breakneck journey through the preceding decades of European horticulture.

It seems fitting, therefore, that the early reception of Boehme, who had in his teaching on the "signature of things" set out what was to become one of the foundational premises of later Russian religious thought—the contiguity of the visible and invisible worlds—should find reflection in the changing patterns of the Russian estate garden. Bruce's Glinki stands at the transition point between a fondness for Dutch and French models, characterized by wide boulevards, trimmed hedges and statuary and, by the mid-1760s, a desire to mirror English horticultural methods with their unexpected, open vistas and intimate spaces.[8] It was necessary, writes one commentator, to "renounce the idea of seeing 'a piece of heaven on earth,' " which the gardens of the seventeenth and early eighteenth centuries had striven to demonstrate in Europe. Instead, one had to understand the garden as a "place, where one can visibly perceive the entire significance of the Divine creation in its totality."[9] This meant doing away with the symmetry and self-contained lines of enlightened reason—the human mind placing its own, rational schema onto untamed nature—and instead becoming part of the "divine enthusiasm" that penetrates all things. Space was not to be enclosed within alleys or symmetrical figurations, but extended, giving the illusion of stretching into infinity. The garden was thus to embody the living experience of the paradoxical indwelling of that which cannot be contained within any given thing. Here, the human being did not reveal the content of eternity through device but rather the Eternal Being; as Andrew Weeks explains, Boehme's concept of the "signature" became "self-transparent through its works of self-revelation."[10] Such a development, involving a withdrawal of the human from its external setting, can be understood as the reflection in externality of what Rémi Brague, in relation to Bernard of Clairvaux, has called the "anthropology of humility,"[11] and whose preeminent representative in Russian masonic circles at this time was Jacob Boehme.[12]

Through their move away from the exertion of control over their environment toward a model where, far from bringing the limitless within the limit, the finite human mind itself was opened up to the infinite, Russians signaled their early departure from the Cartesian mindset with its pretensions to the absolute possession of reality. In the process, the garden ceased to be a product of human ingenuity geared toward embodied perfection and instead began to reflect the stages of a journey undertaken by the soul. The philosopher and agronomist Andrei Bolotov (1738–1833), for example, valued the garden precisely as such a journey into the unknown and was opposed to the imposition of strict geometrical form and symmetry since it "enables the stroller to grasp the plan of the whole garden at once, in an act of totalizing viewing," something he considered inherently sinful for the humble Christian.[13]

Nowhere was this Christian symbolism to be made more explicit than at the estate Savinskoe, belonging to the Lopukhin family (with whom Bruce was on close terms) and a short walk away from Bruce's estate to the north along the River Voria. Although, as with Glinki, nothing today survives of its park and gardens, we have several accounts of their composition. Here, a number of recent trends observed in Western Europe came together. First, like their Georgian counterparts, the gardens at Savinskoe reflected a "specific iconographic program relating to the personal concerns of [their] creator,"[14] wherein, as the poet Dolgorukov wrote after a visit to the estate, "every glance is a teaching/ Every step a hieroglyph."[15] Second, there was a need to see this "program" arise organically, from the creative work of the divine in nature, rather than through human endeavor. Third, the garden was to be constructed narratologically, as a journey that builds a consonance between inner experience and external form. Savinskoe, whose gardens first began to take shape in the 1780s under the influence of Ivan Lopukhin, was in this way in intention similar to the rock garden Sanspareil near Bayreuth where, in the words of its creator Margravine Wilhelmine, "die Natur selbst war die Baumeisterin."[16] Yet Savinskoe was different from Sanspareil in one crucial respect. Sanspareil was based on the adventures of Telemachus (son of Odysseus), especially as depicted in the French Quietist François Fénelon's *Les Aventures de Télémaque*, which the author had written as a moral tale on good rulership. The garden, therefore, like the novel, was highly didactic and was intended to convey the more exigent aspects of benevolent governance to its visitor.[17] Following the rarefied mores of the epoch, archetypes for these ideal qualities were sought in the ancients, and the statuary was overwhelmingly focused on classical themes.

Savinskoe, as well as other masonic estates of the time, operated on a completely different level, and in this, it owes a debt to Boehme. Its symbolism was not didactic but veiled, depending on the "individual perception of the onlooker, capable of discerning esoteric meaning and speculatively transforming the customary elements of Russian estate life into mysterious signs."[18] Here, it was not the designer of the garden that controlled the visitor's experience, but nature itself that opened up to each viewer according to his or her capacities. A stroll around the garden thus amounted to a kind of "spiritual wandering,"[19] where the soul was enabled to read its inherent potentialities from the environment surrounding it.

The centerpiece of the park was Young's Island (named after the English poet Edward Young, discussed in chapter 9), described by contemporaries as a "pantheon to pietism" and containing monuments and buildings dedicated to figures of significance to the Russian masons. Although one could find here monuments to Socrates and Diogenes, these were not the classically inspired busts and statues that littered other European estates of the time. Each figure was identified with a particular object-symbol, which was intended not to memorialize the persons themselves but rather the *path* along which they called humanity to follow. One passed over the waters separating the body of the park from the island (symbolizing baptism as well as the path of unknowing), thence over a small bridge where one was immediately met by a cross dedicated to Jacob Boehme. This monument was described in some detail by Alexander Koval'kov, a student of Lopukhin who may have assisted in the planning of the park.[20]

> The Cross [. . .] is the first sight that one encounters upon crossing over to this blessed island. It is simple; but in its simplicity resides that majesty which is foreign to even the most magnificent obelisks [. . .]
>
> This Cross is dedicated to the great Theosopher Jacob Boehme, whose image is depicted in marble at its foot. Roses and violets, which grow around it, bring him their fragrance as tribute.[21]

Two things stand out here as being of significance. First, the monument to Boehme was the very first encountered upon crossing the bridge onto Young's Island after the path of unknowing. Second, unlike the other monuments, which included obelisks and bas-reliefs (Fénelon and the Bavarian mystic Karl von Eckhartshausen were both commemorated in the form of urns), Boehme was immortalized not through classical motifs but through the cross of Christ.[22] These two facts speak of both Boehme's preeminent position as well as the peculiarity of his Russian reception. Amongst all esoteric writers, it was he who was considered the most authentically Christian. As Nikolai Berdyaev, who himself praised the early Russian masons as the first freethinkers on Russian soil,[23] would later write, Boehme "is the greatest of the gnostics, but also the most Christian of them all."[24] This was an opinion held throughout the nineteenth and twentieth centuries, not only by representatives of the non-churched Russian philosophical community, but also by prominent figures within the most enlightened strands of Russian Orthodoxy itself.[25] This seems puzzling at first, given the alleged absence of the redemptive power of the cross in Boehme, as well as the much greater amount of material dedicated to practical matters of Christian spirituality in writers such as Johann Arndt or Thomas à Kempis. Justifiably or otherwise, the authenticity of Boehme's Christianity was associated with his "simplicity," a characteristic ascribed not so much to his writings (for not even the Russians were eccentric enough to believe this to be true) but to the *style* or spirit of his philosophizing.[26]

Alexander Koval'kov (1795–1852), the exuberant describer of Savinskoe, seemed to model himself on such Boehmean "simplicity." Unique in Russian masonic circles as coming from peasant stock, Koval'kov was one of the first mystics outside the schismatic tradition to lay claim to the role of prophet (a role increasingly assumed by those inspired by Boehme in the nineteenth century), beginning to publish his "revelations" from the age of fourteen. Now largely forgotten, in his time Koval'kov was regarded with devotion by a minority and suspicion by the majority as a channel for Lopukhin's ideas about the "inner church." I think the age needs to be shifted from the Works to Koval'kov himself—perhaps 'Yet by the time of the publication of the *Mystical Works of Alexander Koval'kov* in 1815, he had, at the tender age of twenty-one, developed into a mature religious thinker whose work demonstrates a profound knowledge of the European mystical tradition, enlivened by a palpable spiritual experience that is lacking in the more prominent writings of Lopukhin. The inner consonance between Koval'kov and Boehme is felt on almost every page of these volumes, and in particular in the former's "Thoughts on Mysticism and its Writers." Here, Koval'kov unfolds a sort of diagnostics of mystical experience. Most interesting is his recommendation of the study of different mystical writers in accordance with the varieties of human personality:

> The inner paths leading to the true Light differ from soul to soul, according to their differences in levels of state and abilities. Some are moved by the purity of Love, the way of living Faith in the inwardness of souls. These find their true enjoyment and treasure in the works of Madame Guyon. Others are roused by the Wisdom of Love, its order, and its mysteries in the heavenly Nature: such as these are filled with reverence, gratitude and the pure flame of zeal, receiving into themselves mystic food in the writings of the divinely wise and heavenly crowned Jacob Boehme, that light to the world kindled directly from the fire of Divine love itself, that man of mysteries, I say, in whom Wisdom, as in her own true Temple and element, spoke forth the law of Her Nature.[27]

Koval'kov later restates this comparison between Guyon and Boehme, adding that the former is most suited to those who wish to tend above all to their inner life while "in the works of the divinely wise Jacob Boehme, souls will find all levels both of the external, lower nature, as well as the inner spiritual and Mystic-Divine."[28]

This interpretation of Boehme as synthesizer of the external and internal natures takes Koval'kov beyond Lopukhin's conception of the "inner church" and anticipates the treatment of the same problem in later thinkers such as Vladimir Soloviev and Sergii Bulgakov. Most arresting in this respect is Koval'kov's adumbration of what Bulgakov was to call the "primary sophiological antinomy"—the identity and distinction of Sophia-Wisdom in God on the one hand and in creation on the other—through his development of two central terms from Boehme's corpus: quintessence and tincture.[29]

Though these two categories are often conflated by other alchemical thinkers (such as Paracelsus) and, as a result, by Boehme commentators, the cobbler-mystic is clear in separating the concepts of quintessence (or *quinta essentia*) and tincture. In a passage from *Theosophic Questions*, for example, Boehme enumerates the multiple layers separating created matter from the godhead:

> The four elements are what is outermost; next after them is the astral body; the third in order is the *quinta essentia*, as the principle of the emanated holy Element; the fourth is the tincture, viz. the highest power

Figure 11.1 The only known surviving monument from Young's Island on the Savinskoe Estate, dedicated to Quirinus Kuhlmann. It was found on the estate territory in the 1920s and is now held in the Noginsk Museum of Local History in the Moscow Region. The inscription reads: "Quirinus Kuhlmann was tortured and burnt as a heretic in Moscow in 1689 . . . Passer-by, stop and sigh over this sufferer; bless the enlightenment that scattered the gloom of the ferocity of these times; and learn to be attentive in the very striving toward truth." © Copyright Aleksandr Poslykhalin, 2012

> of the emanated word, in which the two inner central fires lie in one ground. After this, the pure clear Deity is understood.[30]

Quintessence, then, may be described as the heavenly principle inherent in all created matter, a *product* of the heavenly economy, whereas tincture is the "power by which things are changed [. . .] the Word in act;"[31] a kind of "spiritual form that stands betwixt ideal and real being."[32] Koval'kov unfolds precisely this Boehmean understanding of the quintessence and tincture yet adds to this a framework for the further elaboration of their relation. Unlike Boehme, for whom sophianic consummation equated to the reunion of the two tinctures—the tincture of fire and the tincture of light—in the virginal, androgynous Adam, Koval'kov posits the same in the reunion of the tincture (associated with the Son) with the quintessence (associated with the Father), which tincture and quintessence in unity in

Figure 11.2 An etching of Young's Island included in an 1809 edition of the journal *Herald of Europe*. To the left can be seen the urn commemorating Fénelon, while the building in the center is most likely a bell-tower. Boehme's cross was located immediately upon crossing over the bridge on the right-hand side of the picture onto the island. *Vestnik Evropa*, February 1809, No. 4. (out of copyright)

the One yet in separation in the creature. The author then sets out the task of "grasping the character of both tincture and Essence, understanding the means of their union [. . .] and then, with the help of the tincture of substances, purifying and resurrecting bodies."[33]

In this argument, subtly different from that of Boehme yet employing the same terminology, Koval'kov introduces an important alteration to the German mystic's original conception. If, for Boehme, everything "external is a type of the internal"[34] and, in the apposite words of Cyril O'Regan, "sanctification is eternal self-glorification of the divine *in and by the eternal divine milieu*,"[35] Koval'kov adapts Boehmean thinking to reserve a space for a history of the cosmos that is not merely a figuration of the eternal but a temporal movement toward the Divine through conscious human agency. Salvation thus becomes the overcoming of the internal-external division, not through divine fiat but through the mediation of a humanity united with God.

In this process, Boehme and his works themselves take on a distinctly soteriological character. Koval'kov describes the cobbler-mystic as a "messenger" and a "weapon of good news about the heavenly mysteries."[36] Boehme, as "true" mystic, himself becomes the door through which the initiate steps into authentic knowledge of the mystery of God. "The main thing in the teaching of the errant mind consists in theory alone, but in

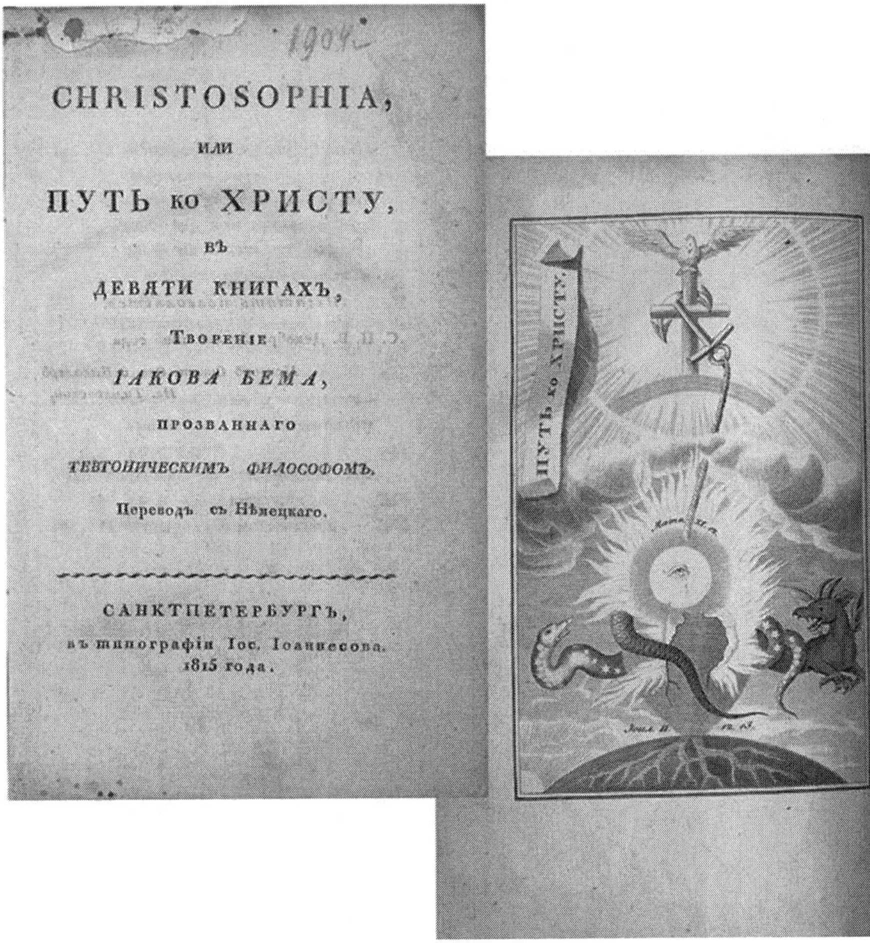

Figure 11.3 An 1815 edition of *Christophia, oder Weg zu Christo*, published in St. Petersburg with an introduction by Ivan Labzin (out of copyright).

Mysticism (*Mistika*)[37] the very spirit speaking is practice."[38] In other words, to read the works of Boehme is not to imbibe the theoretical postulates of the created and uncreated realms, but rather to hear the spirit speaking from its own source, unmediated by human agency. Or, to put it another way, the goal was not so much to master Boehme as to see what he saw and to experience what he experienced. As another member of Lopukhin's circle, Nikolai Kraevich, put it: "the Kingdom of God will not dawn in us through the reading of enlightened authors. We should in ourselves be our own Boehmes."[39]

II

By 1815, the year in which Koval'kov's collected works were published and the Russian version of Boehme's *Christosophia* released in St Petersburg, the German mystic was firmly established as the lodestar of Russian intellectual and religious life. So much so that, in that very same year, the noted poet Ivan Dmitriev complained that he was unable to acquire any novels whatsoever through his book dealer since the latter was no longer importing literature but ordering "Boehme and his comrades" from Paris.[40] The explanations for this are multiple: the heady atmosphere of the early years of Alexander I's reign, under whose rule mystical trends of all kinds were encouraged and materially supported;[41] the perceived closeness of Boehme's writings, with their striking imagery, relating not only to the visual but also to taste and smell, to the richly sensual liturgical life of Orthodoxy; and the general tenor of early Russian freemasonry, which one twentieth-century representative, Boris Ermolov, has described as a "healthy response of the best Russian cultural forces against spiritual dissipation and atheistic currents adopted from without."[42]

The rapid ingestion of Enlightenment ideas, particularly under Catherine the Great (who greatly admired the *philosophes*), undoubtedly went hand-in-hand with a diminishment of the spiritual authority of the Church after the transference of its powers to the secular Holy Synod under Peter the Great. A figurehead was therefore needed from outside the Russian tradition who could, through his intellectual might, counter the specious arguments of the Deists and atheists while at the same time embodying the kind of personal sanctity and zeal that had been all but exterminated from Russian church life. All the same, that amongst the legion of Pietist writers this figurehead should be Jacob Boehme was due in no small part to an elite group of mystic-intellectuals from Moscow who gathered under the aegis of the so-called Learned Society of Friends and met at a number of masonic lodges. In the half-century extending from the last years of Catherine's reign to the peak of Alexandrine mystical enthusiasm and ending with the banning of freemasonry in 1822, their frenetic activity in the realms of publishing, public speaking, and education laid the foundations for a peculiarly Russian Rosicrucianism, often referred to in the literature, somewhat misleadingly, as "Martinism" (after the French Behmenist Louis Claude de Saint-Martin).

The lectures of Ivan Shvarts (1751–1784) demonstrate a profound knowledge of—though not complete dependence on—the teachings of Boehme.[43] Shvarts sets Koval'kov's belief in the salvific power of Boehme's writings in an historical perspective, promoting the notion of an Adamic revelation preserved from the time of the first human being to the present day by certain "friends of God," amongst whom he highlights in particular Boehme and Johann Lavater.[44] Meanwhile, Koval'kov's later accommodation within a Boehmean schema of a cosmic history with its own independent being and dignity can be observed, albeit less emphatically, in a lecture by Shvarts dating to 1782. Here, Shvarts follows Boehme in unfolding an understanding of the human being as an "instrument of God." Yet whereas, for Boehme, the human being is an instrument on which the divine *plays*, for Shvarts, the human being is an "instrument, through whom and in whom God Himself wishes *to act*."[45] Again, the difference is a subtle but important one. For Boehme, as we have said, salvation is fulfilled within the divine environment and, if human beings are participants, it is only insofar as they enter wholly into the resignation of the will that allows the heavenly tincture contained within them to "spring into action." Although Shvarts is not yet as daring as Koval'kov, he builds a scriptural foundation for regarding the material world as a genuine participant in salvation history. In this vein, and surely influenced by the Orthodox veneration of relics, he writes that

> God, having created the perishable and the imperishable, desired through the human being to bring the dark and perishable into the light and imperishable. This imperishable matter is contained in our bones. Carefully inspecting the bone one may see within a certain luminous tint.[46]

This inclusion of the material body within God's salvific economy allows Shvarts to suggest a concrete role for the temporal activity of the human being: "we should try to refine or purify our body to make it less perishable."[47]

Nevertheless, the central human activity that Shvarts highlights in the lecture—imagination—coincides almost entirely with its treatment in Boehme. "Imagination," he writes, "is our most fundamental power. It is the mouth of our soul, through which we taste of spiritual and moral knowledge."[48] Shvarts goes on to outline two types of imagination: one he calls "tasting" and the other "visual," the first leading to the disintegration of the soul and the second to its integration with God. The "main responsibility" of the human being, from this perspective, is to "recognize in oneself the diverging ways of the imagination,"[49] and from there, consciously to strive along the path that leads to the divine.

A counterpart of Shvarts, Semyon Gamaleia (1743–1822), together with the most tireless mason of the age, Nikolai Novikov (1744–1818), conceived a scheme to build a "hermetic library" of some fifty volumes, consisting of Russian translations of esoteric philosophy. The project was brought to an abrupt end by Novikov's arrest in 1792, after which he and Gamaleia worked in solitude on the translations at the former's estate, Avdot'ino. Here, Gamaleia undertook the central aspect of this project: a translation of the complete works of Boehme, which he completed in twenty-two volumes between 1790 and 1795. Because of the prohibition on the activities of this group, these translations were never published, although several have survived in manuscript.[50] Nevertheless, they were copied by hand multiple times and held in the proliferating number of masonic libraries across Russia by the beginning of the nineteenth century. In one collection alone (that of Vasilii Arseniev), Boehme's works numbered sixty volumes.[51]

Gamaleia left little behind by way of original work, yet in his role as translator and model of sanctity, he was greatly esteemed by Russian masons. As Raffaella Faggionato has noted, the "traditional medieval concept of the writer who humbles himself completely in his text to become a divine instrument retained a sense of relevance and importance for the Rosicrucians."[52] In this context, Gamaleia, perhaps more than any other figure of his age, was the archetype of the aforementioned "anthropology of humility," inspiring many by his example. The prominent historian Vasily Kliuchevsky even went so far as to claim that Gamaleia "deserves a hagiography rather than a biography [. . .] Blessed in the best sense of the word, his contemporaries justifiably called him a 'man of God.' "[53] Gamaleia's letters bear witness to the centrality of humility to his worldview (the true Christian, he wrote, must "constantly immerse himself in humility"),[54] as well as his adoption of a peculiarly Boehmean approach to the description of the *via mystica*, which draws on the full range of human sensual experience. Consider, for example, the following passage:

> Whatsoever the human being is inwardly concerned with, with that he communes, and from that receives the qualities, just as when someone prepares various fragrant oils and balsams, she bears the smell of them. So that whoever with his entire soul is forever meditating on the life, example and teaching of Christ our Lord invariably gives off the smell of humility, meekness and tolerance.[55]

Gamaleia's use of the sense of smell here, which Boehme employs in abundance,[56] sounds peculiar indeed outside the alchemical context of the latter's writings. It is indicative of the seriousness given to Boehme's corpus, as well as the Russian tendency to read the German mystic as synthesizer of inner and external natures, that the empirical data of sensuality should be employed so readily for the purpose of disclosing the spiritual.

Gamaleia was also amongst the first to elucidate the role of Sophia, or Divine Wisdom, in his worldview. Although Shvarts had spoken, in Boehmean terms, of the "marriage of Sophia" in which Wisdom, in the most inward space of the heart, "gives [to the soul] the heavenly tincture," he refrained from further speculation on the matter by noting that "this transition is so great that it is impossible to have any conception of it."[57] Gamaleia, on the contrary, went into some detail on the subject in a 1782 speech to members of the Devkalion lodge, to which he belonged. While his treatment of Sophia-Wisdom leans more on Kabbalistic teaching and scriptural precedent, he adds to these former some elements of Boehmean discourse surrounding the idea of "eternal Nature" (*die ewig Natur*). Thus, his statement that "before creation Divine Wisdom played in the eternal Nature in upwardly soaring and mutually penetrating powers,"[58] has the disconcerting effect of co-opting Boehme into the creation account of Proverbs 8.

In many of Gamaleia's letters, he takes on the role of mentor, constantly discouraging pupils from engaging in their own mystical speculations and redirecting them toward prayer, the reading of scripture, and conversion of heart. In a particular letter, he advises that "some authors wrote (particularly one of them) purely for the reborn, and not for everyone [. . .] This is why we're better leaving certain authors until such a time as we become more able to receive them."[59] In another, he advises a friend that it is more fitting for his wife to read the New Testament and that "to give her the notebooks, it seems, is not necessary."[60] The particular author to whom Gamaleia alludes was certainly Boehme, translations of whose works were passed from hand to hand in small, annotated notebooks. His comments expose a conscious strategy on the part of Russian mason-mystics to control the writings of certain authors, especially Boehme, making access to them dependent on having reached a certain stage of spiritual maturity; a practice echoing the hierarchical approach to knowledge acquisition of the masonic degrees.[61]

One document that commanded tremendous authority in masonic circles was that containing the transcripts of talks given by Iosif Pozdeev (1746–1820),[62] a pupil of Gamaleia who later severed ties with Novikov in an argument over the direction of Russian freemasonry. In these talks, Pozdeev outlines a conception of God permeated by Boehmean dynamism: "in eternity one can find birth, for His desire consists only in a ceaseless fecundity or, so to say, a desire to ceaselessly give birth to himself." Pozdeev then permits himself a delightful paraphrase of Boehme's doctrine of creation, saying that "God became Creator in order to see himself in miniature," just as "human beings love to see themselves in their miniatures."[63] Through the circulation and reading of texts such as these, Boehme's view of creation not as the establishment of an independent "Other," but rather as a form of divine self-generation and self-perception, made a profound mark on the psyche of Russian freemasonry.

The influence of Gamaleia and his school was so large that he even saw fit to appear to people in their dreams, appearing in 1810 to the mason Kondrat Lokhvitsky (1774–1849).[64] Two years previously, Lokhvitsky had recorded in his diaries a conversion experience that had occurred while reading Boehme's *Christosophia*, a translation of which had been sent him by Labzin. Upon reading the words "Spirit of God," he was "possessed both inwardly and externally with an inexplicable yet pleasant spiritual dread," thanking "God the Saviour for his mercy in sending this word" to him "through the righteous Jacob," whom he elsewhere calls "St Boehme."[65] Lokhvitsky's account is merely the most striking of an influence that had, by the early nineteenth century, begun to reach beyond the masonic context.

III

From the 1820s onward, two different German thinkers—Schelling and Hegel—were to exercise ever greater command over the minds of Russian intellectuals. This was a time of immense hardship for freethinkers, with the ban on freemasonry in 1822 and the thirty-year reign of the über-autocratic Nicholas I, under whose police state all publications were rigorously censored, and the rights of free association wholly disbanded. Not all believed that German idealism represented a step forward, however, and esoteric currents of thought continued to win over new recruits. On the question of Boehme, upholders of the old ways of Christian theosophy often made uneasy bedfellows with adherents of the new, "scientific" thinking.

Stepan Shevyrev (1806–64), a conservative writer and critic, believed that Hegel had ignored the warnings of Boehme, "the true Founder of German Philosophy and Theosophy," in conflating the "principle of nature with nature itself." For, as Boehme had shown, Shevyrev counters Hegel in distinctly Hegelian terms: "the realization of the idea, as being-for-itself, is conditioned through the being of the principle of nature not-for-itself."[66] Meanwhile, Alexander Herzen (1812–70), a radical Hegelian, wished no less to reserve a place of honor for the German mystic, whose "mystical contemplation, deriving from a holy source, led him to a conception of a breadth the likes of which the science of his time could only dream."[67]

Herzen seemed to esteem Boehme almost despite himself and was at pains to point out that, despite the greatness of the man, all manner of detritus took its source from him, including the thought of Swedenborg, Eckhartshausen, Jung-Stilling, and other "hysterics of sundry unreadable journals and madhouses."[68] In opposition to these peddlers of esoteric nonsense, Boehme, for Herzen, is the founder of a scientific method, a precursor to the Hegelian dialectic, where "the *yes* cannot exist without the *no*."[69] In his restless search to discover movement in every principle, Boehme had demonstrated beyond any doubt that "exclusive, inner being is unbearable; the inner strives to be external." In such a way, Herzen perpetuates the view of Boehme as synthesizer of inner and external natures that he shares with his forebears. Seen in this light, Schelling is no more than "Boehme stood on his head."[70] To be sure, it was unfortunate that Boehme had used the ridiculous language of alchemy to expound his ideas; yet, despite everything, he had "arrived at a profoundly philosophical worldview." Schelling, by contrast, had gone in the reverse direction, descending from "a pseudo-scientific conception to mystical somnambulism."[71]

The cobbler-mystic was exercising not only the minds of philosophers and critics, but making an appearance in Russian literary life as well. During the 1830s, Vladimir Odoevsky, novelist, music critic, and member of the secret society of Wisdom-Lovers, assiduously studied Boehme alongside his successors Pordage and Gichtel. His short story *Salamandra* (1841) provides a striking narrativization of the diverse worldviews that battled for the heart of the Russian enlightenment, from the scientific on one hand to a form of prelapsarian naïveté on the other. The representative of the latter, the Finnish Elsa, whose apparent simplicity conceals her alter-ego Salamandra (the "fire-spirit"), utters words toward the end of the tale that strongly recall Boehme's metaphysics of will and desire: "There's nothing . . . that's impossible . . . for the human will," she explains, "you just have to desire."[72]

The influential poet and literary critic Apollon Grigoriev (1822–64) flirted with Boehme's writings as a young man. In 1842, he wrote to his friend Sergei Soloviev, father of the philosopher Vladimir, that he had "I have greedily thrown myself into reading all the mystics I could find in our library, particularly Boehme," the result being the "conviction that mysticism is just as far from the Truth of Christ as pantheism" and that "venerating the inner life of *man* leaves the same emptiness in the soul as the veneration of the external world."[73]

Perhaps more than any other literary figure of the mid-nineteenth century, however, it was the poet Fyodor Tiutchev (1803–73) whose work most resonated with that of Boehme.[74] In a letter of the early 1860s, Tiutchev referred to Boehme as "one of the greatest minds to have ever lived on this earth," and situated him on the "intersecting point between two entirely contradictory teachings—Christianity and pantheism." Tiutchev was amongst the first to give due attention to the rich language of Boehme, commenting that to do him justice in Russian would mean to adopt some of the linguistic devices found in the expressive language of Russia's sectarian communities.[75] The verse of Tiutchev, whom Berdyaev would later call the "poet of elemental night,"[76] proliferates with imagery of the "abyss" and "chaos," whose contours are more than reminiscent of Boehme's *Ungrund*. Like Odoevsky, Tiutchev points to the instability of modern civilization's accommodation with, even occlusion of, the darker, irrational aspects of being. In some of his most famous lines, he warns: "Do not awaken storms long stilled / For under them chaos stirs."[77]

At the same time, Boehme was beginning to infiltrate the spiritual academies of Russia, where Orthodox clerics prepared students for the priesthood or religious life. Petr Avsenev (in monastic life, Archimandrite Feofan; 1810–52) taught History of German Literature at the Kiev Spiritual Academy, in the process gaining a substantial knowledge of mystical literature, in particular Boehme, to whose "fundamental ideas, character and direction of thinking," if not "the form of exposition" he was extremely sympathetic.[78] In one section of his lectures on psychology, Avsenev notes that contact with certain materials can produce a "certain, almost magical, effect on the nerves and, through them, the soul," offering his students the following example: "just a glance of a shiny surface of metal once led an inspired tradesman-philosopher (Boehme) into a state similar to clairvoyance."[79] In another section, Avsenev provides a pseudo-scientific explanation for the difficulty of Boehme's language. The most elevated state of clairvoyance, asserts Avsenev, lifts its possessor above the life of the soul and into a certain "spiritual consciousness [. . .] in union with the purely spiritual world." In this context, the "loftiness of the language" is a "natural consequence of the disclosure in them of such a higher consciousness."[80]

Avsenev's lectures are written in the style of contemporaneous German philosophy but give away several likely points of convergence with Boehme, amongst them his advocacy of the original androgynous condition of humanity, and the innate striving to reunite the male and female principles.[81] A student of Avsenev's in Kiev, Pamfil Iurkevich (1826–74) later introduced his own version of religious idealism, again not uninformed by Boehme, into the heady environment of Moscow intellectual life from his academic position there. One of his students recalled a conversation in 1873 in which Iurkevich issued the rather counter-intuitive declaration that real philosophy had ceased with the birth of Kant and that its last genuine representatives had been Boehme, Leibniz, and Swedenborg—a comment that carries added resonance in the light of Kant's dismissal of Swedenborg's writings as "dreams of a spirit-seer."[82] This student, Vladimir Soloviev, was to place Boehme at the very center of the Russian religious renaissance of the early twentieth century that followed his death, and which he in large part instigated.

Soloviev, for whom both Iurkevich and Tiutchev were central influences, was an archetypal product of the Russia of his time: a theoretical philosopher with an unparalleled command of classical and modern thought, he was at the same time the father of Russian poetic symbolism and a mystical visionary. Inspired by three visions of Sophia, the first at the age of nine in a Moscow chapel and the others in 1873 while studying in the Reading Room of the British Library and wandering the Egyptian desert respectively, Soloviev's philosophical works can be understood in part as an attempt to explicate his visions of a transfigured nature. It was with this purpose that he set about studying esoteric literature on Sophia from Gnostic, Kabbalistic, and mystical sources in the following years. In a letter of 1877, he sums up these studies:

> In the mystics are many confirmations of my own ideas, but no new light. Moreover, almost all of them are incredibly subjective by nature and, so to say, drivelling. I found three specialists on Sophia: Georg Gichtel, Gottfried Arnold and John Pordage. The most interesting thing is that all three have had personal experiences almost the same as mine. But in theosophy proper all three are quite weak; they follow Boehme but are below him. I think that Sophia had dealings with them more for their innocence than for anything else. As a result, only Paracelsus, Boehme and Swedenborg are real people, which leaves me with a rather open ballpark.[83]

Seeking to build on the teachings of Boehme and Swedenborg, which he calls the "full and highest theosophic expression of old Christianity," the early Soloviev strove to create a "new," universal religion of the Holy Spirit, whose embryonic form he found in Schelling.[84] The influence of Boehme is writ large over Soloviev's unfinished *Philosophical Principles of Integral Knowledge*, where he attempts to practice a new kind of "organic logic" by coaxing out the determinations of the absolute principle. Soloviev rejects the notion that ultimate reality can be entirely contained within the human mind, instead beginning his account from a statement, taken largely as a matter of faith, of the absolute's own putative division within itself:

> The absolute in all eternity necessarily divides itself into two poles or two centers: the first, the principle of absolute unity or oneness as such, the principle of freedom from all forms, all manifestation and, consequently, from all being; the second, the principle or productive power of being, i.e. the multiplicity of forms.[85]

The term "two centers" is taken directly from Boehme,[86] and the overall intention of Soloviev's early project is resolutely Boehmean: namely, to avoid what he considered the hubris of the Hegelian dialectic, which sought to produce the entire content of thought from its own resources; Soloviev would instead operate within the context of divine *self*-revelation. The first motion in Soloviev's system was to remain, not the dialectical or a priori unfolding of the human mind, but, as in Boehme, the prior motion of the absolute in its desire for perceptibility.

Many other points of convergence with Boehme can be found in Soloviev: his development of androgyny, which no doubt also drew on the Kabbala, which he knew well; his determination to posit an anti-divine principle within the divine itself; speculation on the existence of a certain kind of ethereal, holy corporeality that humanity might eventually inherit; and the richly sensual depiction of mystical experience.[87]

Nevertheless, Soloviev was a consummate synthesizer, and to reduce his thought to the influence of any one thinker would be mistaken. If, as it appears, he first turned to Boehme for traces of experiential contact with Sophia that would help explain his own, it should be said that Soloviev's Sophia is very different from that of Boehme. He might not have fully agreed with his successor Sergii Bulgakov's (1871–1944) definition of Boehme's Jungfrau Sophia as "faceless and impersonal, just as the deity itself is impersonal in Boehme's system."[88] However, the Russian philosopher's deeply eroticized vision of Sophia is surely located at some distance from her Boehmean counterpart. A greater distance is opened up between the two when one considers Soloviev's embracing of the doctrine of *apokatastasis* (universal salvation) and denial of the eternity of hell. Most important, perhaps, is the attempt that Soloviev makes to give real substance to world history.

This last distinction between Boehme and the Russian sophiological school emerges most strongly when we consider a thinker who falls outside this tradition, indeed outside any definite school of thought, and in whom Boehme finds his most consistent champion on Russian soil: Nikolai Berdyaev. Berdyaev's reception of Boehme betrays both continuity and discontinuity with the fate of the cobbler-mystic in Russia up to that point. He explores more deeply than ever before the question of the Boehme-event itself: how such an apparent depth of penetration into the core of the divine mysteries was realized by a simple cobbler. Strange indeed to the modern ear sounds his review of Alexandre Koyré's 1929 monograph on Boehme where, in a distinctly precritical vein, Berdyaev objects to the French author's distance from his object of study and his dryly academic lack of spiritual sympathy with Boehme. Challenging Koyré's appraisal of Boehme as primarily a metaphysician, Berdyaev counters that "Boehme was above all a visionary and theosopher" and even questions how an author who is "alien to the Spirit" of Boehme could write such a book.[89]

Yet Berdyaev's approach did not issue exclusively from a bygone form of medieval religiosity. The Boehme-event for him did not simply involve grace acquired through simplicity as it did for Gamaleia. Berdyaev sought to provide a philosophical foundation to the question of how there can exist a personal sanctity that has only itself as its own guarantee, outside of any institutional or social framework:

> The problem which is posed by the phenomenon of Boehme is the problem of gnostic giftedness, a peculiar gift of vision which does not exist in direct proportion to the level of sanctity endowed by the Church.[90]

This problem was made all the more acute as it was being simultaneously posed in disputes over the role of the prophet as the ideal of human activity in Soloviev's thought and life.[91] Although Berdyaev was one of very few to see a positive side to Soloviev's development of prophecy within the framework of a "free theocracy," the two thinkers parted ways on the question of the individual path to its realization. Soloviev and other sophiologists, grounded in the theanthropic (divine-human) Christology that he had first outlined in his *Lectures on Godmanhood*, tended to foreground the self-renunciation of will as a condition of participation in God. Berdyaev instead saw the condition for true gnosis (which for him amounted to the same thing) as contained within a "particular cognitive charisma" of a highly individualized nature.[92] In Soloviev, he believed, the "eternal significance of the principle of personality had not been sufficiently recognized" and his pretensions to prophetic authenticity as a result severely compromised.[93] Boehme's personalistic vision, on the contrary, meant that the German mystic "should enter into our spiritual life as an eternal element, for never before has human gnosis risen to such superhuman heights."[94]

Berdyaev's critique of the Russian intellectual tradition that had preceded him can only be adequately understood within the context of his interpretation of Boehme. It is only, for example, when we make the comparison with the cobbler-mystic that the meaning of Berdyaev's at first puzzling criticism that Soloviev had "objectivized his own subjectivity" becomes clear.[95] For Boehme, writes Berdyaev, "knowledge of the spiritual world [. . .] was a dwelling in that spiritual world [. . .] Being for him did not turn into an object opposed to the subject."[96] Yet while Soloviev, Berdyaev grants, possessed a certain prophetic charisma, it was one insufficiently strong to withhold from transforming the experiential data gained from "gnostic" perception into an objective, and thus static, presence in transcribed thought. Boehme, for him, was so great precisely because he consistently refused to turn the absolute into a possession, forever seeing it in the *dynamis* contained within the perpetual striving that united his own subjective being to the being of God.[97]

Strangely enough, Sergii Bulgakov's critique of Boehme arises from the same ground as Berdyaev's but arrives at precisely the opposite conclusion. It, too, is best understood in the context of Bulgakov's critique of Soloviev. Yet instead of distancing the German mystic from his Russian successor, Bulgakov finds in both the self-same malaise. Boehme, according to Bulgakov, suffered from a kind of self-delusion: imagining himself the channel of divine revelation, he had no idea that he was in actual fact "in captivity to *l'ésprit de systême*."[98] *Aurora*, which Boehme later considered his first, immature attempt at articulating his vision, was for Bulgakov characterized by an "immediacy of 'inspiration.'" If he had stopped writing here, Bulgakov reflects, he would never have arrived at the unfortunate brand of "mystical rationalism" or "theosophism" with which his remaining work is permeated.[99] As it is, Boehme, for Bulgakov, turns the central mystery of Christianity into a rational schema, failing to realize that "hypostacity is not a 'deducible' moment in the godhead but its living essence."

Bulgakov's attention to apophatic (negative) theology was on this point influenced by his recognition of Soloviev's flawed approach, whose teaching he had previously followed more unreflectively and whom in the same work he criticizes from a similar perspective: "although [Soloviev] characterizes the transcendental absolute [. . .] in the terminology of negative theology, he then rationally deduces, unlawfully and without any explanation of its application to the first hypostasis, its relationship to the world and, as a consequence, their mutual determination."[100] In the same way, Boehme's handling of the "leap from impersonality to personhood" on the part of the putatively Christian godhead is therefore for Bulgakov a "very dark teaching,"[101] and results in the opposite effect: the dissolution of personhood in abstract schematizing.

Berdyaev, in sharp opposition to Bulgakov, saw Boehme's metaphysics as grounded in a type of personalism that had subsequently "disappeared from German Idealism in its tendency toward monism."[102] Central to this personalism was Boehme's concept of the *Ungrund*, to which he dedicated the first of two "études" published in 1930, and which he equates with a certain kind of "meonic [from the Greek, *me on*, non-being] freedom undetermined even by God."[103] The significance of this concept is that the *Ungrund* should be understood as more fundamental even than the Trinitarian godhead; as a result, God's being must be viewed *tragically*, as a necessary "battle with the darkness of nonbeing" that eternally overshadows it.[104] Yet this tragic battle is one waged not only by God; all being participates in it, within that faculty Berdyaev calls the "will," which he again takes from Boehme and sees as synonymous with "freedom." Human beings, too, must enter into the "tragedy of the groundless will-desire, to be tinctured by Christ only to lose themselves in darkness once more." Only Boehmean voluntarism has made possible the "philosophy of freedom," Berdyaev wrote.[105]

Among the Russian Behmenists, Berdyaev was the most faithfully Boehmean, yet he viewed himself as no mere disciple. In 1940, near the end of his life, he felt confident enough to proclaim his superiority over his great predecessor: "The particular distinction of my philosophical type," he wrote, "is that I have put at the foundation of philosophy not being, but freedom [. . .] In such a radical form, it seems, this has not been done by any other philosopher."[106]

Berdyaev's philosophical statements often suffer from hyperbole and betray a tendency to underplay affinities with other thinkers. Yet, in one respect, he is surely right to distinguish himself so definitively from other Russian religious philosophers. Berdyaev, like Boehme, was principally a metaphysician of the will, an epithet one can only apply to other Russian sophiologists with a great number of qualifications. Soloviev's thought, for example, evolved from wholesale acceptance of Boehme's positing of a primordial will at the heart of being to a certain distance from the concept in his middle period. His repulsion from Nietzschean voluntarism was surely a factor here. The sophiologists' attempt to build a religio-philosophical system that would do justice to a God in whom eternity and time are already one, without abrogating the rights of temporal becoming, took them away from an association of will with the "first mover."

Their approach did not necessarily jar with the notion of meonic freedom at the core of being, though it does mark sophiology off as a distinctly unvoluntaristic teaching. Nevertheless, that both strands of this argument—the Berdyaevian and Solovievian—should draw on Boehme and that the assessment of Soloviev's legacy should so closely parallel that of the cobbler-mystic is indicative of the latter's consummate ability to inspire diverging trends in thought.

IV

By the first decades of the twentieth century, Boehme had become such an integral part of the Russian intellectual and cultural landscape that to enumerate all who fell under his influence would amount to a roll call of most of the representatives of the Russian Silver Age. They included the majority of those who looked to Soloviev as the progenitor of Russian symbolism, such as the poets Alexander Blok (1880–1921) and Fyodor Sologub, the philosopher-novelists Andrei Belyi (1880–1934) and Dmitry Merezhkovsky (1865–1941), philosopher Semyon Frank (1877–1950), and the "peasant poet" Nikolai Kliuyov (1884–1937). The cobbler-mystic was even beginning to make incursions once more into the royal court, with the wife of Nicholas II, the Empress Alexandra, reading and appreciating Boehme.[107]

One of the more surprising statements of support for Boehme was made by the founder of the Soviet system himself. No doubt influenced by the positive treatment of the German mystic in Herzen and Feuerbach, Vladimir Lenin calls Boehme a "materialistic theist" insofar as "he divinizes not only spirit but also matter. For him God is material; in this is his mysticism."[108] Despite Lenin's personal respect for him, however, the ideological consolidation of Marxism-Leninism in the late 1920s and the distaste for mystical writings of all kinds meant that those who wished publicly to discuss Boehme mainly had to do so in émigré settings.

From his adoptive home of Kulu, India, the painter and orientalist Nikolai Rerikh (1874–1947), whose ideas continue to influence the New Age movement in Russia, saw a direct correlation between mundane "labour" and supernatural revelation as embodied in Boehme, who "worked out his philosophical systems whilst making boots."[109] Meanwhile, in Milan, the émigré poet Georgii Eristov penned a poem called "Misterium magnum" in which he exalted the dual nature of the cobbler and mystic in similar tones.[110]

The influence of Boehme was, however, once more to spring up in the unlikely conditions of Moscow under the Soviets, just as it had in the same city 350 years earlier. The so-called "Moscow esoteric underground" that emerged at the end of the 1950s has received sparse attention, largely because it was so very different from the other alternative, "dissident" culture that emerged at the same time. Yet figures such as Yuri Stefanov (1939–2001) and Evgenii Golovin (1938–2010) in Moscow and, a little later, Elena Shvarts (1948–2010) in Leningrad were tremendously influential in battling for the rights of the numinous in poetic, religious, and academic discourse. These were gifted poets with an immense breadth of interests who were drawn toward contemporary esoteric trends in European thought. Writers such as René Guénon and Algernon Blackwood, who had found new avenues for the esoteric in the modern age, were among their most admired authors. Yet they turned to Boehme not as a precursor to these modern authors but as a thinker whose relevance was no less diminished than it was in seventeenth-century Germany. Golovin, for example, disputes both Bulgakov's contention that the earthly realm has no value for

Boehme and Berdyaev's classification of the German mystic as "gnostic," writing that, in opposition to the Gnostics, Boehme does not hold that creation is the "work of an evil demiurge or the result of the degradation of the Deity. Instead, for Boehme, this world is called to a greater or lesser extent to "apply the brakes" to Adam's fall into demonic chaos."[111] Golovin ends his article with a quote from Boehme that conjures up the terrors of the twentieth century, as well as Dostoevsky's comparison of communist society to an anthill: "And the human being will acquire an ant's face and say: there is no god or gods, though there is a piece of straw on my back. It would be good to burden another back with this straw." For Golovin, such words are "more comprehensible today than they were in the seventeenth century."[112]

The religious poet Elena Shvarts has also added another layer to the modern Russian interpretation of Boehme, this time not in the context of the tragic twentieth century, nor the esoteric penetration into the mysteries of the cosmos; rather, the reverse: Shvarts brings the mysterious in Boehme down to the level of the mundane and familiar. In a delightful short essay titled "Any Old Borscht," Shvarts writes:

> Boehme wrote (as anyone will recognise as true) that the sweet, the bitter, the sour and the salty are the primary elements, the bricks of the universe. From this point of view even a bowl of borscht, in the battle of these elements, hints at the mystery of life. Food can be an adventure.[113]

These few lines are testament to the fact that the Russian reception of Boehme continues to draw on new sources of creative energy. Indeed, in recent decades, Russian translations of the German mystic, as well as monographs and dissertations, have proliferated.[114] The Russian Boehme may have more to tell us yet.

NOTES

1. For studies in English, see Z.V. David, "The Influence of Jacob Boehme on Russian Religious Thought," *American Slavic Review* 21.1 (1962): 43–64; J. Billington, *Icon and the Axe* (New York: Vintage Books, 1970), 171–75, 310–11.
2. One of the most powerful voices against the promulgation of Boehme's ideas was Archimandrite Photios (1792–1838), who did much to inflame the anti-mystical bent of the late Alexandrine period, which contrasted sharply with the atmosphere of the early nineteenth century. In one work, Photios contrasts the German mystic with the purity of the Church fathers, writing of the "mire of erudition in the impious Jacob Boehme." See Arkhimandrit Fotii (Spasskii), *Bor'ba za veru: protiv masonov*, (Moscow: Institut russkoi tsivilizatsii, 2010), 99. On the religio-philosophical level, Boehme's expansion of sensuality beyond the empirium to the realm of the Godhead was perhaps the

major sticking point amongst Orthodox. The early nineteenth-century mystic Savva Moskotil'nikov, while reading *Aurora*, was "struck by the strangeness of the comparison of human feelings produced by means of the five senses with actions of the same order in the highest being [. . .] I am terrified even to think that this pious writer had the thought of indivisibly uniting God with nature." Cited in E. Bobrov, *Literatura i prosveshchenie v Rossii XIX v. Materialy, issledovaniia i zametki* (4 vols., Kazan: Tipo-lit. imp. un-ta, 1901–02), vol. 4, 196–97.

3. The Russian publication of Boehme's *Christosophia* in 1815 cited the author as "Our Holy Father Jacob Boehme," while one of the early readers of the volume, Maksim Nevzorov, referred to Boehme in 1825 as "the true angel described in Revelation 14.6–7." A. Pypin, *Religioznye dvizheniia pri Aleksandre I* (St. Petersburg: Akademicheskii proekt, 2000), 295.
4. A.P. Bogdanov, *Russkie patriarkhi (1589–1700)* (2 vols., Moscow: Respublika, 1999), vol. 1, 297–303.
5. A.N. Andreev, "Kvakery na zapade i v Rossii," *Novaia i noveishaia istoriia* 4 (2010): 167.
6. Inside the Ambassadorial Chancellery, Nordermann, against the advice of Kuhlmann (who saw the Russian tsars as the vanguard of his new kingdom), presented a radically egalitarian vision to the authorities: "Tsars, kings, grand lords and princes, and other grandees will be no more, but all will be equal, and all things will be held in common, with no one calling anything his own." Bogdanov, *Russkie patriarkhi*, 299.
7. R. Collis, "Freemasonry and the Occult at the Court of Peter the Great," Aries: Journal for the Study of Western Esotericism 6.1 (2006): 13–14.
8. A. Schönle, *The Ruler in the Garden: Politics and Landscape Design in Imperial Russia* (Oxford: Peter Lang, 2007), 19.
9. V.S. Turchin, "Vzgliad russkogo masona na prirodu estestvennuiu i iskusstvennuiu," *Russkaia usad'ba: Sbornik obshchestva izucheniia russkoi usad'by* 8.24 (2002): 43.
10. Andrew Weeks, *Boehme: An Intellectual Biography of the Seventeenth-Century Philosopher and Mystic* (Albany, NY: State University of New York Press, 1991), 192.
11. R. Brague, "L'anthropologie d'humilité," in *Saint Bernard et la philosophie*, ed. R. Brague (Paris: Presses universitaires de France, 1993).
12. "The humble, tolerant actions of the enlightened Boehme, with which he had to endure the persecution of his detractors," said the mason Nikolai Kraevich in conversation with a pupil, "are more important than all his writings." N.A. Kraevich, *Luch blagodati ili pisaniia N.A.K.* (Moscow, 1804), 59. The idea of humility as a transformative principle, which facilitates a new kind of anthropology, permeates Boehme's oeuvre; see, J. Boehme, *The Way to Christ* (New York: Paulist Press, 1978), 45.
13. Schönle, *Ruler in the Garden*, 123.
14. K. Rorschach, *The Early Georgian Landscape Garden* (New Haven: Yale Center for British Art, 1983), 6.
15. I.M. Dolgorukov, *Sochineniia Dolgorukova* (2 vols., St Petersburg: A. Smirdin, 1849), vol. 1, 144.
16. Cited in M. Roberts, "*Les Aventures de Télémaque*: A Reading of the Franconian Rock Garden, Sanspareil," *Eighteenth-Century Life* 28.3 (2004): 93.
17. Roberts, "*Les Aventures*," 113. Here, as elsewhere, the spirit of Boehme proved more congenial to the tenebrous environment of Moscow than to Peter's new capital on the Neva.
18. M.V. Nashchokina, "Russkii masonskii sad," in *Russkaia usad'ba. Sbornik OIRU* (Moscow: Zhiraf, 2006), 520.

19. Ibid., 524.
20. On Koval'kov, see Iu. E. Kondakov, *Liberal'noe i konservativnoe napravleniia v religioznykh dvizheniakh v Rossii pervoi chetverti XIX veka* (St. Petersburg: RGPU, 2005), 87–105.
21. Cited in N. Gavriushin, *Iungov ostrov: Religiozno-filosofskii etiud* (Moscow: Logo-N, 2001), 30.
22. The only other crosses on the island were carved into the stone commemorating none other than Quirinus Kuhlmann (see plate 12.1). Gavriushin, *Iungov ostrov*, 41.
23. N. Berdyaev, *Russkaia ideia* (Moscow: Eksmo, 2005), 555.
24. N. Berdyaev, "Novaia kniga o Iakove Beme," *Put'* 18 (1929): 118.
25. There is scant space here to document the complex relationship between the ecclesiastical powers and the early masons, or between these same and later Russian religious philosophers. Suffice it to say that there was a great deal of mutual cross-pollination. Metropolitan Platon (1737–1812), the greatest churchman of his age, for example, supported much of the work of the Masons, believing them to be far less dangerous than the "atheist-Voltairians," and was deeply upset when the state moved against Novikov. Masons such as the priest Fyodor Golubinsky (1797–1854) occupied prominent positions in many spiritual academies. While the Russian Church took a skeptical stance toward representatives of Russian religious philosophy, this did not stop many defining themselves as "Orthodox." Many philosophers likewise saw themselves as the heirs of the early Russian masons. The so-called "Brotherhood of the Argonauts," to which Berdyaev and others amongst Soloviev's successors belonged in pre-revolutionary Russia, was an organization with distinctly masonic practices and mores.
26. Berdyaev compares the "stylized Orthodoxy" of Pavel Florensky unfavorably to that of Boehme, writing "however hard [Florensky] tries to style himself in the key of simplicity, in him there is less simplicity than in any of the gnostics, for example Jacob Boehme, who possessed great simplicity of heart and immediacy (*neposredstvennost'*)." See N. Berdyaev, *Sobranie sochinenii* (5 vols., Paris: YMCA Press, 1983–97), vol. 3, 545. It was this "immediacy" that Soloviev would also value most highly in Boehme.
27. A.I. Koval'kov, *Mysli o mistike i pisateliakh eia* (Orel: Gubernskaia tipografiia, 1815), 31–32.
28. Ibid., 103.
29. S.N. Bulgakov, *Sophia the Wisdom of God: An Outline of Sophiology* (Hudson, NY: Steiner Books, 1993), 66–67.
30. J. Boehme, *On the Election of Grace and Theosophic Questions* (Whitefish, MT: Kessinger, 1992), 299.
31. P. Erb, "Introduction," in Boehme, *Way to Christ*, 23.
32. J. Hamberger, ed., *Die Lehre des Deutschen philosophen Jakob Böhme* (Munich: Verlag der Literarisch-Artistischen Anstalt, 1844), 343.
33. Koval'kov, *Mysli o mistike*, 134.
34. J. Boehme, *Mysterium Magnum* (2 vols., London: John M. Watkins, 1965), vol. 1, 74.
35. C. O'Regan, *Gnostic Apocalypse: Jacob Boehme's Haunted Narrative* (Albany, NY: State University of New York, 2002), 167 (my emphases). Boehme clarified his eschatology in an important letter of 1620 to Paul Kaym; see, J. Böhme, *Theosophische Sendbriefe* (2 vols., Freiburg: Aurum-Verlag, 1979), vol. 1, 80.
36. Koval'kov, *Mysli o mistike*, 104.
37. Vladimir Soloviev, like Koval'kov, would make a strict distinction between the terms *mistitsizm* and *mistika*, the former relating to "the direct,

unmediated (*neposredstvennyi*) relation of our spirit to the transcendental world," and the latter to "the reflective activity of our mind on this relation." V.S. Solov'ev, *Polnoe sobranie sochinenii* (20 vols., Moscow: Nauka, 2000-), vol. 2, 195.

38. Ibid., 15–16.
39. Kraevich, *Luch blagodati*, 67.
40. Cited in A.D. Tiurikov, "Podvizhnik russkoi kul'tury," in I.G. Shvarts, Lektsii (Donetsk: Veber, 2008), 158.
41. Though Alexander I was aware of Boehme, he seems to have held him in low esteem. In a note to his sister written around 1810, he comments that although Boehme seems to have been led by "some sort of supernatural enlightenment," his works belong to a group of writings he calls "theoretical," and which contain "a great mixture of truth and error." See Aleksandr I, "O misticheskoi slovesnosti," in *Perepiska imperatora Aleksandra I s sestroi, Velikoi kniaginei Ekaterinoi Pavlovnoi* (Saint Petersburg: Velikii kniaz' Nikolai Mikhailovich, 1910).
42. G. Adamovich, "Istoriia lozhi Iupiter (Okonchanie)," *Zapiski otdela rukopisei* 53 (2008): 520.
43. Vladimir Tukalevsky's contention that Ivan Shvarts's lectures represent no more than a transcription of Boehme's ideas (even going so far as to conflate the two figures "Shvarts-Boehme") has recently been disproved by Yury Kondakov, who illustrates many points of divergence between the two. See V.N. Tukalevskii, "N.I. Novikov i I.G. Shwarts," in eds. S.P. Mil'gunov and N.P. Sidorov, *Masonstvo v ego proshlom i nastoiashchem* (2 vols., Moscow: Zadruga, 1914–15); Iu. E. Kondakov, *Rozenkreitsery, martinisty i 'vnutrennie khristiane' v Rossii kontsa XVIII – pervoi poloviny XIX vv.* (St. Petersburg: RGPU, 2011), serialized in *Apokrif,* www.cardshouse.castalia.ru/apokrif.
44. Cited in ibid.
45. Shvarts, *Lektsii*, 31. Boehme's thought is redolent with musical metaphors of the relationship between God and humanity; see, J. Boehme, *The Works of Jacob Behmen* (4 vols., London: G. Robinson, 1764), vol. 4, 98–99.
46. Shvarts, *Lektsii*, 18–19; cf. J. Boehme, *Threefold Life of Man* (London: John M. Watkins, 1909), 223, 474.
47. Shvarts, *Lektsii*, 18.
48. Ibid., 48.
49. Ibid., 49; cf. Boehme, *Threefold Life*, xxxvi.
50. Amongst the manuscripts held at the Russian National Library are translations of the following: *De Testamentis Christi*; *Christosophia, oder der Weg zu Christo*; *De signatura rerum*; *De triplici vita hominis*; *De electione gratiae*; *Tabulae principorium*; *Clavis*; *The First Epistle*; and a compendium personally compiled by Gamaleia in 1794 under the title of *Serafim's Garden, or a Spiritual Extract from the Complete Writings of Jacob Boehme.*
51. Gavriushin, *Iungov Ostrov*, 30.
52. R. Faggionato, *A Rosicrucian Utopia in Eighteenth-Century Russia: the Masonic Circle of N.I. Novikov* (Dordrecht: Springer, 2005), 137; see also R. Faggionato, "Un personaggio dimenticato del settecento Russo: Semen Ivanovič Gamaleja," *Rivista Storica Italiana* 102.3 (1990): 955–57.
53. V.O. Kliuchevskii, *Istoricheskie portrety. Deiateli istoricheskoi mysli* (Moscow: Pravda, 1990), 382.
54. S.N. Gamaleia, *Pis'ma* (3 vols., Moscow: Mosk. univ. tip., 1832–39), vol. 2, 16.
55. Ibid., 3:22–23.
56. J. Boehme, *Six Theosophic Points* (Ann Arbor, MI: University of Michigan Press, 1958), 199.
57. Shvarts, *Lektsii*, p. 50.

58. S. N. Gamaleia, "Rech' o sotvorenii mira," in *Rechi Gamalei v lozhe Devkalion 1782–83*, held in Otdel rukopisei, Russian State Library, Moscow. Fond 14, no. 315, 92 (2). I am grateful to Yuri Khalturin for providing me with a copy of this manuscript.
59. Gamaleia, *Pis'ma*, 3:136.
60. Ibid., 1:19.
61. Nikolai Kraevich, too, argues that the reading of certain authors may do great harm to those as yet unprepared for their reception. "Whoever does not become Boehme, let him throw all his labours, knowledge and reading into the manure. And yet: let only the one who is able become Boehme, according to how far the eternal Spirit of each can receive him into themselves." Kraevich, *Luch blagodati*, 28.
62. Yuri Khalturin writes that these speeches acted as "texts of a kind amongst many lodges and, though written by a concrete author, can be seen to reflect the views of the majority of masons from this circle." Y. Khalturin, "Filosofiia russkikh masonov XVIII-nachala XIX vekov: kriticheskaia rekonstruktsiia" (PhD diss., UrGU, Ekaterinburg, 2010), 22–23.
63. Cited in ibid., 148.
64. F. Ternovskii, "Materialy po istorii mistitsizma v Rossii. Zapiski K. A. Lokhvitskogo," *Trudy Kievskoi dukhovnoi akademii* 11 (1863): 173.
65. Ibid., 179.
66. S. P. Shevyrev, "Khristianskaia filosofiia. Besedy Baadera," *Moskvitianin* 3 (1841): 394–95.
67. A. I. Herzen, *Sobranie sochinenii* (30 vols., Moscow: Izd. Akademii nauk SSSR, 1954), vol. 3, 237.
68. Ibid., 238.
69. Ibid., 238.
70. Ibid., 117.
71. Ibid., 118.
72. Ibid., 209.
73. A. Grigor'ev, *Pis'ma* (Moscow: Nauka, 1999), 5.
74. The philosopher Semyon Frank wrote that "Tiutchev's lyricism can be considered as a poetic restatement of Boehme's theosophy." S. N. Frank, *Russkoe mirovozzrenie* (St Petersburg: Nauka, 1998), 195.
75. F. I. Tiutchev, *Polnoe sobranie sochinenii i pisem* (6 vols., Klassika: 2002–05), vol. 6, 66.
76. N. A. Berdyaev, *Smysl istorii. Novoe srednevekov'e* (Moscow: Kanon, 2002), 223.
77. Tiutchev, *Polnoe sobranie*, vol. 1, 133.
78. D. Pospekhov, "Biograficheskaia zametka," in *Sbornik iz lektsii byvshikh professorov Kievskoi dukhovnoi akademii* (Kiev: Tipografiia gubernskogo upravleniia, 1869), viii.
79. F. Avsenev, "Iz zapisok po psikhologii," in ibid., 95.
80. Ibid., 207–08.
81. "Having created them as one person in the beginning, he then divides the whole human being into two halves or sexes—man and woman [. . .] Only in conjugal union the *natural human being becomes a complete*, true human being: in it each individual loses itself in order to find itself once more in the other." Ibid., 142, 147–48.
82. V. S. Solov'ev, *Sobranie sochineniia* (12 vols., Brussels: Zhizn's Bogom, 1966–70), vol. 9, 395; I. Kant, *Theoretical Philosophy 1755–1770* (Cambridge: Cambridge University Press, 1992), 301–60.
83. Solov'ev, *Sobranie sochinenii*, vol. 12, 200.
84. Solov'ev, *Polnoe sobranie*, vol. 2, 177.
85. Ibid., vol. 2, 264.

86. Boehme, *Threefold Life*, 110.
87. In Soloviev's poem "Three Meetings," the sense of smell is the first to greet him after his final "meeting" with Sophia: "The scent of roses filled earth and heaven's sweep." J.D. Kornblatt (ed.), *The Wisdom Writings of Vladimir Solovyov* (Ithaca, NY: Cornell University Press, 2009), 270.
88. S.N. Bulgakov, *Svet nevechernii* (Moscow: Respublika, 1994), 235.
89. N. Berdyaev, "Novaia kniga o Ia. Beme," 117.
90. N. Berdyaev, "Novye knigi o Iakove Beme," *Put'* 5 (1926): 120.
91. Berdyaev would describe prophecy as the "intimate theme of [Soloviev's] entire spiritual life." N. Berdyaev, "Osnovnaia ideia Vl. Solov'eva," in *Sobranie sochinenii* (5 vols., Paris: YMCA Press, 1983–97), vol. 3, 209.
92. N. Berdyaev, "Iz etiudov o Iakove Beme: Etiud I. Uchenie ob Ungrund'e i svobode," *Put'* 20 (1930): 49.
93. N. Berdyaev, "Solov'ev i my," *Sovremennye zapiski* 63 (1967): 371.
94. N. Berdyaev, *Sobranie sochinenii*, vol. 2, 95–96.
95. Berdyaev, "Solov'ev i my," 373.
96. Berdyaev, "Etiud I," 51.
97. This is the core contention of one of the most compelling recent interpretations of Boehme's project, Aleksandr Fedorov's characterization of it as an "attempt to create the whole within a personal space-time [. . .] to express the dynamics of totality." A. Fedorov, "Sozdanie personal'nogo mira i etika nerazlichiia: Ia. Beme i ego posledovateli," *«Istoriia menia»: Traditsiia evropeiskoi filosofskoi mistiki i stroitel'stvo personal'nykh mirov* (St. Petersburg: Izd. SPU, 2006), 127.
98. Bulgakov, *Svet nevechernii*, 144.
99. Ibid., 145. Although Bulgakov is on the whole more sympathetic to Soloviev than to Boehme, he sees exactly the same contamination of an original, intuitive vision by excessive rationalization in both; see, S.N. Bulgakov, "Priroda v filosofii Vl. Solov'eva," *Voprosy filosofii i psikhologii* 5 (1910): 693.
100. Bulgakov, *Svet* nevechernii, 129–30.
101. Ibid., 283.
102. Berdyaev, "Novaia kniga," 121.
103. Berdyaev, "Etiud I," 57.
104. Ibid., 60.
105. Berdyaev, "Etiud I," 56.
106. N. Berdyaev, *Sobranie sochinenii*, vol. 1, 60.
107. On Alexandra's reading of Boehme and his influence on her relationship with her husband, see J. Ashton, "God in All Things: The Religious Outlook of Russia's Last Empress," *Electronic British Library Journal* (2006): 12–14.
108. V. Lenin, *Filosofskie tetradi* (Moscow: Izd.-vo TsK VKP, 1965), 65. Lenin is here summarizing the opinions of Feuerbach. The second part of the quote ("Jakob Böhme nicht nur den Geist, sondern auch die Materie vergöttert") is a direct translation from the latter. See L. Feuerbach, *Sämmtliche Werke* (10 vols., Leipzig: Otto Wigand, 1846–66), vol. 8, 222.
109. N. Rerikh, *Derzhava sveta* (Moscow: Eksmo-Press, 2001), 19.
110. G. Eristov, "Misterium magnum (Iakov Beme)," in *Vernut'sia v Rossiiu – stikhami*, ed. V. Kreid (Moscow: Respublika, 1995), 554. The poem begins: "The summer evening in a purple cloak, / In the shop the acerbic smell of leather, / And the echo of the inspired speech / Of the sage-cobbler" (my translation).

111. E. Golovin, "Murav'inyi lik (Iakob Beme o grekhopadenii)," *Priblizhenie k snezhnoi koroleve* (Moscow: Arktogeia-Tsentr, 2003), 236.
112. Ibid., 246.
113. E. Shvarts, *Opredelenie v durnuiu pogodu* (Moscow: Pushkinskii fond, 1997), 59–60.
114. Since 1990, Russian editions, many newly translated, of the following works by Boehme have been published: two separate editions of *Aurora* (1990, 2008); *Christophia, oder Weg zu Christo* (1994); *Mysterium pansophicum, oder Gründlicher Bericht von dem Irdischen und Himmlichen Mysterio* (1996); *Theosophische Sendbriefe* (2001); *Ein einfaches Leben in Christus* [anthology] (2001); *Clavis* (2001); *Psychologia vera, oder Viertzig Fragen von der Seelen* (2004); and *De triplici vita hominis, oder Von dem Dreyfachen Leben des Menschen* (2011).

12 Hegel's Reception of Jacob Boehme[1]

Glenn Alexander Magee

I INTRODUCTION

Hegel's relation to Jacob Boehme is a controversial topic among historians of philosophy. As I shall demonstrate, it is undeniable that Hegel had a strong interest in Boehme. However, Hegel scholars have often been eager to minimize this and have, in some cases, misrepresented the available evidence in order to make him seem harsh or dismissive in his treatment of Boehme. There is no mystery behind this. Historians of philosophy are trained philosophers, and Hegel scholars tend to be self-identified Hegelians. Many find it simply unacceptable that Hegel might have been seriously interested in (or—worse yet—influenced by) one of the most obscure mystics in the Western canon. To most professional philosophers, mysticism is not merely a non-rational enterprise, but an *irrational* one: one contrary to reason. Thus, their attitude tends to be that we must save Hegel from Boehme.

Part of the problem here is that Hegel does indeed send mixed signals. It is obvious from what has come down to us that Hegel made a careful study of Boehme, and he continually compliments Boehme on his profundity—while simultaneously criticizing him for the "barbarity" of his mode of expression. (At some point Hegel seems to have decided that *Barbarei* would be his standard term of disapprobation for Boehme, because he uses it again and again.) As we shall see, Hegel finds in Boehme ideas quite similar, in certain respects, to his own. And here we run up against some legitimate problems of interpretation and of questions concerning the provenance of ideas. First, does Hegel interpret Boehme correctly, or does he read himself into Boehme? This is a difficult question to answer, owing mainly to the obscurity of both Boehme's and Hegel's writings. Further, if Hegel's interpretation of Boehme is defensible, is he being honest when he suggests (as he clearly does) that Boehme's ideas are anticipations of his own philosophy? Or is Hegel indebted to Boehme for certain insights? Would his philosophy have been the same had he not encountered Boehme?[2]

It seems likely that Hegel took up Boehme for the first time in Jena in the period 1801–07. This was the period during which Hegel formulated his philosophical system, leading to the writing of *The Phenomenology of Spirit* in 1806. But our questions cannot really be settled by determining when it was that Hegel first read Boehme, or even by taking into account his considered judgment about Boehme in the *Lectures on the History of Philosophy*. One reason has to do with another problem for historians of philosophy: the influence of Boehme on Schelling, who was in turn, of course, a major influence on Hegel. As I shall argue, it is highly probable that Boehmean ideas were communicated to Hegel by Schelling in Jena and that they exercised a strong influence on him. Indeed, during this period, Jena was a major center of interest in Boehme. A brief sketch of the Jena "Boehme revival," and specifically of Schelling's interest in his writings, seems in order here.

Many of the greatest figures of the German Romantic movement were assembled in Jena in the late eighteenth and early nineteenth centuries: Friedrich Schlegel (1772–1829); August Wilhelm Schlegel (1767–1845); Novalis (1772–1801), Ludwig Tieck (1773–1853); Johann Gottlieb Fichte (1762–1814); and, of course, Friedrich Wilhelm Joseph von Schelling (1775–1854) himself, whose career would peak during his time there. It is probable that Ludwig Tieck introduced Schelling, Novalis, and the Schlegel brothers to Boehme's writings in 1799. The first mention of Boehme by a member of the Jena circle comes a year earlier, in a letter from Friedrich Schlegel to Novalis, dated December 2nd, 1798, in which Schlegel mentions that Tieck has been studying Boehme. Tieck had discovered Boehme's *Aurora* in a Berlin bookstall. Informed that it was despised by the rationalists, he immediately purchased the volume and proceeded to devour its contents. As a result, one of Tieck's biographers states that "None of his works written between 1799 and 1801 is free of Boehme . . . "[3]

Under Tieck's influence, Novalis began to study Boehme carefully in the winter of 1799–1800. It has been conjectured that Boehme was being read aloud at meetings of the Jena Romantics' circle during this period.[4] Friedrich Schlegel also fell under Boehme's spell, calling his work "the greatest, most profound, most individual, most admirable work of idealism."[5] He believed there were correspondences between the ideas of Boehme and Fichte (who, for his part, dismissed Boehme as an "enthusiast").

Speaking years later about his time in Jena, Tieck recalled that he found Schelling particularly receptive to Boehme's ideas.[6] Indeed, over the course of several years, Schelling set about trying to obtain Boehme's writings for his own library, finally acquiring a complete set only in 1804 (or so his correspondence would indicate). Interestingly, years later, in 1809, Schelling was faced with the problem of acquiring *another* edition of Boehme since he had given his away to his friend Franz von Baader (1765–1841), who was one of Boehme's principal interpreters (often referred to as "Boehmius redivivus"). Schelling wrote to a friend imploring him to obtain a replacement edition of Boehme "at any price."[7] Needless to say, it is certainly very likely that Baader encouraged Schelling's interest in Boehme.

There is a possibility, however, that Schelling may have encountered Boehme's ideas well before 1799, through the works of the Swabian "speculative pietist" Friedrich Christoph Oetinger (1702–1782). The story of Schelling's connections to Oetinger, who was himself heavily influenced by Boehme (and Emmanuel Swedenborg), is an interesting one. We know that Schelling's father owned Oetinger's works, which means that he could have delved into them at a very early age. Schelling's first published work was a poem written on the occasion of the death of P. M. Hahn, an important follower of Oetinger. Schelling's friend Christian Pregizer (1751–1824), the founder of a Pietist sect called the "Joyous Christians," reported that when he first met Schelling in 1803, they spent almost their entire meeting discussing Boehme and Oetinger.[8] Schelling is also known to have remarked to one of his students in Jena that Oetinger was "clearer" than Boehme.[9] And it has also been argued that Schelling's terminology (especially in the 1809 *Freiheitschrift*) shows his familiarity with Oetinger's work.[10] Ernst Benz has demonstrated, furthermore, that in his work, Schelling occasionally employed unorthodox translations of biblical passages made by Oetinger without attributing them to him.[11]

In sum, the Jena that Hegel encountered in 1801 was one where Boehme was "the latest thing" in prominent intellectual circles. And Schelling, Hegel's best friend and roommate, was one of the leading "Boehme enthusiasts," one who had likely been interested in Boehmean theosophy years prior to his appointment in Jena. There is thus abundant *prima facie* reason to believe that Hegel would have received a hefty dose of Boehme upon moving to Jena. Furthermore, we must note that Hegel was initially, for all intents and purposes, Schelling's follower, and that his intellectual (and personal) debt to Schelling was very great. It is therefore likely that Hegel—at least at first—would have been predisposed to take Boehme very seriously and to have allowed Boehmean ideas to enter into his own thinking. (As we shall see, the documentary evidence bears this out—though the story of Boehme's "influence" on Hegel is a far from simple one.)

Hegel came to Jena after some depressing experiences as a household tutor in Bern and Frankfurt. He wrote to his old friend Schelling—his former classmate at the Tübingen theological seminary—asking if he could secure for him a position at Jena. The two men had certainly followed different paths after leaving the seminary. In contrast to the unhappy Hegel, Schelling (who was five years younger) had already published several important works and had come to be seen as the rising star of German philosophy. (In fact, he had taken Fichte's place at the University of Jena after the latter was dismissed due to accusations of atheism.) Schelling responded to Hegel's request by inviting him to Jena and offering him a place to stay. Hegel accepted with great relief, and relocated there in January of 1801.

In Jena, Hegel managed to get his degree from Tübingen, counted as a doctorate, and began giving classes to university students. He was paid nothing by the university itself (which was the practice then with junior academics), though he could charge students individually for instruction. Schelling himself left Jena for a post at the University of Würzberg in 1803. To some extent, his departure seems to have had a liberating effect on Hegel. From 1803 to 1806, he produced a large amount of work, setting out various versions of a new "system of philosophy." In the process, Hegel took a good deal of inspiration from Schelling's ideas but he recast them in a new, more rigorous form, and greatly amplified them.

I would argue that Hegel's dalliance with Jacob Boehme played a significant role in this formative period of his philosophical career. The real evidence for this is in the fragmentary manuscripts Hegel produced during this time. However, I will deal initially with another text, Hegel's *Lectures on the History of Philosophy*, delivered for the first time to students in 1805–06 but not published until after Hegel's death. They contain an entire chapter on Boehme, which is the only material Hegel wrote on him that has come down to us in its entirety.

II THE LECTURE ON BOEHME

Hegel's discussion of Boehme in the *Lectures* comes at the beginning of his treatment of modern philosophy, which Hegel links to the Reformation. For Hegel, modern philosophy, like the Reformation, challenges authority and accepts only "the inward personal spirit."[12] Hegel argues, plausibly, that modern philosophy proceeds from the idea of self-consciousness. We can see this dramatically illustrated, of course, in Descartes's *Meditations on First Philosophy* (1641), in which no philosophical progress is made until Descartes recognizes the indubitable truth of his own existence. In modern philosophy, Hegel tells us, the individual is the "absolute beginning point of determination" (*absoluter Anfang des Bestimmens*).[13] Modern philosophy's emphasis on self-consciousness is highly significant for Hegel because his own system (which he sees as the culmination of the history of philosophy) argues that in human self-consciousness, God and nature are brought to completion.

Hegel argues that modern philosophy initially divides into two streams. The first he calls "realism" (*Realismus*), though it would be called empiricism today. The second is "idealism" (*Idealismus*), which would include what we now call rationalism. Hegel's account of modern philosophy begins with two figures representative of these streams. The first, who represents "realism," is Francis Bacon. Surprisingly, the second figure, representing a kind of proto-idealism, is Boehme. It may seem surprising to find Boehme termed a "modern philosopher" at all (he is, of course, often referred to as a mystic or theosophist, precisely, so as to set him apart from the philosophers).[14] This is not eccentricity on Hegel's part, however, but a genuine insight. Hegel sees Boehme's thought as issuing from that same "inward personal spirit" that is the fountainhead of all modern philosophy. Hegel writes that Boehme

> is the first German philosopher; the content of his philosophizing is genuinely German [*echt deutsch*]. What makes him excellent and noteworthy is the aforementioned Protestant principle of placing the intellectual world within one's own heart [*Gemüt*] and in one's self-consciousness gazing upon, knowing, and feeling all that formerly was [conceived as] beyond.[15]

Like Bacon and the rest, Boehme does not appeal to authority; his ideas flow from his own peculiar, authentic soul-searching. Further, Hegel goes on to argue that Boehme also makes self-consciousness and the *Ich* (ego) central to his thought as well.

Hegel's juxtaposition of Bacon and Boehme is meant, of course, to suggest that they are opposites and represent opposite philosophical tendencies. This is obviously true, in that no philosopher could be further from empiricism than Jacob Boehme.[16] It is also obvious where Hegel's sympathies lie. It is clear from Hegel's account of Bacon that he regards him as a shallow philosopher. The account of Boehme is much longer (close to thirty pages in a recent edition) and much more respectful. It is also very apparently the result of a good deal of work and careful study. Hegel's account of Boehme's ideas is remarkably detailed (indeed, but for the obscurity of some of Hegel's sentences, one could almost recommend it as a good, brief outline of Boehme's thought). Further, Hegel quotes from or cites several of Boehme's works. His main source is *Aurora*, but he also relies upon *Theosophische Sendbriefe*, *Beschreibung der drey Principien Göttliches Wesens*, *Mysterium Magnum*, and others. Anyone who reads these pages with an open mind will be struck by the fact that Hegel's interest in Boehme was quite serious.

Hegel makes his transition from Bacon to Boehme by referring to the latter as "philosopho teutonico," and insisting that "we" (namely, "we Germans") have no reason to be ashamed of him. Right away we therefore get the suggestion that Hegel recognizes that many will object to his decision to include Boehme in an account of modern philosophy. But Hegel is obviously concerned here, at least in part, to rehabilitate Boehme in the eyes of his students and colleagues. Hegel notes that the Enlightenment caused Boehme's name to lapse into obscurity in most learned circles, as a result of which he came to be dismissed as an enthusiast. It is only recently that Boehme's profundity has come to be recognized. Hegel is clearly thinking of the Romantic movement. It may seem at this point as if Hegel has been swept up into the Romantic celebration of Boehme, but he immediately signals that he intends to be even handed. "It is certain, on the one hand," Hegel writes, "that he did not merit the disdain accorded to him; on the other, however, he did not deserve the high honor into which he was elevated."[17]

Hegel notes that "philosophia teutonica" was an older term for mysticism. It would be useful here to pause by briefly considering Hegel's basic understanding of mysticism. His most significant statement on the subject occurs in a remark appended to a paragraph in the *Encyclopedia of the Philosophical Sciences* (1817): "It should also be mentioned here that the meaning of the speculative is to be understood as being the same as what used in earlier times to be called 'mystical' [*Mystische*], especially with regard to the religious consciousness and its content."[18] This is a striking assertion, because in fact speculation (*Spekulation, spekulative Philosophie*) is the term Hegel uses to describe his own philosophy, and here he seems to be identifying speculation with mysticism. Hegel defines speculation as the "positive moment" of reason (*Vernunft*) itself (the "negative moment" being dialectic). Ordinary thought (what Hegel calls "the understanding," *Verstand*) is preoccupied with conceptual "either-ors" and unable to think beyond them. Speculation transcends opposites, reconciling them in some greater whole. This is a description of Hegel's philosophical "method" (if it can be called that), and he sees the same approach at work in mysticism. Hegel makes it clear that he sees Boehme as a speculative philosopher in this sense, though one with a crucial flaw.

Hegel's attitude toward the mysticism of Boehme and others is precisely analogous to his attitude toward religion in general. Like religion, mysticism has the same content or the same object as philosophy—but it can only imperfectly approximate to a truth that philosophy alone can fully articulate. Hence, the study of mysticism, like religion, may offer the philosopher important signposts pointing the way to philosophy's goal. Hegel states that, "It is the distinctive task of philosophy to transform the *content* that is in the representation of religion into the *form* of thought; the content [of religion and philosophy] cannot be distinguished."[19] Hegel's treatment of Boehme is fundamentally no different from his treatment of any number of other figures in the history of ideas: he sees him as in certain ways approaching the ideas that only he, Hegel, fully and adequately articulates.

So what are those ideas? I will summarize them here for the uninitiated (though the reader should bear in mind that there are fierce disputes among Hegel scholars about what the Master "really meant"). In brief, Hegel's philosophy holds that the ultimate goal of existence is its coming to consciousness of itself through human beings. Hegel articulates this process into three moments, and he makes it clear that these correspond to the Christian Trinity. The first is an absolutely self-related Idea, which Hegel identifies with God *in himself*; God considered apart from creation. God in this form is not truly God, because he is still *merely* idea. In nature, the second moment, we find a concrete expression of God. Hegel treats nature as a great chain of being approximating to the perfect self-relatedness of Idea. However, it is only in the third moment, Spirit (or humanity) that God/Idea finds its true embodiment. In Absolute Spirit, the self-related Idea becomes a self-thinking, self-conscious thought. Thus, Hegel weaves a tale in which God begins as inchoate and comes to full expression through creation and, ultimately, only through humanity (though Hegel is careful to tell us that this is not a temporal process).

As we shall see, there are rather striking parallels between these ideas and Boehme's—at least as presented by Hegel. Though Hegel sees Boehme as a philosopher, and a speculative one at that, Hegel's major objection to Boehme is that he expresses ideas in "sensuous" form. In Hegel's philosophy, this is called *Vorstellung* (or *das vorstellende Denken*), often translated into English as "picture thinking": the tendency to think in terms of images rather than abstract concepts. Earlier, I noted that, for Hegel, the *content* (i.e., inner truth) of religion and philosophy is identical. The form, however, is quite different. Philosophy is purely conceptual, whereas religion uses "picture-thinking": myths, allegories, images, and the like. For Hegel, what keeps Boehme from being a great philosopher is his almost complete, and often singularly bizarre, reliance upon sensuous images to express ideas. Hegel refers to Boehme as being, in this respect "a complete barbarian" (*vollkommen Barbar*).[20] In Hegel, oppositions are normally seen to conceal an underlying identity, and we are now in a position to see the fundamental identity between Bacon and Boehme. Both are "sensuous" philosophers: Bacon with his empiricism and insistence on sensory observation, and Boehme with his much more profound philosophy, which nevertheless relies upon the sensuous image as a vehicle to know the supersensible.

Following his introductory remarks, Hegel offers a brief biographical sketch of Boehme, including a long, vivid account of Boehme's mystical visions. Hegel's treatment of these visions is devoid of both sarcasm and skepticism. This is in keeping with his attitude of open-mindedness—best exemplified by passages in the later *Encyclopedia of the Philosophical Sciences*—toward paranormal phenomena in general.[21] Hegel speculates that Boehme must have read "mystical, theosophical, and alchemical writings," including those of Paracelsus.[22] He begins his actual account of Boehme's ideas by saying that "Boehme's profoundest interest is in the Idea, and he struggles hard to express it."[23] In Hegel's philosophy, "the Idea" has a special, technical meaning, one which I alluded to earlier. The Idea is, in fact, the final major division of Hegel's *Science of Logic*. In it, subject and object are overcome, so that Idea is ultimately idea of itself (or Absolute Idea, the final category of the *Logic*). However, this self-related Idea becomes truly actual only in self-related *thought* (i.e., self-consciousness). So, when Hegel refers to Boehme being profoundly interested in the Idea, we are again dealing with the issue of self-consciousness and the nature of the "I."

Hegel is famous for having said (in *The Phenomenology of Spirit*) that "the true is the whole [*Das Wahre ist das Ganze*]." And the whole must include the negative: the whole contains evil as well as good, darkness as well as light. Negativity is one of the leading motives of Hegel's system. The dialectic is driven by conflict; within it, concepts spar against one another in order to generate new concepts. Hegel sees history as driven by negativity, as well. Hegel's famous concept of the "cunning of reason" involves war, conflict, and destruction, all tending to advance the revelation of the Absolute in time. Indeed, at the root of all forms of human Spirit, Hegel sees Desire (*Begierde*) as a kind of negative will to absolutize the self, to annul the subject-object distinction. This negative force is actually made use of in the coming into being of science and philosophy; the negative in a sense is transmuted into the positive, into an essential part of the whole. Hegel sees the same basic thought-pattern at work in Boehme. He sees Boehme as struggling to articulate a conception of God that draws unity out of opposition, finding everything within God, even the Devil. Hegel writes:

> The fundamental idea in Boehme is the effort to comprise everything in an absolute unity—the absolute divine unity and the union of all opposites in God. Boehme's chief, and one may say, his only thought, is the divine threefoldess; to perceive all things as the revelation and representation of the Holy Trinity, so that it is the universal principle in which and through which everything exists; in such a way, moreover, that all things have only this Trinity in themselves, not as a Trinity of the ordinary conception [*Vorstellung*], but rather as the actual [trinity of] the Absolute Idea.[24]

Hegel is here noting the similarity between the Trinitarian structure of Boehme's thought and his own. (As I will discuss later, however, Hegel had only recently arrived at the familiar tripartite structure of system—and Boehme may have influenced him in this.) Hegel claims, however, that Boehme's particular use of the Trinity is part and parcel of his picture thinking. Hegel believed that he himself had *not* modeled his philosophy on the Trinity. He held that the true form of philosophy resembles the Trinity simply because the Trinity is an anticipation of true philosophy, in the form of a sensuous image. Of course, this may be an instance (of which there are many) of a philosopher failing sufficiently to understand himself.[25]

Hegel then launches into a detailed discussion of the Trinity he finds in Boehme. God the Father contains an internal division. Hegel quotes Boehme as saying that God is simultaneously "darkness and light, love and wrath, fire and light," etc. God is one essence or substance, separated by anguish (*Qual*). What this represents for Hegel is the "absolute self-related negativity" of the Absolute Idea, which is simultaneously absolute affirmation. The self-relation of Absolute Idea is negativity because, in it, subject and object have been overcome and all externality banished. Anguish is the duality of self-consciousness in God. Yet this duality is also one and simple: "I = I." In God the Father, however, there is still only an unactualized *will* to self-consciousness. Hegel mentions that Boehme refers to God as *salitter* or *salniter,* saying "this great salitter is the hidden, unrevealed essence."[26] It contains all powers or qualities *in potentia*. Hegel charges that Boehme's attempts to define these qualities are exceedingly obscure (as any honest reader of Boehme will readily admit). And he offers a long quotation from Boehme seemingly in order to illustrate this.

Commentators on Boehme always seem to differ in their lists of his "qualities" or "source spirits." Hegel lists the following: "cold, hot, bitter, sweet, wrathful, sour, rough, soft quality [*weiche Qualität*], sound, etc."[27] Hegel's chief criticism of the doctrine of source spirits is that Boehme fails to show that there is any necessity to there being just these spirits or qualities, rather than some others. There is a loose parallel to be drawn here between Boehme's qualities and the categories of Hegel's Logic. Hegel argues that his categories are all part of an organic system, in which each is necessary and each is what it is in relation to all the others. He is looking for that same sort of necessity in Boehme and finds it lacking.[28]

Hegel reports that Boehme characterizes the second person of the Trinity not just as "Son" but as "the Word, the Separator [*der Separator*], the anguish, the revelation, and generally the "I"ness [*Ichheit*], the source of all difference, of will and being-in-itself."[29] The Son is a necessary complement to the Father because, as Hegel puts it, expounding Boehme's ideas, "God as the simple, absolute essence is not the absolute God; in him is nothing to be recognized."[30] Whereas God the Father is "source and germ" (*Quellen und Keimen*) of all powers and qualities, the Son is their unfolding. Compare this to what Hegel has to say in the later *Encyclopedia of the Philosophical Sciences* when he discusses the relation between God, as Absolute Idea, and nature: "God, as an abstraction, is not the true God, but only as the living process of positing his other, the world, which, comprehended in its divine form is his Son; and it is only in unity with his other, in Spirit, that God is subject."[31] As we shall see, Boehme's Trinity works differently from Hegel's, but obviously both the language and ideas here are strikingly similar.

In any case, for Boehme's God to be revealed to himself, a kind of separation must take place. Hegel quotes Boehme as saying "Nothing can be revealed to itself without opposition." Just a year or so after giving his lecture on Boehme, Hegel would write his own account of self-consciousness in *The Phenomenology of Spirit*, in which he argues precisely that self-consciousness is achieved through the opposition of otherness. Fichte, in his *Foundations of Natural Right* (1797), argued that opposition is a necessary condition of self-consciousness—specifically the opposition of other self-conscious human beings. So, it is unlikely that Hegel derived this view from Boehme—but he must have found this coincidence between Fichte and Boehme to be remarkable. Hegel goes on in the lectures to quote Boehme at length, speaking of the necessity of conflict and adversity to the development of self-consciousness, and everything else.

As Hegel tells it, Boehme's "Son" is the reflection of the powers within the Father. In the Son, God contemplates himself, and Boehme identifies this as "knowledge of the *Ichts*." As Hegel points out, *Ichts* is a play on *Nichts*, "nothing," but also upon *Ich*, "I" or "ego." Hegel states that "the *Ich* of self-consciousness is contained within it."[32] Hegel writes that "The Son, the something [*das Etwas*] is therefore I, consciousness, self-consciousness; the abstract neutral is God, the gathering himself together into the point of being-for-self [*Fürsichseins*] is God."[33] The Son is the great Separator, who takes the qualities and powers that are bound into one within God the Father and "separates" them so that God comes face-to-face with himself. Hegel mentions in this context that Boehme also refers to the Son as Lucifer and remarks, "This is the connection of the devil with God; that is to say other-being and then being-for-self, being-for one [*Für-Eines-Sein*], so that the other is for one. And that is the origin of evil in God and out of God. This is the highest profundity of thought of Jacob Boehme."[34] The "fall of Lucifer" involves the inward-fashioning [*Hineinbilden*] and inward-imagining [*Hineinimaginieren*] of the I as the fire which consumes all. This is the negative aspect of the Separator and the "wrath [*Zorn*] of God." Hegel comments that "This is very bold and speculative. . . . Indeed Boehme has here penetrated into the entire depth of the divine being; evil, matter, or however it is called, is the I = I, the being-for-self—this is the true negativity."[35]

However, God's othering or self-revelation is not complete until his powers are expressed in creation. And this, according to Hegel's account, is the coming-into-being of the Spirit, the third person of the Trinity. Spirit is the unity of the light (the Son or Lucifer) with the powers latent in God the Father: the creation of an independent world that is a continual revelation or expression of the powers of God. Hegel notes that, for Boehme, the Trinity is continually born in all things. All of reality is the revelation or unconcealing of God.

Hegel concludes his account of Boehme by summing up what he takes to be his most profound ideas. Hegel names two: "the generation of the light, of the Son of God out of the qualities" and "the diremption [that is, tearing apart or separating] of [God] himself." He then goes on yet again to comment on the "barbarism" of Boehme's form of expression, to which he says he cannot reconcile himself. But he closes the chapter by insisting on the profundity of Boehme's ideas and by saying that "we cannot fail to see the profound craving for speculation which existed in this man."[36] In the foregoing, I have chosen to limit myself to Hegel's account of Boehme's Trinity, as it is the major focus of his discussion, but there is more to Hegel's discussion of Boehme in the *Lectures*. For example, Hegel also discusses Boehme's treatment of philosophy, astrology, and theology. And he deals with "three kinds of powers or *Spiritus*" in Boehme, which may provide the key to decoding the mysterious "triangle diagram" found in Hegel's *Nachlass*.[37]

In the final analysis, what is clear in the *Lectures* is that Hegel admires Boehme and takes his thought very seriously but is concerned to distance himself from it at the same time. Hegel treats the parallels between his thought and Boehme's as merely, it would seem, accidental: Boehme *anticipates* much in modern, speculative philosophy. But Hegel never once says anything that would indicate that he is indebted to Boehme or that Boehme in some way influenced him. To build a case for this influence, we must look at the fragments from the Jena period.

III THE JENA THEOSOPHIC WRITINGS

We know that, beginning in the Frankfurt period and while he was at Jena, Hegel was struggling to develop a philosophical style all his own. What we find when we turn to the Jena fragments and notes, none of which were published until many years after Hegel's death, is Hegel essentially "trying on" the ideas and vocabulary of Boehme. It is clear that, despite his reservations, Hegel was strangely attracted to Boehme's way of expressing himself. He admits this, in a way, in the *Lectures*. After noting that Boehme uses the term *Urstand* (which might be translated "original condition") for "substance," Hegel remarks "it is a shame that we cannot use this and many other such striking expressions."[38] In fact, as we have already seen and will see again, Hegel did go on to employ some Boehmean expressions and now and then what can be characterized as a vaguely Boehmean "style."

The first Jena fragment we shall consider is a "myth" about Lucifer thought to have been composed by Hegel in 1804–05 (prior to the composition of Hegel's lecture on Boehme—though precise dating of some of these texts is impossible). Hegel writes in this text:

> God, having turned toward nature and expressed himself in the pomp and dull repetition of its forms, became aware of his expansion . . . and became angry over it. Wrath [*Zorn*] is this formation, this contraction into an empty point. He finds himself in this way, with his being poured out into the unending, restless infinity, where there is no present but an empty transcendence of limit, which always remains even as it is transcended.[39]

In Hegel's "myth," God externalizes himself in nature but becomes "angry" over it, and through this becomes conscious of himself. God's wrath becomes the spirit of Lucifer, which reflects God back to himself. Hegel criticized his own myth as "the intuitions of barbarians" (*die Anschauungen der Barbarei*) because of its reliance on "picture-thinking." The language and style of this fragment are echoed in the "Revealed Religion" section of the *Phenomenology of Spirit* (1807). David Walsh states accurately that this section is "from start to finish identical with the theosophic Christianity of Boehme."[40] There, Hegel writes of the "first-born Son of Light" (who is Lucifer), "who fell because he withdrew into himself or became self-centered, but that in his place another was at once created."[41] (Walsh has also argued that Hegel's use in the *Phenomenology of Spirit* of such terms as "element," "aether," "expansion," and "contraction" has its roots in his acquaintance with Boehme and Paracelsian alchemy.)[42]

In the same period (1804–05), Hegel produced a work that has come to be called the "divine triangle fragment." The original text no longer exists, but Hegel's early biographer, Karl Rosenkranz, quotes from it and describes it at length.[43] Rosenkranz maintains that the text was heavily influenced by Boehme (and Franz von Baader) and he summarizes it as follows:

> To express the life of the idea, [Hegel] constructed a *triangle of triangles*, which he suffered *to move through one another* in such a way that each one was not only at one time extreme, and at another time *middle* generally, but also it had to go through this process internally with each of its *sides*. And then, in order to maintain the ideal plasticity of unity amid this rigidity and crudity of intuition, to maintain the fluidity of the distinctions represented as triangle and sides, he went on consistently to the further barbarity of expressing the totality as [a] *square resting* over the triangles and their process. But he seems to have got tired in the following out of his labour; at any rate he broke off at the construction of the *animal*.[44]

Hegel's first triangle ("God the Father") describes a "Godhead" closed inside itself, similar to Boehme's primordial trinity of conflict within God, preceding his manifestation. In "God the Son," the second triangle, God recognizes himself in the form of otherness. This otherness must be brought into unity with God, or it has the potential to become evil. Hegel states that "the Son must go right through the earth, must overcome evil, and in that he steps over to one side as the victor, must awaken the other, the self-cognition of God, as a new cognition that is one with God, or as the Spirit of God; whereby the middle becomes a beautiful, free, divine middle, the Universe of God."[45] A third triangle, that of the Holy Spirit, then comes into being. Hegel writes that "the Earth as the self-consciousness of God is now the Spirit, yet it is also the eternal Son whom God intuits as himself. Thus has the holy triangle of triangles closed itself. The first [triangle] is the Idea of God which is carried out in the other triangles, and returns into itself by passing through them."[46]

It seems clear that in this fragment (as well as in the "Lucifer myth" of the same period), Hegel is developing the outlines of his philosophical system. And to do so, he is employing the language and style of Boehme. Hegel's first triangle, "God the Father," is analogous to the later *Logic* (with its threefold structure of Being-Essence-Concept), while the second triangle, of the Son or earth, corresponds to the *Philosophy of Nature* (Mechanics-Physics-Organics). And the relationship between the two triangles is strikingly similar to the relationship between Hegel's Logic and

Nature: it is the *telos* of Idea to become embodied as the natural world. (In Hegel's words, the "Idea of God" becomes "the universe of God.") In the third triangle, God intuits the Son, or earth, as himself, and achieves self-consciousness, a moment that approximates the role played by Spirit in Hegel's mature system. Spirit—human Spirit—brings the system, and reality itself, to completion when it recognizes that it itself is the embodiment of Idea, and that all of nature (as well as history) is intelligible as a kind of progressive unfolding of its own being.

What is particularly odd about the triangle fragment is that it is so close to Hegel's own description in the *Lectures* of Boehme's Trinity. We know that during roughly the same period in which he wrote the triangle fragment, Hegel altered his philosophical system from four divisions to the familiar triad of Logic, Philosophy of Nature, and Philosophy of Spirit—the same triad seemingly depicted in mythic, Boehmean style in the fragment. I would like to suggest the possibility that Hegel's study of Boehme's Trinity played a role in helping him to formulate his system as tripartite. I do not mean that Hegel got from Boehme merely the idea of a three-part system. Rather, I am suggesting that it may have been Boehme's peculiar interpretation of the Trinity that helped Hegel to see specifically *how* his own system could be unified in a tripartite form.

To put things in the starkest possible terms (and at the risk of repetition), the tripartite system that Hegel eventually arrived at in Jena:

(1) begins with the *Logic*, which expresses a self-related Idea that is nevertheless *mere* Idea; an inchoate reality ("God in himself"), which then,

(2) "freely releases itself" as nature, a scale of forms (described in *The Philosophy of Nature*), imperfectly expressing or embodying Idea, culminating in,

(3) Spirit (the subject of *The Philosophy of Spirit*), which understands itself as the final flower of all that has gone before—as the fully adequate embodiment of Idea; self-related Idea made flesh in the form of living, human self-awareness.

Stated in its essentials, this tripartite system of thought is strikingly reminiscent of Boehme's Trinitarian speculations. Given Hegel's close reading of him, the resemblance between their philosophies cannot easily be attributed to coincidence. It thus seems quite plausible that Hegel was positively influenced by Boehme, and in a significant way.

Of course, there are serious difficulties with such a claim. Hegel's system, in its broad outlines, *is* strikingly reminiscent of Boehme—as interpreted by Hegel. It remains an open question as to whether Hegel has simply read himself into Boehme. If so, then it is entirely possible that Hegel arrived at the basic form of his system (described above) quite independently of his encounter with Boehme and that he is simply viewing Boehme in a distorted manner, through the lens of that system.

The question of whether Hegel has read himself into Boehme remains unsettled largely due to the fact that Boehme's writings are so obscure and open to a variety of interpretations. The only way, therefore, to make the above argument fully convincing would be by supplementing it with a careful and unbiased study of Boehme, taken on his own terms. Anyone undertaking such a study would have to be fully attuned to the danger of reading Hegel (or any other thinker) into Boehme. (For this reason, studies of Boehme produced by scholars who are relatively *unfamiliar* with Hegel are actually more valuable to those who wish to explore the Hegel–Boehme connection.) My own study of Boehme's writings inclines me to the view that Hegel *has* accurately described his Trinity, and that the ideas he attributes to Boehme are really to be found in the mystic himself. Needless to say, however, that is not a point I can prove in the present essay.

IV BEYOND JENA

Hegel's interest in, and sympathy for, Boehme must have been widely known. In 1811, one of Hegel's former Jena students, Peter Gabriel van Ghert (1782–1852), a Dutchman, sent him Boehme's collected works as a gift. Van Ghert would not have done this unless it was plain to those who knew Hegel in Jena that Boehme was very important to him. Hegel thanked van Ghert in a letter of July 29th, 1811:

> Now I can study Jacob Boehme much more closely than before, since I was not myself in possession of his writings. His theosophy will always be one of the most remarkable attempts of a penetrating yet uncultivated man to comprehend the innermost essential nature of the absolute being. For Germany, he has the special interest of being really the first German philosopher.[47]

Hegel writes further in the same letter that Boehme's endeavor "constitutes the most arduous struggle both to bring the deep speculative [content], which he holds in his intuition, into representation and so to master the element of representational [thinking] in order that the speculative content might be expressed in it."

There are those who might prefer to believe that Hegel's interest in Boehme was an aberration of youth, but that does not appear to be the case. Hegel never wrote extensively on Boehme again, but in addition to the 1811 exchange with van Ghert, there is ample reason to believe that Hegel remained interested Boehme and never changed his evaluation of him.

A case in point is Hegel's preface to the 1827 edition of the *Encyclopedia of the Philosophical Sciences*. Introducing some of his basic ideas, Hegel mentions Boehme more than once. He writes, "The spirit is essentially consciousness, and hence [consciousness] of the content made into an object. As feeling, the spirit is just the not yet objective content itself (only a *quale*, to use an expression of Jacob Boehme); it is just the lowest stage of consciousness, in the form of the soul, which we have in common with the lower animals."[48] Hegel goes on to write of Boehme:

> The name 'Teutonic Philosopher' has rightly been conferred upon this mighty spirit. On the one hand, he has enlarged the basic import of religion, [taken] on its own account, to the universal Idea; within that basic import he formulated the highest problems of reason and tried to grasp spirit and nature in their determinate spheres and configurations. [All this was possible] because he took as his foundation [the thesis] that the spirit of man and all things else are created in the image of God—and, of course, of God as the Trinity; their life is just the process of their reintegration into that original image after the loss of it. On the other hand (and conversely), he forcibly misappropriated the forms of natural things (sulphur, saltpeter, etc.; the sharp, the bitter, etc.) as spiritual forms and forms of thought.[49]

In the same text, Hegel also makes several admiring references to Franz von Baader. In support of his own attempt to "rationalize" religious doctrine, Hegel quotes volume five of Baader's *Fermenta Cognitionis* (1824). There, Baader claims that the treatment of religion as only a "matter of the heart" is a view dear to atheists, who know that to undermine religion they must undermine the notion that a rational theory of religion is possible.[50] After quoting Baader, Hegel goes on to state that:

> What is most sublime, most profound, and most inward has been called forth into the light of day in the religions, philosophies, and works of art, in more or less pure, in clearer or more obscure shapes, often in very repulsive ones. We can count it as a particular merit of Franz von Baader that he not only goes on bringing such forms to our recollection, but also with a profoundly speculative spirit he brings their basic import expressly into scientific honor because on that basis he expounds and confirms the philosophical Idea.[51]

In an extraordinary footnote, Hegel writes "I am certainly delighted to learn that Herr von Baader agrees with many of my propositions—as is evident both from the content of several of his more recent writings and from his references to me by name. About most of what he contests—and even quite easily about everything—it would not be difficult for me to come to an understanding with him, that is to say, to show that there is, in fact, no departure from his views in it."[52] Hegel then goes on to take issue with a criticism Baader made of one aspect of his *Philosophy of Nature*.[53]

Although Baader does make some favorable remarks about Hegel in the first volume of *Fermenta Cognitionis*, Hegel's assessment of his relationship with Baader seems to have been highly unrealistic. Baader, for his part, appears to have been simply puzzled by Hegel's attention, and his insistence on their ability to "come to an understanding." Clark Butler has referred to "Hegel's abortive courtship of von Baader," writing, "despite apparent differences, Hegel sought to persuade both the public and von Baader himself that their positions were reconcilable. . . . Von Baader responded negatively to such overtures, though he respected Hegel as a critic of Kant, Fichte, and Schelling."[54] It is not unusual for one prominent scholar to "court" another, for career advancement or often simply to establish an intellectual friendship. Baader, however, was a decidedly strange and marginal figure for Hegel to court. Nevertheless, this is in keeping with what I see as an increased openness in Hegel's later career concerning matters relating to mysticism and esotericism.

We find a further illustration of this pattern in Hegel's revision of the first book of his *Science of Logic*, which he completed not long before his death. In the original 1812 edition, Hegel offers the following in a remark concerning "quality" in the section on *Dasein*:

> *Qualierung* or *Inqualierung*, [which are terms from] a philosophy which goes deep but into a murky depth, refers to determinacy as in itself, but at the same time is another in itself. Or it refers to the familiar nature of opposition, as it is in its essence. In this respect, opposition constitutes the inner nature of quality and is essentially its self-movement in itself. *Qualierung* means therefore, in the aforementioned philosophy, the movement of a determinacy in itself, in which respect it situates and fastens itself in its negative nature (in its *Qual*) from out of another, signifying in general the quality's own internal unrest through which it produces and holds itself only in conflict.[55]

In the revised 1832 edition, the above passage has been significantly altered and now mentions Boehme by name. The new version reads as follows:

> *Qualierung* or *Inqualierung*, an expression of Jacob Boehme's, whose philosophy goes deep, but into a turbid depth, signifies the movement of a quality (of sourness, bitterness, fieriness, etc.) within itself in so far as it situates and fastens itself in its negative nature (in its *Qual*) from out of an other—signifies in general the quality's own internal unrest by which it produces and maintains itself only in conflict.[56]

Perhaps Hegel felt that he could not mention Boehme openly in the original edition. In the last years of his life, however, he had established himself as the leading philosopher in Germany and so seemed to feel more comfortable acknowledging his interest in Boehme. Thus we are faced with exactly the opposite of what many commentators on Hegel's relationship to Boehme would have us expect: instead of moving away from Boehme in his mature period, Hegel actually seems to be moving, in a very public manner, *toward* him. Hegel's attempt to ally himself with Baader only reinforces this impression.

To conclude, it is worth noting that, during Hegel's lifetime and in the years following his death, it was quite common for him to be linked with mysticism in general, and Boehme in particular. Friedrich Theodor Vischer (1807–1887) remarked that the Hegelian philosophy had come forth "from the school of the old mystics, especially Jacob Boehme."[57] In his 1835 work *Die christliche Gnosis*, Ferdinand Christian Bauer claimed that Hegel was a modern Gnostic and argued for his philosophical kinship with Boehme. Finally, and most amusingly, we must note the words of Schelling. In a lecture given in the 1830s, Schelling remarks disdainfully, "Jacob Boehme says: divine freedom vomits itself into nature. Hegel says: divine freedom releases nature. What is one to think of this notion of releasing? This much is clear: the biggest compliment one can pay to this notion is to call it 'theosophical.' "[58]

NOTES

1. I wish to thank Andrew Weeks for his helpful comments on an earlier draft of this article.
2. There is a fair amount of literature treating the Boehme-Hegel relationship, dating back to the first half of the nineteenth century. See for example E. Haldane, "Boehme and Hegel," *Philosophical Review* 6 (1897): 146–61; Ingrid Schussler, "Boehme und Hegel, "*Jahrbuch der Schlesichen Friedrich Wilhelms Universität* 10 (1965): 45–58; David Walsh, "The Esoteric origins of modern ideological thought: Boehme and Hegel," (PhD diss., University of Virginia, 1978); David Walsh, "The Historical Dialectic of Spirit: Jacob Boehme's Influence on Hegel," in *History and System: Hegel's Philosophy of History*, ed. Robert L. Perkins (Albany, NY: State University of New York Press, 1984), 15–46; Karin Atala, "A study of the nature of reality and language in J. Boehme's *Aurora* and G. W. F. Hegel's *Vorlesungen ueber die Philosophie der Religion III*," (PhD diss., Catholic University of America, 1988); S. J. McGrath, "Boehme, Hegel, Schelling, and the Hermetic theology of evil," *Philosophy & Theology* 18 (2006): 257–86.
3. Roger Paulin, *Ludwig Tieck: A Literary Biography* (Oxford: Clarendon Press, 1985), 100.
4. Paola Mayer, *Jena Romanticism and Its Appropriation of Jacob Boehme* (Montreal: McGill-Queen's University Press, 1999), 182.
5. Quoted in Mayer, *Jena Romanticism*, 140.
6. Edwin H. Zeydel, *Ludwig Tieck, The German Romanticist: A Critical Study* (Princeton: Princeton University Press, 1935), 130.
7. See the translator's introduction in *Schelling: Of Human Freedom*, trans. James Gutmann (Chicago: Open Court, 1936), xlvi.
8. Ernst Benz, *The Mystical Sources of German Romantic Philosophy*, trans. Blair R. Reynolds and Eunice M. Paul (Allison Park: Pickwick Publications, 1983), 13–14.
9. Mayer, *Jena Romanticism*, 185.

10. See for instance, Benz, *Mystical Sources*, 30; also Robert Schneider, *Schellings und Hegels schwabische Geistesahnen* (Würzburg: Tiltsch, 1938), 10. Gershom Scholem also states that he discerns Oetinger's influence in the thought of both Schelling and Hegel. See Scholem, *Kabbalah* (New York: New American Library, 1974), 200.
11. Benz, *Mystical Sources*, 54–56.
12. Hegel, *Lectures on the History of Philosophy*, 3 vols., trans. E. S. Haldane and Frances H. Simson (London: Kegan Paul, Trench, Trübner, 1892), vol. 3 [henceforth "LHP III"], 159; *G. W. F. Hegels Werke* [henceforth *Werke*], 20 vols., ed. Eva Moldenhauer and Karl Markus Michel (Frankfurt am Main: Suhrkamp, 1986), vol. 20 (*Vorlesungen über die Geschichte der Philosophie* vol. 3 [henceforth "VGP III"], 63. The translation by Haldane and Simson is, unfortunately, not very reliable. I have therefore in a great many cases amended their translation of certain passages, or produced entirely new translations of my own.
13. LHP III, 164; VGP III, 68.
14. Boehme's early followers referred to him by the code-name "Teutonicus Philosophus," though this fact on its own would not have induced Hegel to count Boehme as a philosopher.
15. LHP III, 191; VGP III, 94.
16. Boehme certainly appeals to experience, of a kind. But he does not insist, as an empiricist would, that all claims be supported by evidence drawn from mundane sensory observation.
17. LHP III, 189; VGP III, 91.
18. *Werke*, 8, 178 (Hegel's paragraph # 82, *Zusatz*). *The Encyclopedia Logic*, trans. T. F. Geraets et al. (Albany, NY: State University of New York Press, 1991 [henceforth "Geraets"]), 133. Hegel makes similar remarks elsewhere, seemingly identifying speculation and mysticism. See especially *Vorlesungen über die Philosophie der Religion*, 3 vols., ed. Walter Jaeschke (Hamburg: Felix Meiner, 1983–87), vol. 1, 333; vol. 3, 125.
19. Hegel, *Lectures on the Philosophy of Religion*, 3 vols., ed. and trans. Peter C. Hodgson et al. (Berkeley, CA: University of California Press, 1984), vol. 1, 333; *Vorlesungen über die Philosophie der Religion*, vol. 1, 235.
20. LHP III, 189; VGP III, 92.
21. See Glenn Alexander Magee, "Hegel on the Paranormal: Altered States of Consciousness in the Philosophy of Subjective Spirit," *Aries: Journal for the Study of Western Esotericism* 8 (2008): 21–36; and "The Dark Side of Subjective Spirit: Hegel on Mesmerism, Madness, and Ganglia," in *Essays on Hegel's Philosophy of Spirit*, ed. David Stern (Albany, NY: State University of New York Press, forthcoming).
22. LHP III, 191; VGP III, 94.
23. LHP III, 193; VGP III, 95.
24. LHP III, 196; VGP III, 98.
25. J. N. Findlay once observed that "[Hegel's] whole system may in fact be regarded as an attempt to see the Christian mysteries in everything whatever, every natural process, every form of human activity, and every logical transition." Findlay, *Hegel: A Re-Examination* (London: Allen and Unwin, 1958), 131.
26. LHP III, 198; VGP III, 101.
27. LHP, 200; VGP, 104.
28. Nevertheless, there is a greater similarity between Boehme's system and the Logic than Hegel himself will allow. Specifically, there is a strong parallel to be made between the "circularity" of Boehme's system of "source spirits" and the "circularity" of the system of concepts in the Logic. Boehme claims

that his first and final spirits are one, just as Hegel claims that the end of the Logic returns to the beginning. Whereas Hegel employs the image of the circle to describe the structure of the Logic and the system as a whole, Boehme employs the image of the wheel. Boehme writes in *Aurora*, "But if I should describe the Deity in its birth in a small, round circle, in the highest depth, then it is thus: Suppose a wheel standing before you, with seven wheels one so made in the other that it could go on all sides, forward, backward and cross ways, without need of turning back. In its going, that always-one wheel, in its turning about, generates the others, and yet none of them vanishes out of sight, but all seven are visible. . . . The seven wheels are the seven spirits of God. They are always generating one another, and are like the turning of a wheel . . . and the seven wheels are hooped round with fellies, like a round globe," *Aurora*, chap. 13, §§ 71–2; *Aurora*, trans. John Sparrow (London: John M. Watkins, 1914), 328–29. Boehme describes his spirits as "generated one in another," whereas Hegel speaks of the concepts of his Logic as implying one another, and of all of them as "contained in" the final concept, Absolute Idea. For a more extensive discussion of this issue, see Glenn Alexander Magee, *Hegel and the Hermetic Tradition* (Ithaca, NY: Cornell University Press, 2001), 160–65.

29. LHP III, 202; VGP III, 105.
30. LHP III, 202; VGP, 105.
31. Philosophy of Nature § 246, *Zusatz*; *Werke* 9, 23.
32. LHP III, 205; VGP III, 108.
33. LHP III, 205; VGP III, 108.
34. LHP III, 205–206; VGP III, 109.
35. LHP III, 206; VGP III, 109.
36. LHP III, 216; VGP III, 119.
37. Magee, *Hegel and Hermetic Tradition*, 104–19. See also Helmut Schneider, "Zur Dreiecks-Symbolik bei Hegel," *Hegel-Studien* 8 (1973): 55–77.
38. LHP III, 203; VGP III, 106.
39. Johannes Hoffmeister, ed., *Dokumente zu Hegels Entwicklung* (Stuttgart: Fromann, 1936), 364–65.
40. Walsh, "Boehme's Influence on Hegel," 28.
41. Hegel, *The Phenomenology of Spirit*, trans. A.V. Miller (Oxford: Oxford University Press, 1977), 468; *Phänomenologie des Geistes*, ed. Hans-Friedrich Wessels and Heinrich Clairmont (Hamburg: Felix Meiner, 1988), 504.
42. Walsh, "Boehme's Influence on Hegel," 28. Walsh believes that only the influence of Boehme can explain why Hegel believes that history has a structure, and that it is to be understood in terms of the development of Spirit.
43. Karl Rosenkranz, "Hegels ursprüngliches System 1798–1806," *Literarhistorisches Taschenbuch* 2 (1844): 157–64. Translated in H. S. Harris, *Hegel's Development: Night Thoughts (Jena 1801–1806)* (London: Oxford University Press, 1983), 184–88.
44. Rosenkranz, 160; Harris, 185. Harris (in *Night Thoughts*) attempts to reconstruct the strange geometrical theosophy of the "Triangle Fragment." See also Helmut Schneider, "Anfänge der Systementwicklung Hegels in Jena," *Hegel-Studien* 10 (1975): 133–71.
45. Rosenkranz, 163; Harris, 187–88.
46. Rosenkranz, 162–63; Harris, 187.
47. See *Hegel: The Letters*, trans. Clark Butler and Christianne Seiler (Bloomington: Indiana University Press, 1984), 573; *Briefe von und an Hegel*, 4 vols., ed. Johannes Hoffmeister (Hamburg: Felix Meiner Verlag, 1952–81); Hoffmeister numbers the letters; this is number 192.

48. Geraets, 12; *Werke* 8, 24.
49. Geraets, 15; *Werke* 8, 28–29.
50. Baader, *Fermenta Cognitionis* (Berlin, 1824), preface, ix ff (quoted in Geraets, 14; *Werke*, 8, 27).
51. Geraets, 15; *Werke* 8, 29.
52. Ibid.
53. Baader replied to Hegel's defense of himself in an 1824 essay entitled "Hegel on My Doctrine in the Preface to the Second Edition of the Encyclopedia." See his *Sämtliche Werke*, ed. F. Hoffmann et al. (Leipzig, 1851–60), Folge I, 10:306–309.
54. Butler, 570.
55. *Wissenschaft der Logik: Das Sein* (1812), ed. Hans-Jürgen Gawoll (Hamburg: Felix Meiner, 1986), 82. Since A. V. Miller bases his translation on the 1832 edition, this passage is not to be found in the English edition of the work.
56. Hegel, *The Science of Logic*, trans. A. V. Miller (London: George Allen and Unwin, 1969), 114; *Wissenschaft der Logik: Die Lehre vom Sein* (1832), ed. Hans-Jürgen Gawoll (Hamburg: Felix Meiner, 1992), 109.
57. See Benz, 2.
58. F. W. J. Schelling, *On The History of Modern Philosophy*, trans. Andrew Bowie (New York: Cambridge University Press, 1994), 155.

13 H.L. Martensen on Jacob Boehme

George Pattison

The main focus of this chapter will be the interpretation of Boehme by the nineteenth-century Danish theologian Hans Lassen Martensen. In addition to producing what was intentionally a "popular" book on what many regarded as an exceptionally obscure body of writings,[1] Martensen is significant and perhaps even unique amongst Boehme's post-1800 theological interpreters in the extent to which he interprets and appropriates some of the most speculative elements in Boehme's thought as being essentially compatible with an ecclesiastically orthodox theology.[2] However, even though he also shows awareness that Boehme is not an entirely unproblematic figure in relation to the mainstream of Christian dogmatic thinking, Martensen's work exemplifies the perils as well as the attractions of using Boehme as a resource for doctrinal theology. I shall conclude this chapter by using two other theological appropriations of Boehme, by William Law and Paul Tillich, to bring into focus how Martensen ultimately succumbs to these perils.

I

But who was Martensen, and why should his work on Boehme attract our special attention? Martensen is chiefly remembered today as being the object of many of Kierkegaard's attacks on Hegelianism—Jon Stewart's *Kierkegaard's Relations to Hegel Reconsidered* singles him out as the most frequent target of Kierkegaard's most bitter sarcasm.[3] Martensen, born in 1808 (and thus five years older than Kierkegaard, whom, at one point he tutored on Schleiermacher's *Glaubenslehre*), had a brilliant early theological career and went on to even greater success when, in 1854, he was appointed Bishop of Sjelland and Primate of the Danish People's Church.[4] A blurb by T. & T. Clark, who published the English translations of his *Christian Ethics* and *Christian Dogmatics*, declared him to be "the greatest Scandinavian, perhaps the greatest Lutheran, divine of our century".[5] That Martensen has been reduced to a footnote to Kierkegaard should not therefore lead us to minimize his significance for his own time or the value of taking him as a case-study for the nineteenth-century theological reception of Boehme. Part of his interest in this latter regard is, as we shall see, how his intellectual career stretched from the post-Hegelian debates of the 1830s through to the very different horizons of the later nineteenth century.

A key term in Martensen's reading of Boehme is "speculation," a notion that was central to the intellectual context in which he made his academic debut. In 1836, he returned to Denmark after a study tour of Germany. This had exposed him to a range of contemporary influences, including not least the Catholic mystical writer Franz von Baader and the speculative theologian K. Daub, although Martensen's biography suggests that an interest in speculation on the "inner life-process" of God was already established by 1834, when Hegel, Schelling, Baader, and Boehme were amongst those occupying his thoughts. In lecture series in 1837 and 1838, he was largely responsible for introducing Hegelian terminology and method into Danish theology, causing an effect not dissimilar to the vogue for postmodernism on American campuses in the 1980s. Martensen himself was probably not far from the truth when in rather self-satisfied terms he described the impact of these lectures as follows:

> The effect of my lectures can certainly without exaggeration be characterized as great and exceptional. A new life and feeling showed itself among the theological students. Philosophical studies worked their enticing power, and the students were constantly discussing the highest problems. Certainly there were those, who are unavoidable in such circumstances, for whom the whole thing was just a matter of fashion. Hegel was the man of the moment, and if one had his stamp of approval, one stood at the summit of the age. Others were more serious about Hegel and studied him deeply.[6]

Hegel subsequently disappeared from Martensen's work, although, in truth, even in these early lectures Martensen did not so much identify himself as a Hegelian but, in the terminology of the day, as a "speculative theologian," a term that encompassed both Hegelian and non-Hegelian thinkers. The latter included I.H. Fichte, P. Marheineke, J.G. Erdmann, K. Rosenkranz, and K. Daub, several of whom published work in Fichte's *Zeitschrift für speculative Theologie*. What, in this context, did "speculative" essentially mean? Basically, the claim was that the structures of human knowing—the forms and modes of human consciousness—were appropriate receptors of divine knowledge and that the phenomenological analysis of the content of the religious consciousness could yield an objective knowledge of God.

In the opening paragraph of the doctoral thesis that established his reputation in Denmark, Martensen claimed that such "speculative understanding of God and the divine things" was in basic accord with "the philosophizing Fathers of the Church, as well as with the scholastics of the Middle Ages who taught that theology was philosophy, that true philosophy was theology, and thus claimed a unity of both."[7] Both philosophy and theology are rooted in the desire for knowledge of the truth, and if one distinguishes them on the grounds that one approaches truth through faith and the other through knowledge, this runs the risk of splitting truth into two, as happened in "a bad scholasticism."[8] To avoid this, the search for truth begins neither in "pure thought" nor in doubt; rather philosophy itself must be relocated to the "*inside* of faith."[9] This means that a modern philosophical approach to God will have its starting-point in human beings' religious self-consciousness. In Descartes, Kant, and Schleiermacher, this approach is unable to overcome the limits of subjectivity. Hegelianism, however, lays the basis for a genuine and objective speculative knowledge of God. In accordance with this program, his early lecture series had titles such as *Lectures on the Introduction to speculative dogmatics* (Winter Semester 1837–8) and *Speculative Dogmatics* (Summer 1838).

At the same time, and like many contemporaries (again including Kierkegaard), his interest in the latest ideas from Germany was closely connected with issues of literature and aesthetics. The notion of "fantasy" played an important part in bridging these two fields (i.e., logic and ontology on the one hand and aesthetics on the other), and it is striking that he himself says of his late book on Boehme that, more than any other of his works, it exemplifies his belief in the positive role of fantasy in the representation and understanding of Christian truth. In the specific sense used by Martensen, "fantasy" is what Romantic philosophers and poets understood as the active power of imagination and which they saw as integral to any act of consciousness, including knowledge of the external world. In other words, knowledge is not just a matter of organizing and reproducing the data of sense-experience, passively received, but is itself constructive. Against accusations that this was "fantastic" in a merely negative sense, the argument was that such a procedure was the only way to do justice to the freedom that was the basic reality of human and divine life. At the same time, the image-making power of fantasy legitimates the use of myth and symbol in theology and gives them a role greater than providing mere "illustrations" to truths known more appropriately in a purely intellectual way.

Martensen's "discovery" of Boehme was part of this ferment of ideas—Hegel himself had, after all, identified Boehme as "the first German philosopher," and references to Boehme are found in Martensen's early lectures—paradoxically most accessible today in Kierkegaard's lecture notes—where, for example, he is used to illustrate the basic difference between Catholic and Protestant views of Christ (with Anselm offered as the counter-pole to the *philosophus teutonicus*).[10] But Boehme was also part of a larger reappropriation of mystical sources, including preeminently Meister Eckhart, to whom also Martensen dedicated a monograph (published 1840).[11]

It is, in fact, in this monograph that we first encounter a significant comment on Boehme in Martensen's published writings. Boehme is introduced as the "foremost representative" of mysticism in the evangelical churches.

As in Kierkegaard's lecture notes, the distinctively Protestant nature of Boehme's thought is emphasized, as is its difference from the mysticism of the Middle Ages: his "contemplation could only appear on the basis of Protestantism and is saturated by the Reformation's principle."[12] Like the medieval Catholic mystics, "he knew that it was egoity which removed the human being from God" ("egoity" in the sense of both oral and epistemological self-centeredness).[13] But whereas the medieval thinkers understood this in a "one sided ascetic self-preoccupation," Boehme "considered this from its universal, cosmic aspect and expressed his conception as a representation of Lucifer's falling away from and struggle against God. The unfolding of this struggle, the light's gathering triumph over the darkness, is world history." And, adds Martensen, it is "this universal and objective tendency" that earns Boehme's thought the epithet "theosophy."[14]

However, despite references to Boehme in these early works, there is little extensive engagement with his work. Again, there is relatively little direct discussion in the *Christian Dogmatics*, the work that in 1847 gave a rounded exposition of Christian doctrine in terms that were in significant continuity with the earlier lectures. Nevertheless, here too, and with the benefit of being able to look back from the later monograph on Boehme, we can see several aspects of Martensen's theology where there is a clear influence from Boehme. Take the case of Martensen's Trinitarian speculations. Whereas Schleiermacher had seen the doctrine of the Trinity as an attempt to explain and interpret the Christian experience of God as love and not to encourage any speculation as to the internal life of the Trinity over and above that general affirmation, Martensen believes that there is a "knowledge" given in this experience and that it is possible to explicate this knowledge speculatively. The economy of Trinitarian revelation—human beings' historical experience of God—also reveals God's "essential relation to himself."[15] Whilst our human limitations mean that we can only attain a "shadowy knowledge" of the essential Trinity, this same shadowy knowledge is nevertheless said to be "ontological," that is, a knowledge of the real being of God.[16] "God could not be the revealed, self-loving God, unless He had eternally distinguished Himself into I and Thou (into Father and Son), and unless He had eternally comprehended Himself as the Spirit of Love."[17]

All of this could be said within the parameters of Hegelianism, however.[18] But the way in which Boehme has helped lead Martensen beyond a purely Hegelian speculation can be seen in his sophiology. Sophiology is best known today in the context of nineteenth- and twentieth-century Russian religious philosophy[19] and relates to speculation as to the status of the divine Wisdom (Greek: *sophia*). In full-blown sophiology, "wisdom" is not a mere attribute of divine nature but a distinct divine principle, possibly constituting a fourth divine entity in addition to the Trinity of Father, Son, and Holy Spirit. We encounter Martensen's own sophiological tendencies when, in §56, in a section on "The Divine Hypostases," he describes how, in contemplating "the heavenly image of the world as it arises out of the depths of His own nature," the primal Ego of the Father "sees the image of His own essence, His own Ego in a *second* subsistence." This divine reflection on the "heavenly ideal world" is possible only when God knows Himself not only as Ego but as Logos, as speaking and spoken Word, as revealed and revealing. This "inner revelation," in which God reveals Himself to Himself, is the dividing line between Christianity and Judaism. At its maximum, the Old Testament could only conceive of this self-revelation of the divine life as occurring via the divine Wisdom that as an eternal image of the world spoken by God in the act of creation is not itself divine but a kind of middle term between creator and creation. In Christianity, however, God is in Himself Logos, in Himself Wisdom. Divine self-consciousness does not require there to be anything other than God, merely for God "to think of Himself as another."[20] In an earlier treatment of Wisdom in the section on the attributes of God, Martensen speaks of Wisdom as "what speculation calls the idea, the world-forming thought."[21] He also notes that "the theosophists" (which is how he characteristically refers to Boehme) speak of her as "the heavenly maiden, the divine *sophia*,"[22] and he depicts this Wisdom as the "artist" who worked with the Most High in creation but which completes its work only in human beings, in holy souls that know Christ.[23] Recalling again Martensen's affirmation of myth and symbol as legitimate modes of the knowledge of God, the implication lies near at hand that the creative *poiesis* (that is, productive activity) of the imagination is the ultimate means in and by which the "divine depths" are revealed to human beings. And it is somewhere in this area, we might say, that speculation changes from being a way of stating the intuitive dimension of any act of knowledge to being a means of extending knowledge beyond the range of experience. Knowledge of God derived from the revelation of divine love in the experience of redemption is on the edge of being transposed into something else, into an essentially poetic and imaginative mythology—but one that is at the same time being proposed as having genuine cognitive and ontological purchase.

II

Despite the evidence for the early and significant influence of the German sage, it is not until 1881, 40 years later, that Martensen publishes his monograph on Boehme. He states that, in the meantime, since his younger days, Boehme had "gradually faded away" from his attention, "although," he adds, "modern philosophy and theology still kept me in contact with his ideas, during the whole of my life."[24] Now, however, "a point in Böhme which has formed the subject of much philosophical discussion, and with which I had long been occupied, compelled me to return to the fountain head, to seek for myself grounds of a more solid and independent conviction."[25] He does not directly state what that "point" is, but the fact that he then goes on to discuss the subtitle "theosophical studies" and that both the beginning and end of the book focus on the theme of theosophy suggest that the point is the nature or possibility of "theosophy." It is suggestive that the Theosophical Society had been founded in 1875, six years before the publication of Martensen's book, although I have not as yet been able to trace any direct connection. However, it is a striking thought that a career that began by reworking Hegel for theologians, might, at its conclusion, have engaged with the followers of Mme. Blavatsky.[26]

Central to Martensen's study are the claims that Boehme the man and Boehme's main ideas—not least the idea of theosophy—are both essentially Protestant and essentially congruent with orthodox Christian teaching. Like Hegel, Martensen acknowledges the possible distortions that arise from Boehme's vivid, materialistic, and unschooled language. "Many have regarded him as a visionary," he notes, "and have placed his teaching in the history of human follies. In many libraries his writings are to be found under the rubric '*Fanatici*.'"[27] However, Martensen's own view soon becomes apparent, namely, that Boehme "combined with simple Christian faith and piety the most profound philosophical speculation" and that "one is surprised, amidst the obscurity and the gloom, by lightning which now gladdens and anon appals by the glimpses it affords us of Time and Eternity, of the Divine, human, and demonic depths."[28] Moreover, "he sought to promote a true and practical Christianity which should not be confined to the 'sphere of the letter': in this he coincides with the nobler pietism."[29] After listing his subject's influence on Hegel, Schelling, Franz Baader, Saint-Martin, and even Charles I, Martensen then gives a brief outline of Boehme's life, emphasizing that his ecclesiastical enemies were driven more by malice than by any actual heterodoxy on Boehme's part, and that both the philosophical and personal qualities of Boehme's thought were essentially in accord with Christian doctrine.

This remains a guiding thread of the exposition of Boehme's ideas that follows. Martensen begins, as I have said, with the notion of theosophy itself. "[I]ts form," he writes, is "that of intuition, immediate perception, central apprehension of God and existence."[30] This might seem to make it a branch of speculative theology, but, he states, "Theosophy seeks to embrace far more than Theology. Out of the idea of God it seeks to apprehend the world, in all the circles of the universe to see things as they are in God."[31] By this means it seeks to prove "that the principles of Christianity are identical with those by which the world itself subsists, and on which the foundation of the world is laid."[32] As such, it bears comparison with the positive philosophy of Schelling.

As in the brief comments in the Eckhart book, this kind of "objective, theoretical mysticism" is contrasted with the typical mysticism of the Middle Ages, which is seen as "subjective" and "practical": "it is the mysticism of the mind as distinguished from that of the heart."[33] It looks to understand nature, the macrocosm, and yet "there is no genuine theosophy which is not qualified by the mysticism of the heart."[34] Martensen reiterates this point by appealing once more to biographical data, saying of Boehme that he had "from the first, sought only the Heart of Jesus Christ" until his vision of "the gracious maiden," "the Eternal idea, the precious Sophia, the heavenly Wisdom," who opens up the realm of theosophic knowledge.[35] As a Christian thinker, Boehme is essentially scriptural and, even though some of his interpretations are clearly eccentric, "he lives and breathes in the fundamental perception of Scripture" as he seeks in it "a cohesion between the historical and the metaphysical."[36] He is, as has been said, essentially a Protestant phenomenon, and yet his focus on super-historical principles also makes him a "super-confessional" thinker, a claim that Martensen backs up by reference to Baader, a Catholic thinker, having called Boehme "his real teacher."[37]

Martensen proceeds to give a broad-brush setting of Boehme's thought in a history of ideas that involves the Kabbalah, Gnosticism (of which Boehme is cleared), and the intellectual life of the Renaissance with its interest in alchemy and magic. In connection with the influence of Paracelsus, we see in Boehme the interrelationship of microcosm and macrocosm focusing on the idea of life: "in this natural philosophy, Boehme is confronted by a *living intuition of nature . . .* "[38] Nature is not only object, but subject: "a universal life is diffused throughout nature. Will and imagination are everywhere at work, although not self-conscious, but plastically-working will and imagination."[39] Because these are not merely harmonious but develop through discord, the outcome is precisely *life*.

It is this understanding of life as the dynamic interplay of difference that is also encountered in Boehme's idea of God, where his central concern is "*the apprehension of the God of Revelation as the Living God*."[40] In making this claim, Martensen once more adverts to the essentially Protestant nature of Boehme's project. Insisting (again) that Boehme's God "is the God of Christianity, the God of revelation and of the Church," and emphasizing Boehme's Trinitarian orientation, Martensen asserts that "whereas the Reformation had contented itself with reviewing and refashioning the dogmas that belong to practical soteriology, Boehme took up the speculative dogmas which the Reformation had passively accepted from Catholicism, at the head of which stands the doctrine of the Trinity."[41]

These comments implicitly ascribe an enormous importance to Boehme's role in the history of modern Protestant dogmatics. Martensen is in effect claiming that Boehme is pointing the way to the theological completion of the Reformation and, as such, also defining the trajectory of future Protestant theology. Furthermore, if we look back to the earlier work, especially the *Christian Dogmatics*, with these remarks in mind, we can see that it is Boehme, even more than Hegel, who powers Martensen's attempt to explicate the inner divine life of the Trinity. Given the turn to Trinitarian thinking in Protestant theology in the twentieth century, one might regard this as fulfilling Martensen's prognosis, even if it was Barth rather than Boehme or Hegel who directly initiated this turn.[42]

As Trinitarian, Boehme's God is fundamentally different from the God of mysticism: "while Mysticism, from Dionysius Areopagiticus down to Schleiermacher, defines God as the unvarying nameless One . . . Boehme demands a God who manifests Himself in differences, in contrasts, in defining relations; and only this God is to him the true God"[43]—and readers are scarcely in any doubt that Martensen agrees.

It is this dynamic view of God and of God's inner, living drive to manifestation in and through "differences" that provides the theoretical basis for Boehme's positing of "nature in God." Here too, Martensen defends Boehme's orthodoxy against the charge of conflating God and nature. It is not a question of "matter" in God, "but rather a source for matter, a plenitude of living forces and energies."[44] Nor is it a matter of a developing or emergent God—for which Jacobi had reproached Schelling. Christianity (and Boehme) "proclaims a God who is perfect and blessed in Himself from all eternity, and where love is not the *result* of the world's development, but its postulate."[45] Hegel is criticized for interpreting Boehme in a pantheistic way, and Schelling is also found wanting. Only Baader (it seems) correctly sees that "Böhme's God . . . is the God who is perfect in Himself, prior to creation and the world."[46] Martensen now sets out to show that, despite Boehme's use of alchemical terms such as salt, mercury, sulphur, and so forth, his doctrine of the divine life is authentically Christian.

I shall not now renarrate Martensen's entire exposition, but it is worth noting how he gives special emphasis to the question of wisdom. In the section on "God and the Uncreated Heaven," he explains how Boehme's system begins with the simple indifference of the Abyss, within which "*mysterium magnum*, there is a bottomless unoriginated Will."[47] Since nothing else is, the only possible object for this will is itself: it can and must only desire itself. Yet in order to desire itself, it must in some way represent itself to itself; therefore, "the first thing it does is to fashion for itself a Mirror, in which it can behold itself."[48] In Boehme's thought—as opposed to that of Kant—this "is not only a reason-mirror, a thought-mirror, but also a mirror of imagination and fancy." Therefore, "To the imaginative Eye that looks into the mirror it reveals the whole pleroma,—shapes, colours, and figures; indeed as we shall find in the sequel, it reflects the image of the Triune God Himself. There is nothing either in heaven or upon earth which did not, at the beginning, become manifest in this mirror."[49] However, as Martensen also goes on to point out, Boehme not only refers to this mirror as the eternal wisdom or eternal idea, but he "also calls this idea a Maiden . . . who stands, in the dawn of eternity, before the God who gives himself up to Self-manifestation, and who, so to speak, allures Him to manifest Himself, by showing Him the exceeding riches of His glory."[50] This, of course, is Sophia, "co-eternal with God" but "not God of God, but simply the friend of God."[51] This maiden Sophia "stands before God as if in a vision, a morning-dream of Eternity, which prophetically reveals to Him what He *can* become, what He *can* make Himself."[52] Aroused to the desire of manifestation by the

"Magia" of sophianic maidenhood, a process is set in motion that issues in the full Trinitarian development of the divine life.

However, this does not exhaust the role of Sophia since, thus far, all that has been discussed is the immanent development of the Trinitarian life or how God becomes manifest to himself as Father, Son, and Holy Spirit. But how does God become manifest in creation, and how does God therefore become manifest to the creature, that is, to us? Here too, Sophia plays a vital part, since what the divine will chooses to bring to manifestation in creation is only what it has already beheld in the internal, primal, esoteric "mystical self-contemplation" or the "magical self-mirroring, the tranquil wisdom, where God, in pure introspection, converses only with Himself."[53] If "eternal nature" is the material in which this manifestation occurs, the eternal wisdom or idea is the pattern that shapes it in its manifestation. "There is here," writes Martensen, "an eternal going-forth and an eternal entering-in. God eternally goes forth out of His inwardness to manifest Himself again in externality, and from this externality He again returns, enriched, into the tranquil inwardness."[54]

In reviewing this account, Martensen returns to the matter of the unfinished business left by the Reformation. Boehme's Trinitarian speculation, he states, represents a real advance on the Athanasian Symbol, of which Martensen says that its God is "a god for mere thought," whereas Boehme's God is "a living Trinitarian God" who is not only capable of loving but of being love.[55] As such, his is a God corresponding to the evangelical breakthrough and capable of founding the ethical consequences that follow. That God is revealed as the eternal overcoming of darkness by light, grounds the dynamics of the religious life itself: "the contrasts of manifestation, which constitute the regenerated personality."[56] Whereas Calvin and Luther seemed to allow for a distinction between the secret and the revealed will of God, Boehme's God is as He is in His manifestation, and His manifestation manifests Him as He is. This God is the living God, the God who is love, the God who grounds reconciliation. Therefore, this God "is, in his inmost Being, kindred to man, as man is kindred to God."[57] But this, after all, was always the implicit assumption that allowed speculative theology to regard the analysis of human beings' religious self-consciousness as a reliable guide to the real essence of the divine Being.

Nevertheless, Martensen also has a number of critical objections to Boehme, not least the fact that the latter begins his account with the Abyss or absolute indifference, something that, despite generally clearing Boehme of charges of Gnosticism, he does see as essentially Gnostic. Against this, he says, "Unless we begin with Consummate Love in perfect reality, we shall never find it. The commencement must be ethical."[58] Moreover, Boehme generally gives far too great a role to nature, which Martensen regards as merely "a condition and medium" for God's self-manifestation,[59] but not itself divine. This is especially problematic with regard to Boehme's discussion of a "dark nature-principle" in God.

Martensen's approach to Boehme's theogonic and Trinitarian writings set the tone for the rest of his exposition. Leaping over much of his discussion, I turn to the concluding sections and especially to the section dealing with the state of the soul after death, in which Martensen allows his own speculative tendencies fullest rein.

What Martensen finds decisive in Boehme's teaching on the state of the soul after death is the latter's description of this state as "a state of Inwardness and of the Kingdom beyond as a Kingdom of Inwardness, in which there is no outward corporeity."[60] Not that there is *no* corporeity, since "spirit and nature, the inward and the outward, cannot be entirely separated [but] Böhme teaches . . . that there is an inward and finer corporeity imperceptible to the senses,—a corporeity which we do not acquire beyond, but take with us from this world."[61] This is linked by Martensen to Paracelsus's idea of a "sidereal" or "Light-body, which the pious and blessed develop into greater perfection as their heavenly attire."[62] Martensen declines to pursue these questions further, "because they lead us into obscure subtleties,"[63] but he nevertheless affirms the idea of the soul existing in what he calls "a certain intermediate corporeity . . . or, as modern students have called it, a symbolical body, which can only make itself known by shining and sounding, and which is destined to be succeeded by an actual body, when the hour of Resurrection arrives."[64] The dead are like dreamers, "They are in a '*magia*,' that is, they are self-conscious in a condition of relative non-corporeity; they perceive and comprehend, independently of a material sense-apparatus."[65] The analogy with the dream-state is strengthened, he claims, by scriptural references to the dead as "those that sleep." A "symbol" for this "magical" post-mortem state may also be found in "the dream which takes place in the Mesmeric sleep . . . the so-called clairvoyant and ecstatic states, in which the soul is, as it were, rapt from the body."[66] However, he characteristically goes on to warn against confusing the two since there is no idea of eternity operative in the magnetic[67] and mesmeric states, so the analogy is merely formal. Bound as we are to the corporeal forms of this world, we cannot comprehend the magical condition of the soul after death, in which time-space relations as we know them are abrogated. And yet, he insists, even in heaven itself there is "a contrast between *near* and *far*, *here* and *yonder*."[68] Against Boehme, who, according to Martensen, distinguishes solely between heaven and hell, we may suppose there to be "many mansions" beyond death, and many "intermediate regions." Furthermore, where Boehme supposes that the soul can no longer change its mind after death, Martensen argues that we cannot exclude the possibility

> that the world and the scenes that surround the soul [after death] may not set it new tasks, inasmuch as time is not, in every sense, excluded. . . . How does [Böhme] know that, in that higher world, there may not be new manifestations of the Divine Will, with regard to which the soul may have to determine itself? And how does he know but that fresh problems may arise out of the native depths of the soul itself?[69]

Martensen focuses these questions on the issue of Christ's descent to the Dead. Here, Boehme follows the standard Lutheran view that sees this as having a solely judicial and not a redemptive significance, that is to say, that Christ went only to confirm judgment on the devil and destroy his power, not to redeem the righteous kept until then in the underworld (as in Catholic and Orthodox teaching). In fact, Boehme effectively excludes the idea of such a descent because of the perfect reconciliation of wrath by love effected on the cross. However, Martensen deems Boehme's deficiency on this point to have been corrected by another theosophical theologian, Friedrich Christoph Oetinger (1702–1782). Oetinger not only allows for the possibility of post-mortem repentance, but says that even the saved do not immediately enter into the fullness of eternal blessedness. "[H]e teaches that they advance from class to class, from grade to grade, from Abraham's bosom, or the lower Paradise, to the higher heavenly region. After death we shall most certainly not at once be at home with the Lord, but there are many degrees of progress. Jesus guides us from station to station with his shepherd's staff."[70]

Oetinger finds support for "his doctrine of the great diversity of souls and of spiritual states after death" in reports of appearances of departed spirits, a source of information that, as Martensen notes, is continued in contemporary spiritualism. As for Martensen's own view, he comments at the outset that "unless one professes pure materialism, and denies the conceptions of spirit and the spirit-world, one cannot deny the possibility that spirit may be able to manifest itself to spirit; nor is it possible to perceive what natural laws can prevent a purely spiritual 'commercium' "[71]—a position for which he also finds support in Kant. However, he also notes that the majority of these reports concern spirits that are in one way or another incapable of entirely freeing themselves from their earthly bodies and that must therefore be presumed to be positioned rather low in the hierarchy of post-mortem states. More advanced souls will have more completely separated themselves from their earthly bodies and will therefore not appear in such sensuous forms. "[C]oming into closer relations with these souls" cannot therefore be expected to lead to "deeper insight into the mysteries of the world beyond, and perhaps even apprehend eternal truths, which one cannot already know from Revelation".[72] It also follows that such spirit-phenomena as spiritualism concerns itself with cannot be "a consoling substitute for that Christian faith in immortality which many have lost."[73] Nevertheless, Oetinger's view is both a corrective to his master, Boehme, and "betokens a new momentum of development in Protestant eschatology, which has attained wider expansion only in the dogmatics of the present century."[74]

In fact—but without mentioning the influence of theosophy on his own thought—the points developed here are very much the points Martensen made in his own name in the *Christian Dogmatics*, especially in §276 "The Intermediate State in the Realm of the Dead" where he argues for a Protestant analogue to purgatory, albeit one purged (so to speak) of the "many crude and false positions" associated with the "Romish" doctrine.[75] As often with regard to Martensen, it is once more Kierkegaard who supplies the clearest counter-position. In one of his Christian Discourses of 1848, "There will be the Resurrection of the Dead, of the righteous—and of the unrighteous," Kierkegaard states that the Christian position effectively says:

> 'Nothing is more certain than immortality; you are not to worry about, nor to waste your time on, not to seek an escape by—wanting to demonstrate it or wishing to have it demonstrated. Fear it, it is only all too certain; do not doubt whether you are immortal—tremble, because you are immortal'.[76]

Why "tremble"? Because the resurrection is a resurrection to judgment:

> Immortality is not a continued life, a continued life as such in perpetuity, but immortality is the eternal separation between the righteous and the unrighteous . . . immortality and judgment are one and the same.[77]

The outcome of preaching immortality, then, is to direct the question back to the whole manner of a person's life, so that Kierkegaard effectively repeats in modern form the teaching of the *Imitation of Christ*: "Very soon the end of your life will be at hand: consider, therefore, the state of your soul."[78] The topic of immortality is not to offer a subject for speculation, but is there to incite us to self-examination and amendment of life here and now!

There is no evidence that Kierkegaard is intentionally rebuking Martensen in the discourse on Resurrection, although it is possible, but the question itself was one of the earliest explicit points of contention between them. In 1841 Martensen had published a review of a collection of poetic works by J.L. Heiberg, who had been the first major figure in Danish intellectual life to explicitly align himself with Hegelianism. One of these, the dramatic poem *A Soul After Death*, tells in a rather humorous fashion the peregrinations of a recently deceased soul who, refused entrance to both heaven and Elysium, is accosted by Mephistopheles who invites him back to his place, assuring him that everything there is just like what he is used to in Copenhagen, and many of his neighbours are indeed already there. It is entirely boring and in bad taste, but what's to worry about in that? Martensen, perhaps extravagantly, compared Heiberg to Dante, and even ranked him higher with regard to his understanding of the metaphysical relationship between essence and appearance. In the final line of his thesis *On the Concept of Irony*, Kierkegaard remarks that, if any reader wants further "food for thought" on the question of the relationship between irony and actuality, he recommends they read Martensen's review. I take this remark as itself ironic and as indicative that Kierkegaard did not regard either Heiberg's poetic irony or Martensen's speculative interpretation of *A Soul after Death* as being able to deal with the real issues of life in all its complex and difficult actuality. Or, to put it otherwise, the speculations offered by Heiberg and Martensen were a matter of myth, symbol, imagination, and poetry and not, as they themselves believed, a significant contribution to knowledge: it is not the mythology or the poetic that is the problem, but simply its being confused with knowledge and with life.[79]

III

I should like to bring out further the problematic features of Martensen's use of Boehme by contrasting it with that of two other major theological figures, one from the eighteenth century and one from the twentieth: William Law and Paul Tillich.[80] Doing so will help us see what is distinctive in the Danish theologian's approach and also to identify in external terms the weaknesses that, otherwise articulated, were already apparent to his one-time student, Kierkegaard.

Law sees Boehme (whom he calls God's "chosen instrument")[81] as helping to resolve major issues of doctrinal theology, particularly with regard, first, to the relationship between reason and revelation and, second, to the nature of the atonement—both of which were prominent in the ecclesiastical disputes of Law's time. In both cases the key is found in God's consistent and persistent character and presence as pure, unqualified love.

Law sees the question of reason and revelation as hinging on a proper understanding of the relationship between God, creation, and fall. In classic Christian theology, God's original creation was, of course, good and, as such, testimony to the goodness and wisdom of its creator. However, Christian theologians diverged significantly with regard to how far this testimony remained valid subsequent to the Fall. For those in the mainstream Catholic tradition, the fall diminished but did not eclipse or annihilate the image of God in human beings nor did it alter the fundamental relationship of creature and creator that provided the basis for an analogical knowledge of God from our knowledge of created things. This tradition was significantly transformed but, in its way, also continued in early modern English natural theology, with the new "experimental" science of Bacon and the Royal Society playing the part assigned to Aristotelian metaphysics by Thomas Aquinas. However, a further development of this tendency led some in the direction of deism, namely, the view that nature has been constituted as a self-contained system subject to unalterable laws. In this situation any intervention or revelation by a supernatural being could only occur as an act of violence against the normal course of nature. A very different approach, however, had been developed in the Augustinian tradition, an approach that was radicalized and acquired normative status in the Reformed and Lutheran Churches. This view saw the fall as not merely marring but utterly destroying the image of God in human beings, and also distorting the non-human creation in such a way as to render knowledge of God apart from revelation impossible.

In works such as *The Spirit of Love*, Law deliberately uses Boehme to help his readers through the impasse offered by the implacable opposition between deism and supernaturalism. The error of both, he suggests, is precisely to think of God and the world as related only in an external way. Even natural theology falls into the same trap and therefore cannot provide a secure defence against deism (a point that Law's contemporary, David Hume, would also argue). However, "creation" is not an ensemble of beings outside of or external to God in any simple way, although neither is it a direct manifestation of the divine life itself. Rather, the basis of creation is an "eternal nature" that is the "outward Manifestation of the invisible Riches, Powers, and Glories of the Deity."[82] Moreover, "creation" is not a once-for-all act that occurred at a specific point in the past: it is "not *once done*, but ever doing, ever standing in the *same Birth*, for ever and ever breaking forth and springing up in new Forms and Openings of the abyssal Deity."[83] The implication of this is that we can, in fact, have no full or adequate knowledge of finite, temporal nature without also taking into account its grounding in the eternal nature that, in turn, is a manifestation of the invisible life of God. The testimony of nature to the divine life is not a matter of external testimony or inference, as in natural theology, but it itself is one aspect of what is essentially a "twofold state": in its perfection, nature "is Nature, and it is God manifested in Nature."[84] Ultimately, reason and revelation are therefore two approaches to the same basic reality and the basis for an opposition between them is carried away.

The same logic extends into Law's treatment of the interrelated topics of the fall and the atonement. Here, he uses Boehme to argue that even in its most chaotic and "dark" states, creation is never without a possible connection to the mystery of the divine life: "all that is called *Nature*, *Darkness*, or *Self*, not only has no Evil in it, but is the only Ground of all possible Good"[85]—except when it disconnects itself from its relation to God. Equally, God never ceases to be love in His dealings with fallen nature. Where the Reformed tradition—strongly reflected in the Church of England's Book of Common Prayer—consistently portrayed God as revealing Himself to sinners in the form of wrath, Law emphasizes that both in creation and in redemption God is nothing but love: it is not, as in both medieval and Reformation teaching, that a wrathful Father needs to be placated and propitiated by the sufferings of His obedient Son. Rather, the Son is nothing other than the expression of the Father's constant and enduring love. Such a God of love is only to be known through love, that is, through the heart giving itself over to the "spirit of love." But this is possible only because Christ is not given to us in a merely external way, as in the Reformed doctrine that Christ's righteousness is merely imputed to the ungodly, but, as Law puts it, "Christ given *for us*, is neither more nor less, than Christ given *into us*."[86] The work of redemption thus continues the work of creation, bringing to perfection the twofold inter-involvement of creature and creator.

Now I am not saying that Law does not affirm and make extensive use of the speculative aspects of Boehme's thought—he does—but the point is that he does so precisely in order to resolve specific and controversial points of doctrine. Moreover, as the titles of such works as *The Spirit of Prayer* and *The Spirit of Love* suggest, Law saw his own task in essentially practical terms, perhaps intuitively if not actually applying Luther's dictum that theology is a practical rather than a speculative science. In other words, the questions he addresses and his manner of addressing them relate directly to concrete issues in living the Christian life. To the extent that his work is "speculative" it is so only in the service of practice. It is not knowledge of the abyssal being of God that is at issue, but whether it is really possible to live our lives in loving response to the experience of God's love.

Paul Tillich (1886–1965) is a thinker of a very different kind from Law, and Boehme is only one of many sources flowing into his mature theology, especially, we may say, Boehme as mediated by Schelling. However, whilst we can find in Tillich elements that use Boehme in something like a speculative way, he seems especially to emphasize what we might call the apophatic element in Boehme.[87] He typically sees Boehme as representing a mystical tradition that also includes Plotinus, Eckhart, Nicholas of Cusa, and Spinoza and he says of this tradition that:

> it is the permanent function of mysticism to point to the abysmal character of the ground of being and to reject the demonic identification of anything finite with that which transcends everything finite.[88]

Tillich sees human existence as structured according to a sequence of interconnected polarities, primarily individuality and participation, dynamics and form, and freedom and destiny. In these terms, all of us are, for example, individuals but also participants in a larger social reality and although the balance will be constantly shifting, there can never be a purely individual human being or a human being entirely without individual character. Similarly, everything is both in a process of becoming and to that extent cannot be tied to or grasped by any particular form we impose upon it, but, equally, nothing is ever entirely without any element of form, since this would mean that there was simply nothing there to be talking about at all. In discussing the dialectics of dynamics and form Tillich says of "dynamics" that it represents "the *mē on*, the potentiality of being, which is non-being in contrast to things that have a form, and the power of being in contrast to pure non-being . . . It underlies most mythologies and is indicated in the chaos, the *tohu-va-bohu*, the night of emptiness, which precedes creation. It appears in metaphysical speculations as *Urgrund* [sic] (Böhme), will (Schopenhauer) will to power (Nietzsche), the unconscious (Hartmann, Freud), élan vital (Bergson), strife (Scheler, Jung)."[89] And, he adds, this dynamic element "is open in all directions; it is bound by no a priori limiting structure."[90] Although he does not make the connection with Boehme explicit (mentioning Kant and Schelling), this *Ungrund* is also akin to what he calls "the '*Unvordenkliche*' (that principle prior to which thought cannot take place, the *Prius* of thinking)." In all these ways, then, Boehme's thought is used to indicate that which sets a limit to all thought and speculation, to what cannot be thought conceptually or can only be thought negatively, paradoxically, or apophatically. It is that with which thought must reckon, but which cannot itself be thought.

If I am correct in characterizing Law's and Tillich's relations to Boehme as, respectively, practical and apophatic, they offer a clear counterpoint to Martensen's approach, which is unashamedly speculative. However, this is also a pointer to what—from the point of view of the Christian orthodoxy he claims to expound—is problematic in his approach. Although, as author of a three-volume *Christian Ethics*, Martensen was well aware of Christianity's practical dimension, he was consistently drawn by theoretical speculations and by the intellectual desire to advance cognition beyond the boundaries of pure reason set down by Kant. At the same time, he was almost gratuitously dismissive of the apophatic element in theology.

In his *Christian Dogmatics* he argues that "if God is personal, we should expect Him to reveal Himself in the realm of personality, in a sphere of created spirits, by whom He can be believed in, known, and loved."[91] The God who is believed in the covenantal relationship made concrete in the Church, the community of faith is therefore a God who, in faith, is *known*. In the Spirit, the believing community becomes capable of searching out the hidden things of God. This leads Martensen to some critical remarks on apophatic theology:

> When Dionysius the Areopagite and John Scotus Erigena teach that God is absolutely incomprehensible, not merely for us, but also in Himself, on the ground that if He were known, the comprehension of Him would subject Him to finitude, antagonism, limitation; when they assert God to be an absolute mystery, above all names, because every name drags Him down into the sphere of relations; when they refuse to conceive of God save as the simply one (*to haplōs hen*), as pure light, which does not differ from pure darkness, in which neither way nor path is discernible; when they object to calling God anything but "pure nothing," not because of His emptiness, but because of His inexpressible fullness, in virtue of which he transcends every "something,"—on which ground they also define Him as super-essential (*huperousios*)—they give utterance, no doubt, to their sense of the unfathomable depth of the mystery; but still such a mystical, neo-platonic mode of looking at the subject is an error—is a falling back on the indeterminate absolute of pantheism. By excluding the idea of understanding the Divine nature, mysticism excludes also the possibility of a revelation. For to comprehend a being is to know it in its relations; and if it did not pertain to the nature of God to enter into relations, to make Himself intelligible, He would not have revealed Himself.[92]

It is, I suggest, precisely the problem with Martensen that not only does his work pursue a speculative interest that has become separated out from its practical context, but he does so without retaining what has been called the "apophatic marker" that, in my view, should accompany all good theology. This also suggests that I believe that Kierkegaard was right to see Martensen as having signally failed to recognize the necessary limitations of human knowledge with regard to God and, for all his brilliance, as having been "speculative" in a derogatory sense. That, however, does not foreclose on the question as to the value of a creative and visionary approach to theology that is appropriately balanced by the wisdom of unknowing.

NOTES

1. In his memoirs, Martensen writes approvingly of the fact that the book has been read by laypeople and adds "I have even met women who have read my book." See H. L. Martensen, *Af mit Levnet*, Part 3 (Copenhagen: Gyldendal, 1883), 210.
2. In the memoirs, Martensen insists that Boehme can only be understood "by those who stand within the Christian world-view" (Martensen [1883], Part 3, 209).
3. Jon Stewart, *Kierkegaard's Relations to Hegel Reconsidered* (Cambridge: Cambridge University Press, 2003).
4. The title *Folkekirken*, The People's Church, as opposed to "National" or "Established" Church reflects the constitutional position that it will remain the national Church only as long as it also remains the Church of the majority of the Danish people. Unlike the establishment of the Church of England, this means that if membership falls below 50% of the franchised population, it will cease to be "established." It was just this "democratic" element that Kierkegaard, for example, especially objected to.
5. This is printed in, e.g., the Publications advertised at the back of Volume 1 of Martensen's *Christian Ethics* (Edinburgh: T. & T. Clark, 1873).
6. Martensen (1883), Part 2, 5–6.
7. H. L. Martensen, "The Autonomy of Human Self-Consciousness in Modern Dogmatic Theology," trans. and ed. C. J. Thompson and D. J. Kangas, in *Between Hegel and Kierkegaard: Hans L. Martensen's Philosophy of Religion* (Atlanta, GA: Scholars Press, 1997), 76.
8. It is unclear whether Martensen is specifically referring to the thought of Averroes or to Latin Averroism, with its doctrine of two kinds of truth, the one philosophical and the other theological (such that a thing could be true in one and untrue in the other).
9. Martensen (1997), 77.
10. See, e.g., Søren Kierkegaard, edited by Niels Jørgen Cappelørn et al. *Journals and Notebooks*, Vol. 3 (Princeton, NJ: Princeton University Press, 2010), 128 (Notebook 4:5).
11. English translation included in *Between Hegel and Kierkegaard*, 149–243.
12. Martensen (1997), 240
13. Ibid., 241.
14. Ibid., 241.
15. H. L. Martensen, trans. W. Urwick, *Christian Dogmatics* (Edinburgh: T. & T. Clark, 1866), 106.

16. Martensen (1866), 107.
17. Martensen (1866), 107.
18. Although, just to complexify matters, Hegel too had developed his own Trinitarian speculations with help from Boehme. See Glenn Magee's chapter on "Hegel's reception of Jacob Boehme" in this volume.
19. See Oliver Smith, "The Russian Boehme," in this volume.
20. Martensen (1866), 109.
21. Ibid., 96
22. Ibid., 96.
23. Ibid., 96–7.
24. H. L. Martensen, trans. T. R. Evans, *Jacob Boehme. His Life and Teaching or Studies in Theosophy* (London: Hodder and Stoughton, 1885), vi.
25. Martensen (1885), vi.
26. It has to be acknowledged that neither in the Boehme book nor in his memoirs does Martensen himself suggest this. However, his work was commented on (with specific reference to Boehme) in *The Theosophical Quarterly*, (1913), vol. 10, 279–82.
27. Martensen (1885), 1.
28. Ibid., 2.
29. Ibid., 2.
30. Ibid., 17.
31. Ibid., 17.
32. Ibid., 18.
33. Ibid., 19.
34. Ibid., 19.
35. Ibid., 21.
36. Ibid., 24.
37. Ibid., 25.
38. Ibid., 32.
39. Ibid., 33.
40. Ibid., 37.
41. Ibid., 36–7
42. Although, equally, one might reflect on whether Barth does not, in fact, have more in common with the speculative theologians than some accounts of his thought might suggest. See my article "Martensen, Speculation and the Task of Modern Theology," in J. Stewart ed., *Hans Lassen Martensen. Theologian, Philosopher and Social Critic* (Copenhagen: Museum Tusculanum Press, 2012), 17–45.
43. Martensen (1885), 38–9.
44. Ibid., 41.
45. Ibid., 44.
46. Ibid., 46.
47. Ibid., 57
48. Ibid., 58
49. Ibid., 59.
50. Ibid., 59.
51. Ibid., 59.
52. Ibid., 62.
53. Ibid., 97.
54. Ibid., 97.
55. Ibid., 99–100.
56. Ibid., 104.
57. Ibid., 106.
58. Ibid., 124.

59. Ibid., 125.
60. Ibid., 303.
61. Ibid., 303.
62. Ibid., 303.
63. Ibid., 303.
64. Ibid., 304.
65. Ibid., 304.
66. Ibid., 306.
67. Many nineteenth-century theories sought to link hypnotism (mesmerism) to electro-magnetism.
68. Martensen (1885), 312.
69. Ibid., 316.
70. Ibid., 321.
71. Ibid., 323–4.
72. Ibid., 326.
73. Ibid., 327.
74. Ibid., 327.
75. Martensen (1866), 457.
76. S. Kierkegaard, *Christelige Taler* in *Søren Kierkegaards Skrifter*, vol. 10 (Copenhagen: Gad, 1997), 205.
77. Kierkegaard (1997), 205.
78. Thomas à Kempis, trans. L. Sherley-Price, *The Imitation of Christ* (Harmondsworth: Penguin, 1952). Thomas also emphasizes the link between "immortality" and responsibility.
79. For a full discussion of what Kierkegaard might have meant by this comment, see my *Kierkegaard, Religion, and the Nineteenth Century Crisis of Culture* (Cambridge: Cambridge University Press, 2005), 96–115.
80. On William Law, see Alan Gregory's contribution to this volume.
81. William Law, ed. S. Spencer, *The Spirit of Prayer* and *The Spirit of Love* (Cambridge: James Clarke, 1969), 220.
82. Law (1969), 221.
83. Ibid., 221.
84. Ibid., 222.
85. Ibid., 276.
86. Ibid., 235.
87. Apophatic theology is theology that "describes" or defines God solely by means of negations.
88. Paul Tillich, *Systematic Theology* vol. 1 (Welwyn Garden City: James Nisbet, 1968), 156.
89. Tillich (1968), 198.
90. Ibid., 199.
91. Martensen (1866), 83–4.
92. Ibid., 88.

14 The Place of Jacob Boehme in Western Esotericism

Arthur Versluis

Historically, one can find many efforts to label or "place" the vast and complex work and thought of Jacob Boehme. For some, Boehme is best understood in the context of Pietism;[1] for others, he exemplifies enthusiasm, often more or less synonymous with irrationalism;[2] for others, there is a Boehme most important for his philosophical influences;[3] for others, he represents mysticism;[4] and at least in the case of Romanian physicist Basarab Nicolescu,[5] his work is even interpreted as shedding light on some discoveries of modern physics! One could say that there is a Boehme for every generation and purpose. While recognizing that no label or categorization schema is sufficient for a figure of Boehme's magnitude, nonetheless, when we survey Boehme's place in the growing literature on Western esotericism, we find many contradictions. In fact, Boehme's inconvenient place in the study of Western esotericism is both central and revealing.

The academic field of Western esotericism, for its part, is comparatively recent, dating to the end of the twentieth and the beginning of the twenty-first centuries.[6] In this field, different scholars have offered alternative models for understanding or mapping what is included and what is excluded. Virtually every model includes Jacob Boehme. Yet even here, interpretations of Boehme's work and its significance differ. Boehme has a central place in the field of Western esotericism because of the historical role that he played: he represents the confluence and synthesis of a whole array of esoteric currents, including alchemy, astrology, Christian Kabbalah, magic, and mysticism, into a sophisticated body of work influential not only for all those in the subsequent tradition of Christian theosophy, but also for many others outside that current as well. Boehme looms so large in the history of esotericism that he cannot be excluded from it, yet his inclusion actually compels scholars to reconsider what a term like "Western esotericism" demarcates. Boehme's role in histories of Western esotericism is significant, to be sure. But he also presents a very real challenge for understanding what these latest labels, "esotericism," and even more, "esoteric," really mean.

Historically, Boehme has been in a category termed "mysticism," but in the period from the 1990s to the present, some scholars have sought to create a new category, "Western esotericism," and to place Boehme as an exemplary figure within that. Why create this new category, and how is it to be distinguished from "mysticism," if indeed such a distinction holds? And if one accepts this new category, what advantages does it offer for understanding a complex figure like Boehme? To answer questions like these, we first must consider Boehme as a mystic.

I BOEHME AS MYSTIC

Let us begin with an overview of the secondary literature "placing" Boehme as a mystic. Secondary literature of the early twentieth century tended to position Boehme as central among mystics, albeit often with various caveats. Rufus Jones (1863–1948), a professor at Haverford College, author of various books on mysticism, and a Quaker, emphasized as central to Boehme's work his "way of salvation" or experiential "process of salvation."[7] For Jones, Boehme is not so much a nature mystic as he is a premier exponent of "spiritual religion," exemplified best for him by the Quakers. And Rudolph Steiner (1861–1925)—founder of the spiritual/occult philosophy of Anthroposophy, and of its allied movement, the Anthroposophical Society—emphasized about Boehme his possession of the keys to nature, although Steiner did also acknowledge and indeed directly "place" Boehme in the tradition of European mysticism going back to Eckhart and Tauler.[8] Evelyn Underhill also refers frequently to Boehme in her seminal work *Mysticism*.[9]

Indeed, Boehme, during much of the twentieth century, was placed by most scholars into the perhaps nebulous category of mysticism. But "mysticism," as is well known, is a category often freighted with opprobrium. Standard definitions of mysticism, even into the twenty-first century, included connotations like irrationalism and delusion. Many scholars of mysticism, in response, overcompensated with what we might term hyperanalysis of categories and types of mysticism. In secondary literature that analyzes mystical literature and phenomena, Boehme is largely noticeable by his absence. Classical examples of this literature include the pugnacious R.C. Zaehner, as well as W.T. Stace and Paul Marshall.[10] Some, in analyzing mysticism, so intensify their rational faculties as to attempt to analyze mysticism more or less out of existence, as Steven Katz does, claiming it as fundamentally a constructed or, in other cases, a linguistic phenomenon.[11]

Here, too, Boehme is either peripheral to the respective authors' cases or, in fact, entirely ignored. Boehme is notoriously difficult for the creativity and density of his language, for the volume of his writings, for his unique vocabulary drawn from sources as varied as astrology and alchemy, and for the magisterial quality of his declarations. For these and many other reasons, Boehme is often problematic as an example. Furthermore, if one's case is that Boehme's work is largely or purely a linguistic construct, such a claim goes entirely against Boehme's own clear assertions that in fact he possessed direct spiritual knowledge and that those who would judge him unfairly would be better off not opening his works at all.[12] That is, Boehme emphasizes his own spiritual authority and direct gnostic experience.[13] When a secondary author contravenes these claims, he effectively places himself above his subject, claiming in effect to know more than Boehme about Boehme's claims to knowledge. Such implied scholarly claims of supervenience of their subjects come freighted with their own issues.

Boehme is a reference point for Paul Marshall, for instance, who includes him in a list of "extrovertive" mystics. The term "extrovertive," coined by W. T. Stace, presumes that there is a class of mystical phenomena to be differentiated from "introverted" or inward experiences of transcendence.[14] Marshall lays great emphasis on this notion, claiming that "a special category of experience deserves to be recognized, a type of experience in which the world is seen anew, transformed by unity, knowledge, light, love, eternity."[15] "To qualify as extrovertive, a mystical experience should bring a transformed apprehension of the natural world," Marshall continues, through such experiential qualities as "unity," "intuitive comprehension of the world," "luminous transfiguration of the environment," and/or "an altered temporality that includes all times and places." Boehme, he thinks, exemplifies an extrovertive mystic because his mysticism emphasizes insight into hidden aspects of nature.[16]

Other secondary literature on mysticism emphasizes direct individual experiences of unity. Here we might mention especially Robert K. C. Forman, who emphasizes Pure Consciousness Events, or PCEs, as central to mysticism.[17] Allied in some respects to Forman is some of the neuroscientific literature on mysticism, notably works written or coauthored by Andrew Newberg, who, from the 1990s onward, advanced a model of understanding mysticism as the progressive transcendence of subject-object differentiation, during which process emotional attachments drop away. This "deafferentation" can occur as a function of aesthetic experience, but it becomes stronger or more complete as one approaches what Newberg and d'Aquili term "Absolute Unitary Being" (AUB).[18]

Physicist Basarab Nicolescu, a central figure in the transdisciplinary movement, in turn regards Newberg as a preeminent example of a transdisciplinary researcher who is open to transcendence and is not a reductionist. Nicolescu is author of *Science, Meaning, and Evolution: The Cosmology of Jacob Boehme*, among other works, and interprets Boehme through a lens rather akin to that of those who claim him as an "extrovertive" mystic, that is, as primarily offering insights into nature and cosmology.[19] Such a perspective on Boehme does ignore the nondual aspects of Boehme's work—in particular, concepts like the *Ungrund* (not-ground) and *Nichts* (Nothingness), which signify different aspects of sheer transcendence of self-other. But the importance of Nicolescu's work is that for him, even more than for a scholar of mysticism like Marshall, Boehme provides the ideal exemplar of cosmological insight or gnosis.

There is, of course, a very different mode of "placing" Boehme, which is to condemn him as "heretical." From the seventeenth century onward, Boehme in particular and Protestant "enthusiasts" more generally were sometimes derogated as akin to the Gnostics of antiquity. Richard Baxter (1615–1691), for instance, the bitterly anti-enthusiast author of the well-known *Reliquiae Baxterianae* (1696) regarded Boehme's "cloudy nonsense" and "enigmatical expressions" as having their roots in the "hideous bombardical words" of the "first heretics," Basilides and Valentinus.[20] These kinds of condemnations correspond to the classification "mysticism" for Boehme, who is placed in a cluster of other authors, some of whom were clearly mystics, like Johannes Tauler, and others of whom are more ambiguous. The category "mysticism" is thus typically allied with "heresy" and "Gnosticism," as well as with individualist "enthusiasm," and opposed to Baxter's Puritanism or to some other doctrinal constellation represented as synonymous with "orthodoxy," "faith," and "truth".[21]

Even more specifically, for a recent anti-Gnostic theorist like Cyril O'Regan who writes in the tradition of anti-Gnostics Eric Voegelin and Hans Blumenberg, Boehme represents the reintroduction of Valentinian Gnosticism into the early modern and modern periods. Like his predecessors Voegelin and Blumenberg, O'Regan is keen on the scent of "Gnosticism" as that projected category for heretics which "modernity" has to vanquish once again, and he sees Boehme as pivotal for the surreptitious reintroduction of Valentinian Gnosticism into the modern period.[22] O'Regan's work demonstrates once again how Boehme's mysticism can become a kind of screen for a projected image. But once again, Boehme is the required screen. Even as a foil in O'Regan's prolix argument, Boehme is central.[23]

These remarks on (sometimes polemical) scholarship on mysticism provide a context for understanding how Boehme subsequently appears in scholarship on Western esotericism. Boehme's mysticism is depicted often as cosmological, as nature-mysticism, or as "extroverted," but the category "mysticism" definitely comes first. Indeed, even in the early twenty-first century, Boehme remained classified first as a mystic and only secondarily as a figure in Western esotericism. Why is this important? To answer this question, we should survey how Boehme appears in scholarship on Western esotericism.

II BOEHME AND WESTERN ESOTERICISM

The founding figure of the academic study of Western esotericism as its own category is Antoine Faivre, who had published a great deal on *naturphilosophie* and related subjects before turning his attention more specifically to an area he termed "Western esotericism." The slightly ungainly suffix to "esoteric," "icism," came about because "esoterism" was already in use by Traditionalists in the line of René Guénon (1886–1951) to signify the esoteric center or essence of religion. "Traditionalism" is a loose term applied to Guénon, A.K. Coomaraswamy (1877–1947), Frithjof Schuon (1907–1998), and others of this school, who assert an esoteric *prisca theologia* or *religio perennis* at the center of the world's great religious traditions. Since "esoterism," in this school, designated an approach to the hidden primordial center of all religions, "esotericism" became a preferred term so as to demarcate an area of academic inquiry without the Traditionalist connotations of "esoterism." Those who use the term "esoterism" "tend," Faivre writes, "just like mystics, to maintain a discourse marked by subjectivity." He demarcates, rather, an "historical survey" that "treats essentially the modern period of Western esotericism" based on a "methodological base" of "guiding criteria."[24]

Why are both mysticism and Traditionalism a problem here, right at the founding of the modern study of "Western esotericism"? Both mysticism and Traditionalism tend to make truth claims—and mystics in particular do so as a matter of course. To establish the field of "Western esotericism" within late twentieth-century academic discourse, it was necessary to clearly differentiate it from mystics and from Traditionalists, that is, from those who assert that there is the possibility of direct spiritual insight or realization, or gnosis. But that is in some respects an ironic distinction because some central figures (including Boehme) who are included by Faivre as exemplary of "Western esotericism" in fact assert quite boldly that they are in possession of direct cosmological and metaphysical insight into the hidden aspects of nature and the divine. They make "truth claims." But the term "Western esotericism" was invented to avoid the "mysticism" and "subjectivity" implied by "esoterism" and its truth claims, so there is an implicit conflict between the category "esotericism" and its exemplars. We will return to this question.

But first, let us see how Boehme appears in various surveys of Western esotericism, beginning with Faivre's own *Access to Western Esotericism* (1993), a founding work for the field. For Faivre, notwithstanding the underlying problem that Boehme is frequently categorized as a mystic, Boehme and Boehmean theosophy play a central role in what he construes as Western esotericism. Indeed, after the term "gnosis," comes for Faivre, "theosophy," which "confers on esotericism this cosmic, or rather cosmosophic dimension."[25] Boehmean theosophy, writes Faivre, "renders possible a philosophy of nature." Yet at the same time, it is in itself "an amalgam between the medieval mystical tradition (that of fourteenth-century Germany) and the *Naturphilosophie* inspired by Paracelsus." And in fact, Faivre explicitly acknowledges not only Boehme's debt to fourteenth-century German mysticism, but also refers specifically to the importance of the *Ungrund* in Boehme's esotericism.[26]

Faivre uses a typological approach that proposes Western esotericism to consist in (1) a practice of correspondences, (2) living nature, (3) imagination, (4) transmutation (5) a praxis of concordance, and (6) transmission.[27]

A predominance of these characteristics marks a work or figure as belonging to the category "Western esotericism." Although he does allude to a pivotal *via negativa* concept like *Ungrund* in Boehme's work, nonetheless, both Boehmean theosophy and Western esotericism are defined by Faivre in such a way as to exclude mysticism and to emphasize esotericism as cosmological in nature. To use the term derived from Stace's assertions about mysticism, Faivre in effect characterizes Boehme's esotericism as "extrovertive." The fundamental question, of course, is why Boehme in particular, or Christian theosophy more broadly, should be classified as belonging to the category "Western esotericism" as opposed to the category "mysticism."

Faivre writes that "the difference with mysticism appears especially, of course, in the fact that the contemplative claims to abolish images, while for Boehme and theosophers generally, the image is the fulfillment."[28] Theosophy is, he continues, "a theology of the image," for "each being possesses a finality of perfection, which passes through the image and its incarnation."[29] Hence, Faivre lays primary emphasis on the symbolic aspects of Boehmean theosophy and on Boehme as a philosopher of Nature.[30] These aspects are certainly there in Boehme's work. However, there remains a fundamental question as to why, nonetheless, *in toto* Boehme's work should not belong to the category of "mysticism" to which it had long been assigned in scholarship. For that matter, Boehme could be classified as "visionary religion"; it is not clear why the category "esotericism" is actually necessary. After all, a theology of the image is another way of describing *via positiva* mysticism from Dionysius the Areopagite onward.

In a later work, in French *Accès de l'ésotérisme occidental, Tome II* (Paris, 1996) and in English *Theosophy, Imagination, Tradition* (2000), Faivre again returns to the centrality of Boehme and theosophy for the category "Western esotericism," and once again grapples with the awkward category of "mysticism." In this case, he draws on the work of Bernard Gorceix, and in particular on Gorceix's *Flambée et agonie*, a work whose subtitle is *Mystiques du XVIIe siècle allemand.*[31] Gorceix inconveniently and clearly describes Boehmean theosophy in terms of mysticism, and hence Faivre has to remark that "Not that the theosophical element is always absent among these mystics, but mysticism is not theosophy."[32] Yet the "theosophical tradition is presented in *Flambée et agonie* as inseparable from the religious context, principally mystical, in which it could flower."[33] Gorceix, in other words, demonstrates that the seventeenth century is in fact "the third peak in the history of German mysticism."[34] Hence, the fundamental problem of developing a distinction between mysticism and esotericism, or even mysticism and Boehmean theosophy, remains unresolved here for Faivre.

Subsequently, in his revised version of an earlier brief handbook, *L'Ésotérisme* (1992), published in 2010 as *Western Esotericism: A Concise History*, Faivre seeks to demarcate "mysticism" from "esotericism," noting various cosmological themes like "transmutation" that he finds characteristic of esotericism, and then noting that "certain [of his ideal] components can be common to several forms of thought, for example, both to 'mysticism' and to 'esotericism.'"[35] But here he does not further explain how those characteristics might correspond to anything like *via positiva* or *via negativa* mysticism. And in a subsequent chapter, he places Boehme in the broader current of Germanic *Naturphilosophie*, remarking that "Christian theosophy shares the characteristics enumerated above with the other Western esoteric currents. It nevertheless possesses certain characteristics that, taken together, serve to specify its originality."[36] These characteristics are (1) a God-Humanity-Nature triangle, (2) direct access to higher worlds leading to a "central vision," and (3) the primacy of the mythical.[37] In Faivre's discussion of Boehme in this book, he takes care never to use the word "mysticism," and although he makes mention of Boehme's important concept of the *Ungrund*, it is primarily in an attempt to distinguish him from a mystic like Meister Eckhart. Thus, here too, many foundational questions regarding efforts to distinguish "mysticism" and "esotericism"—especially as regards the pivotal figure of Boehme—are elided.

For a resolution to such questions, we might turn to a book with the promising title of *Gnosis: An Esoteric Tradition of Mystical Visions and Unions* (1993) by Canadian scholar Dan Merkur. Merkur's first chapter is entitled "The Study of Mystical Experiences," and he briefly surveys the twentieth-century history of the study of mysticism without showing whether or how mysticism and esotericism might coincide or differ. Later in the book, Merkur does refer to Boehme (or Boehme's philosophy) at the end of a chapter on spiritual alchemy, as well as in relation to Merkur's discussion of Gnosticism.[38] But Boehme remains more or less clearly here an example of a mystic, and the relationship between Boehme and terms like mysticism and esotericism remains unexamined.

Might we find clarification in Kocku von Stuckrad's *Western Esotericism: A Brief History of Secret Knowledge* (2005)? He offers a new approach to the study of esotericism, one deeply influenced by (de-)constructionist approaches to the study of religion, arguing that "esotericism" does not really exist except as a discursive concept in the heads of scholars, and that one would be better off using a term like "the esoteric."[39] Von Stuckrad argues for the study of the esoteric as a discourse analysis that focuses on particular motifs like "the dialectic of the hidden and revealed" or "eternal knowledge."[40] As regards Boehme, he straightforwardly places him in the tradition of German mysticism, remarking "the influence of the German mystical tradition (Meister Eckhart, Johannes Tauler) . . . is clearly evident."[41] Hence von Stuckrad resolves the "problem" of Boehme's place in Western esotericism fairly simply: Boehme is a mystic; one can analyze his work *as* esoteric, and one does not need to resort to "tautological" *Idealtypen* like Faivre's cosmological characteristics to do so.[42]

A subsequent survey of Western esotericism was offered by Joscelyn Godwin in a work with the title *The Golden Thread: The Ageless Wisdom of the Western Mystery Tradition* (2007). Originally published as a series of lapidary essays in *Lapis* (New York Open Center), this collection was eventually published as a book by the Theosophical Society Press. Characteristically elegant, Godwin's prose offers us not an academic model for the study of Western esotericism, like the other titles more or less do, but rather a graceful introduction for the general reader to a variety of esoteric subjects. He offers some succinct observations on Boehme and theosophy, remarking that "what most differentiates Christian theosophy from the mainly Catholic tradition of mysticism is that, as an experiential path, it addresses the intellect as well as the emotions."[43] Further, "the intellectual side of theosophy is more than the mere satisfaction of curiosity: it is a gnosis, that is to say the conscious integration of the human subject with its own transcendent nature."[44] In Godwin's work, one finds no taxonomical anxieties, but instead highly unusual, provocative, thoughtful essays in which Boehme naturally has his place in the broader currents of the "Western mystery traditions."

Akin to Godwin's work in at least some respects is my own *Magic and Mysticism: An Introduction to Western Esotericism* (2007). This survey offers a different solution for "placing" Boehme and mysticism in relation to Western esotericism: rather than avoiding the category "mysticism," I foreground it as one of two organizing themes, the other being "magic."[45] Mysticism, in this schema, is associated with what I term "metaphysical gnosis," characterized by *via negativa* language, whereas magic is associated with what he terms "cosmological gnosis," characterized by the use of symbols and images as well as by efforts to produce results in the physical world.[46] Both of these broad categories can be esoteric, but I use this term in a dynamic and functional sense akin to what von Stuckrad has proposed. Further, I observe that both categories have historically been marginalized, "in part because of the longstanding anti-esoteric bias in the West, and by the related desire to turn both subjects into objects of rationalist discourse and manipulation."[47] Hence, I encourage an open, empirical approach to the esoteric, whatever "vectors" one uses to define it in terms of social dynamics or otherwise.

In any case, in this model, Boehme inherits the German mysticism of Meister Eckhart and Tauler, and "maintains a balance between imagery and the transcendence of imagery, the *via positiva* and the *via negativa*."[48] Boehme, I suggest, represents the union in one figure's work of both cosmological and metaphysical gnosis. Boehme thus becomes not a problematic figure, but an emblematic one: seen functionally, his work in its baroque complexity, even majesty, is certainly esoteric or initiatory, and indeed Boehme himself emphasizes that it is intended only for some people, not for all; while historically, Boehme represents the synthesis of numerous prior esoteric currents, including alchemy, astrology, mysticism, and perhaps a mediated (Christian) Kabbalah. He thus is categorizable without conflict both as a mystic and as a primary figure/exemplar of Western esotericism.[49] Of course, this begs the question of whether a new category of "Western esotericism" adds to our understanding of Boehme.

The final survey of Western esotericism we will cover here is that of Nicholas Goodrick-Clarke, *The Western Esoteric Traditions: A Historical Introduction* (2008). Goodrick-Clarke, since his is the final survey among these books, helpfully and elegantly summarizes the works of his predecessors, including Faivre, Versluis, and Stuckrad, alluding, like several of the others, to Wouter Hanegraaff's empirical methodology and to Pierre Riffard's taxonomy of the esoteric.[50] But Goodrick-Clarke's approach is that of an historian, and because he does not offer a model or particular taxonomy of his own for esotericism or the esoteric, he is free simply to place Boehme and Christian theosophy within their historical contexts from the seventeenth century onward, and that is that. Earlier terms that situate Boehme, like "Pietism," are still employed here. For instance, Goodrick-Clarke asserts that "given its emphasis on interior spirituality, Pietism fostered an intellectual atmosphere receptive to esotericism."[51]

Goodrick-Clarke does begin his chapter on Boehme by remarking forthrightly that Boehme "early established his reputation as a leading Protestant mystic." But Goodrick-Clarke, following Faivre, by and large avoids the term "mysticism" in his discussion of Boehme and Christian theosophy. Instead, we find references to Boehme's "interior spirituality," his "spiritual-philosophical system," his "inner vision," and grounding in "individual visionary experience."[52] The particular kinds of questions we have been pursuing are mostly elided by this elegantly told historical approach: Boehme as a mystic is acknowledged, but so is his importance as a major figure in the history of Western esotericism. Once again, the various categories overlap without too much difficulty.

From our survey of these surveys, we can see that, while there is some minor disagreement, broadly speaking, the majority of these scholars have no difficulty in placing Boehme and Christian theosophy in both the categories of mysticism and Western esotericism. Certainly there is no disagreement at all that Boehme represents a major figure in the history of Western esotericism, whatever taxonomy or historical demarcation is used. But the implications of Boehme's work as esoteric are another matter, and it is to those that we turn in the final section.

III BOEHME AS ESOTERIC

Ultimately, the problem that Boehme exemplifies in much of this academic discourse is taxonomic, but underlying the terminological questions are methodological ones. Fundamentally, the challenge Boehme represents—and of course, not Boehme alone—rests in the nature of Boehme's work as esoteric and in the way one "places" or interprets him and his significances. Here we are taking up the idea—put forward by both von Stuckrad and me in different ways—that, as von Stuckrad has it, it may be better to refer to "the esoteric" than to "esotericism" as a construct. And further, as I have suggested, it may be important to think about the esoteric dynamically or functionally. The case of Boehme is instructive for exactly these kinds of approaches.

Here, of course, we cannot offer a complete analysis of Boehme's work as esoteric using these ideas: his work is simply too vast and too complex. But we can begin to point out how Boehme's work can be understood first in terms of social dynamics. With regard to the social dynamics that produce the esoteric, elsewhere I suggested as examples esoteric/exoteric, gnostic/rationalist, and heterodox/orthodox as types of dynamic social polarities that shape esoteric discourse.[53] All of these dynamics are clearly visible in Boehme's work and life. We will recall that Boehme himself frequently derogated those who merely attended "stone churches" and insisted on the central importance of direct inner spiritual rebirth, awakening, and transmutation; that he was during his life and afterward attacked as an "enthusiast" or irrational without regard to the subtleties of the gnosis that he encouraged; and that he was opposed and forbidden to write by his Lutheran pastor, Gregor Richter.[54] I offer these only as famous instances of exactly these kinds of social dynamics at work in the case of Boehme because he would seem to be an ideal subject for understanding more clearly and deeply how they operate. But these kinds of analysis, although they may augment historical study, still do not address the more fundamental methodological and taxonomic questions raised by a figure like Boehme.

Significantly more provocative is what I am terming a "functional" analysis of Boehme's work. By that I mean the way that his work encodes and discloses secret knowledge and/or gnosis. In Boehme's case in particular, but in many other works of Christian theosophy as well, the text is itself initiatory. The text largely consists in spiritual guidance. Sometimes these texts are epistolary, like Boehme's own letters, or the letters of Johann Gichtel, and sometimes they describe a sequential process, for instance an alchemical process using astrological, that is, planetary symbols and associations as signposts for inner ascending stages of purification, transmutation, and illumination.[55] Other texts describe "travel" through visionary landscapes or intermediate realms rather like those by Suhrawardi and others as elucidated by Henry Corbin.[56] Still others are straightforward descriptions in the form of an experiential journal chronicling the transformative process undergone by an individual or a group.[57]

But virtually no attention to date has been given to these kinds of texts as initiatory documents.[58] Clearly, they are describing changes in consciousness, sometimes also expressed as visionary experiences. But if we think about them functionally, we have to ask questions like: How do they reveal such changes or a larger spiritual process? What signals and means do they use? What are the more subtle aspects of their disclosures? The more we engage in close reading of these dense and often mysterious texts and images, the more profoundly and clearly we may begin to understand them. In some respects, this kind of reading is similar to working with literature.

But there is a difference. In the case of Boehme, and of theosophy more generally, the authors make clear that in their view, the stakes are much higher. Literature often has a ludic aspect, and one cannot so easily say that one particular reading of *Moby Dick* is absolutely correct, and another wrong, if both can be corroborated. However, the assertions of Boehme himself are not ludic, and he is relatively clear in many of them. There is, in his experience, he claims, a particular kind of spiritual awakening. It is, he says, necessary to experience it for oneself. Rationalists should not attempt to analyze it via logic-chopping, and religious opponents ought to let it go and not comment on it. Boehme unambiguously tells us that he has direct spiritual knowledge both cosmological and metaphysical. He unambiguously makes what has become known as "truth claims."[59]

Hence, Boehme offers a particularly strong example in "Western esotericism"—however one happens to construe that term, if one accepts it at all—of assertions concerning cosmological and metaphysical truth. The problem this poses for the contemporary scholar would seem self-evident. It is the same kind of issue that confronts scholars of Platonism and Neoplatonism, which, frankly, is no doubt why these areas are not exactly well represented in the contemporary academy. Contemporary scholars of religion are frequently told that there is no such thing as religion in itself, that to commit "essentialism" is a mortal sin, and that even mystical experiences themselves are merely discursive constructions.[60] Boehme's own work represents the exact antithesis of this kind of reflexive, timid rhetoric, and hence is actually somewhat inconvenient if we begin to take any part of it seriously on its own terms.[61]

But a functional reading of the initiatory dimensions of a text means that, in some sense at least, one has to accept it as at least provisionally real, as describing, let us say hypothetically, an actual inner process and set of experiences. One has to engage at minimum in the kind of suspension of judgment, the "willing suspension of disbelief" that Coleridge said was vital to reading literature. Because to understand the text on its own terms, one has to set aside one's own layers of interpretive opposition, "postmodern" or otherwise, even if "religionism" or "essentialism" remain mortal sins for many in contemporary academic orthodoxy. This, of course, is Boehme's challenge for us; this challenge is his "place" in the study of Western esotericism. He is not the only one who poses such a challenge, but he does pose it very clearly nonetheless.

The challenge that Boehme's work poses is still to be addressed in at least two different ways. One is a close reading of how a particular work functions as an initiatic text, that is, what its markers and keys are, what it appears to be alluding to in kinds of consciousness, and so forth. This is not particularly easy, and even it requires at minimum what I am terming a hypothetical approach to the text as reflecting and, to some extent, itself embodying or evoking particular changes in consciousness. At the very least, to engage in such a reading, one has to accept the possibility that such changes in consciousness hypothetically could exist. Already, this threatens to go beyond a mere "suspension of disbelief"; and it is also more than a matter of empathy or seeking to "think like" another, because what is under consideration may include but is not necessarily limited to discursive thought. Such a reading accepts the possibility of changes in consciousness not accessible to (exoteric) discursive thought or analysis. But the second answer to the challenge is more difficult and is suggested by the first. It is the question of how and to what extent one accepts as real or, if one prefers, "real," the claims of, for instance, Boehme.

Although one does not find much concerning this line of inquiry in recent scholarship on either mysticism or Western esotericism, at least as yet, that is not the case with neuroscientific literature. A succession of recent articles, books, and multivolume series on neuroscience and religion have tended to focus on the study of mysticism or mystical phenomena, often with extremely interesting implications.[62] Whereas most works belonging to the academic study of religion stay far away from the "experiential" questions that Boehme's work might raise, for the neuroscientific study of religion, the "experiential" is in fact closer to the starting point, the actual starting point for neuroscience of course being that which can be measured, for instance, via functional magnetic resonance imaging of brain activity. I allude to the rapidly developing area of neuroscientific research because it may well, over time, encourage scholars to more forthrightly address the fundamental experiential kinds of questions that Boehme's work raises.

For ultimately, it is in answering the looming challenge posed by Boehme's work that we may begin to understand what a term like "esoteric" means in a particular case, not only in terms of historical context and categorization, but also as describing the esoteric process whereby the reader engages with a mystical text. Ultimately, whether one classifies Boehme under the category "mysticism" or as exemplifying "Western esotericism" is not so important—what matters most is whether these categories or contexts shed light on Boehme's work. Much scholarship on both "mysticism" and "Western esotericism" has elided essential aspects of Boehme's challenging work, in particular those aspects that exhort the reader toward what we might term changes in consciousness.

Should Boehme's work be labeled "mysticism," "esotericism," both, or neither? In the end, the value of such categories for scholars is the light they shed on the author and his work. It may well be that the category "mysticism" is more appropriate than "esotericism" if it offers the scholar a greater purchase on the peculiar challenges posed by Boehme's work, and Christian theosophy more broadly. By contrast, if the study of "esotericism" genuinely demarcates a separate field of inquiry, what does that field contribute to our understanding of history, philosophy, literature, and religion? An obvious answer is that it contributes the study of what is distinctively "esoteric," meaning also "initiatic," in a particular author's work. And while much has been written on Boehme in various contexts from Pietism to mysticism to Western esotericism, we still await investigation of his work as esoteric; how, and in what senses this is so; and ultimately, what "esoteric" means in such a case. Despite all that has been written, that is still a challenge that lies, not behind us, but ahead.

NOTES

1. Peter Erb, *The Pietists: Selected Writings* (Mahwah, NJ: Paulist Press, 1983); Peter Erb, *Pietists, Protestants, and Mystics* (Lanham, MD: Scarecrow Press, 1990).
2. See for instance, Ben-Ami Sharfstein, *Mystical Experience* (Oxford: Blackwell, 1973), 133, where Sharfstein blithely asserts, without bothering with troublesome evidence, that Boehme was "psychotic."
3. Glenn Magee, *Hegel and the Hermetic Tradition* (Ithaca, NY: Cornell UP, 2008).
4. See, for instance, the work of Rufus Jones or Evelyn Underhill, discussed and cited below.
5. Basarab Nicolescu, *Science, Meaning, and Evolution: The Cosmology of Jacob Boehme* (New York: Parabola, 1991).
6. The American Academy of Religion began offering regular panels on Western esotericism in the early twenty-first century (they had existed intermittently in the 1990s), and the European Society for the Study of Western Esotericism and the Association for the Study of Esotericism only began holding regular conferences in 2007 and 2004, respectively. There had been sections of the International Association for the History of Religion conferences devoted to Western esotericism since 1995.
7. Rufus Jones, *Spiritual Reformers in the Sixteenth and Seventeenth Centuries* (London: Macmillan, 1914), 190.
8. Rudolf Steiner, *Mysticism at the Dawn of the Modern Age*, in German *Die Mystik im Aufgange des neuzeitlichen Geisteslebens*, vol. 7 of *The Complete Works of Rudolf Steiner* (also under the title *Eleven European Mystics* (N.P.: Rudolf Steiner Press, 1960–71).
9. Evelyn Underhill, *Mysticism* (New York: E.P. Dutton, 1961), 255–57, where Boehme is offered as a classical example of "The Illumination of the Self."
10. R.C. Zaehner, *Mysticism, Sacred and Profane* (Oxford: Oxford University Press, 1957); W.T. Stace, *The Teachings of the Mystics* (New York: Mentor, 1960); Paul Marshall, *Mystical Encounters with the Natural World: Experiences and Explanations* (Oxford: Oxford University Press, 2005).
11. See primarily Steven Katz, ed., *Mysticism and Language* (New York: Oxford UP, 1992); see also *Mysticism and Religious Traditions* (New York: Oxford UP, 1983). For an even more extreme form of constructivism, see Don Cupitt, *Mysticism After Modernity* (New York: John Wiley, 1998).
12. Jacob Boehme, *Aurora*, xx.87, xxvi.142 and *Signatura Rerum*, 1.1—to give only two examples.
13. The term "gnostic" in lower case signifies the generic use of the term to mean direct inner knowledge or spiritual intuition; it does not connote "Gnostic," which conventionally designates various "heretical" groups or individuals belonging to the period of late antiquity.
14. W.T. Stace, *The Teachings of the Mystics* (New York: Mentor, 1960) and *Mysticism and Philosophy* (London: Macmillan, 1961), as well as *Man Against Darkness and Other Essays* (Pittsburgh: University of Pittsburgh Press, 1967).

15. Paul Marshall, *Mystical Encounters with the Natural World: Experiences and Explanations* (Oxford: Oxford University Press, 2005), 25.
16. Marshall, 40. Of course, it is entirely possible that the "introvert/extrovert" distinction is only a matter of the area under consideration, and that extrovertive mysticism, so called, is only an epiphenomenon of non-dual experience.
17. Robert K.C. Forman, ed., *The Problem of Pure Consciousness* (New York: Oxford University Press, 1990); see also Forman, *Mysticism, Mind, Consciousness* (Albany, NY: SUNY Press, 1997), and Forman, ed., *The Innate Capacity: Mysticism, Philosophy and Psychology* (New York: Oxford University Press, 1998).
18. Andrew Newberg and Eugene D'Aquili, *The Mystical Mind* (Minneapolis: Fortress Press, 1999), 188–190, 199–203.
19. Basarab Nicolescu, *Science, Meaning, and Evolution: The Cosmology of Jacob Boehme* (New York: Parabola, 1991).
20. Richard Baxter, *Reliquiae Baxterianae* (London: T. Parkhurst, 1696), part i, 74–77; Richard Baxter, *The Practical Works of the Rev. Richard Baxter*, William Orme, ed. (London: James Duncan, 1830), vol. 20, 294–95.
21. Examples include John Anderdon, *One Blow at Babel in those of the Pepole called Behmenites* (London: 1662), or Thomas Tenison, *An Argument for Union* (London: 1683). For an overview of some of the seventeenth-century controversies in this regard, see Margaret Bailey, *Milton and Jakob Boehme: A Study of German Mysticism in Seventeenth-Century England*, (New York: Oxford University Press, 1914), 95–96. Some related background is to be found in Ariel Hessayon, "*Gold Tried in the Fire*"*: The prophet Theaurau-John Tany and the English Revolution*, (Aldershot: Ashgate, 2007).
22. Cyril O'Regan, *Gnostic Apocalypse: Jacob Boehme's Haunted Narrative*, (Albany, NY: SUNY Press, 2002). See also Cyril O'Regan, *Gnostic Return in Modernity* (Albany: SUNY Press, 2001). Hans Blumenberg, Robert Wallace, trans., *The Legitimacy of the Modern Age* (Cambridge: MIT, 1983), and Eric Voegelin, *Science, Politics and Gnosticism* (Chicago: Regnery, 1958). See also Arthur Versluis, "Voegelin's Anti-gnosticism," *Telos*, 124 (Summer 2002): 173–82, as well as Arthur Versluis, *The New Inquisitions* (New York: Oxford University Press, 2006), 69–84, and *The Mystical State* (Minneapolis: New Cultures, 2011), 103–04.
23. See also Philip Lee, *Against the Protestant Gnostics* (New York: Oxford University Press, 1993), for an example of analogously misleading treatment of "Gnostics."
24. Antoine Faivre, *Access to Western Esotericism* (Albany, NY: SUNY Press, 1994), 5.
25. Faivre, *Access*, 23.
26. Ibid., 63.
27. Ibid., 10.
28. Ibid., 27.
29. Ibid., 28.
30. Antoine Faivre, *Philosophie de la Nature: Physique sacrée et théosophic* (Paris: Albin Michel, 1996), 76.
31. Bernard Gorceix, *Flambée et agonie*: *Mystiques du XVIIe siècle allemand* (Sisteron: Présence, 1977).
32. Antoine Faivre, *Theosophy, Imagination, Tradition: Studies in Western Esotericism* (Albany, NY: SUNY Press, 2000), 64.
33. Faivre, *Theosophy*, 65.
34. Ibid., 77.
35. Antoine Faivre, *Western Esotericism: A Concise History* (Albany, NY: SUNY Press, 2010), 14.

36. Faivre, *Western Esotericism*, 41.
37. Ibid., 42.
38. Dan Merkur, *Gnosis: An Esoteric Tradition of Mystical Visions and Unions* (Albany, NY: SUNY Press, 1998), 75, 151, 288. In the last reference, in the notes, Boehme is described as a "seventeenth-century Rosicrucian theosopher."
39. Kocku von Stuckrad, *Western Esotericism: A Brief History of Secret Knowledge* (London: Equinox, 2005), 9–10.
40. Stuckrad, 10–11.
41. Ibid., 97.
42. Ibid., 5.
43. Joscelyn Godwin, *The Golden Thread: The Ageless Wisdom of the Western Mystery Traditions* (Wheaton: Theosophical Publishing House, 2007), 114.
44. Godwin, *Golden Thread*, 115
45. Like some scholars of esoteric Judaism, I posit a spectrum with overlap that includes "magico-mysticism" and "mystico-magic." See, for instance, Moshe Idel, *Kabbalah and Eros* (New Haven: Yale University Press, 2005) or Elliot Wolfson, *Language, Eros, Being: Kabbalistic Hermeneutics and Poetic Imagination* (New York: Fordham University Press, 2005).
46. Arthur Versluis, *Magic and Mysticism: An Introduction to Western Esotericism* (Lanham, MD: Rowman Littlefield, 2007), 2–5.
47. Versluis, *Magic and Mysticism*, 5.
48. Ibid., 109.
49. Although he does not apply the term, presumably Boehme in my model would exemplify "magico-mysticism" because, for Boehme, mysticism is primary but has cosmological implications as well.
50. Nicholas Goodrick-Clarke, *The Western Esoteric Traditions: A Historical Introduction* (New York: Oxford University Press, 2008), 3–14.
51. Goodrick-Clarke, *Western Esoteric Traditions*, 104.
52. Ibid., 87–104.
53. Versluis, *Magic and Mysticism*, 5–6.
54. Boehme certainly can be seen as representing a post-Reformation radical Protestant tradition of anticlericalism and individualism, but here I am concentrating on the dynamics in his work as esoteric in opposition to exoteric religion.
55. "Epistolae Theosophicae," in Johann Georg Gichtel and Johann Wilhelm Ueberfeld, eds., *Theosophia Revelata: Das ist: Alle Göttliche Schriften des Gottseligen und Hocherleuchteten Deutschen Theosophi Jacob Böhmens*, vols. XVIII, XIX, XX, & XXI (Amsterdam: 1730). See also Jacob Boehme, *The Epistles of Jacob Boehme* (Glasgow: John Thomson, 1886) and Johann Georg Gichtel, *Theosophia Practica*, 7 vols., (Leiden, 1722), which consists primarily in a collection of letters of spiritual advice.
56. John Pordage, *Sophia, das ist, Die holdseelige ewige Jungrau der Göttlichen Weisheit* (Amsterdam, 1699).
57. Thomas Bromley, *The Way to the Sabbath of Rest*, (London: 1655 [1692, 1710 rpt.]; Ann Bathurst, *Journals*, 2 vols., 1693–1696, Bodleian Library, Oxford, MS Rawlinson D 1263.
58. Some scholars have approached esoteric texts (sometimes ritual texts) as initiatic. See for instance Jason Winslade, *Thinning the Veils: Initiation and the Performance of Occultism* (PhD. diss., Northwestern University, 2008); see also Karen-Claire Voss, "Spiritual Alchemy: Interpreting Representative Texts and Images," in Roelof van den Broek and Wouter Hanegraaff, eds., *Gnosis and Hermeticism: From Antiquity to Modern Times* (Albany, NY: SUNY Press, 1998), 147–82.

59. The problem of "truth claims" with regard to mysticism is touched upon by John Danvers's recent study of mysticism and literature, *Agents of Uncertainty* (Amsterdam: Rodopi, 2012), 67–68. He questions the claims of Katz and Cupitt as regards an asserted primacy of language over direct experience. It is true that mystical texts are linguistic products, but that does not warrant the implication that there is no experiential reference point or basis for what is conveyed or alluded to in a mystical text.
60. See the earlier discussions of the works of Katz and Cupitt, and also those of Faivre, for some examples.
61. For a survey that demonstrates just how widespread anti-essentialist kinds of assertions or presuppositions are in the academy, see Kevin Schilbrack, "Religions: Are There Any?" in *Journal of the American Academy of Religion*, 78 (2010) 4: 1112–38.
62. The leading researcher in the neuroscientific study of religion is Andrew Newberg, MD, author of *The Mystical Mind* (Minneapolis: Fortress, 1999), *Why God Won't Go Away* (New York: Ballantine, 2002), and *Principles of Neurotheology* (New York: Ashgate, 2010). Other resources in the field include Patrick McNamara, *The Neuroscience of Religious Experience* (Cambridge: Cambridge University Press, 2009) and McNamara, ed., *Where God and Science Meet*, 3 vols., (Westport: Praeger, 2006), to give just a few examples of leading work.

15 Conclusion

Why Boehme Matters Today

Bruce B. Janz

In the almost 400 years since Boehme's death, he has been revived, reappropriated, and rediscovered repeatedly. For someone often seen as marginal in Western thought, he has certainly reappeared regularly over the years as intellectually significant. And yet, it still seems necessary to consider the question of whether Boehme continues to matter today. In my own field of philosophy, I have sometimes encountered quizzical looks and questions from other philosophers wondering why anyone would be interested in this seemingly incidental figure. Why should a philosopher be concerned with an undisciplined "picture-thinker," to quote Hegel? Why indeed. But my sense of philosophy has always been that it is sometimes found in unexpected places, and finding philosophy in a figure generally situated in the history of mysticism and spirituality should not, after all, be a surprise. More importantly, for philosophy at least, is this: an encounter with Boehme potentially brings philosophers back to the well-spring of philosophy, the question of what makes philosophy what it is. Philosophy turns to first things, in a variety of ways, and Boehme, too, drives us in that direction. That is not yet a guarantee of philosophical usefulness or profundity, but it is an intriguing start.

Even if Boehme potentially matters to philosophy, though, this does not in itself tell us much yet about academia in general. For whom does he matter? For what reason might he matter? These are always the first questions. We could look at this in terms of different disciplines—historians will ask different questions of him from those of philosophers, or linguists, or cultural theorists, or those looking for spiritual insight, even though there may be and has been some overlap. This does not yet guarantee that he *does* matter now, but again we move closer to asking a useful question about Boehme's place today.

The mattering of someone like Boehme will, of course, be different depending on the kinds of questions your discipline has trained you to ask. I hope to suggest that Boehme's way of mattering today goes beyond just the historian's impulse to "get him right," or to trace the lines of influence and connection, important as that is. Moreover, it is not just a matter of getting the texts about Boehme straight so that we can understand other texts more clearly, important as that also is. The texts, and the concepts, are interesting in their own immediate context, but that does not mean that they might not also be interesting for other reasons and in other settings. And, it is more than just decoding him—despite what Herman Vetterling in *The Illuminate of Görlitz* might have thought, when he compiled his massive, limited-edition work, there is no prize for the intellectual cryptographer deciphering some esoteric code.[1] It is also more than the philosopher's impulse to sketch out a contained and coherent system. No, "mattering" has to do with what Boehme might make possible today, what doors he might still open for us now. One must be true to him, but being true means being faithful to his creative impulse as much as it means expounding correctly the details of his system or his place in an intellectual genealogy.

Mattering starts with one thing, in my mind, and it is going to be something that is not intuitively obvious. It is this: *mattering means to work as Boehme worked, that is, to learn to create as he both described and modeled the creative process*. This does not, of course, mean that we should go out and get a pewter dish and stare at it until something happens. Working as Boehme worked means focusing on at least three issues: Boehme's intellectual strategies, his creation of concepts, and his formulation of questions. We will consider each in turn.

I INTELLECTUAL STRATEGIES THAT MATTER

My first introduction to Boehme was as an undergraduate by a German culture professor who told me that Boehme should be avoided because he was "too difficult and kind of strange." He was, I think, trying to spare me some frustration, but all he did was to give me a reason to look deeper. I started reading and found at the time that, yes, he was both difficult and strange to my twentieth-century eyes. And yet, his strange syntax, myriad allusions, and apparent leaps of logic had a kind of order and rhythm to them. I eventually came to recognize the word-play, neologisms, and parallelisms—*Ichts/Nichts, Vernunft/Verstand, Gefassete, Ungrund,* and so many others (terms which we will shortly consider in more detail), which gave evidence of a structured and disciplined mind. This did not necessarily require the elaborate linguistic work that some, such as Stephen Konopacki, have done, but it was enough to pique my interest.[2] It seemed to me that he was willing to create concepts when needed, in response to the central vision that stayed with him ever since he set his eyes on that pewter dish (if, indeed, he ever did).

Boehme's incredible creativity seemed to spring from the necessity of creating concepts that were adequate to his circumstances. Of course, his creation of concepts does not necessarily begin with him—the list of his precursors and influences is long, as is the list of his intellectual children and grandchildren. But the creation of concepts (and I use "creation," rather than "production" or "adaptation," in a manner similar to Gilles Deleuze, which we will discuss shortly) does not necessarily mean creation *ex nihilo*. It is tempting with almost any historical figure to construct a narrative of change or crisis to which they were responding, but in Boehme's case, it seems clear that he was faced with shifts in theology and epistemology that required a new set of intellectual tools to express and explore. We can, in retrospect, chart the development of those tools, those strategies that allowed him to address the problem of evil in a new way, that allowed a new sense of the *ex nihilo* of creation, and that related individuals to the divine in a manner not seen before. This gets more interesting, though, when we consider what it would be like to make similarly daring moves today, in the face of our own questions. If Boehme is not just giving us a set of propositions that fit together like architecture, but a chart that allows us to act as he acted, we may find him mattering to us today as something more than the historical curiosity that much of the academic world sees him to be. To use an analogy, Nietzsche excoriated Christians, not because they believed in Jesus, but because they derived the wrong message from him: that it was his words and system that were to be followed, rather than his creative and affirmative manner of life that was to be emulated (incidentally, I think Nietzsche is one of the most indebted nineteenth-century thinkers to Boehme in his style of thought despite, to my knowledge, never having read Boehme).

As this volume illustrates, we have any number of examples of thinkers who have seen Boehme as a creative force. It seems he made an appearance everywhere, as an influence on major figures, even if in some cases they saw in him only what they wanted to see. The results of a quick survey of philosophers and theologians over the past hundred or so years (and the list would be much longer with literary and artistic figures) would turn up references to Boehme as a precursor to or influence on at least the following: Friedrich Nietzsche (1844–1900), Sigmund Freud (1856–1939), Henri Bergson (1859–1941), Rudolph Otto (1869–1937), Nicolai Berdyaev (1874–1948), Carl Jung (1875–1961), Martin Buber (1878–1965), Paul Tillich (1886–1965), Martin Heidegger (1889–1976), Gabriel Marcel (1889–1973), Hans-Georg Gadamer (1900–2002), Emmanuel Levinas (1906–1995), Simone Weil (1909–1943), Thomas Altizer (1927-), Gilles Deleuze (1925–1995), Jacques Derrida (1930–2004), and Giorgio Agamben (1942-). And beyond these individuals, one can sense the effect of Boehme's questioning and concepts in phenomenology and hermeneutics in general. Paul Tillich is surely correct when he says that Boehme has had "an astonishing influence on the history of Western philosophy."[3]

Boehme, then, has mattered a great deal in our intellectual history. The interesting issue, though, is not whether we can in fact draw a direct line of influence between Boehme and any of these figures just listed, but is rather the question of how a creative thinker like Boehme is used to create concepts adequate to circumstances after his own time. There are reasons why

Boehme keeps showing up, but those reasons shift at different times. At one time, it is his form of dialectic that provides a suggestive mode of thought. At another, it is his voluntarism, and at another again, it is his way of making individuals productive without losing that which brings them into being. And at still other times, it is his way of radicalizing ontology, forcing us to ask the most basic questions about existence in perhaps the most original way since Aristotle. We can see this modeled at the beginning of *Mysterium Magnum*[4] as he gives a sense of an emergent God that does not negate the myriad of wills striving for their own emergence and that are allowed to realize that desire through the collaboration with that emergent God. *Lust*,[5] a blind, free, affirmative force, does not, in fact, overcome and negate *Begierde*, that is, a craving for manifestation and flourishing, but fulfills it and brings it into manifestation. Individuals have some form of status, then, as far back as their roots in *Begierde*. In the chaos of conflicting forces that is the *Ungrund*, *Lust* emerges through the myriad forces of *Begierde* as the foundation for the Godhead, while the forces Boehme describes as *Begierde* become actual through the inflowing and dynamic creation of *Lust*.

Boehme's own creativity, then, is rooted in his sense that creativity is the very nature of reality, and so that must be reflected in how one engages in thought. And, that creativity manifests itself through Will and Understanding as "color, power, and virtue" (*Farben, Kraft und Tugenden*), or as the drive to differentiation, manifestation, and creativity (since for Boehme, creation is just virtue, and un-creation, the move back to *Turba* or destructive Chaos, is the essence of evil). In other words, while some have seen him as restless, always looking for a new system adequate to express his mystical insight, I think it is more likely that his thought is a model of creation itself, which is always to create anew. It is, of course, true that some of his later works develop earlier concepts, in some cases, replacing them with richer ones (his move from his early use of *Abgrund* in the *Aurora* to the later *Ungrund* in *Mysterium Magnum* is a case in point), but this seeming restlessness can just as well be seen as successive manifestations of a central *Lust*.[6] All existing intellectual systems are, for Boehme, craving to be completed and brought into reality. He works his way through the currents of thought available at his time, showing that they all have the creative spark within them that allows something new to emerge (and, at the same time, they all have the ability to become ossified and inert, a shadow of their real potential).

As we look at the figures who have seen Boehme as interesting, we see some who self-identify as "Behmenists," that is, followers of Boehme's method or cosmology, and some who do not. The second group is in some respects the more interesting one, and in fact, those whose minds Boehme changed, or at least challenged, as opposed to those who "applied" Boehme's thought to some problem or issue, are particularly rewarding to examine. This, I think, is what he did for thinkers such as Buber, Berdyaev, Koyré, Tillich, and even Hegel. In all these cases, the thought of the individual became an updated dialogue with Boehme. These thinkers used aspects of Boehme to address questions that were at least partially different from those that Boehme himself had struggled with.

There is, in fact, another subgroup—those who used or absorbed elements of Boehme without acknowledging it. This is perhaps an even more interesting group, and would include thinkers such as Friedrich Nietzsche, Jacques Derrida, and probably Gilles Deleuze. This approach will not necessarily lead to traditional historical analysis, for how do we know that these figures used Boehme if there is no direct or textual evidence? What I have in mind, though, are the concepts that pass from Boehme into more general cultural usage, at least within intellectual culture. The specifics of Boehme's system may require careful study, but some Behmenist version of God as negation (different from classic apophatic approaches), some version of signatures in which Boehme (along with others such as Paracelsus) had a hand, would owe at least partial debt to the general cultural dissemination of Boehme's thought. He was, after all, popular enough among preachers and lay scholars that his ideas were disseminated from pulpits and circulated in compilations, annotated texts, and pamphlets in several countries. Not everyone took the radical steps that the Philadelphians took of weaving Boehme explicitly into the warp and woof of a theology. For some, it simply became part of what I call the "conceptual ecology" of the time. This, clearly, is not enough to argue for any specific influence of Boehme, but what is noteworthy is that as concepts become part of the intellectual currency of a place, they both enhance and limit the development of other concepts.

In that regard, it is worth thinking about who those people were, and are, who mediate that ecology, and which Boehme they are mediating. Who were the intermediaries from whom people would learn about Boehme? Around the turn of the twentieth century in the English-speaking world, it might have been A.J. Penny or Evelyn Underhill, which would have given us a particular kind of Boehme, one who might have been useful to those who saw mysticism as fundamental to religion (this is the same time as Baron von Hügel was doing similar work, and William James talked about mysticism in *Varieties of Religious Experience* in almost phenomenological ways).[7] Before that, at least in Germany, Boehme was in every history of philosophy text, so that would have accounted for his transmission there. He was in Hegel's and Feuerbach's histories of philosophy, as well as others.[8] We might describe that version of Boehme as the idealist, or perhaps as the Romantic thinker. In France, it would have partly been the work of Alexandre Koyré, in which case it would have been the phenomenological Boehme, or perhaps the cosmologist, but also still Saint-Martin, which would have shown Boehme as the esoterist.[9] Mid-twentieth-century in the English-speaking world, it might have been Howard Brinton, in which case we would have Boehme as evolutionist.[10] Surely John Joseph Stoudt would have been one access point, in which case it is Boehme as a good Lutheran after all, with a system to rival anything the neo-Thomists were coming up with.[11] Sheldon Cheney, who gives us Boehme as a holy, almost evangelical figure, might be another version that resonated with some.[12] And today? Perhaps the most common access point would be Andrew Weeks's intellectual biography, in which case we would have Boehme, the man of his time, the thinker embedded in his religious and social context.[13] We would also have Boehme as transmitted by the Internet, in which case we see him in many different lights, from mystical seer to theosophist to esoterist to precursor of quantum theory.[14] The point is, the mattering of Boehme today has to do with what kind of Boehme we are talking about, and how that particular Boehme became part of the conceptual ecology of the time in question. Boehme is not infinitely malleable, despite what some might think, but his work has been taken as inspiration for thinkers of vastly different agendas and interests. The most interesting Boehme today is the one we don't know is there, the one who has become part of the backdrop against which other concepts strive for manifestation.

II CONCEPTS THAT MATTER

Intellectual strategies produce concepts that are adequate to a place. Boehme is a model of a thinker who did not allow the minor inconvenience of the lack of a concept stop him from producing one that would accomplish a task. Of course, we can trace his influences through a myriad of sources such as Paracelsus, Weigel, and Schwenckfeld. Weeks's intellectual biography is an excellent account of those sources. But it is my view that Boehme was no mere cataloguer of others' ideas, or even a translator of those ideas into his modern idiom. He did have concepts at his disposal that might have been adapted, in the hands of a less skilled, less imaginative thinker. *Urgrund* and *Abgrund* existed in the tradition, for instance—did he need *Ungrund*? Of course he did—it is not quite the same, and it is a concept adequate to the attempt to establish the plenitude of forces striving for manifestation. Why does he invent *Ichts* as a counterpart to *Nichts*, why not just use *Etwas*, or at least, why take so long to get around to *Etwas*? Why create a new word? It is not an arbitrary choice—*Ichts*, far better than *Etwas*, captures the possibility of some rudimentary level of subjectivity. Is what he does with signatures just a version of the medieval "book of the world" theology we find in earlier in Alan of Lille and later in Paracelsus? The ties are there of course, but he is doing something new. When I began looking into Boehme's work, I had been led to believe that he was undisciplined, erratic, and that his use of words and concepts was inconsistent. When one actually considers his concepts and the alternatives he had before him, though, it seemed to be anything but erratic. The evident care I saw convinced me that his concepts were not just derivative of all the influences we can rightly see in him, but that he was doing something new and creative every time he appropriated a term or concept. This creative impulse was often an experimental one (Boehme's concepts do not come fully formed, and some are discarded along the way in favor of other, better adapted concepts in his ecology), and as such, not part of a linear or deliberate process. But this experimental creativity is far from the image of the undisciplined and erratic writer.

We find this constantly in Boehme's work, and the fact that we find it should provide for us a model of creativity, not merely a model of a creation that has already happened and is now settled. Boehme, despite what Hegel might have thought, does not subsume individuals under a more general universal. Those individuals, the diverse manifestation that springs ultimately from *Ungrund*, never leave behind the productive capacity of those individuals. There is, of course, *Verstand*, which for Boehme, suggests the difference between a surface and depth understanding of the world (*Vernunft* being the surface knowledge that Boehme continually rails against, and which Hegel eventually sees as the genuine form of reason in contrast to Boehme's "picture-thinking"), but one must never forget that for Boehme, all parts of the creative moment are present at all times in all things. The place of the individual in creation, the will that chooses to move with *Lust* into manifestation, is always there. This is new, but what it means, past the significance of a concept like that for Boehme's own work, is that Boehme gives us a model of conceptual creation, even as he describes ontological creation. In other words, while his system is explicitly about the nature of creation, he shows that that creation is not just the creation of entities or beings. It is also the creation of ways of understanding. *Verstand* is simultaneously the understanding of the common thread that makes all life possible and the extreme diversity of both life and thought that allows God to emerge in concert with beings. We should think about what it would mean to work as Boehme worked, not to emulate his specific ontology, but to be creative in this manner. In the midst of the cross-currents of influences that existed in Görlitz, Boehme found successive ways throughout his writings to put those influences into productive relationship.

Boehme's choice of *Ungrund* is an interesting case in point. A scan of the history of philosophy makes clear that there were many versions of negation and nothingness available to him. He created something new (although he clearly drew on existing elements to formulate that new concept). Why did he do that? Because nothing that had come before was adequate to the world in which he found himself. *Ungrund*, as already mentioned, is not the same as earlier concepts such as *Abgrund* or *Urgrund*—"un" can designate plenitude rather than lack. "*Unmasse*" is an uncountably large number of things, and "*Unmaessig*" happens whenever one has had a little too much to drink. And so, in the chaos of *Ungrund*, there is an infinite plenitude. Of what? Of wills, all striving for manifestation, all unable to achieve it. Boehme calls these wills *Begierde*, or craving, and they wait for *Lust* to come and, in a kind of divine creative economy, agree to flow through those who would allow it and bring them to manifestation. *Lust* consolidates into

God, and the familiar development of the Trinity happens in conjunction with this. The myriad wills of *Begierde* show *Lust* in all the ways it can be shown. They are the mirror. And so, individuals in some form go back much further than previous accounts. The unfolding of God goes forward, in the three principles and seven spirits, and comes prior to the full realization of creatures. And, along the way, the problem of evil is also solved—it is now a matter of uncreating. A fake *Lust* comes along, Lucifer, and tries to infuse those elements of *Begierde* that did not cooperate at the beginning and "uncreate" the rest. That is what Boehme calls *Turba*, the chaos that comes from uncreating. Evil is uncreation, not just a matter of disobeying some random rule that God decided to institute for our own good.

So, Boehme offers a system, surprisingly (although not completely) consistent despite its complexity, but it is a system in which he feels free to create concepts, partly from intellectual necessity and partly from an aesthetic sensibility that connect the beauty and balance in his thought to its intellectual utility.

One example of a contemporary figure who exemplifies Boehme's creative mode is Gilles Deleuze. Deleuze and his colleague Felix Guattari, with whom he sometimes wrote, did not talk about Boehme, to my knowledge. A friend of Deleuze's told me that he thought Deleuze would probably have avoided Boehme based on a stereotypical sense that he was primarily a religious figure. Yet, Deleuze was both a philosopher of creativity and a creative philosopher, and he wrote on other figures, such as Henri Bergson, who had clear religious agendas. Explicit connections have rarely been made between Boehme and Deleuze (the only recent attempt was by Mark Bonta), but Boehme's relevance becomes apparent as we see a similar appropriation and creation of concepts, and a similar model of creativity in both.[15]

In *What is Philosophy?*, Deleuze and Guattari's final work, the philosopher is called the "friend of the concept" and also the "potentiality of the concept."[16] Deleuze, in his work before *What Is Philosophy?*, had assembled a cast of characters whom he did not think of as influences, but as thinkers who contributed something central to the way concepts developed. Leibniz, for instance, contributed "the fold" (*le pli*), which is perhaps best exemplified by the way that sculptors treated draped cloth—folding back on itself, doubling over yet continuous. Deleuze was interested in the path the concept took as it developed and changed, and the fold was an element of that. Other thinkers he focused on included Spinoza, Hume, Nietzsche, Freud, Kafka, Bergson, and Francis Bacon (the painter, not the philosopher). Each was in some way or other heterodox, and each contributed some element that was useful in thinking about how concepts take on a life of their own. Strange terms, almost Behmenist in their complexity, emerge—exteriority, intension, lines of flight, rhizomatic thought, schizoanalysis, deterritorialization, reterritorialization, and so forth. It becomes a story about life and creativity—resolutely materialist, and yet vitalist in a way not seen before (that is, not a vitalism that posits a soul in all things, but rather a vitalism that posits inorganic life in a process of emergence). It is a story about the "becoming" of all things. Deleuze shows the continual creation of things, the reality of both the virtual and the actual. He does not pit humanity against nature, such that if one is free the other is not.

Now, what I have just described is all Deleuze, but there are echoes of Boehme here as well. There is a sense that life exists in these concepts, that they could easily be covered over, put into a narrative of some sort, and rendered impotent. These concepts must create their own ecologies, gathering other concepts around. I almost expect to see the word *Gefassete* when I read Deleuze, Boehme's portmanteau word that connects *Gefaß* (container) with *fassen* (to grasp). Deleuze's concepts, like Boehme's, create their own container in their grasping. And, potentially, this same action also ossifies them. Boehme has his signatures for that reason, and Deleuze has his deterritorialization and reterritorialization. But as important as the concepts are, both Boehme and Deleuze are concerned with the emergence of life itself. Howard Brinton saw Boehme as an evolutionist, and in a way, he was correct.[17] Brinton's version of evolution, though, was far more mechanistic than either Boehme or Deleuze would have considered correct. He imagined in Boehme a sort of teleological panentheism (that is, the position that God exists in and through nature as well as beyond and before it) and redemption of nature, whereas it can be argued that in fact both Boehme and Deleuze are more interested in the emergence (actualization) of virtual beings into actuality.

As I said earlier, Boehme never let the lack of a concept stop him from writing. He engaged in portmanteau, he played with words, he made up etymologies, he used Latin—all of it meant that he could allow concepts to live, which is to say, the concepts, like the cosmology he described, were one of profound and diverse new production. Whatever differences there may be between Boehme and Deleuze, the impulse to explicate life itself, and not just the markers or signifiers of life, is something they share.

Another example of a concept that Boehme pressed into service, and which has been altered and adapted to contemporary purposes, is the "signature." Boehme adapts it most directly from Paracelsus,[18] but also from the older "book of the world" tradition extant in the Middle Ages in theologians like Alan of Lille and Hugh of St. Victor. *Signatura Rerum* is generally understood as his version of inner/outer signification. There is, though, something more provocative suggested here, that contemporary thinkers such as Giorgio Agamben develop. But first, a reminder about Boehme's treatment of signatures.

Signatura Rerum was written in 1622, two years before Boehme's death. It is addressed to physicians in the broadest sense of the word—all who are concerned with healing in any part of creation. Boehme's therapeutic program is an alchemical one that recognizes that physical suffering has a metaphysical cause and that cure is effected through the transformative powers of the elements. Boehme's particular alchemical structure is in one sense not novel. It is a seven-fold set of properties that describe creation. There is an upper and lower ternary separated by a *Schrack*, a lightning stroke; the first three properties describe the genesis of spirit, while the last three describe the genesis of body. The properties all worked in harmony in the prefallen state, or in eternal nature; however, since the fall into temporal, tainted nature, these properties have been out of tune. Boehme uses a metaphor of music several times to make this condition clear. Each existing thing is like an instrument, which God plays. The Fall "broke" the world and all the instruments in it. It was therefore up to God to fix the creation, to repair the instrument. This is the meaning of redemption. But, that repair does not mean that all creation works properly again. The instruments must still be tuned. That tuning is Boehme's concern in *Signatura Rerum*. The various forms or properties are at present out of balance. It is the job of the healer to understand how the forms are out of balance and to bring them back into balance. Then there will be something like sympathetic vibrations that run through all creation. God is the movement of the strings and the wind in the organ and, ideally, all creation responds in perfect harmony.[19]

This is a more or less standard version of Boehme's concept of signatures. Boehme is taken as sketching out a hermeneutic of divine presence, one in which those who have the eyes to see the signatures have access to a "true" version of the world. And yet, it is possible to see something else happening, if we allow ourselves to be nudged out of the metaphysical framework of presence.

There is a classic tension in theories of meaning between those derived from or related to structuralism (semiotics, post-structuralism) and those derived from phenomenology (e.g., hermeneutics). The tension is between a set of theories that locates meaning in a network of some sort, and a set of theories that locates meaning within human existence. Both of these families of theories are powerful and useful, and they are not easily reducible to each other. Each, in a certain sense, fundamentally questions the starting point of the other. Structuralist theories treat the subject as another signifier in a system, not privileged in any way (a challenge to phenomenological theories, which begin from human experience), whereas phenomenological theories start from the premise that the subject is revealed through its encounter with other meaningful entities. The first has as its central model the system, while the second has the text in mind, along with related skills such as reading.

The clear usefulness of both of these approaches to theorizing meaning has prompted some to seek rapprochement between them. This is not as easy as it sounds, though, since each questions the foundational assumptions of the other. Paul Ricoeur solved the problem by putting the two in a dialectical relationship.[20] Gadamer and Derrida found themselves in a discussion over exactly this issue, one that many see as having ended inconclusively and unsatisfactorily.[21] Foucault addressed the impasse as well, or rather attempted to move past it, while acknowledging the pull of both structuralism and hermeneutics.[22]

Giorgio Agamben sees in Boehme's notion of signatures another answer to the problem. For Agamben, the signature stands before the signifier and the signified. It is "what makes the sign intelligible." The signature is "what makes the mute signs of creation, in which it dwells, efficacious and expressive."[23] Agamben sees in Boehme's idea of the signature not a dialectical move to bring together the hermeneutic and semiotic (*à la* Ricoeur), but an attempt to link signs to ontology in a new manner. Agamben walks a careful line between the potential problems inherent in using theories only derived from structuralism or theories derived entirely from phenomenology. In the first case, there is the risk of the endless freeplay of the signifiers. Significance is the meaning assigned by the relations in a network, the significance that comes from having the most Facebook "likes" or YouTube hits or ad views. It is a significance that tells us nothing about what made the thing significant, only that it was significant. On the other hand, meaning within the phenomenological sphere is constructed differently. It tends to be meaning that does not rely on network connections but on interpretation, the kind that brings order (i.e., a single narrative, a sense of the whole) to the chaos of particularity. What is the risk with this? It is the risk that comes from multiple versions of the whole that can never come to a clear resolution. How can these coexist? Must one predominate? What if my synoptic and comprehensive truth differs from yours? How can it do this, in the end, other than through a mystical sense of a narrative's "rightness"? The hermeneuticist's answer to this is dialogue, but it is worth noting that this is a process rather than a guide for decision-making and does not necessarily guarantee a resolution.

The signature stands prior to both of these modes of understanding. It is meant to address both the problems that come with too much particularity and the problems that come with potentially arbitrary or incommensurable versions of the whole. But does this solution not simply put a third entity prior to the structural and phenomenological approaches, which settles the impasse by fiat? No, because, in the process, Agamben essentially redefines the problem at hand. It is no longer a matter of enabling two paradigms of interpretation to coexist. It is now a matter of showing how both require something more to be other than "inert and unproductive." Signatures do not so much show us what matters, but how mattering happens. They are fundamental to creative activity. One reviewer speaks of it as the "problem that every scholar today faces concerning the 'selection criterion' for everything from a particular document in an archive, to an entire field of research, to which book I should read next, even how should I live if I am to think something new and creative."[24] The analogy here is the creation of knowledge within a discipline. We can either become overwhelmed by the profusion of information available today, or we can approach the problem of creating knowledge by holding to a preexisting narrative. Neither of those, in the end, are a successful solution to the creation of knowledge that is adequate to the questions at stake in the discipline. In other words, it is one thing to have a pure signifier, but quite another to have signifiers that are attuned to particular kinds of outcomes, to creative potential.

One might just see Agamben as a particularly astute interpreter of Boehme's, one who sees the potential of Boehme's concept of signatures as something more than just an element of a mystical cosmology. And he certainly is that. But what he demonstrates is that Boehme's concepts can be brought into contemporary conversations, not anachronistically but creatively. Those concepts exist in an ecology of other concepts (and Boehme's ecology is extremely rich and nuanced). When concepts are carefully introduced into other ecologies, not as invading species but as new elements in tension and cooperation with existing concepts, what results is creative growth. In the example given here, Boehme's notion of signatures is used to interrogate a contemporary problem. It helps us to recognize some of the limits of current answers to that problem and suggests a way forward. This is the way that Boehme's rich ecology can continue to help us engage our thought-world.

III QUESTIONS THAT MATTER

These intellectual strategies lead to concepts adequate to their place. Adequate concepts lead to new questions. Boehme, I think, allows us to think those new questions, not because he was a visionary, or someone who was "ahead of his time," but precisely because he was in his time. He asked the right questions of and for his time, and the concepts that came out of those questions were adequate to his place. "Adequacy" does not mean that no one disagreed with them, or that everyone immediately recognized them to be true and correct, or that their adoption was universal. Adequacy means that he kept the creative momentum alive. He was not interested in merely consolidating the gains of previous intellectual revolutions (that is what he saw the Lutherans as doing, particularly Gregor Richter, his adversary in Görlitz), but rather, he laid the groundwork for the next creative shifts by asking new questions.

What kind of new questions? Here are a few:

1. What is freedom? Boehme re-asks this very old question in the context of an ontology that posits freedom as existing everywhere. Boehme does not prefigure the later Enlightenment versions of freedom, which are rooted in choice along with the absence of barriers for the will's exercise of that choice. Freedom is not earned through hard work, nor is it realized through the self-understanding that God comes to. Freedom is part of the system from the beginning. And, everything—every will, every person—chooses. We sometimes think that what differentiates humans from the rest of nature is that our choice still lies before us. But we must not forget that all parts of the emergence of God and of nature are simultaneously present at all times in all things. In this sense, the choice, for Boehme, is being made at each moment. There is not as radical a version of freedom until Sartre.

2. What does it mean to know something? This is not just a Platonic dialectic, moving toward a unified truth currently covered over by opinion. Boehme does, of course, rail against those who have a superficial and fragmentary knowledge of things. And yet, despite this, I think we would be too restrictive to see him as advancing the position that there is only a single form of knowledge in the end. I read him as setting the table for us, or as preparing the way for the vast diversity of creation to show the infinite kinds of knowledge possible. Of course, there is still *Verstand*, the understanding that sees the unified nature of things. But there is also *Vernunft*, Boehme's term for reason about discrete particulars. Whereas he seems to reject this form of reason in favor of *Verstand*, he in fact recognizes its necessity.[25]

3. How do we account for evil in the world? Again this is an old question to which Boehme gives a new answer. The classic problem, of how we might avoid laying evil on God's doorstep, is given a new strategy. If all that exists does so because God flows through it, and if it is all constituted by will, then the move toward un-creation, toward unraveling the creative cooperation between the joyful *Lust* and the desiring *Begierde* that produces the wild diversity we see, would be evil, it would be *Turba*. It makes one wonder whether Boehme might have an interesting response to the contemporary environmental crisis, which surely must be seen as a move to un-creation if ever there was one. At any rate, whether or not his "theodicy," or defense of God in the face of the presence of evil is successful, it does represent a new question: How does evil relate to God if we conceive of God as an eternally creative impulse?

4. How can creativity occur continually, and not just as an initial act? This is a question that we have already been dealing with. Signatures figure into this, and a new explication of Boehme's use of *Weisheit* would also help to explicate creativity. Boehme extends and makes practical the question of creativity. It is not just a description of the divine economy, but it is a model for how humans live at their best. They remain, in every way, creative.

Now, these new questions are his. They are new not because they've never been asked before, but because they have never been asked in this way before, with this set of concepts available, with this set of social and cultural forces bearing down. We have to find our own new questions. But I think this happens. We hear the echoes of Boehme as Nietzsche defends and elaborates the will, and those echoes come down through Derrida, and even more through Deleuze, in his philosophy of creativity. We hear the echoes of Boehme in Heidegger, as he describes a world that requires us to learn to see, almost as if we look for signatures, and almost as if we are apprehending truth as "*alethia*," or uncovering/unforgetting. We hear the echoes in the current wave of philosophy of religion, which is untethering itself from using analytic Christian theology as its starting point, and reimagining the central questions as they might be asked from a different set of reference points.

The point is, we have new questions, and those questions force us to appropriate concepts from different places, to adapt them to new circumstances, and to recognize the inadequate questions we have worked with in the past. We need not just to study the creative thinkers who appropriated Boehme. We can, in fact, ask a new question, one appropriate to our place, and we can create the concepts adequate to that question, and to that place. This is why Boehme matters today: he gives us a model, and a reason, for creative thinking.

NOTES

1. Herman Vetterling, *The Illuminate of Görlitz or Jakob Böhme's Life and Philosophy* (Leipzig: Markert and Petters, 1923).
2. Stephen Konopacki, *The Descent into Words: Jakob Boehme's Transcendental Linguistics* (Ann Arbor: Karoma Publishers, 1979).
3. Paul Tillich, in John Joseph Stoudt, *Sunrise to Eternity: A Study in Jacob Boehme's Life and Thought* (Philadelphia: University of Pennsylvania Press, 1957), 7.
4. Jacob Boehme, *Mysterium Magnum* (London: John M. Watkins, 1965), 1–2.
5. Often left Latinate as "Lubet" in early English translations, which serves to obscure the term more than necessary.
6. Jacob Boehme, *The Aurora* (London: James Clarke, 1960), chaps. 5, 22; Boehme, *Mysterium Magnum,* chap. 1.
7. A.J. Penny, *Studies in Jacob Böhme* (London: John M. Watkins, 1912); Evelyn Underhill, *Mysticism* (London: E.P. Dutton, 1911); Baron Friedrich von Hügel, *The Mystical Element of Religion as Studied in Saint Catherine of Genoa and her Friends* (London: J.M. Dent, 1909); William James, *Varieties of Religious Experience* (London: Longmans, Green, and Co., 1902).
8. G.W.F. Hegel, *Lectures on the History of Philosophy Vol III: Medieval and Modern Philosophy* (Berkeley: University of California Press, 1990), 110–17; Ludwig Feuerbach, *Geschichte der neueren Philosophie von Bacon bis Spinoza* (1833).
9. Alexandre Koyré, *La Philosophie de Jacob Boehme* (Paris: J. Vrin, 1929).
10. Howard Brinton, *The Mystic Will: Based on a Study of the Philosophy of Jacob Boehme* (New York: The MacMillan Company, 1930).
11. Stoudt, *Sunrise to Eternity.*
12. Sheldon Cheney, *Men Who Have Walked with God* (New York: Alfred A. Knopf, 1945).
13. Andrew Weeks, *Boehme: An Intellectual Biography of the Seventeenth-Century Philosopher and Mystic* (Albany, NY: SUNY Press, 1991).
14. For example, Basarab Nicolescu, *Science, Meaning and Evolution: The Cosmology of Jacob Boehme* (New York: Parabola Books, 1991).
15. Mark Bonta, "Rhizome of Boehme and Deleuze: Esoteric Precursors of the God of Complexity," *SubStance* 39:1 (2010): 62–75.
16. Gilles Deleuze and Felix Guattari, *What Is Philosophy?* (New York: Columbia University Press, 1994), 5.
17. Brinton, *Mystic Will,* 131ff.
18. Paracelsus, "Concerning the Nature of Things, Book the Ninth: Concerning the Signature of Natural Things," in *The Hermetic and Alchemical Writings of Paracelsus, Vol. 1: Hermetic Chemistry,* ed. Arthur Edward Waite (Berkeley, CA: Shambhala Publications, 1976), 171–94.
19. Jacob Boehme, *Signature Rerum* (1622). Reissued in translation as *The Signature of All Things* (Cambridge: James Clarke, 1969), 10–11.

20. Paul Ricoeur, *Interpretation Theory: Discourse and the Surplus of Meaning* (Fort Worth, TX: The Texas Christian University Press, 1976).
21. Diane Michelfelder and Richard Palmer (eds.), *Dialogue and Deconstruction: The Gadamer-Derrida Encounter* (Albany, NY: SUNY Press, 1989).
22. Hubert Dreyfus and Paul Rabinow, *Michel Foucault: Beyond Structuralism and Hermeneutics,* 2nd ed. (Chicago: University of Chicago Press, 1983).
23. Giorgio Agamben, *The Signature of All Things: On Method* (New York: Zone Books, 2009), 42–3.
24. John V. Garner, "Giorgio Agamben: The Signature of All Things: On Method, Luca D'Isanto with Kevin Attell (tr.)," *Continental Philosophy Reviews* 43 (2010): 583–84.
25. This is reminiscent of how Martin Buber handles the I-Thou and the I-It—and it should be remembered that Buber did his doctoral dissertation partly on Boehme. Martin Buber, *Zur Geschichte Des Individuationsproblem (Nicolaus von Cues und Jakob Böhme)* (PhD diss., University of Vienna, 1904).

Contributors

Alan Gregory has taught historical and systematic theology on both sides of the Atlantic and is currently serving as Professor of Church History and Historical Theology at the Seminary of the Southwest in Austin, Texas. He is the author of *Coleridge and the Conservative Imagination*, and *Quenching Hell, the Mystical Theology of William Law.* He is also a contributor to the *Oxford Guide to Romanticism* and a collection of essays on Coleridge's "Opus Maximum," *Coleridge's Assertion of Religion.* At present, he is completing a book on Science Fiction and Christian theology.

Kristine Hannak studied German, English, and Theater Arts at the University of Tübingen, Germany and at the University of Oregon. She has taught German literature courses at the Universities of Marburg and Tübingen. She is a Research Fellow at the Center of Excellence *Enlightenment—Religion—Knowledge* at the University of Halle, Germany where she has worked on Boehme in a research group for three years. In 2011, she earned her PhD at the University of Tübingen with a book on the contribution of early modern mysticism and spiritualism to the beginnings of the Enlightenment.

Bruce Janz is Professor and Chair in the Department of Philosophy and director of the Center for Humanities and Digital Research at the University of Central Florida. His PhD is from the University of Waterloo in Canada. He is the author of *Philosophy in an African Place*, and articles and chapters on African philosophy, place and space, environment and technology, contemporary philosophical theory, contemporary culture, and the history of mysticism. He has taught in Canada, the Unites States, Kenya, and South Africa.

Elisabeth Engell Jessen has studied at the universities of Copenhagen and Oxford. She has published a monograph in Danish on Blake's reception of biblical motifs, *Bibelske Motiver hos William Blake*, and wrote her PhD thesis on Blake and conversion. Her primary research interests are literature and theology, conversion narratives, romanticism and religion, and eighteenth-century Moravian art and spirituality.

Glenn Alexander Magee is Associate Professor and Chairman of the Department of Philosophy at the C. W. Post Campus of Long Island University. He is the author of *Hegel and the Hermetic Tradition*, *The Hegel Dictionary*, co-translator of *Kant and Swedenborg: Dreams of a Spirit-Seer and Other Writings*, and editor of *The Cambridge Handbook of Western Mysticism and Esotericism*. He received his PhD from Emory University in 1998.

Lucinda Martin earned her PhD in Germanic Studies at the University of Texas at Austin in 2003. She has taught language, culture, and religious studies courses at the University of Texas, the University of Würzburg, and the Martin Luther University in Halle, Germany. She is a Fellow of the Young Center for Anabaptist and Pietist Studies in Pennsylvania and is currently a Research Fellow at the Center of Excellence *Enlightenment—Religion—Knowledge* in Halle, Germany where she is completing a book on Pietist women.

George Pattison is 1640 Professor of Divinity at the University of Glasgow. He has previously held posts at King's College, Cambridge, the University of Aarhus (Denmark), and the University of Oxford. His interest in Martensen relates to his long-term study of nineteenth-century theology and philosophy of religion, with particular emphasis on Hegel and his critics. His most recent books include *Kierkegaard and the Theology and the Nineteenth Century* and *Kierkegaard and the Quest for Unambiguous Life*. He is co-editor of *The Oxford Handbook of Kierkegaard*.

Leigh T.I. Penman is a Research Fellow at Goldsmiths, University of London. He graduated with degrees in arts and law from the University of Melbourne. He is the author of the forthcoming monograph *Unanticipated Millenniums: The Lutheran Experience of Chiliastic Thought, 1600–1630* as well as more than a dozen articles on aspects of early modern history. His current research concerns intellectual geographies of Protestant dissent in northern and central Europe.

Nigel Smith is William and Annie S. Paton Foundation Professor of Ancient and Modern Literature at Princeton University. His principal publications are *Perfection Proclaimed: Language and Literature in English Radical Religion, 1640–1660*; *Literature and Revolution in England, 1640–1660*; the Longman Annotated English Poets series edition of Andrew Marvell's *Poems*; *Andrew Marvell. The Chameleon*. He has also edited the Ranter pamphlets and George Fox's *Journal*. He is currently writing a comparative study of the relationship between the state and literary production in early modern Europe and a book about the interaction of words and music.

Oliver Smith is Lecturer in Russian at the University of St Andrews. His publications include the monograph *Vladimir Soloviev and the Spiritualization of Matter* and numerous articles on the Russian theological and philosophical traditions, as well as on Russian environmental thought. He is currently working on biblical reception and the prophetic tradition in Russian cultural history.

Arthur Versluis is Professor and Chair of Religious Studies at Michigan State University. He is the founding president of the Association for the Study of Esotericism, he served as editor of the journal *Esoterica*, and he is founding co-editor of *JSR: Journal for the Study of Radicalism*. A longstanding member of the American Academy of Religion, he is author of numerous books, including *Magic and Mysticism: An Introduction to Western Esotericism*, *The New Inquisitions*, *Restoring Paradise*, *The Esoteric Origins of the American Renaissance*, *Wisdom's Children*, and *American Transcendentalism and Asian Religions*. He is also lead editor of the book series *Studies in Esotericism*.

Andrew Weeks is Professor of German at Illinois State University with a doctorate in Comparative Literature from the University of Illinois in Urbana-Champaign. He has published intellectual biographies of Jacob Boehme, Paracelsus, and Valentin Weigel, as well as a history of German mysticism and translations of the writings of Paracelsus and Weigel. His scholarly interests include Reformation-era anticlericalism and dissent, the cultural history of the late Reformation, and editions of early modern literature.

Select Bibliography

Boehme's first biographer, Abraham von Franckenberg, reckoned that he wrote thirty works. Following an adaptation of von Franckenberg's numbering by the translator John Sparrow, the English titles are given below in chronological order, with date of completion, transcription, or publication in brackets. Those that are incomplete are indicated with an *.

1. * "Aurora" (June 12, 1612)
2. "The Three Principles of the Divine Essence" (1619)
3. "A book of the Threefold Life of Man" (September 1620)
4. "Forty Questions concerning the Soul" (August 1620)
5. "The Incarnation of Jesus Christ"; "The suffering, death and resurrection of Jesus Christ"; "The Tree of Christian Faith" (May–August 1620)
6. "A book of the small six points, and a book of the great six points" (1620)
7. "Of the Heavenly and Earthly Mystery" (May 8, 1620)
8. "Of the Last Times, or of the 1000 year Sabbath, being two epistles to Paul Kaym" (August 14–November 19, 1620)
9. "Signatura Rerum: or the signature of all things" (August 1621)
10. "A consolatory treatise of the four complexions" (March 1621)
11. "The first apology to Balthaser Tilke concerning the *Aurora*" (1621); and "The second apology to Balthaser Tilke concerning Predestination, and the person of Christ and the Virgin Mary" (July 3, 1621)
12. "Considerations upon Esajas Stiefel's book of the threefold state of man, and his new birth" (April 8, 1621)
13. "A large book of the errors of the sects of Ezechiel Meth, or an apology to Esajas Stiefel concerning Perfection" (April 6, 1622)
14. "Of True Repentance" (1622)
15. "Of True Resignation" (1622)
16. "Of Regeneration, or the New Birth" (June 24, 1622)
17. "Concerning the Election of Grace, or of God's will towards man; commonly called Predestination" (February 8, 1623)
18. "An appendix to the book on Predestination, being a short compendium of Repentance" (February 9, 1623)
19. "Mysterium Magnum, or the Great Mystery, being an exposition of Genesis" (September 11, 1623)
20. "A Table of the Divine Manifestation, or an exposition of the Threefold world. Showing what God is in Himself, without Nature and Creature: and how he

is to be considered in Nature according to the Three Principles"; annexed to a letter concerning knowledge of God, of all things, and of the true and false light (November 11, 1623)
21. "A Dialogue between a scholar and his master, concerning the Supersensual life" (January 1624)
22. * "The Highly precious Gate of the Divine Vision" [also known as "A little book of Divine Contemplation"] (1622–24)
23. "Of Christ's two Testaments, viz. Baptism and the Lord's Supper" (May 7, 1624)
24. "A dialogue between an enlightened and unenlightened soul" (1624)
25. "An apology for the book of True Repentance, upon a pamphlet of the primate of Görlitz, Gregor Richter" (April 10, 1624)
26. * "The 177 Theosophic Questions, with answers to 13 of them" (1624)
27. "An epitome or abstract of the Mysterium Magnum" (1624)
28. * "The Holy Week or a Prayer Book for every day of the week; with prayers as far as the end of Tuesday" (1624)
29. "A Table of the Three Principles, or a key to his writings"; being an appendix to an epistle addressed to Johann Sigismund von Schweinichen and Abraham von Franckenberg (February–August 1624)
30. "Of the Last Judgment" (1624?)

In addition, there is "A Clavis or Key, being an exposition of some principal matters and words in Boehme's writings" (March–April 1624), while Boehme's extant correspondence for the period from January 1618 to June 1624 has also been published.

The standard modern German edition of Boehme's works is the *Sämtliche Schriften* edited by August Faust and Will-Erich Peuckert, 11 vols. (Stuttgart: Bad-Canstatt: Frommann, 1955–1961)

For reasons of space, a full bibliography for this volume has had to be omitted. Readers can find it at the following web page: http://www.gold.ac.uk/history/research/panaceasociety/

Extensive Boehme bibliographies are also available here:

http://pegasus.cc.ucf.edu/~janzb/boehme/boehmebib.htm
http://www.jacob-boehme.org/html/bibliography.php

Index